D1597626

REVITALIZING
AMERICAN INDUSTRY

Sponsored by the Amos Tuck School of Business Administration, Dartmouth College, with the support of the Exxon Education Foundation and the General Electric Foundation.

REVITALIZING
AMERICAN INDUSTRY
Lessons From Our Competitors

Edited by
MILTON HOCHMUTH with WILLIAM DAVIDSON

BALLINGER PUBLISHING COMPANY
Cambridge, Massachusetts
A Subsidiary of Harper & Row, Publishers, Inc.

Copyright © 1985 by Ballinger Publishing Company. All rights reserved. No part of this publication may be reproduced, stored in a retrieval system, or transmitted in any form or by any means, electronic, mechanical, photocopy, recording or otherwise, without the prior written consent of the publisher.

International Standard Book Number: 0–88730–019–7

Library of Congress Catalog Card Number: 84–18471

Printed in the United States of America

Library of Congress Cataloging in Publication Data
Main entry under title:

Revitalizing American industry.

   Includes bibliographies and index.
   1. United States—Commerce—Case studies.   2. United States—Industries—Case studies.   I. Hochmuth, Milton S.   II. Davidson, William Harley, 1951-   .
HF3031.R48 1985   338.0973   84–18471
ISBN 0–88730–019–7

To Raymond Vernon,
our mentor

CONTENTS

LIST OF FIGURES

LIST OF TABLES

PREFACE

Toward the middle of the 1980s the fact was clear that with very few exceptions the United States could not successfully compete, unaided, with foreign manufacturers in the world marketplace.

To a great extent only those U.S. industrial firms producing abroad—through subsidiaries, joint ventures with foreign firms, or subcontracting or purchase of parts and components from other countries—were able to compete without some form of government help. Examples of such ventures abound. The so-called smokestack steel and auto industries succeeded in claiming a U.S. market share thanks only to such protectionist palliatives as "trigger price mechanisms" for steel imports and "voluntary restraints" on the part of the Japanese auto industry. In the field of consumer electronics, American manufacturers maintained a share in the television receiver market only through "orderly marketing agreements" with Taiwan and Korea. At the same time, America's aircraft industry was losing market share to European manufacturers.

Europe and Japan are no longer the only challengers. In the 1980s an ever-growing number of "newly industrialized" countries (NICs) were joining Taiwan and Korea as important exporters of manufactured goods. Automobile engines, computer components, integrated circuits, and even modern commercial aircraft from Mexico, Brazil, Singapore, and Indonesia were capturing a share in the U.S. and world market.

As a result of the growing U.S. merchandise trade imbalance, which was $123 billion for 1984 and estimated to be as much as $150 billion for 1985, advocacy of a U.S. industrial policy similar to those formulated by competing nations increased. Such a policy would replace the ad hoc and fragmented measures now current.

How well have these policies worked for our competitors? Do, in fact, U.S. industries need such help? How would such policies aid higher technology industries?

The chapters that follow examine the changes in economic strength and competitiveness that have occurred among the principal trading nations of the Western world over the last two decades. Our purpose is not merely to trace the growth of America's industrial competitors but to probe for the reasons that lie behind major changes in the world economic order. Issues such as national industrial policies (or the absence of them), national "indicative" planning, the encouragement (or discouragement) of capital investment, the role of banks and other financial institutions, research and development investments, labor costs and degree of labor diligence, labor attitudes, and unique national cultural contexts—all bear on the central question underlying recent changes in a nation's ability to compete in the world marketplace.

The book will examine this question from two viewpoints. The first is the national perspective of each of the leading Western industrial nations, plus Brazil and Mexico as representatives of the newly industrialized countries. The second viewpoint is based on selected industrial sectors that most vividly exemplify the fundamental changes that have taken and are taking place: the mature —some economists have termed them "declining"—sectors of steel, automobiles, textiles, and the two largest advanced-technology sectors: information technology and aerospace. Together, these two viewpoints allow a fairly comprehensive picture of how nations and their industries are competing—or failing to compete —in today's world.

There is always a danger in the kind of "committee" approach we have taken here in analyzing such a broad and complex situation. But in this case the varied yet complementary national perspectives, together with in-depth sectorial analyses, provide a much more balanced examination than any individual view, however brilliant. Indeed, this approach seemed necessary, and to this end a colloquium was held at Dartmouth College's Amos Tuck School of Business in 1982. During and after the colloquium the essays presented were critiqued and revised in order to focus their content and aim for this book.

We are indebted to Dean Richard West of the Tuck School for his encouragement. Our efforts could not have succeeded without financial support and we wish to acknowledge with gratitude grants from the Exxon Education Foundation and the General Electric Foundation. Last but not least, we acknowledge the uncomplaining efforts at Dartmouth's Tuck School of Holly Lanagan, Paula Sweeney, and the Tuck School staff, and Bette Collins of the University of Virginia's Darden School of Business. We are grateful to Eunice Ballam at Tuck School, who accomplished the arduous task of typing and retyping the manuscript.

Milton Hochmuth and
William Davidson

1 FROM CHALLENGER TO CHALLENGED

Milton Hochmuth

Despite their best efforts, social scientists often find it difficult to present a true picture of reality and nowhere is this difficulty more evident than in the field of economics, and particularly international economics and international business. A related problem, because it delays constructive policy changes, is the inertia or persistence of once factual perceptions in the minds of laymen and scholars alike, long after conditions have changed. Here, Britain provides a sterling example.

During the nineteenth century, Britain was unquestionably considered the strongest economic power in the world. It possessed over half the world's merchant sea tonnage—a key indicator of economic prowess at the time—and was indisputably the greatest trading nation of the world and center of international finance. As the birthplace of the industrial revolution, Britain also possessed the natural resources constituting that era's principal ingredient for national economic power, coal, and iron; in 1870 Britain generated over half the world's entire production of iron ore. The perception of what the French called *la suprématie anglaise* was widely prevalent on the eve of World War I. And if we take the percentage of world exports of manufactured products as indicating an industrialized nation's relative international economic strength, Britain

1

earned and retained its palm as "workshop of the world" well into the 1920s. Moreover, Britain was generally accepted to be the world's preeminent financial power even into the 1930s.[1] Closer examination, however, reveals a different story.

Most economists would agree that the single best index of a nation's economic strength is the sum total of the goods and services it produces or its gross domestic product (GDP). As a corrallary, the GDP per capita may be used as an equally good measure of a market-economy nation's economic well-being as differentiated from its overall economic strength. Comparisons between nations can then be made at current rates of exchange. But even given these measures comparisons are difficult because of exchange rate distortions. It is only recently that economists have made comparisons more meaningful by taking into account the actual purchasing powers of equivalent amounts of currency in different countries. This has been termed *real* GDP per capita as measured on a "purchase power parity" basis.[2]

What is interesting here is that available statistics show that the United States, not Britain, became the nation with the largest GDP and the nation with the largest *real* GDP per capita as early as the 1840s and has not lost that lead since.[3] (At *current rates of exchange* the U.S. 1979/1980 GDP per capita was temporarily lower than that of all the Common Market countries except Britain and Italy.) Because quantifying economic strength is not a simple concept, it was perhaps due to Europe's colonialist outward-looking economies (as compared to the inward-looking American economy) that America's economic strength was not fully sensed in the pre-World War II era.

THE PERCEIVED AMERICAN CHALLENGE

Perception finally caught up with the economic facts when, after World War II, the United States became widely viewed as the most powerful economic power in the world. That the rest of the post World War II world would come to view the United States—now variously called the economic giant, economic imperialist, or Colossus of the North—with mixed feelings is understandable. Envy, fear, uneasiness, resentment, frustration, and only occasionally admiration or understanding, are words that come to mind to describe the attitude of the world's nations toward America's economic ascendency.

Not until the late 1960s, however, did these feelings crystalize and form the basis for the national politicoeconomic policies of the industrialized democracies of Europe vis-à-vis the United States. (In Japan, this policy formulation occurred at a much earlier date.) No single intellectual incident was more influential in catalyzing European, and even world, opinion than J.J. Servan-Schreiber and Michel Albert's *The American Challenge,* first published in French in 1967.[4]

The basic premise of the book was that the United States, with its multinational corporations as the soul and cutting edge of its economic might, was in the process of effectively carving up the world—and Europe in particular—into bite-size pieces that it was contentedly digesting. By 1982, the authors intoned, "the World's third greatest industrial power, just after the United States and Russia, may not be Europe but American Industry in Europe." There followed a litany of examples of American dominance in business, industry, and finance. While U.S. multinationals were using their immense financial strength to create or "seize control" of European subsidiaries, through which they could exploit their considerable and continuing technological superiority, Europeans were content with "little more than the purchase of securities [in the United States]."[5]

If the agent of dominance was seen as the multinational corporation and the weapon the dollar, it was U.S. technological superiority and its huge domestic market that were the roots of power. Unless the Common Market were made to work for Europeans instead of American multinational corporations, unless Europe created large industrial firms that could compete head-on with Americans, unless Europe successfully forged into the front ranks of high-technology innovation, Europe would be condemned to second-rate status with a second-rate standard of living.

THE ERA OF THE "GAPS": DOLLAR, TECHNOLOGICAL, AND MANAGERIAL

The gathering alarm over U.S. economic power originated with what became known as the "dollar gap." Though the term had been used in the 1940s it did not become widespread until the early 1950s when Europe and Japan were emerging from the ashes of World War II. Economists and politicians then became increasingly preoccupied by a "dollar shortage."[6]

A great deal of the post-World War II "dollar gap" in Western Europe was caused by the imbalance between consumption and production over and above U.S. aid.[7] In Japan, on the other hand, a positive balance of payments was rapidly achieved by restraining consumption. (But the "cost" to the Japanese in terms of standard of living was high. On a "real" or "purchase power parity" basis, Japan's gross domestic product per capita did not reach the British level until 1972.)

An American economist and key adviser to congressional committees on matters of trade, Howard S. Piquet, summed up the situation in 1952:

> Two world wars have accelerated and accentuated the transfer of the center of economic power from the Old World to the New . . . the countries of Western Europe find it difficult to buy what they need from the Western Hemisphere. They have not the dollars with which to pay . . . . Europe has largely recovered from the effects of the War as far as physical productivity is concerned, but increased productivity alone is not enough to bring about balance in the international accounts. That can come about only through expanded international trade. Modern Europe has never been self-sufficient and is not likely to become so.[8]

Piquet then concluded from his analysis that, even if the United States were to suspend all quotas and tariffs on a temporary basis, the resulting increase in imports would fall short of solving the dollar gap. Moreover, such additional imports of manufactured goods, he estimated, would have displaced only 1 percent of the total U.S. value added by manufacture for 1951. "The number of individuals and establishments that would be injured would undoubtedly be small . . . and would not be burdensome to the economy as whole."[9]

In light of the current high level of imports to the United States, it is interesting to note which industries would have been hardest hit according to Piquet's calculations. U.S. watches and silk fabric manufacturers, he felt, would have lost significant market shares, with lesser losses to producers of optical instruments, sewing machines, and apparel.[10]

In 1953 the dollar gap continued unabated, and Professor Roy Harsod, in the 1953 Sir George Watson Lectures, could still speak of "despondency" over the matter.[11] He offered the Korean War as one reason for the trade disequilibrium, which he felt to be at the root of the problem. In addition,

> . . . industrializing tendencies in certain countries that might otherwise have strongly expanded food production have made the world more dependent on American food supplies. Large investment programs have created demand for capital equipment that the U.S. has been well-qualified to supply . . . . The ability of the U.S. economy to meet foreign needs in the post-war quinquenium . . . may have enabled American producers and traders to build up customer connections which once formed are not easily altered . . . . [12]

Harsod concluded that to "get a bilateral balance [of trade between Europe and the U.S.] even by expanding exports, Europe would have to double its exports from their present [1952] value. Each doubling could not take place without large price concessions; therefore, volume would have to increase four-fold. This is beyond the realm of practicality." He felt that only through multilateral trade with the Third World was there a chance of establishing equilibrium.[13]

Yet in spite of these gloomy prognostications Western Europe and Japan began closing the dollar gap as well as their real GDP per capita gap with the United States during the mid-1950s. These advances reflected Western Europe's and Japan's aggressive drive for exports of manufactured goods and their increasing competitiveness in the world marketplace. By 1955 West Germany, France, and Japan had balanced their overall merchandise trade. Only Britain showed a negative trade balance, while the United States continued to enjoy a positive balance. Then, at the end of 1958, *Fortune* wrote:

> During the past decade it has become an axiom of economic policy that the U.S. exports too much, imports too little, and hence, in addition to private overseas investment [and invisibles], must pour out a flood of government money abroad to help plug what is called the "dollar gap." *But as 1958 ended it became apparent that the real gap in U.S. foreign accounts is of a very different nature* . . . . [14] (italics added)

As early as February 1958, European central banks had begun converting their growing dollar reserves into gold, which soon triggered a "gold flow" problem for the United States. With very little public awareness, over \$2.3 billion was converted by the Europeans alone in 1958. Ascribed to an "unfavorable trade balance" for the United States, an even greater loss of gold was predicted for 1959. The tide had turned.

While there was only muted concern in the United States due to the gold flow, the Europeans and the Japanese were not content to rest on their laurels. As U.S. multinational corporations continued to invest abroad rather than to export, the industrialized democracies now sought to get at the root of what they still perceived to be their major weakness vis-à-vis the United States—a "technology gap." In 1964 the responsible ministers of the Organization for Economic Cooperation and Development (OECD) countries formally addressed themselves to what was euphemistically called "national differences in scientific and technical potential." Although Europe (except Britain) and Japan had corrected their trade imbalances, they still felt the United States was able to maintain its hold of the world economy through sheer know-how. Closely associated with this "technology gap" was the perception of a related "managerial gap." Not only was the United States scientifically and technologically ahead in critical industrial sectors, but U.S. firms were better at exploiting their technological advantages than other countries (the gold flow and a falling dollar notwithstanding). Later, in 1968, the OECD published a series of studies detailing Europe's lag in eight key high-technology sectors, from computers to metallurgy.[15]

IS THE PAST A PROLOGUE?

In a widely discussed 1978 paper issued by the Cambridge Economic Policy Group (CEPG), Cripps and Godley postulated the concept of "relatively unsuccessful" (RU) industrialized countries as opposed to "relatively successful" (RS) industrialized countries.[16] By their definition, based on competitiveness in the world marketplace, Britain was clearly an RU country. In a later article, the CEPG took off the velvet glove and changed "relatively unsuccessful" to "'senile' industrial countries" and again singled out the United Kingdom. Are there are other industrialized countries that are RU or "senile" (or becoming so)? More specifically, in which camp does the United States fall?

To answer these questions, the concept of RU and RS must be objectively measured. One could argue that "competitiveness" in international trade is not the best objective criterion. As mentioned earlier, a nation's relative well-being is perhaps best measured by relative GDP per capita or, better, by real GDP per capita based on the "purchase power parity" exchange. *Still, proof is not required to project a relative drop in GDP per capita (real or otherwise) for an industrialized nation in today's interdependent world if that nation's products are consistently not competitive in the world marketplace.*

Looking first at the trends in the growth of real GDP per capita, it is evident that the United States rivals Britain as the laggard. Taking 1955 as a base year, ten years after the conclusion of World War II but before the creation of the European Common Market, we have in Table 1–1 the following indices of growth (in constant 1982 dollars and on a "purchase power parity" basis with the United States).[17]

The data in Table 1–1 show that although the U.S. standard of living is improving but slowly, the United States still enjoys a significant lead over the rest of the industrialized world as far as real GDP per capita is concerned. But the gap is closing. We are not implying that this U.S. lead is desirable or even "good"; the statistics do reveal, however, that America no longer appears to be the "challenger" but the "challenged." At any rate, no nation can be content to see its standard of living rise at a lower rate than in other countries at a comparable stage of development.

Table 1–1. "Real" Gross Domestic Product Per Capita.

Year	Japan a	Japan b	France a	France b	Germany a	Germany b	United Kingdom a	United Kingdom b	United States a	United States b
1955	23.7	100	53.6	100	58.8	100	61.1	100	100	100
1965	43.6	221	67.2	151	77.0	157	63.5	125		120
1975	68.7	415	82.5	220	83.5	203	64.6	151		143
1980	74.8	509	84.3	254	88.4	242	62.3	164		161
1983	79.7	551	84.1	257	87.1	242	63.4	170		164

Notes:
a. "Purchase power parity" basis, with U.S.=100 for given year.
b. Growth in (a.) with 1955=100 (constant currency).
Source: U.S. Bureau of Labor Statistics, May 1984 (unpublished data).

As far as measuring industrial competitiveness in the world marketplace is concerned, the single best index is a nation's world marketshare (including its domestic market) of manufactured goods.[18] Supporting this view is the fact that the world's largest homogeneous market, the United States, has been relatively very open and the rest of the world markets reasonably open, with important exceptions, since the advent of the General Agreement on Tariffs and Trade (GATT) in 1948 and the subsequent multilateral trade agreements held under its auspices.

Table 1–2 shows the exports of manufactured goods from the five largest industrialized countries for 1951, the years 1962–1964 serving as a basis for comparison, and then for the most recent years that data are available. The countries' percentage share of total world exports of manufactured goods from the fifteen "industrialized nations" of the world is also shown. Comparable data for three "newly industrialized" countries are given in the last columns. (Exports from these three are not included in the totals for the fourteen.)

Clearly, the star performer according to Table 1–2 is Japan, and the undisputed laggard is Britain. But if these figures support Britain's position as an RU nation, they also confirm the United States as equally relatively unsuccessful.

We do not intend here to discuss a causal relationship between export performance and relative lack of growth in GDP per capita; but we do wish to establish some objective criteria for measuring *relative* national success and trends in *relative* economic power. There can be no argument that for an industrialized nation to lose world market share for its manufactured goods, including an important share of its home market, is cause for significant alarm. The United States faces this predicament now, just as Britain did in the past. The extent to which this loss of competitiveness has affected the U.S. balance of trade is shown in Table 1–3. Here we see that in the 1965–1987 period, exports of manufactured goods increased eightfold while imports increased thirteen times. Significantly, the only category listed in Table 1–3 that showed an increase in the recession year of 1982 was imports of manufactured goods. Somehow, this imbalance, which does not even address the imbalance due to petroleum imports, must be corrected.

Agriculture has been one of the few bright spots in recent U.S. international trade. Can agriculture be expected to compensate for

Table 1–2. Exports and Percent of World Exports of Manufactured Goods (SITC 5–8) from the Fifteen Industrialized Supplier Countries and Three Newly Industrialized Countries (billions of current U.S. dollars).

YEAR	Total Exports From 15 Countries	Index 1962 = 1.0	U.S.		France		Germany		Japan		UK		Taiwan	Korea	Brazil
1951[a]	31.8[b]	.5	8.8	28.9%	2.8	8.8%	2.8	8.8%	1.2	3.7%	6.1	19.3%	NA	NA	NA
1962	62.3	1.0	13.7	22.0	5.4	8.7	11.7	18.8	4.4	7.0	8.8	14.2	0.1	0.01	.04
1963	67.5	1.1	14.3	21.2	5.8	8.7	12.9	19.1	4.9	7.3	9.4	14.0	0.1	0.04	.04
1964	77.1	1.2	16.5	21.5	6.5	8.4	14.4	18.7	6.1	7.9	9.9	12.8	0.2	0.06	.08
1978[c]	634.3	10.2	94.5	14.9	58.8	9.3	125.2	19.8	94.2	14.9	57.6	4.3	11.3	11.2	—[d]
1980	878.0	14.1	144.0	16.4	84.0	9.6	166.9	19.0	124.4	14.2	86.4	3.9	17.5[e]	15.7[f]	—
1981	852.5	13.7	154.3	18.1	75.2	8.8	150.8	17.7	146.9	17.2	70.4	4.4	—	—	—
1982	807.5	13.0	139.7	17.3	69.7	8.7	152.6	18.9	134.3	16.6	65.3	4.7	20.5	18.1	7.5
1983	797.6	12.8	132.4	16.6	68.5	8.6	146.5	18.5	142.2	17.5	60.5	5.1	23.4	20.4	9.3

Notes:

a. 1951–1964 data from United Nations Secretariat

b. Total World Exports of Manufactures

c. Data for 1978 on for industrialized countries is from *International Economic Indicators,* U.S. Department of Commerce, June 1984 pp. 28 and 34. Percentages do not agree exactly with total exports.

d. Data for 1978 on are from the Bank of Brazil and may not correspond to United Nations data.

e. Data for Taiwan are from "Monthly Statistics of Exports and Imports," Ministry of Finance, Republic of China, various issues

f. Data from Republic of Korea consulate, Atlanta, Ga. July, 1984.

Table 1-3. U.S. Merchandise Exports and Imports, 1965=100 (millions of current dollars).

YEAR	Exports f.a.s.[a]			Imports f.a.s.[a]			
	1 Total	2 Agricultural	3 Manufactures	4 Total	5 Petroleum & Products	6 Total less Petroleum	7 Manufactures
	($26,399)	($6,305)	($17,433)	($21,427)	($2,034)	($19,393)	($11,244)
1965	100	100	100	100	100	100	100
1975	402	353	407	460	—	369	454
1980	820	669	825	1,143	3,904	853	1,113
1981	867	702	885	1,218	3,814	946	1,267
1983[b]	742	582	701	1,204	2,788	1038	1,456
	($195917)	($36700)	($132408)	($258000)	($56700)	($201300)	($163730)

Notes:

a. Free alongside (excluding international transportation and insurance). If the data were on a c.i.f. basis (including cost of the goods plus international freight and insurance), the already unfavorable U.S. balance would be much worse because of the use of non-U.S. ships and insurance. Some data are customs value, approximately same as f.a.s.

b. Some 1983 data estimated.

Sources: Columns 1,3,4,6, and 7. *Economic Report of the President* (Washington, D.C.: U.S. Government Printing Office, 1984), p. 336. Columns 2 and 5: Ibid., p. 334.

the lagging industrial sector? A glance at Table 1–3 shows that agricultural exports have grown even more slowly than export of manufactures. Moreover, given the increasing export competition in agricultural products from Europe, Brazil, Canada, Australia, and eventually other Latin American and African countries, together with increasing mechanization worldwide, a significant growth in agricultural exports is unlikely. Indeed, in 1983, the long U.S. dominance in world grain trade was seen as slowly diminishing.[19]

U.S. economists often cite the export of services as a potential offset to the unfavorable merchandise trade balance. Services are part of the rapidly growing "tertiary" sector of the U.S. economy which in 1982 employed 74 percent of the total U.S. wage and salary workers as opposed to only 21 percent in manufacturing and a mere 3 percent in agriculture. The tertiary sector is here taken to include wholesale and retail trade, transportation, public utilities, finance, insurance, real estate, local and federal employees, as well as "services" proper. Mining and construction are not included. As will be seen in Professor Neil Hood's essay (Chapter 5), gargantuan increases in the export of services would be needed to compensate for each percentage point in share of world export of manufactures.

Closely related to economic well-being and to share of the worldmarket in manufactures is this question of employment. Table 1–4 presents employment trends in the United States, including data on the individual sectors analyzed in this book.

From Table 1–4 we see that while employment in the United States has grown much faster than the population (due to the increased percentage of women in the workforce, etc.) the old "key industries" such as steel, automotive, textiles, and apparel have actually suffered a drop. Moreover, the high-technology sectors such as electronics and aerospace have not been able to compensate for the drop in the rest of the manufacturing sectors, as many observers had hoped. On the whole, manufacturing employment is increasing at a substantially lower rate than either the population or employment as a whole. Only the tertiary sector is growing at a faster rate. But a nation cannot maintain a high standard of living based on this largely domestically oriented sector alone. Of course if the U.S. manufacturing sector could have increased its productivity sufficiently, it is conceivable

Table 1–4.   Employment in the U.S. 1965 (millions) = 100.

YEAR	Total Popula- tion	*d* Agri- cultural Employ- ment	*d* Total Wage & Salaried Non- Agricul- tural	*d* Total all Manu- fac- tur- ing	*d* All Services "Tertiary Sector"	*e* Steel	*a,e* Motor Vehicles & Compon- ents
1965	(194.3)	(4.4)	(60.8)	(18.1)	(38.8)	(0.657)	(0.843)
	100	100	100	100	100	100	100
1970	106	80	117	107	122	95	95
1975	111	77	126	101	140	83	94
1978	115	77	143	113	157	85	119
1981	118	77	150	112	170	77	93
1982	120	77	147	104	169	65	82
1983	(234.2)	(3.4)	(90.0)	(18.7)	(66.3)	(0.336)	(0.727)
	121	77	148	103	171	51	86
Gain/ (Loss) 1965–83 millions	+40	(−1.0)	+29.2	+0.6	+27.5	(−0.321)	(−0.116)

Notes:

a. Does not include automotive supplier or other automotive related industries.

b. For historical reasons non-electrical machinery normally includes the office and computing machines sub-category which is now largely electronic. Therefore this category has been subtracted out and listed separately in the table

c. Also included in Electrical and Electronic Machinery

Sources:

d. Economic Report of the President, February 1984, pp. 253ff.

e. U.S. Bureau of Labor Statistics, Labstat series, April, 1984.

f. Aerospace Industries, Association of America, 1984.

that a relatively smaller number of employees could have produced enough goods for those displaced to the service sector, either directly or indirectly by exporting sufficient goods to cover imports. But this has not happened.

THE EVOLUTION OF FOREIGN DIRECT INVESTMENT (FDI)

Before examining the changes that have occurred in greater detail we must consider the earlier predictions about the power of

b,e	e	e	e	f	e	c,e
Non-Electrical Machinery	Electrical & Electronics	Textile Mill Products	Apparel & Other Textile Products	Aerospace	Office & Computing Machines	Electronic Components & Accessories
(1.545)	(1.615)	(0.926)	(1.354)	(1.175)	(0.191)	(0.307)
100	100	100	100	100	100	100
110	116	105	101	102	151	119
115	105	94	92	80	150	110
128	124	97	98	83	184	149
132	130	89	92	102	243	182
116	125	81	86	99	257	185
(1.556)	(2.045)	(0.744)	(1.169)	(1.151)	(0.489)	(0.593)
101	127	80	86	98	256	193
+0.011	+0.430	(−0.182)	(−0.185)	(−0.024)	+0.298	+0.286

American multinational corporations (MNCs) in Europe. Certainly, American foreign direct investment (FDI) has grown since 1966. In that year, American FDI totalled $51.8 billion, 30 percent of which was in Europe. By 1980 the total reached $213.5 billion, 45 percent of which was in Europe. Does this make American MNCs in Europe the third largest economic power in the world?

Here it is instructive to see if the ratio of U.S. FDI in Europe to European gross domestic product had indeed increased. Table 1–5 summarizes this data for the period 1963–1980.[20]

From the table it appears that the relative importance of U.S.

Table 1–5.   United States Direct Investment in Europe.

Year	1963	1970	1978	1980	1982
U.S./FDI in Europe ($billion U.S.)[a]	10.3	25.3	70.6	95.7	68.5
European GDP ($billion U.S.)[b]	426.0	763.0	2,484.0	3,091.8	2,989.5
Ratio *U.S./FDI* % European GDP	2.4	3.3	2.8	3.1	2.3

Sources:
a. U.S. Department of Commerce "Survey of Current Business," February 1981, pp. 39 ff., August 1981, and August 1983, p. 36.
b. *U.N. Yearbook of National Accounts, 1979,* and OECD "Main Economic Indicators," April 1984, p. 182.

FDI in Europe peaked by the end of the 1960s and dropped significantly by 1982.

More informative than these European data are the long-term trends in FDI flows. The U.S. share of all outward FDI flows from thirteen leading industrial countries went from 61 percent in the 1961–1969 period to 46 percent in 1968–1973 to 29 percent during 1974–1979. West Germany's shares were, respectively, 7, 12, and 17 percent; and Japan's were 2, 7, and 13 percent.[21] On a purely numerical basis, the number of annual *new* foreign affiliates of U.S. firms has steadily decreased since a peak in 1967.

NOTES

1. Reliable pre-World War I economic statistics are not easily obtained, particularly comparative international statistics. Production statistics are more reliable than income statistics, certainly before 1947. See, for example:

   W. W. Rostow, *The World Economy* (Austin: University of Texas Press, 1978).

   Angus Maddison, *The Economic Growth in the West* (New York: The Twentieth Century Fund, 1964).

   Simon Kuznets, *The Economic Growth of the Nations* (Cambridge, Mass.: Belknap Press, 1971).

   Simon Kuznets, "Foreign Trade: Long Term Trends," *Econ-*

omic Development and Cultural Change 15, no. 2 (January 1967): 53.

Robert Baldwin, "The Commodity Composition of Trade: Selected Countries, 1900–1954," *Review of Economics and Statistics* (vol. 40, February 1958): 50–68.

2. See:

Irving Kravis, Alan Heston, and Robert Summers, *International Comparisons of Real Product and Purchasing Power* (Baltimore: Johns Hopkins University Press, 1978).

Various issues of the *Review of Income and Wealth,* in particular the March 1980 issue, pp. 19–66.

For an early study, see Milton Gilbert and Associates, *Comparative National Products and Price Levels* (Paris: OEEC, 1958).

Comparative Real Gross Domestic Product, Real GDP per Capita, 1950–1981, U.S. Bureau of Labor Statistics, Washington, D.C., May 1983 (unpublished data).

3. Kuznets, *Economic Growth,* pp. 11–14 and 45–47; also Maddison, *Economic Growth,* p. 40 (using Kuznet's growth rates).

4. Jean-Jacques Servan-Schreiberand Michel Albert, *The American Challenge* (New York: Atheneum, 1967).

5. Ibid., p. 147.

6. Charles P. Kindelberger, *The Dollar Shortage* (New York: The Technology Press, John Wiley, 1950).

7. Ibid., p. 47.

8. Howard S. Piquet, *Aid, Trade, and the Tariff* (New York: Thomas Crowell, 1953), p. 347.

9. Ibid., p. 47.

10. Ibid., p. 349.

11. Roy Harsod, "The Dollar," *Sir George Watson Lectures 1953* (New York: Harcourt Brace, 1954), p. 117.

12. Ibid., p. 135.

13. Ibid., p. 145.

14. *Fortune* (January 1959): 51.

15. *Gaps in Technology,* General Report to the Third Ministerial Meeting on Science of OECD Countries, March 11 and 12, 1968 (Paris: OECD, 1968), p. 5.

16. Francis Cripps and Wynne Godley, "Control of Imports as a Means to Full Employment and Expansion of World Trade: The UK's Case," *Cambridge Journal of Economics,* no. 2 (1978): 327–34.

17. See introduction and note to U.S. Bureau of Labor Statistics: Comparative Real GDP per capita . . . for nine countries 1950–1979, October 1, 1980 (unpublished data). See also Kravis, Heston, and

Summers, *International Comparisons;* and various issues of *Review of Income and Wealth.*

18.   Manufactured goods are taken to be U.N. SITC categories 5 through 8.

19.   *Wall Street Journal,* May 19, 1983, p. 1.

20.   See *Recent International Direct Investment Trends* (Paris: OECD, 1981) for a detailed discussion with extensive data.

21.   Ibid., p. 40.

2 THE ANALYTICAL CHALLENGE

Raymond Vernon

The previous chapter describing the fading position of the United States reflects very well the feelings and anxiety that recent developments have generated. The essays that follow, by exploring the developments in individual industries and by analyzing similar problems in other countries, are intended ultimately to help policymakers understand the nature of the problem and devise appropriate responses. Before we plunge into these studies, however, it may help to examine a little further some of the obscurities in the present U.S. position and the anxieties that the position evokes.

It is not difficult to understand why so many Americans are concerned about the slowing absolute growth rates of the U.S. economy. At home, this slowing up has made it harder to cope with the country's social problems, harder to mount an adequate defense, harder to maintain open markets, and harder to contribute to foreign aid. Abroad, because of the sheer size of the U.S. economy, America's feeble growth rate bears significantly on the economic well-being of other countries.

But why should Americans worry about the U.S. loss of ground in relative terms—that is, relative to our global allies? The reaction of Americans could stem from a quite human, prideful unwillingness to relinquish our position as number one, together with a desire to cling to the advantages of hegemonic power. Or it may be that, reflecting a persistent tilt toward isolationism in the U.S. tradition, Americans are unsure whether allies such as Japan and France will continue in their friendly role and are, therefore, fearful to see them developing independent strength. Finally, the U.S. reaction could be the result of a fear that such relative slippage is likely to go on forever. If so, there are cases in history that seem to support the concern, such as the empires of Rome, Spain, and Britain, but there are more ambiguous cases as well, such as those of France and Germany, whose historial vicissitudes have been much more complex. In any case, so far as history is concerned, one cannot be certain what the recent changes in the U.S. economy presage for the future; and, so far as economic theory can tell us, there is no reason to believe that the country's growth could not speed up again. The reasons for the widespread concern over America's waning relative economic position, therefore, have still to be clarified.

Another ambiguity of the U.S. position needs to be addressed in defining the problem and prescribing the appropriate remedies. If the problem has been described as a slippage in the U.S. economy, it has sometimes been viewed as a slippage in the performance of U.S. industry as well. And when reference is made to U.S. industry, there are usually clear indications that this reference encompasses the performance not only of U.S. parent firms at home but also of their subsidiaries abroad.

To include the performance of U.S. subsidiaries in foreign countries, however, is to alter the focus of the problem in critical respects. In the first place, the worldwide performance of U.S.-owned industry has been rather different from that of industry located in the United States. In 1957, for instance, the sales of U.S.-owned manufacturing subsidiaries abroad amounted to only 8 percent of the output of manufacturers in the United States, but in 1966 that figure had risen to 13 percent, and in 1977 to 23 percent.[1]

More important, however, is the fact that the welfare implications of the of industry growth in the United States are different in some vital respects from the welfare implications of growth by U.S.-owned subsidiaries abroad. Although U.S. stockholders receive the lion's share of the dividends generated by such foreign subsidiaries, the largest part of the value added by those subsidiaries accrues to the labor, suppliers, and governments of the countries where they are located.[2] Accordingly, while U.S. stockholders and conceivably U.S. managers benefit from the performance of subsidiaries in foreign countries, the position of U.S. labor, U.S. suppliers, and the U.S. government is much more ambiguous.

Analyses of the distribution of benefits provided by subsidiaries usually concentrate on the effects of such subsidiaries on U.S. exports or on the U.S. balance of payments.[3] All that one can say at this stage is that there have been diverse effects from such subsidiaries, if one is trying to compare the situation with a hypothetical world in which such subsidiaries did not exist. Some subsidiaries appear to have stimulated the innovational tendencies of the parent, or added to the exports of the United States, or both; but others seem to have actually reduced the parent's need for innovation, or reduced U.S. exports.

With such diverse and uncertain consequences at work, no good reason exists for the U.S. government to place obstacles in the way of continued growth of foreign subsidiaries; but these uncertainties also raise understandable doubts over the justifiability of policies that unselectively foster the growth of such subsidiaries. In any event, the uncertainties underline the importance of distinguishing between the growth of the U.S. national economy and the global growth of U.S.-controlled industry.

SCIENCE, INVENTION, AND INNOVATION

A great deal more is known today about the process of industrial innovation than was the case thirty years ago,[4] but considerable uncertainty still surrounds the conditions necessary for bringing about the sort of innovative advances that contribute to a country's growth.

Industrial innovation entails a mix of activities that range from the most mundane kind of "cutting and pasting" to the most challenging use of advanced scientific principles. If the findings involve basic research, industry cannot exploit these findings unless its engineers and technicians are aware of them. But the availability of information is only a beginning. At least two other intangibles may be critical: the credibility of the information as perceived by the prospective user and the existence of a powerful motivation for applying the information. It is not surprising to learn, therefore, that engineers and technicians commonly ignore useful technological advances that are called to their attention from sources outside the firm, and that the stimulus for many industrial innovations is often traced to salesmen, customers, or industrial competitors.

Moreover, a country's innovation is no guarantee that that country will be its principal beneficiary. The concept of interchangeable parts, which was invented in Europe, for example, was adopted first and most widely used in the United States. The industrial robot, an idea developed in the United States, was first applied extensively in Japan, along with the application of electronic controls to camera shutters and numerous other U.S. innovations. The diffusion of an invention, as distinguished from its initial creation, can be quite complex, and the process has been the subject of numerous studies.

Not surprisingly, therefore, the rate of pure scientific activity and pioneer invention in a country has not proved to be an accurate indication of that country's level of successful industrial innovations. The rate of U.S. industrial innovation in the nineteenth century, for example, was high, while the country's contributions to pure science were quite limited; England's contributions to pure science and breakthrough inventions in the twentieth century have been considerable, but the national record of successful industrial innovation has been poor; Japan's performance since World War II is rich with innovations but almost totally lacking in achievements in pure science or with regard to breakthrough inventions. As if to complete the cycle, the United States in recent years has exhibited a sustained capacity for contributing to pure science and invention, but a less striking capacity for successful industrial innovation.

The tenuous link between pure science and invention on the one hand and industrial innovation on the other is no doubt caused in part by what economists like to call the nonappropriability of the information generated by scientists and inventors. The results of pure science are published for the use of all who have the capability and the incentive to interpret their significance. Technical breakthroughs, such as the splicing of genes or the development of optical fibres, are also widely available in one important sense: the long lead times and large scale that typically mark the development of such inventions usually offer attentive observers in foreign countries the opportunity to detect the useful possibilities well in advance of the inventors' application as a successful industrial product. With continuous improvements in transportation and communication, a strong possibility exists that the work of scientists and pioneer inventors will become increasingly appropriable and that the level of industrial innovation in any country will grow increasingly independent of the level of the purer scientific activities conducted in that country.

The implications of these observations for national policy are profound. The expansion of government-supported basic research may be neither necessary nor sufficient for an expansion in industrial innovation; on the other hand, a global scanning of the world's scientific research may be indispensable. If industrial innovation is a national objective, it may be necessary to recast governmental policies to respond to this imperative for global scanning.

MEASURING THE IMPUTS TO INNOVATION

Another issue of considerable importance for policymakers is whether the amount of successful industrial research and development in any country bears a systematic relationship to the volume of the inputs directly committed to R&D activity in that country. There is a clear assumption that the relationship must be positive and strong, and because that assumption exists, concern was expressed when U.S. commitments to such activities seemed to be declining in the late 1960s. The declining could be seen both in the number of scientists and engineers engaged in R&D and in the national level of R&D expenditures.[7]

That R&D inputs have some relationship to subsequent R&D outputs no doubt has some validity, but whether a decline in inputs can be taken as a certain signal for a subsequent decline in outputs is another matter.[8] R&D budgets are typically influenced by the anticipation that investments will be profitable, but these estimates are characteristically subject to large margins of error. Other factors also influence the R&D budget, such as the firm's desire to imitate competitors as a form of hedging, the level of the firm's R&D expenditures in years past, and the firm's conception of some sort of appropriate long-run ratio between its R&D expenditures and its sales.[9] Factors such as these could produce a correlation between inputs and outputs in any given industry or firm, without any implication of substantial causality running from input changes to output changes.

In any case, the statistical record of U.S. inputs to R&D activities in recent years presents an ambiguous picture. Although the growth of such activities seemed to be slowing in the period from the latter 1960s to the mid-1970s, it picked up again about the mid-1970s, and since then has kept pace with the trends of other countries.[10]

Interpreting the figures on R&D investments is complicated further by some familiar statistical problems of coverage, composition, and weighting. What is labelled as an R&D input varies over time in any country. The differences begin on the shop floor and in the laboratory. If development work is being conducted in relatively small manufacturing firms, there is a good chance that it will not be sharply distinguished from production costs or marketing costs; if it is being conducted in machinery rather than in chemical industries, the possibility of such lack of differentiation is increased; if the development entails the packaging of components produced by others, rather than the design of new components, the risks of omitting the distinction are also relatively high. As a result, advances in technology, in the number of innovating firms, and on the mix of the innovating industries in any country cause variations in the coverage of the data made available which may be misinterpreted as a signal of a national changing level of effort. Comparing the level of innovation being carried out in different countries may also be difficult due to national definitions. For example, the USSR reports about twice as many scientists and engineers engaged in R&D as the United States,[11] even though the innovational output of the USSR is quite small.

As a rule, when analysts measure the level of R&D effort, they normalize the figures in some way in order to improve the comparability of the figures among countries and across time. Where the number of scientists and engineers in R&D is being monitored, for example, the numbers are usually normalized by the aggregate size of the workforce. Where R&D expenditures are being studied, a common method of normalization is to calculate a ratio of national R&D expenditures in any year to the gross national product (GNP) for that year.

It is hard to know how to interpret changes in the ratios that emerge from these normalization methods, however. In a period of rising GNP, for instance, a less-than-proportionate increase in R&D expenditures could be a sign of increasing efficiency in the application of such expenditures—that is, a sign that a given dollar of R&D effort generates more added product at the margin than in the past. In any event, just because GNP is increasing, the idea that expenditures on research and development ought to be increasing in equal proportion is not self-evident; and if GNP is declining while R&D expenditures are declining at a lesser rate, the improving ratio may offer no grounds for complacency.

MEASURING INNOVATIONAL OUTPUT

When we turn from measuring inputs to measuring outputs, a few points of fact are reasonably clear. On any measure, there is no doubt that Japan has improved its performance spectacularly in the past few decades, and there are hints that U.S. innovations have not been appearing in recent years as frequently as in the past. Indeed, the Japanese trend has been so vast that no systematic documentation is needed to confirm it. Lesser shifts, however, such as the putative decline in U.S. innovation, involve greater uncertainty.

The problems of measuring the output of innovational efforts take a number of forms, but one set of such problems is reminiscent of the difficulty encountered in measuring inputs. When attempting to define a successful industrial innovation, it soon becomes evident that objective standards are hard to establish. Researchers have found various ways of evading the daunting problem of defining what constitutes an innovation, but in the end they usually fall back on the strategem of calling an innovation whatever industry specialists choose to designate. Using that criterion, for instance, one study shows that a group of fifty-seven U.S.-based multinational enterprises introduced only thirty-four innovations between 1971 and 1975, as compared to over sixty innovations in most of the preceding five-year periods.[12]

But can we be sure just what the figures mean? We cannot, for instance, exclude the possibility that innovations in machinery are of quite different proportions and significance from innovations in electronics, as the specialists in the respective industries see them, so that differences in industrial mix over time can create the illusion of a shift in innovative output.

Of the various efforts to measure innovational output, those that are based on counts of patents issued are probably the least ambiguous in their coverage. Sophisticated econometric analyses of national and individual firm patent data are going on now that promise to ferret out the underlying tendencies concealed in these data.[13]

Despite the care with which scholars are now beginning to plumb the patent data, the ambiguities associated with the data continue to be overwhelming. Once again, however, the Japanese performance is clear: Japan's inventors are increasingly prominent among holders of newly issued patents in practically all major countries.[14] But weaknesses in the data place in serious doubt many other inferences, including the inference regarding the absolute decline of U.S. innovational activity.

The number of patents filed by inventors of any country is a function of several variables. Obviously, the paramount variable is the existence of innovations with sufficient novelty to be accepted by patent examiners. A second variable is the inventors' strategy —their choice between attempting to keep the invention an unpatented secret or disclosing the invention and securing legal protection. A third variable is inventors' expectations of doing business in the patent-issuing jurisdiction—that is, the expectation that there will be a commercial interest to protect.

We are, unfortunately, back to the ineluctable fact that all of these judgments differ according to industry, country, and timing. Patents in some branches of electronics are of little value because they are so swiftly overtaken by subsequent developments; patents in pharmaceuticals or in machinery may be quite another matter. Patents in some countries may be useless to the inventor because the prospects of doing business in those countries are slight at the time of invention, but the picture can change within a decade, as it has for many Japanese enterprises.

The U.S. case is of particular importance in the context of this book since the patent data so clearly display a decline during the 1970s in the relative position of U.S. inventors, both at home and abroad.[15] This decline has been much greater than the concurrent decline in R&D expenditures. At the same time, in practically all industrialized countries, real R&D expenditures per patent issued have risen considerably.[16] Numerous factors could explain these interesting trends, including some of the definitional and weighting possibilities mentioned earlier. But one hypothesis applies to U.S. inventions with particular force.

Recall that the 1950s and much of the 1960s were periods in which U.S. technological supremacy was largely unchallenged. During this period, however, inventors in other countries, notably those in Japan, were scanning U.S. inventions with increasing intensity. As foreign inventors began to press closer to the U.S. technological frontier, the possibility of rivalling the Americans, rather than simply accepting their innovations in the form of products, became increasingly real. It is not easy to say exactly how U.S. inventors responded to the increased scanning and rivalry of foreigners; from some points of view, the patent could have grown more important, from other points of view, less. On balance, however, it is possible that the advantages of secrecy have grown in the eyes of inventors everywhere, but especially of inventors in the United States.

All this, of course, is conjecture, to be explored and tested with more study. Meanwhile, we have come away from repeated scrutinies of the data on the absolute and relative trends in U.S. innovation not quite sure what the data were implying. Japan's rapid expansion has seemed evident enough; some slowing up in the pace of U.S. innovations has seemed a possibility, although far from a certainty. The length of time that any innovator—American, Japanese, or any other—can hope to retain an unchallenged lead has probably been considerably shortened. But why such changes would suggest a grave problem is not evident. Up to this point in the analysis, therefore, the nature of the problem remains obscure.

THE SLIPPERY PRODUCTIVITY CONCEPT

A more sweeping and more inclusive concern on the part of observers than concern for the obscure problem of innovation is that the long-term growth of U.S. productivity may be coming to an end. In the hands of U.S. industry, according to the usual assumption, given inputs of labor, capital, and raw materials can no longer be counted on by enterprises hoping to expand their foreign interests. Although developments of a similar sort have occurred in most of the countries of Western Europe (and even Japan), the decline in the ability of U.S. enterprises to increase their output from a given input appears to have been more pronounced than elsewhere.

A decline in U.S. productivity usually conjures up a picture consisting of four general trends: aging factories incapable of delivering as much as they did in the past; indifferent labor, less attentive to the job and prone to work stoppages; increasingly costly raw materials, drawn from deeper mines and wells or remote foreign sources; and more restrictive governmental regulations that raise costs in order to protect the environment, to increase health and safety, to reduce job discrimination, or to serve other social objectives. A wealth of individual illustrations puts meat on the arid bones of such possibilities and demonstrates beyond serious doubt that each of these scenarios is actually happening in at least some sectors of U.S. industry.

Worries over the apparent decline in U.S. productivity have produced a number of careful and perceptive econometric studies of the recent behavior of the U.S. economy.[17] These studies have generally confirmed the fact that the statistics on U.S. inputs and outputs were reflecting some substantial changes in the U.S. economy in the first half of the 1970s, but the obvious possibilities, such as a decline in the willingness of labor to work or the failure of new machines to provide higher output, did not seem to be the culprits. Studies of this sort, by disposing of these obvious possibilities, have tended to focus attention on the role of "advances in knowledge" as the possible cause of the declining trends recorded by the statistics. But the link between the supposed productivity decline and the role of knowledge has been almost purely inferential; some researchers have simply used the "knowledge" rubric as an explanation for an otherwise unexplained outcome.

Although some of the econometric analyses that are attempting to capture the underlying factors in the trend are of unexceptionable quality, they are obliged to rest on data that are imprecise in meaning.[18] We have already explored some of the problems associated with the data that purport to measure the inputs and outputs associated with innovation. Where the larger issue of productivity is involved, questions about the meaning of the underlying data proliferate.

As with the analysis of innovation, econometric efforts require measures of output and input. The output in this instance is national product or national income, while the inputs cover labor, capital, and national resources, including land. Measuring total output for a nation over a series of years is never an easy exercise. A major source of potential statistical error lies in the prices that are used to deflate figures purporting to represent the value of output. One bold study, for instance, demonstrates that the gyrations in productivity data in the early 1970s—which reflected sharp rises followed by sharper declines—could have been due almost entirely to the price run-up in oil and the sporadic attempts at price control during the interval.[19]

More generally, it is difficult to produce appropriate price deflation when products are being greatly modified, when production processes are in flux, and when the relative number of units of the various products is changing. Consider, for instance, the output of the construction industry, an industry that is usually identified as one of the principal culprits in the reported decline of U.S. productivity.[20] The problem in this case is to find a measure of output that combines in one overall total a constantly changing mix of residences, skyscrapers, warehouses, roads, and bridges. The starting point in such an exercise is to find the aggregate value of the output, then to deflate it by some appropriate index that eliminates the effects of price changes from one year to the next. In this particular case, there is ample evidence that the deflator that is being officially used significantly overstates the actual increase in costs, largely because it fails to take into account the various ways in which the construction industry has been conserving on the use of high-cost union labor. As a result, the deflated figures that purport to measure the trends in construction output appear to be understating such output by considerable amounts.

Consider, too, the problems of measuring automobile output in a period such as the present, when quality standards are on the rise. In industries such as automotives, one begins with what look like hard numbers, namely, the number of cars produced. If the changes in models are minor, one would be tempted to use the number of units produced—or some deflated index of the value of production—as a guide to output. Yet to do so would be misleading; the change in quality could be overlooked in the measure of output.

When measuring the output of any industry over long periods

of time, other problems crop up. How is one to compare, for instance, the DC-6s of the 1950s with the DC-10s of the 1970s? Relative prices may provide some basis for comparing the output represented by a new product with that represented by an existing one; on that basis one DC-10 could be thought of, say, as the equivalent of four DC-6s. But if the analyst is interested in the productivity of the industry, relative prices are a treacherous basis for comparing output. The price of the existing product may reflect quite different factors from that of the old, such as a different competitive position in the market including a different stage in the product cycle. Factors such as these may conceivably create offsetting biases in the data; but the biases can also be systematic, pushing the aggregate figures in one direction or the other.

Whereas some of the shifts in output may take place within a given product line such as aircraft, others will occur between different types of products or services. Output may shift, for instance, from more cigarettes to more medical services, or from more automobiles to more traffic direction. Such shifts present a familiar statistical problem, even more difficult than the problem of the changing qualities of aircraft: how to find a common point of comparison for the output of the assembly line worker and the output of the traffic policeman. In practice, as it turns out, the output of each is measured quite differently: the first, by some proxy for the output of automobiles; the second, by a measure of inputs rather than outputs, such as the cost of the labor, gasoline, and equipment used in the directing of traffic.

The problems of measuring output in a rapidly changing environment are compounded even further by messy questions of accounting. Change is characteristically accompanied by abnormally high expenditures of a nonrepetitive kind; these are usually lumped together under such deceptive rubrics as start-up costs or learning costs. Such costs, being nonrepetitive and having a lasting impact on subsequent output, could as well be dubbed capital expenditures. In some cases, the classification chosen may not affect the statistician's measure of industry output; in other cases, it may depress the total output measure (while at the same time understating investment in the industry).

Still another kind of problem in measuring output—especially in the 1970s—has already drawn considerable attention. This is the question of whether a nation's output should be increased by some amount to reflect industry's added expenditures aimed at preventing the destruction of the environment or prolonging the lives of workers. Two rather different kinds of additions to output may thus be justified: benefits that are immediately generated as free goods, such as cleaner air, and benefits that will appear much later, such as the lengthening of worker lifespan.

When attempting to evaluate the effect of factors such as these on changes in the output of the United States, the bias they introduce may not matter a great deal, provided their influence does not vary much over the course of time. And comparisons of U.S. data with those of other countries need not be greatly imperiled, provided the size of the biases introduced in all the various countries has been more or less the same. Unfortunately, however, the decades of the 1960s and 1970s were periods of extraordinarily rapid change, periods in which existing products and services were being modified and new products introduced at a dizzying rate. It was a period, too, in which environmental, health, and safety efforts all over the world were vastly expanded, but at rates and in forms that varied from one country to the next.

The problems associated with output are matched by equally difficult problems on the input side. Labor hours, for instance, are not a homogeneous input: there are hours on the assembly line or the farm and hours in the laboratory, hours of the inexperienced young worker and hours of the superannuated worker, hours of men and those of women. During the past few decades, as we have already noted, the U.S. economy and the economies of other countries were changing rapidly, and not altogether synchronously. In the United States, for instance, an influx of young workers, minority workers, immigrant workers, and women substantially changed both the size and composition of the workforce, changes that were not matched by Europe or Japan. One ambitious study concludes that an apparent reduction in U.S. labor productivity for the period 1965–1978 as compared with prior years can be entirely explained by the decline in the "quality" of the U.S. labor force. In any case, there is strong support for the proposition that such factors had a material effect upon the changes in the U.S. data between the 1960s and 1980s, as well as in the comparisons of performance between countries.

As noted earlier, there have been some quite valiant efforts on the part of inspired econometricians to find statistical adjustments for the various factors that might be distorting the interpretation of productivity measures. Even the most inspired efforts at statistical adjustment, however, have their pronounced limitations. An increase in the number of inexperienced workers in a factory, for instance, can create new work norms and thereby affect the productivity of all the workers in the factory, as well as the productivity of other factories that they supply; but it is too much to expect the econometrician to be able to pick up effects such as these. Similarly, adjusting an output measure for such factors as the decline in the corrosive effects of the atmosphere on people and materials has to be a grossly arbitrary exercise at best, however skillful the econometric technique may be.

Of course, it can be argued that many of these factors require no adjustment; after all, when the output per hour declines as a result of the inexperience of workers, the resulting decline is just as certain as if it were due to an increase in the laziness of workers. The ultimate object of most studies, however, including those in this book, is surely to find remedies by studying causes, and the remedy for inexperience is different from that for laziness. Curing laziness may require changes in policy, the curing of inexperience may require nothing more than the passage of time.

AN INTUITIVE LEAP

There is no ignoring the fact that a great deal has changed in the position of the U.S. economy over the past thirty years and that some of the changes are not cause for self-congratulation. Nor are we optimistic that some perceptive analyst will eventually put a finger on some primary cause for the seeming decline in U.S. activity. The list of candidates for investigation as possible villains in the piece is depressingly long. At the macroeconomic level, for instance, there is the low propensity of the U.S. public to save— a factor that is thought to elevate the cost of capital and increase the risks of inflation. In the field of industrial organization, barriers to exit confront large industrial firms in mature industrial societies such as the United States, which inhibit them from dropping their senescent lines of activity in favor of newer ones. In the field of regulation, there is the special nature of the U.S. regulatory process, which entails acute uncertainties and extraordinary delays as the parties exhaust their endless rights of argument and appeal. And there is the increasingly bureaucratic and technocratic character of U.S. business management, with its concentration on managing the price of the company's equity securities and avoiding takeover bids that threaten the managers' tenure.

Yet, if one is looking for factors that may have inhibited the industrial growth of the United States more than that of other countries, a few stand out as the most plausible. The relative decline in the U.S. economy, it should be emphasized, goes back to the 1950s and 1960s, when other countries began to close the gap in per capita income, in exports, and in various other measures. In the 1950s and the 1960s, you will recall, U.S. management and U.S. labor were still being extolled by most observers for their outstanding capabilities. Were the evaluations of observers in that earlier era wrong, or was the subsequent relative decline in the U.S. position the result of other factors?

We intuitively believe that some of the key forces that had elevated U.S. income beyond those of other industrialized countries during much of the nineteenth and early twentieth centuries began losing some of their power during the 1950s. One of these forces was the abundance and richness of the country's natural resources, including land. The other was the nature of U.S. innovations: under the special circumstances of the century-long period from the mid-1850s to the mid-1950s, U.S. innovations were mainly of a kind that would soon have a market in other countries.

Neither of these points needs a great deal of elaboration. The natural-resource position of the United States bestowed large Ricardian and monopoly rents upon the country for much of the century-long period—a situation reflected in heavy exports of resource-intensive products. But the country's export dominance in raw materials began to shrink visibly after World War I, and drastically after World War II, culminating in a great flood of oil imports in the 1970s. In the process, the United States lost its absolute advantage in many industries that drew on these raw materials. Moreover, U.S. manufacturers did not develop any great efficiency in procuring their needed materials from foreign sources, such as Japan succeeded in developing. U.S. antitrust policy banned the use of import cartels, thereby limiting the country's national bargaining power; U.S. foreign policy proved ineffective in discouraging the nationalization of its raw-material-producing subsidiaries in foreign countries, which were taken over in large numbers in the 1960s and 1970s; and in some cases, as in oil, copper, and timber, U.S. import policy provided some protection to the relatively inefficient domestic producers that remained. The upshot was that the U.S. competitive advantage in the resource industries was greatly narrowed, being retained mainly in agriculture.

Developments on the technological front, however, may have been even more important in determining the recent changes in the competitive position of the United States. Until the 1960s, the new products generated by U.S. industry were of a kind that would encounter rapidly growing demand in other countries. Responding to the relatively high income levels of the U.S. economy that had prevailed over many decades,[21] American entrepreneurs tended to concentrate their innovational activities on the satisfaction of novel, high-income wants and on reducing the use of their relatively high-cost labor; in the process, they tended to use capital and raw materials, including energy, with a profligacy that may have appropriately reflected those resources' relative prices in the United States. The Europeans and the Japanese, on the other hand, tended to concentrate their innovational energies on areas that would allow them to survive in competition with the Americans. That meant a special emphasis on processing techniques that cut costs and improved the quality of the U.S.-innovated products, and on developing variants of those products appropriate for lower-income markets.

For a time, it appeared that the innovational roles that their respective positions had assigned to the various countries were benefiting the U.S. entrepreneurs much more than the Europeans and the Japanese. As incomes rose in Europe and Japan during the 1950s and 1960s, and as labor costs rose in relation to capital costs and raw-material costs, the products created to meet American needs proved increasingly relevant for other markets as well.

That U.S. advantage, however, began to disappear in the 1970s —the victim of several different kinds of forces. First was a radical shift in the perceptions of producers and consumers regarding future trends in relative prices: capital and energy were expected to be the high-cost factors of the future, and the incomes of consumers were not expected to rise very rapidly. In a world of that sort, the innovational bent of the Europeans and the Japanese became much more relevant than before, in the sense that capital and energy became the factors to be saved, and price and quality became more important than novelty. At the same time, differences among the national economic environments that entrepreneurs faced in Europe, Japan, and the United States shrank rapidly. From a factor-cost viewpoint, the U.S. economy lost its distinctive characteristics as the prices of capital and raw materials moved more in line with prevailing factor prices elsewhere; and from a demand point of view, the same convergence occurred as the per capita income lead of the United States melted away. Finally, the Japanese government and a number of European governments systematically offered official support to some industries that faced formidable technological obstacles by helping them to assemble the needed capital and reduce the attendant development risks.

The upshot was that U.S. entrepreneurs confronted a national environment in which the innovational stimuli were no longer very different from those that their competitors faced. And they confronted the new situation with old innovational habits that no longer provided the advantage they once had. It is hardly surprising, therefore, that the innovational efforts of U.S. industry in the 1970s did not produce the competitive results that once seemed so assured.

In a textbook world of efficient markets, of course, none of this hypothesizing would make much sense. One would not expect to encounter a factor bias in the national innovations of entrepreneurs in different countries. In a textbook world, the friction of distance would not have played a role in the responses of entrepreneurs; all entrepreneurs would have been stimulated by the same profitmaking and cost-saving opportunities, irrespective of the country in which they were located. And if, perchance, some such bias did develop, exchange rates or internal price levels would promptly operate to wipe out the overall competitive advantage of any of the competing countries.

But, of course, entrepreneurs have been operating under conditions that do not easily fit the textbook model. The propensity of U.S. entrepreneurs to resist adapting to the market needs of their foreign customers, although documented mainly through anecdotal evidence, has nevertheless been unquestionable. Moreover, the resistance of such entrepreneurs could be explained rationally by the fact that U.S. enterprises have looked on innovational activities and managerial attention as scarce, rationed resources to be doled out in response to those opportunities whose prospective yields seemed highest—opportunities in the huge U.S. market. So long as these activities are considered to be rationed, enterprises will direct them first toward what they perceive to be the most profitable opportunities. The same focus suggests why Japanese managers and innovators have studied U.S. technology and the U.S. market with such rapt attention. For the Japanese, assimilating U.S. technology and penetrating U.S. markets has offered the promise of large profits.

As for the textbook expectation that exchange rates and prices would bring about market equilibrium, those hopes too were repeatedly thwarted. At times, the vagaries of capital-market movements produced exchange rates that inhibited the necessary adjustments, while at other times the sluggishness in the responses of labor and management delayed the adjustment process.

Yet the efficient market model does offer one hint for the future: The disparity between U.S. innovational habits and the needs of international competitiveness are not likely to last forever. In time, U.S. entrepreneurs can be expected to observe the innovational developments of other countries with great care, in the belated realization that those innovations offer relevant profitmaking signals, and they can be expected to innovate in directions that acknowledge the disappearance of the unique factor-cost configurations of the United States. Whether they may also need a boost from official sources in situations where the risks are very high and the scale of needed effort is very large is less certain at this stage, but the possibility is not to be excluded.

CONCLUSION

There is little room for complacency concerning the performance of the U.S. economy over the past decade or so. The degree of economic slowdown may have been overstated, and the causes of the slowdown different from those that conventional wisdom has identified, but the performance of the economy has definitely been disturbing in certain critical respects. But why? And what is to be done about it?

With phenomena as complex as those described in this chapter the researcher invariably is confronted with difficult choices. Investigations may be framed as a series of tests directed toward precise hypotheses, and these tests can lead to the rejection of the hypotheses. However, even the most ambitious analysis turns out to cover only a restricted facet of a very large problem. The tests will be significant in a statistical sense or not, the sign right or wrong, but the questions that have not been addressed are still likely to overwhelm the researcher.

The alternative when dealing with a highly complex problem is to cast a much wider net, albeit with a far coarser mesh, relying on history, case studies, and unstructured data for a hint of the underlying processes and likely solutions. Insofar as hypotheses are implicitly or explicitly tested in this approach, the tests can only be of a low order of rigor and with weak capabilities for discriminating among competing propositions.

The choice of approach is a matter of the researcher's temperament and taste. No single approach, though, is likely to bring the research much closer to a definitive understanding of the processes that appear to have slowed the U.S. economy.

NOTES

1. Calculated from F. Cutler and C. Douty, "Foreign Capital Outlays and Sales of U.S. Companies," *Survey of Current Business* 41 (September 1961): 70; *Economic Report of the President* (Washington, D.C.: U.S. Government Printing Office, 1981), p. 240; U.S. Department of Commerce, Bureau of Economic Analysis, *U.S. Direct Investments Abroad, 1966* and *1977* (Washington, D.C.: U.S. Government Printing Office, 1972 and 1981), pp. 70 and 283, respectively.
2. Data on this point are fragmentary, but see Raymond Vernon *Sovereignty at Bay: The Multinational Spread of U.S. Enterprises* (New York: Basic Books, 1971), p. 101.
3. See, for instance, R. E. Lipsey and M. Y. Weiss, "Foreign Production and Exports in Manufacturing Industries," *Review of Economics and Statistics* 63, no. 4 (November 1981): 488–94.
4. See, for instance, Edwin Mansfield et al., *Research and Innovation in the Modern Corporation* (New York: Norton, 1971); Illinois Institute of Technology Research Institute, *TRACES: Technology in Retrospect and Critical Events in Science,* Vols. 1 and 2 (Chicago: IIT Research Institute, 1968, 1969).

5. See, for instance, T. J. Allen, *Managing the Flow of Technology* (Cambridge, Mass.: MIT Press, 1978), especially pp. 35–56, 126–79.
6. For instance, E. E. Rogers, *Communication of Innovations,* 2nd ed. (New York: Free Press, 1971); Nathan Rosenberg, "Factors Affecting the Diffusion of Technology," *Explorations in Economic History* 10, no. 1 (Fall 1972): 3–33.
7. National Science Board, *Science Indicators 1980* (Washington, D.C.: U.S. Government Printing Office, 1981), pp. 50–70.
8. A review of the evidence on this point, which expresses reservations similar to those in this chapter, is found in Rolf Piekarz, Eleanor Thomas, and Donna Jennings, "International Comparisons of Research and Development Expenditures" (Paper presented at an American Enterprise Institute conference on productivity, September 30, 1982).
9. Edwin Mansfield, *The Economics of Technological Change* (New York: Norton, 1968), p. 64; Mansfield et al., *Research and Innovation,* pp. 84–109.
10. For a careful analysis of U.S. R&D expenditures as compared with other countries during the period 1964 to 1978, see Piekarz, Thomas, and Jennings, "International Comparisons."
11. *Science Indicators 1980,* p. 108.
12. Raymond Vernon and W. H. Davidson, "Foreign Production of Technology-Intensive Products by U.S.-Based Multi-national Enterprises," National Science Foundation, no. PB 80 148638 (Boston: National Science Foundation, 1979), p. 38.
13. See, for instance, a study sponsored by the National Bureau of Economic Research which is beginning to produce a series of working papers. Particularly insightful are: K. B. Clark and Zvi Griliches, "Productivity and Growth at the Business Level" (Discussion Paper no. 910, Harvard Institute of Economic Research, July 1982); and John Bound et al., "Who Does R&D and Who Patents?" (Discussion Paper no. 913, Harvard Institute of Economic Research, July 1982).
14. R. E. Evenson, "International Invention: Implications for Technology Market Assessment" (Center Discussion Paper no. 419, Economic Growth Center, Yale University, July 1982), p. 13.
15. Ibid.
16. Ibid.
17. Notably, E. F. Denison, *Accounting for Slower Economic Growth: The United States in the 1970s* (Washington, D.C.: Brookings Institution, 1979); John W. Kendrick and E. Grossman, *Productivity in the United States: Trends and Cycles* (Baltimore: Johns Hopkins Press, 1980); Zvi Griliches, "R&D and the Productivity Slowdown," *American Eco-*

nomic Review 70, no. 2 (May 1980): 343–48; N. E. Terleckyj, *R&D and U.S. Industrial Productivity in the 1970s* (Washington, D.C.: National Planning Association, 1981).

18. This subject is carefully explored in a number of sources. See especially *Measurement and Interpretation of Productivity,* prepared under the chairmanship of Albert Rees by a panel of the National Research Council (Washington, D.C.: National Academy of Sciences, 1979); also Denison, *Accounting for Slower Economic Growth,* especially pp. 122–47.

19. Michael R. Darby, "The U.S. Productivity Slowdown: A Case of Statistical Myopia" (Working Paper no. 1018, National Bureau of Economic Research, November 1982).

20. For a review of the construction industry data, see Clint Bourdon, "Is Construction Productivity Declining?" (Joint Center for Urban Studies Working Paper no. 68, Cambridge, Mass., April 1981).

21. Michael Darby, "The U.S. Productivity Slowdown."

3 JAPAN'S CHALLENGE TO THE UNITED STATES
Industrial Policies and Corporate Strategies

Yoshi Tsurumi

In 1951 Japan's gross national product was only one twenty-fifth of the U.S. level. By 1984 Japan had closed this gap to about one-half the United States' $3 trillion economy (at current exchange rates). At this level Japan's per capita income approaches that of the United States, which has slipped to tenth place on the per capita scale. According to many economists, Japan's GNP will eventually overtake the U.S. GNP by the year 2000. The once complementary trade and investment relationship between the United States and Japan in the 1950s and 1960s has changed to a competitive one since the early 1970s. As Japan's economic gains are increasingly perceived as being made at the expense of the United States and Europe, many in U.S. business and government circles are troubled by at least two major questions: Is Japan the only country able to achieve industrial growth in the face of chronic shortages of technology, capital, and other necessary resources in an complex, interdependent world? And if the United States follows the examples of the Western European nations by protecting domestic industries against Japanese imports, what will happen to the system of multilateral free-world trade and investment which the United States has helped to shape since the end of World War II?

39

INDICATIVE ECONOMIC PLANNING: JAPAN'S SUPPLY MANAGEMENT

Although popular lore may lead us to believe that Japan's industrial development since the 1870s was brought about by selfless, farsighted, sagacious bureaucrats and patriotic industrialists,[1] in reality, Japan's rapid growth owes to the luck of external factors combined with profit-seeking private initiatives. The Japanese government has, in fact, merely concentrated on building a national consensus around industrial goals and on providing a framework that weeds out weak private firms so that only the strongest emerge as internationally competitive forces.[2]

Legacy of the Pre-World War II Era

When World War II ended with Japan's total defeat, the country had but a few institutional legacies left with which to reconstruct the war-torn economy. In this legacy, however, are the lessons of Japan's cumulative trial-and-error approach to rapid industrialization from the 1870s to 1945.

Japan believed firmly in a model of self-reliant economic development that avoided, where possible, dependence on foreign direct investments for capital, technology, foreign exchange (access to export markets), managerial skill, or ideology. During this period, government policymakers and industrialists remained convinced of the wisdom of turning to the one, renewable resource Japan had in abundance—people.

Early in the 1870s, almost as an act of faith, business and government leaders assumed that hard work coupled with improved technical skills of the Japanese population would make up for their country's scarcity of capital and technology.[3] Three-quarters of a century later, Japan had succeeded in ingraining this approach to economic growth squarely in the minds of the Japanese people. The self-reliant model of economic growth based on the perpetual improvement of human resources, led in time to another Japanese business trait—namely, the practice of scanning the world for any useful hints regarding technological innovations, market developments, institutional reforms, or knowledge of foreign markets.

Always mindful of the fact that Japan must import to prosper, this sense of dependency on the rest of the world for food and raw materials prepared Japan to regard it own exports as public benefits that can be produced alongside the private, profitmaking benefits.

In order to catch up with the West during the prewar period, Japan coordinated the tasks of manufacturers, banks, and trading firms to expand manufacturing and mercantile activities in less time than had been required historically of their American and European counterparts.[4] Out of this "division-of-task" approach arose large, general trading firms (sogoshosha) like Mitsui and Mitsubishi, profit-oriented, institutional innovations of established Japanese industrialists and merchants. By becoming efficient distributors of products, services, financial credits, information, and technologies inside and outside Japan, these sogoshosha and their smaller counterparts, senmonshosha, helped fledgling Japanese manufacturers to service both national and international markets. This system was able to procure necessary raw materials, technologies, and market information from abroad at a fraction of the costs smaller businesses would have had to incur if left alone to develop individually at home and abroad.[5]

Japan's self-reliant model of managing rapid industrial growth despite a chronic shortage of necessary resources assigned the executive branch of the government (more importantly, the central bureaucracy) the function of orchestrating national goals, allocating scarce resources, arbitrating interfirm disputes, and, above all, promoting the industries with future growth potential even at the expense of mature or declining industries. The career bureaucrats, who enjoyed continuous tenure within the central ministries, assured a continuity of industrial policies. Their business counterparts, who maintained equally long careers within their respective firms, in turn made uninterrupted, cumulative dialogue possible between business and government circles concerning the common task of setting and implementing economic goals for the nation as a whole.

The demarcation between public and private domains—the distinction between what governments should do and what private firms should do—has always been blurred and drawn with expediency. Even at the outset of Japan's industrialization, private enterprises believed that the government would turn public business ventures, once successful, into their hands[6] As private firms developed their own manufacturing and mercantile capabilities, the government role was increasingly reduced to that of preparing the national framework for industrial development. On the other hand, backed by the government's pro-business attitude, business circles had long come to regard it as ideologically legitimate for government officials to meddle with their business ventures. For the government to steer national economic and political development, it had to develop intimate knowledge of private firms. Moreover, the fact that leaders of government, business, the mass media, and academic circles traditionally came out of a handful of leading universities facilitated both formal and informal communication between business and other important sectors of Japanese society. A cooperative and consultative mode of business-government interactions was quickly established.

Post-World War II Events

Postwar economic growth in Japan was aided a great deal by a series of political, social, and economic reforms that were carried out by the U.S. occupying forces, but often with the help of eager Japanese who had long been frustrated by imperial Japan's rejection of their reform demands. Land reform, for example, unleashed the productive zeal of previously landless tenant peasants and small farmers. The dissolution of *zaibatsu* combines permitted young managerial cadres to chart rather freely the recovery and growth of their respective firms.[7] Promotion of industrial labor unions legitimized employees' active participation in managing the workplace and led to the growth of enterprise-based unions. The rise of these unions prevented Japanese managers from laying off rank-and-file employees should any effort to shift the blame for managerial mistakes to the employees be made.[8]

Together with the dissolution of the private stockholdings of *zaibatsu* families, the "democratization" of the market paved the way for the subsequent growth of competitive markets, which helped private firms to raise additional capital. General suffrage and a series of political reforms made political parties susceptible to a public demand that the central bureaucracy balance the diverse interests of consumers, laborers, farmers, and other nonbusiness groups. The complete abandonment of imperial army and navy forces not only reduced the financial burden of military expenditures but, more importantly, returned Japanese political power to the technocrats who were concerned only with the industrial recovery of the country. None of these reforms was specifically intended to help the recovery of the Japanese economy; rather, they were intended to excise what the occupying forces believed were the foundations of a militaristic Japan. In retrospect, however, one cannot but greatly appreciate how useful these reforms turned out to be in facilitating Japan's economic growth.

With the dissolution of *zaibatsu* groups, the government of the present Ministry of International Trade and Industry (MITI) emerged as the central governmental unit steering industrial policies. Just as business and government leaders of prewar Japan did, MITI rejected unrestricted laissez-faire, market-based resource allocation in favor of targeted allocations of scarce resources to improve the long-term supply capabilities of key industries. For this purpose, MITI revived the wartime practice of government-business collaboration for distributing scarce resources to a limited number of high-priority projects through industry associations. MITI emphasized the complete metamorphosis of the Japanese economy from a dependence on light goods and low-technology industries to an economic base of heavy industries, and particularly chemicals.

From 1946 to 1948 MITI broke serious production bottlenecks in the coal and steel industries by providing them with the necessary capital and materials and by simultaneously linking them through a strict barter arrangement. As the coal and steel industries regained self-sustaining power they, in turn, pulled the machinery and chemical industries out of their collapse.[9] From this experience, the basic tenet of MITI's management of long-term supply capabilities for the Japanese economy emerged: MITI would identify critical production bottlenecks in the economy and locate key industries with growth potential at home and abroad. Then, MITI would select a number of large, growth-minded firms in the target industries in order to help them become self-sustaining. In turn, the large manufacturing firms, revived or further nourished by MITI's assistance, would pull up small and medium-sized firms clustering around them.

After Japan regained political independence in 1951, Japanese business and government circles continued to concentrate on improving the long-term supply capability of the Japanese economy. Shipbuilding was the first industry to be selected as the "national champion" of the 1950s because a vast world market existed for tankers. Since shipbuilding requires a variety of industrial and electrical equipment, steam turbines and diesel engines, and lots of sheet and slab steel, the widespread "industrial linkage effects" of the shipbuilding industry could be counted on to revitalize both technological innovation and production capacity across a wide range of machinery and heavy industries. With the help of international trading firms, which successfully persuaded Greek shipowners to divert their orders from the United Kingdom and Norway to Japanese shipyards, ships became the leading export product of Japan by the mid-1950s. Product innovations, which allowed mammoth tankers to be produced and delivered in about half the time required of smaller-sized tankers from British and Norwegian competitors, raised the quality image of Japanese tankers and freighters and helped to reverse the prewar, world market perception of things "made in Japan" as shoddy products.[10]

The foreign exchange costs of the shipbuilding industry were financed by MITI. At the time (1950–1951), Japan was experiencing an unusual increase in foreign exchange from sales of goods and services during the Korean War. MITI channeled the foreign-exchange earnings of old, leading export items like toys, textiles, and ceramics into shipbuilding and related industries. Later, in the 1960s and 1970s, it was the shipbuilding industry's turn to earn foreign exchange that could be earmarked for newly targeted industries such as petrochemicals, automobiles, electrical and electronic equipment, and computers.

Three Guiding Principles

From the 1950s to the 1960s, as Japanese business and government circles saw the cumulative benefits of targeted industrial policies, there evolved three guiding principles for the indicative economic planning of Japan. First, the government would promote "the survival of the fittest" in each targeted industry,[11] favoring those firms that demonstrated their viability and competitive prowess at home and abroad. The export performance of manufacturing firms would be the acid test that their technological and marketing capabilities were worthy of international standards. This policy triggered intense vying among industrial firms for the leading positions in their respective industries and for global market standing.

Second, the government would administer market competition to weed out the weaker firms.[12] The increases in the productivity of labor, raw materials, and capital that accompanied technological innovation fueled active price and quality competition not only in such basic industries as steel, nonferrous metals, and chemicals, but also in electrical machinery, shipbuilding, telecommunication equipment, and automobiles. The price and quality consciousness of the large exporting firms was in turn to be transmitted throughout the Japanese industrial structure to firms supplying input to the exporting firms. This "administered market competition," with a pronounced export orientation, proved to be the means by which Japanese indicative economic planning conveyed the discipline of international price and quality competition to both the exporting and nonexporting sectors of the economy. Industrial concentrations were encouraged in order to permit the realization of economies of scale. But the exposure of these large firms to export competition prevented such growing industrial concentration from stifling technological innovation and price competition.

Nowhere is this model of administered market competition more clearly illustrated than in the initial stages of the Japanese computer industry. As in the case of other technology-intensive industries, the growth potential of the computer industry was first recognized around the mid-1950s by a number of Japanese electronic and electrical equipment manufacturers. MITI, however, did not take note of this trend until the early 1960s. By then, thirteen Japanese hopefuls had entered the market, all of which were too technologically and financially weak to combat the dominant force in the market, IBM (Japan).

In 1961 MITI gave financial aid to seven of the hopeful firms who formed a joint computer-lease-financing company with equity capital invested in equal amounts by each of the firms. In the process of subsequent market competition, the more successful firms drew off most of the financial resources of the lease-finance company, and the weaker companies were forced to subsidize their stronger competitors.[13] By the late 1960s three survivors, Fujitsu,

NEC-Hitachi, and Univac-Oki, emerged and they moved on to compete with IBM inside and outside Japan. Mitsubishi Electric and Toshiba had to drop out of the large-scale computer market but reemerged ten years later on their own accord as contenders in the minicomputer field.

The government's use of administered market competition distinguished Japan's indicative economic planning from that of the United Kingdom and France. For instance, France's Plan Calcul and the British government's efforts, both of which were aimed at developing nationally leading computer firms during the 1960s, merely concentrated on financially subsidizing their respective fledgling computer companies without exposing them to market competition at home and abroad as a stimulus for technological and marketing innovations.

As the third principle in Japan's indicative economic planning program, the role of the government as the change agent of Japan's industrial structure was firmly established. Indeed, business leaders, government policymakers, and even academic economists came to regard the industry as something to manipulate so that both the scope and direction of changes in the industrial structure would guide the growth strategies of individual firms.[14]

Implementation of Indicative Economic Planning

The emergence of indicative economic planning can be clearly traced to the first five-year economic plan of 1948.[15] At this time, a broad development goal was set in terms of the targeted growth rate of the economy and the direction of changes in the industrial structure was illustrated by identifying a list of new products (or industries) for Japan to emphasize. During the drawing up of this five-year plan—a broad declaration of future economic scenarios —private businesses became formally and informally involved in debating diverse social and economic goals with government officials and academics. Exposure to market competition at home and abroad acted as stimulus.

The Economic Planning Agency (established in 1946) initiated the first economic plan by feeding various economic forecasts to the advisory councils of different ministries. Business leaders, representatives of regional business and industrial associations, academics, journalists, and labor unionists were appointed to sub-committees to discuss and evaluate, together with government officials, various scenarios of Japan's industrial development for the next five to ten years. These committees dealt with employment, economic growth, balance of trade, income distribution, price trends, technological capabilities and growth, productivity improvement, and other macroeconomic scenarios and then translated them into specific industrial goals. This consultative process permitted government officials to appreciate the needs of private-interest groups and enabled these groups to appreciate the public-policy concerns of the nation. Through the efforts of various mass media, the scenarios were publicly debated throughout their formative stages. Once these scenarios were accepted as national goals, they were widely propagated, again through the mass media, and each business firm was able to tailor its own growth plan according to the macroeconomic framework of the nations's growth.[16]

The First Stage, 1948–1963.   In these first fifteen years, the Economic Planning Agency initiated process quotas, and "government administrative" guidance of selective import restrictions were added to restrictions on foreign direct investments. Only technical licensing agreements—the importation of requisite product and production-process technologies—and joint-venture forms of foreign direct investments were selectively promoted by MITI. This policy helped targeted firms in key industries to acquire necessary technology from abroad. Allocation of foreign exchange, a scarce resource at the time, was used to regulate the inflows of technology and the importation of necessary raw materials and industrial equipment.

Investment capital, another scarce resource, was rationed by the Bank of Japan through the conduits of a select number of commercial banks to targeted manufacturing activities and market developments.[17] Priorities for capital loans were set by the Ministry of Finance in line with the national scenarios of economic development, and these priorities were published and updated as recognized needs changed. However, it was the commercial banks that had to screen in detail the various loan applications from their client manufacturing and trading firms. These commercial banks borrowed heavily from the Bank of Japan but nevertheless had to absorb the economic risks of their own capital loan programs. Decisions in underwriting the financial needs of private industrial development plans were to be based on business judgments, not political ambitions.

Such fiscal incentives as accelerated depreciation, deferred tax liabilities, and exemptions from excise taxes were specifically devised to encourage expansion and improvement of manufacturing capacity, export activities, and development of overseas markets. Those firms that performed well by public-benefit standards in exports, modernization of their manufacturing facilities, and technological innovations were often further rewarded by the government's favorable treatment of the firms' applications for additional technical licensing agreements with foreign firms and by foreign-exchange allotments required for importation of materials and the opening of overseas marketing subsidiaries.

The Second Stage, 1964–1972. Japan accepted Article 11 of the General Agreement on Tariffs and Trade (GATT) in 1963 and moved to dismantle the import quota system. From 1962 to 1963, the number of GATT Residual Quota Items were reduced from 466 to 197, and from 1963 to 1972, they were cut further from 197 to 33.[18] In 1964 Japan joined the Organization for Economic Cooperation and Development (OECD) and accepted Article 8 of the International Monetary Fund (IMF) Charter, thus removing foreign exchange controls on inflows and outflows of capital.

With the progressive dismantling of import restrictions and foreign exchange controls, the Japanese government lost two of its tools for meting out rewards and punishments to selected industries. After the development of domestic capital markets and given the increased cash inflows of many growing firms, capital and credit rationing were no longer effective in motivating firms in a specific direction. Instead, the government promoted the absorption of newer and newer technologies into the hands of private industry.

The Third Stage, after 1973. In addition to the further dismantling of tariff and nontariff impediments to imports, Japan gradually abandoned restrictions on foreign direct investments from the end of the 1960s to early the 1970s. The first oil crisis of 1973–1974 and the second oil crisis of 1979 severely tested the capabilities of the industrial management system of Japan to absorb massive external economic shocks under the floating exchange-rate system. The system demonstrated its ability to adjust itself quickly to such shocks, however.[19] For example, after the first oil crisis triggered a 20 to 30 percent annual rate of inflation in Japan, less than a year was required to bring it down to a single-digit inflation figure and to move the Japanese economy onto a new, steady growth path.

Prior to the first oil crisis, MITI had been trying to contain the influence in the Japanese market of such major international oil firms as ESSO (Exxon's subsidiary), Mobil, Caltex, and Shell Oil. Once the worldwide oil supply was curtailed, MITI quietly shifted its policy to favor foreign oil firms' activities, even at the expense of Japanese oil firms, with the tacit expectation that the deeper involvement of the international firms in a growing and lucrative Japanese market would assure Japan of a continued supply of necessary crude oil.[20] This policy shift was the harbinger of new vistas in Japanese industrial management: an inclusion of foreign firms in the industrial structure of Japan as well as the general encouragement of Japanese firms' direct investments abroad to secure food and raw materials and to expand access to foreign markets for Japanese products and technology.

About a decade earlier, MITI had permitted IBM and Texas Instruments to have fully owned operations in Japan in exchange for Japanese firms' access to these companies' basic patents in computers and integrated circuits (ICs). But this tradeoff was a mere extension of Japan's past practice of acquiring requisite foreign technology in exchange for foreign firms' investments in Japan. However, after the oil crisis of 1973, MITI and to a lesser extent the Ministry of Finance, began to factor the similar positions of foreign firms abroad into the management of Japan's dependency on the rest of the world for necessary capital, technology, and market access. This is why during Mazda's near collapse in the period from 1974 to 1978—the Japanese version of Chrysler—import tariffs on automobiles were cut and eventually abolished. Mazda was left alone to fend for itself. If Mazda failed, its market shares at home and abroad would have been absorbed by remaining Japanese firms. The survival of the fittest took on a distinctly global dimension in MITI's quest for stronger Japanese firms.[21]

Since the early 1960s, when Japanese industries obtained a wide range of technological capabilities, Japan's indicative economic planning had begun to set broader and broader scenarios for Japan rather than the narrow industrial goals of the past. The 1960 "Doubling of National Income" scenarios were to provide much wider vistas and greater leeway to private firms than previously and in 1970 MITI began a new orchestration for the Japanese economy by popularizing the slogan "Transformation of the Japanese Economy from Heavy and Chemical Industries to Knowledge-Intensive Industries."

MANAGEMENT OF TECHNOLOGY: JAPAN'S CHALLENGE TO THE UNITED STATES

Around 1870, when Japanese government leaders of the Meiji Era were choosing the self-reliant model for the country's industrialization, Japan had already signed away its sovereign rights to determine import tariffs and quotas in a series of unequal treaties with the West. Government and industries were left with no choice but to create and develop their infant industries mainly on the basis of joint government and business efforts to absorb foreign manufacturing technology while, at the same time, augmenting the technological capability of Japan.

As selective management of the technological growth of Japan again became the central theme of Japan's indicative economic planning after World War II, Japan upgraded manufacturing technology mainly by infusing massive but selected imports of foreign technology into indigenous technological bases.[22] Acquiring new product-related technology from American and European firms in the 1950s to the 1960s, Japanese firms concentrated on improving their process-related technologies so as to be able to manufacture similar products at a lower cost than their licensor-competitors. In order to avoid the export restrictions placed on licensed-product technologies by American and European licensors, Japanese licensees first adapted these products to the Japanese environment and then improved them. This practice, which characterized Japan's technological efforts in the 1950s and early 1960s,[23] followed the guiding principle of improving the productivity and quality of Japanese-manufactured goods.

Productivity Drive

A number of empirical studies have viewed the causes of Japan's rapid GNP growth during the postwar era as a result of increases in three gross inputs—labor, capital, and technology.[24] These studies indicate that technological development is the single most important contributing factor to Japan's industrial growth (40 to 60 percent of GNP growth has been attributed to "technological progress"). In addition, the GNP growth that is ascribed to the increase in Japanese capital stock masks, in many cases, an underlying expansion of the technological capabilities of Japan; for instance, a large-scale capital-intensive operation requires new production-process technology. Even the technical competence and experience of labor owe much of their improvement to continual on-the-job training. Japan's rapid rise in manufacturing productivity, which in turn sustained the rapid GNP growth, has been made possible by Japan's cumulative augmentation of technological capabilities. This trend is illustrated in Tables 3–1 and 3–2.

Table 3–1 summarizes the growth in labor productivity of manufacturing industries in Japan, the United States, West Germany, the United Kingdom, France, and Italy from 1960 to 1979. Table 3–2 compares labor productivity (value added per worker) of nine manufacturing industries of the United States and Japan from 1967 to 1981. From the two tables, one should note that, of the six industrialized countries, Japan registered the highest productivity growth during the last two decades. One can also observe that some Japanese industries caught up with U.S. industries earlier than others. This disparate growth in the labor productivity of different Japanese industries reflects Japan's changing emphasis on the expansion of various industries' technological frontiers. By

Table 3–1. Growth of Labor Productivity in Manufacturing Industries (value added per worker) 1960=100.

	Japan	West Germany	United States	United Kingdom	France	Italy
1960	100	100	100	100	100	100
1965	141	133	123	118	126	151
1970	258	174	141	142	178	188
1975	333	222	164	167	217	233
1978	413	261	181	175	263	277
1979	445	280	185	180	282	290

Source: *White Paper on International Trade,* MITI (Tokyo, 1980).

Table 3–2. Comparison of United States and Japanese Productivity by Selected Year and by Industry (U.S.=100 for each year).

Industry	1967	1970	1973	1976	1979	1981
Average of all Manufacturing Industry	39	57	69	73	83	98
Steel	62	88	130	185	208	215
Nonferrous Metal	42	78	66	63	82	88
Metal Fabrication	36	52	67	75	86	96
General Purpose Machinery	42	60	63	82	111	120
Electric Machinery	44	64	82	99	119	128
Transportation Machinery (total)	42	67	85	110	124	135
Automobiles (including motorcycles)	38	63	72	86	100	120
Transportation Machinery except Autos	35	54	91	121	—	134
Precision Machinery	26	38	55	73	134	156

Source: Computed from *White Paper on Labor,* Ministry of Labor (Tokyo, 1981). 1981 figures were estimated from the trends of Japan and the United States.

extrapolating the trend shown in Table 3–2, one can safely speculate that the overall manufacturing productivity of Japan caught up with and even surpassed that of the United States by 1982. In three industries, chemicals, aircraft, and farm implements, which are not shown in the industry breakdowns in Table 3–2, the United States still continues to command a distinct advantage over Japan, but these advantages are offset by the productivity lags in the steel, automobile, and machinery industries.

Competition in Research and Development

Japan's single-minded improvement of its technological base is reflected in its incessant increases in R&D expenditures. The ratio of R&D expenditures to Japan's GNP increased steadily from 0.3 percent in 1948 to 1.2 percent in 1960 and even further to 1.7 percent in 1970. Meanwhile, Japan's GNP rose in real terms more

than fifteenfold from 1948 to 1970 . During the 1970s Japan continued to expand R&D expenditures, and, in 1981 the ratio of
Japan's R&D expenditures to GNP passed the U.S. rate of about
2.3 percent.

In contrast to Japan, the U.S. ratio of R&D expenditures to GNP
peaked in 1964, when it reached around 2.9 percent, and it has
steadily declined during the 1970s.[25] Table 3–3 compares such
ratios of the United States and Japan from 1970 to 1981. If you
adjust U.S. R&D expenditures using the U.S. inflation rate, you will
notice that real R&D expenditures have declined throughout the
1970s and during the 1980s so far, whereas the comparable figures
for Japan showed distinct growth. In fact, from 1970 to 1980
Japan's R&D expenditures doubled.

About 69 percent of U.S. R&D expenditures are annually
financed by the federal government, with about half of those expenditures slated for defense-related projects and about 22 percent for aerospace projects. On the other hand, three-quarters of
Japan's R&D expenditures are annually financed by private firms.
Even the bulk of Japanese government-sponsored R&D projects
are directly targeted at the commercialization of scientific and
technological breakthroughs.

Table 3–3. Ratios of R&D Expenditures to GNP for Japan and
the United States, 1960–1981.

Year	Japan	United States
1960	1.20%	2.70%
1965	1.30	2.80
1970	1.70	2.64
1975	2.01	2.28
1976	2.10	2.27
1977	2.21	2.24
1978	2.29	2.24
1979	2.36	2.25
1980	2.48	2.30
1981[a]	2.52	2.30

a. Estimated from R&D trends

Source: Kagaku Gizutsu Hakusho (White Paper on Science & Technology). Agency of
Science & Technology, MITI, Tokyo for appropriate years.

Comparison of R&D Productivity

Japan and the United States now appear to be spending roughly the same amount on R&D for commercial applications. Although the impact of R&D activities on the economic growth of either country is difficult to measure, we can make a few telling observations about plausible differences in R&D productivity between the United States and Japan.

It has been argued that Japan's increases in market share of worldwide manufactured exports can be explained by Japan's cumulative R&D expenditures,[26] and more specifically, by the productivity improvement resulting from the greater technological competence of Japanese firms.[27] Japan's steel exports illustrate this point. For the production of crude steel, the basic oxygen furnace (BOF), which was first developed in Austria around 1953, is considered to be the most significant technological breakthrough in steel making since the Bessemer process of the late nineteenth century. The United States, West Germany, France, the United Kingdom, Italy, Japan, and the Soviet Union adopted the BOF method about the same time, around 1957. By 1972 over 80 percent of Japan's crude steel was being produced by the BOF method, while the diffusion rate of the BOF method in West Germany was only about 60 percent. The rest of the countries were left far behind. Meanwhile, Japan's share in the world steel export market increased from 6.5 percent in 1960 to over 25 percent in 1973.

From 1958 to 1978, Japan's share of the overall world export market increased from about 3.0 percent to 8.2 percent, while that of the U.S. declined from about 18.0 percent to 12.0 percent. If you exclude exports of crude oil, natural gas, raw materials, and food (a minor Japanese export), Japan's share in the world export market of manufactured goods reached about 16 percent in 1980 —thus doubling in about one decade. Since Japan's manufacturing productivity began to catch up with that of the United States, the U.S. trade deficit with Japan jumped from less than $2 billion annually before 1975 to $5.3 billion in 1976 and to about $33 million in 1984.

If the number of patent applications is taken as a gross indicator of the technological results of R&D expenditures, Japan caught up with the United States by 1970. In 1978, about 100,000 new patent applications were filed in the United States; in the same year, 166,000 new patent applications were filed in Japan. During the 1970s, R&D-expenditure elasticity of patent applications was estimated to be about +0.52 for the United States and +0.75 for Japan, indicating that Japan's R&D expenditures were about 40 percent more effective than those of the United States.[28]

Figure 3–1 depicts the trend in cross-patent applications between Japan and the United States. In 1979, the number of Japanese patent applications in the United States surpassed the number of U.S. patent applications in Japan. More importantly, America's relative superiority in technological innovations appears to have peaked in 1970. Of course, R&D expenditures do not necessarily produce patentable results; nor are all of the patentable results of R&D efforts made by private firms. However, there is no denying that the falloff in American R&D activities during the 1970s was accompanied by two negative effects: a decline in export

Figure 3–1. Cross-Patent Application between the United States and Japan.

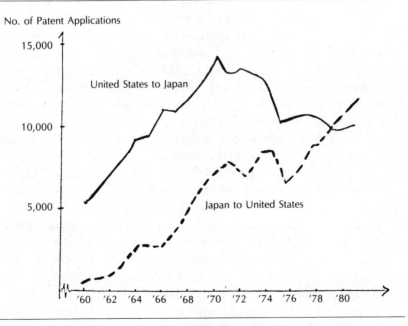

Source: *Patent Applications,* Patent Office, Tokyo, for appropriate years.

strength in the world market for U.S. manufactures, and a decrease in American manufacturing productivity. What might have caused this decline in R&D in the United States?

Differences in Governmental Support of R&D

Earlier we noted the differences between Japan and the United States not only in terms of the scope but in the thrust of governmental support for R&D. Nowhere is this difference more marked than in the rivalry between the United States and Japan in industrial robotics and microelectronics. MITI of Japan and the U.S. Department of Defense have provided roughly the same amount of R&D subsidies to their respective industries,[29] but many observers are now predicting that within a decade, Japanese firms will emerge as the victors in these fields.

Unlike MITI, which has helped a few chosen high-technology firms become internationally competitive through the use of administered market competition at home and abroad, the Pentagon awards many of its large contracts without competitive bidding. Worse, the Pentagon's procurement formulas lack any built-in incentive for awardees to be cost-effective, technologically innovative, or internationally competitive. Cost inefficiencies are in fact rewarded by the Pentagon's blind acceptance of contractors' substantial cost overruns.[30] Unlike MITI, the Pentagon pays little attention to the global market potential of new products resulting from R&D. As a result, much of the U.S. government support of R&D does not, in contrast to Japan, put pressure on a few growth-oriented firms to survive the uncertainties of the market. In addition, emphasis on global market competition requires a long-term commitment to chosen R&D projects. Yet, Pentagon R&D contracts are subject to sudden shifts in the perceived needs of national security and in prevailing domestic politics.

Japanese business has come to accept the government's promotion of joint R&D efforts between otherwise competing firms.[31] In fact, both business and government regard such joint R&D efforts to start new industries as conducive to subsequent market competition among private firms. Joint research efforts assure the development of new products by launching a few firms in fierce competition with one another in order to further technological innovations, improve production processes, and, above all, meet market demands at home and abroad.

In 1950 this government role was firmly established when the Ship Technology Institute was inaugurated. Competing shipyards and shipping firms were invited to participate in joint R&D activities, thus bringing together engineers and scientists from different firms so that innovations might be shared among the leading shipyards.

This model of joint R&D was later applied in the field of high technology. As private Japanese firms improved their own technological abilities during the 1950s and 1960s, the government shifted its emphasis to long-term, "colossal" (*ogata*) projects in order to make technological breakthroughs in a chosen field. For example, in 1970 the semiconductor and microelectronics industries were chosen for such projects; in 1980 the government initiated efforts to design a fifth-generation computer as its *ogata* for the coming decade.[32]

Direct R&D subsidies by the Japanese government are modest. Even when MITI's Agency of Science and Technology appoints its sixteen research institutes to specific projects, such as very large-scale integrated (VLSI) semiconductors, jet engines, water desalinization equipment, advanced composite materials, and natural resource recycling, these projects are invariably co-funded by ad hoc associations of several participating firms and universities.[33] In reality, MITI's role is to help legitimize technological goals and to provide an initial push to the emerging efforts of private firms. In order to encourage private firms' R&D efforts the government links its tax-cut incentives to the growth in R&D investments as well as to meeting the international test for quality of R&D products. Firms are permitted to treat 25 percent of any year-to-year increase in R&D expenditures as a direct tax credit, with a limit of 10 percent of total corporate tax liabilities. In addition, firms can write off up to 60 percent of their initial research facilities, R&D-related equipment, and test plants in the first year of acquisition. High-technology firms are thus helped in conserving cash inflows during the growth stage. In order to encourage private firms to test the innovative quality of their R&D products against international standards, a lower income tax rate is also applied to the corporate income firms receive from the granting of overseas technical licensing agreements.[34] This provision may appear strange to U.S.

firms trying to discourage "technological drain," yet the provision not only helps Japanese companies avoid reliance on domestic applications of technological innovations but, more importantly, encourages the Japanese to acquire new technologies from abroad through cross-licensing agreements with American and European firms.

INDUSTRIAL GROUPS AND INDIVIDUAL FIRMS

Despite government support, it was the competition between individual firms that rescued the Japanese economy after World War II and raised it to its present position in less than twenty-five years. The government has, ultimately, not had the power to dictate its will onto private enterprises. As the Japanese economy was opened to international competition during the 1960s and as firm after firm embarked upon direct foreign investment throughout the 1970s, the government's power over the private sector diminished. At this point, private Japanese firms can, by and large, choose whether or not to cooperate with the government or with other firms, business being guided primarily by self-interest.

In retrospect, two policies of the occupation forces turned out to be extremely important in shaping the industrial structure and corporate behavior of postwar Japan. We referred earlier to the dissolution of *zaibatsu,* a dissolution that loosened hundreds of firms from the control of holding companies and divided a number of large *zaibatsu* into small, independent firms.[35] The occupation forces also removed high-ranking businessmen who had held decisionmaking or executive positions during the war from their seats of power. In 1948 this purge swept senior executives out of their jobs and placed younger managers in charge of rebuilding the nation's businesses. *Zaibatsu*-related firms were the hardest hit by this purge. These practices effectively eliminated out-dated forms of management based as they were on the financial control of various subsidiaries under the tightly knit holding companies.[36] The younger executives, who were very much involved in the manufacturing and sales operations of their firms, concentrated on managing technology and actual operations. Free from the stifling influence of traditional, discredited "Imperial Japan," these managers were free to pick and choose elements of their former management systems they thought were useful, but they were also eager to absorb what they were told were the "best American industrial management systems" and they adopted them to their operations.[37]

Prewar *Zaibatsu* Groups

As we have noted, industrial groupings are not new to Japan.[38] Functionally, the emergence of these industrial groupings reflected a desire to gain internal control over supplies of scarce resources such as capital, technology, trained labor, and managerial skills. The prewar *zaibatsu* structure enabled its affiliated firms to share these resources and to diffuse technological and managerial innovations rapidly among member firms without depending on uncertain developments in external, open markets. The division of manufacturing, mercantile, and financial tasks among a *zaibatsu* permitted the group to grow rapidly by pursuing economies of scale and to enter new industrial fields by pooling the necessary resources. This kind of "group capitalism" did much to shape the industrial structure of prewar Japan.[39] Once *zaibatsu* structures were in place, the prewar Japanese government left the major tasks of industrial policy planning and implementation to several competing groups. By playing one group off another, the government counted on intense rivalry to steer industrial development during a period of acute resource shortages. Because the prewar *zaibatsu* were family-controlled, member firms being mere subsidiaries of the holding company of each owner family,[40] the key decisionmaking power rested with the holding company. Rivalry between a few large groups often replaced market competition among many firms.

On the other hand, the industrial structure was always in a state of flux as Japan continued to absorb new product technology, which permitted many independent entrepreneurs and inventors to launch their own new ventures. Most of these ventures chose to remain outside the *zaibatsu,* although some were subsequently acquired by *zaibatsu.* Of the former, Matsushita, Sanyo, Toyota, Hitachi, and Nissan grew, after the war, to become household words in Japan. Of the latter group, one recognizes Toshiba, NEC, Toray, and Mitsubishi Electric.

Postwar *Keiretsu* Groups

Toward the latter half of the 1950s, when Mitsubishi and Mitsui were reestablished after merging with the remnants of prewar Mitsuihishi Shoji and Mitsui (two former leading *sogoshosha*), journalists and scholars alike wrote somewhat sensationally about a revival of the prewar *zaibatsu* combines.[42] However, these accounts failed to understand the fundamental differences between the prewar *zaibatsu* and the postwar industrial *keiretsu*.

The most striking difference is that the postwar groups do not have any central holding company or any other controlling entity. In addition to the fact that the antimonopoly law of 1947 made holding companies illegal, individual executives of *keiretsu* member firms, who were thrust into top-management positions after the dismissal of senior officers by the occupation forces, were too independently minded and guarded their own businesses too intensely to concede their hard-won managerial autonomy to any central body outside the firm. This lack of a central management company, or of the prewar pattern of pervasive interlocking directorates, explains how, for example, within the Sumitomo *keiretsu* group, both Sumitomo Chemicals and Sumitomo Light Metals entered the aluminum industry and competed fiercely with each other. Mitsubishi Chemicals and Mitsubishi Yuka, other examples, are independent firms within the Mitsubishi Group who compete with one another in the processed-lead market and in other markets. Managerially independent member firms are thus free to compete with other member firms in addition to trading with outside companies.

The emergence of the *keiretsu* can be traced to the government's shipbuilding strategy of the 1950s and early 1960s. Government loans and subsidies were channeled through a handful of large commercial banks, which were responsible for a rigorous economic evaluation of investment projects involving shipyards and shipping firms. Since many fiscal incentives and a favorable allocation of scarce foreign exchange were tied to the export performance, general trading firms became the indispensable core members of the *keiretsu.* Once in place, this clustering of trading and manufacturing firms around a selected number of large commercial banks enabled the government to allocate capital, foreign exchange, and technology to targeted growth industries.

By the mid-1970s, seven major *keiretsu* complexes had emerged. In Japan they are popularly identified by the name of the *keiretsu's* lead commercial bank, for example, the Mitsui Group, Mitsubishi Group, Sumitomo Group, Fuyo Group (Fuji Bank Group), Daiichi-Kangyo Group, Sanwa Group, and Tokai Group. Table 3–4 profiles these seven groups as of March 1974. It should be noted that each core member firm has majority ownership as well as minority participation in literally hundreds of subsidiaries. Joint ownership of these subsidiaries by core member firms of different *keiretsus* is not uncommon.

The heavy-machinery and chemical industries were far more complex technologically than the simple, prototypical industries of the prewar era and required large initial capital outlays. As in the case of the petrochemical complex, technological and market links among the different processing stages of these industries needed to be carefully brought together by the cooperative venture of a dozen or so firms. The economic and technological interdependence of these new firms would provide a mutual guarantee of the minimum market and the resources necessary for the requisite economies of scale in the entire new industry.

True to the time-honored practice of "division of tasks," a group of industrial and trading firms would usually form the "joint-entry," with each independent firm specializing in one or two stages of the processing, from the import of necessary raw materials to the production of various semifinished and finished products. Combined, these independent firms parallel the vertical and horizontal integration that large American oligopolistic firms attained within their own subsidiaries and product divisions. Unlike the integrated operations of their American counterparts, however, the joint-venture form of Japanese industrial and trading firms·permitted each participating company to leave the arrangement even at the expense of the other participants.

The government's task was to ensure that at least two competing rival groups (say, Mitsubishi and Mitsui) would enter the same field. In this way, the rivalry between the two would provide the

Table 3-4. Seven *Keiretsu* Complexes as of March 1974.

	Mitsui	Mitsubishi	Sumitomo	Fuyo	Daiichi-Kangyo	Sanwa	Tokai
No. of Core Member Firms	22	27	16	29	57	36	25
No. of Subsidiaries 50–100% Owned by Core Member Firms	486	399	260	606	674	842	n.a.
No. of Subsidiaries 25–50% Owned by Core Member Firms	975	1,070	578	1,206	1,180	1,548	n.a.
No. of Subsidiaries 10–25% Owned by Core Member Firms	1,367	1,460	781	1,581	1,623	2,003	n.a.

Source: Japan Fair Trade Commission, *The Second Survey on the General Trading Company* (Tokyo, 1975), pp. 17–18.

impetus for technological and marketing excellence. As the domestic markets of various products expanded, the government
further administered market competition by encouraging new entrants from other industrial groups as well as from large independent firms.

Group Capitalism of the Postwar Period

Although member firms of the *keiretsu* own one another's equities,
this ownership averages less than 2 percent per firm—too small to
allow control of one firm by any other. Thirty percent of each
firm's equity is owned by other core member firms, however, which
is large enough to provide the security of interdependence. In
addition, commercial banks are permitted to own equity in their
client firms just as in West Germany. Although Japanese banks'
equity ownership of key client firms is on average less than 3 to 5
percent, this link gives the bank legitimate access to inside information. In exchange for the banks acting as inside referees for
their clients' economic performance, lead creditor banks are expected to rescue faltering client firms by bringing in necessary
managerial, technological, and marketing assistance from other
members of the same industrial group. This explains is why
Sumitomo Bank, rather than the Bank of Japan or MITI, carried
out the rescue operation of Mazda from 1974 to 1978. In reality,
client firms' short-term debts to their lead bank take on the characteristics of "preferred stock."

Manufacturing and trading companies inside and outside the
keiretsu complexes soon found the pace of industrial and mercantile growth after the 1950s too rapid, too uncertain, and too diverse to be contained by the straight-jacketing operations of the
prewar *zaibatsu* groups. Lead commercial banks issued loans just
as often outside as inside their own group. Manufacturing and
trading firms often found more favorable deals outside their member group and challenged their group firms to meet similar terms.
The task of successfully targeting opportunities, given the ever-
widening frontiers of technological innovation within equally diverse and elusive market developments at home and abroad, could
never have been handled by the tightly controlled structures of
family-owned holding companies.

In the United States, the conglomerates that developed in the 1960s and that resemble in essence the *zaibatsu* groups of prewar Japan have often been slow in reallocating resources internally and slow in seizing upon new technological frontiers.[42] On the other hand, firms handling many products but with strong central offices have been quick to move resources around internally and to enter new fields by exploiting technological links with their existing products.[43] The *keiretsu* groups of postwar Japan are similar to these multiproduct U.S. firms. Their lead commercial banks and trading firms act as the organizers, referees, and partners in new ventures and also work to improve the existing businesses of their related member firms. Capital, trained labor, managerial skills, and technology can all be efficiently reallocated from declining firms to growth firms.

In short, the "group capitalism" of postwar Japan functions in much the same way as the "financial capitalism" of West Germany, where the internal capital market of bank-client relationships assures efficient and timely allocation of capital. The Japanese system also shares in the best features of the "managerial capitalism" of the United States in which professional managers adopt a hands-on approach in the allocation of necessary resources to targeted projects.[44]

CORPORATE GROWTH THROUGH TECHNOLOGICAL LINKAGE: THE NONPORTFOLIO APPROACH

Unlike American firms, large Japanese firms have narrow product lines and for a number of reasons.[45] The traditional demarcation of tasks among various Japanese firms inevitably leads to single-product companies. Furthermore, a lack of predatory takeover practices in Japan not only leaves executives free to pursue their own long-term growth goals, but also limits diversification through horizontal and vertical integration of technological links with other existing businesses. Even friendly merger and acquisition moves are socially tolerated only because the acquiring firms are seen as rescuing faltering ones. The absence of a "secondhand corporate market" also discourages engineers and managers from removing one set of their firms' R&D products and starting new businesses.

The absence of a mobile labor market for hourly employees as well as for executives, managers, and engineers leaves firms little choice but to expand geographically from domestic to foreign markets and to upgrade product technology by developing new products for which there appears to be a growing global market. If firms fail to do so, they will soon be weeded out of existence. Bankruptcies involving not only small and medium-sized firms but large obsolete ones as well, like Sasebo Heavy Industry (shipbuilding), are accepted as a way of life in Japan. Sometimes, a whole industry disappears—as coal-mining nearly did in the early 1960s.

This "survival of the fittest" mentality in postwar Japan has produced specific corporate strategies, and they can be characterized by the following two major investment and marketing approaches.

Riding International Product Cycles. [46]   In the early days of reindustrialization, a Japanese firm would first acquire the product's requisite manufacturing technology that had been developed in the West and adapt it to the Japanese market. Since Japan had production cost advantages (mainly due to lower wage rates) and had incorporated some distinctive features (such as "compactness" and "good workmanship") into their products, Japanese firms began successfully to export their products to United States and European markets which were finely segmented and demonstrating high price elasticities of demand. Having gained access to the export markets, Japanese firms increased their production capacities and technological capabilities.

Rather than waiting for Japanese demands for new products to catch up with the United States and Europe, Japanese manufacturers now make major shifts in their production design and processes to mass-produce new goods and introduce them first into U.S. and European markets.[47] The Japanese consumer is, meanwhile, faced with older products—for example, monochrome versus color television sets, straight-stitching versus zig-zag and automatic sewing machines, ordinary steel pipes versus corrosive-proof steel pipes for gas lines.

Meanwhile, Japanese manufacturers are continually ploughing back the cash inflows from domestic and export sales into further modernization of production facilities and into innovative R&D efforts to manufacture new products before their American and

European competitors can do so. They eventually leapfrog foreign competitors, even in product innovation, and garner still larger market shares, first, in the industrialized countries, then in the newly industrializing countries, and finally in the developing nations.

The growth of Sony, Matsushita, Sanyo, Toshiba, Hitachi, and other consumer electric and electronics firms is a familiar story. They entered the U.S. market standard with small electronic and electrical appliances such as transistor radios and then moved into compact, monochrome television sets. In the mid-1960s Japan was the only supplier of compact, solid-state, color television sets. Sony and Matsushita then preempted their American and European competitors (RCA, Philips, and Zenith) by being the first to introduce portable and home-use video cassette recorders (VCRs) in the United States.[48] In 1982 Sony and other Japanese consumer electronics firms were entering the fields of personal computers, word processors, and related products in Japan and the United States.

Japan's conscious riding of international product cycles has taken another form. In this case, manufacturers of appliances and machinery first develop compact models to meet the demand at home. Then, realizing potential markets for these models in the United States and elsewhere, they enter foreign markets in the compact-product segments. Once they establish a beachhead overseas they begin tracking their customers up to medium-sized and large-sized models. This successful strategy, carried out by Honda for its automobiles and motorcycles, is currently being repeated with Honda lawnmowers and outboard marine motors in the United States.

Toray has used the same strategy. This firm was organized by the Mitsui Group in 1926 to manufacture the first popular man-made fiber, staple fiber. By 1940 Toray had developed its own prototype nylon technology (*amiran*),[49] and after 1950 the firm acquired DuPont's nylon technology. By the 1970s, Toray had expanded sales into Korea, Taiwan, Southeast Asia, and Latin America. As Japan lost its production-cost advantages to developing countries, Toray concentrated on spinning off its synthetic fiber technology into potentially lucrative new products. By the end of the 1970s, Toray had emerged as the world leader in carbon fiber,[50] an advanced composite material with wide industrial and consumer uses.

This pursuit of technological innovations is different from the portfolio approach that many American firms use to justify their premature abandonment of existing technologies. Japanese manufacturers are likely to try harder than American managers to identify potential ventures within their familiar product-market lines by applying their knowledge more intensively. For this task, they must remain alert to technological and market developments in their fields inside and outside Japan. Since managers are guaranteed longevity with their firms, they tend to display a long-term commitment to the development of new products and new markets but in familiar fields. For example, from 1970 to 1982, Hitachi, NEC, and other firms transformed Japan's semiconductor industry from infancy to a leading force in the world.

Maximizing Global Market Shares. Domestically as well as internationally, Japanese firms concentrate on maximizing shares in whatever markets they choose to enter rather than maximizing profits on individual projects or in the short run. When a target market is potentially very large or steadily growing, a 1 percent share in the first year of that market is read to mean great sales volume a few years later. In fact, market shares represent deferred and compounded profit returns. By following this strategy, Japanese firms act as if they are trying to maximize seven- to ten-year "moving average profits" for the firm as a whole.

Many American firms, on the other hand, are constrained in their efforts to achieve long-term profit maximization in two ways. First, American firms are far more dependent on external capital markets for their debt and equity funds than their Japanese competitors are; they are, therefore, far more concerned with maximizing quarterly earnings per share to satisfy lenders and professional investors. In addition, low earnings per share, which would depress stock prices, might invite predatory takeover bids.

Second, postwar management thinking in the United States has led many American firms to rely heavily on certain financial-control tools for individual projects, divisions, subsidiaries, and other intrafirm subunits.[51] Each subunit is held as a profit center responsible for reporting quarterly or even monthly profits for budget comparison. This management control method is biased toward motivating each subunit manager to act as if the manager's quarterly behavior had no impact on other subunits of the same firm or on the long-term growth of the firm as a whole.

Use of the discounted cash-flow method (DCF) of evaluating investment projects also encouraged American firms to treat investment proposals as separate and discrete units with no impact on one another. When this financial method of investment evaluation is applied, those projects that promise large short-term cash inflows are favored over long-term projects with their greater future uncertainties. When managers fill in the DCF worksheets, they tend to favor the more certain estimates of revenues, operating costs, and other economic variables for the next three to five years. When promotions, bonuses, and other rewards are closely tied to the short-term economic performance of their own profit centers, they are least likely to submit projects that will have a long-term impact on the firm by fundamentally changing their firm's overall growth and competitive position in the world.[52]

Consider the U.S.-Japanese rivalry in memory chips. When U.S. industry leaders suffered a short-term business decline during the 1974–1975 recession, they cut previously planned investments in R&D and production facilities in order to conserve their financial liquidity. American financial communities, moreover, withdrew their support for semiconductor firms. Meanwhile, their Japanese competitors increased their R&D and capital investments.[53] By the time American firms renewed their investments late in the 1970s, the Japanese had closed the production and technological gaps enough to overtake the Americans by the mid-1980s. Moreover, while American manufacturers were still preoccupied with 16k random access memory (RAM) chips, Japanese memory-chip manufacturers leapfrogged to production of 64k RAM chips. In 1980, Japanese manufacturers were the first with successful 260k RAM chips.

Unlike their American competitors, Japanese firms do not evaluate every investment project as a discrete, incremental additions to their business. They treat investment in R&D, expansion of production capacities, and market development as integral parts in advancing the company's competitive position. It is not that Japanese firms disregard profits. They are very profit-minded, but they have learned that, once their market positions are firmly in place, profits will naturally follow. During the 1960s, when Japanese manufacturers of passenger cars, consumer electronics, steel, fork-lift trucks, office copiers, computers, watches, semiconductors, motorcycles, and pharmaceuticals were competing hard at home and abroad to expand their market positions, they did not hesitate to borrow heavily to finance investment needs.[54] During the 1970s they repaid their debts as they attained steady growth. Today, contrary to popular myth about Japanese firms' high debt/equity ratios, Matsushita, Toyota, Honda, Yamaha, and other firms have no long-term debts.

Japanese Manufacturing Systems: Innovative Institutional Technologies

By the end of the 1970s, many American firms had grudgingly conceded that their Japanese competitors possessed superior process-related technologies. They also had to admit also that, even with seemingly comparable production methods, Japanese manufacturing firms were superior in their management structure and worker skills which enabled them to motivate workers to operate machinery more efficiently than their American counterparts— primarily through quality control. In 1979, for example, Hewlett-Packard tested the failure rates of over 300,000 16k RAM memory chips from three Japanese and three American suppliers and found that the worst Japanese supplier still gave six times more reliable chips than the best American supplier.[55]

Many observers point to the "learning curve effect" to explain the cost advantage of Japanese manufacturing firms. According to this popular version of the theory of economies of scale, for every doubling of production volume, the average production cost is expected to decline by 20 to 30 percent.[56] A number of studies report such results in the case of Japanese manufacturing industries.[57] Little is said, however, about the manufacturing systems of Japanese firms that have attained superior productivity and quality simultaneously.

Table 3–5 compares typical production in car plants in Japan and the United States in 1981. The table also compares the ratio of inventories to total sales of General Motors and Toyota, the two largest automakers in the world.[58] Japanese production systems are far more capital-intensive (that is, have a greater degree of automation) than their American counterparts. More importantly, and in line with conventional wisdom of U.S. industrial engineering and factory management, the machine set-up time of American

Table 3–5. Comparison of Car-Manufacturing Systems in the United States and Japan, 1981.

	United States	Japan
1. Parts stamped per hour	325	550
2. Manpower per press line	7–13	1
3. Time needed to change dies	4–6 hours	5 minutes
4. Average production run	10 days	2 days
5. Time needed per small car	59.9 hours	30.8 hours
6. Average daily absentee rate	11.8%	3.5%
7. Average annual employee turnover	15%–20%	2%
8. Number of Quality Inspectors	1 per 7 workers	1 per 30 workers
9. Inventory/Gross Sales	GM 16.6%	Toyota 1.5%
10. Number of suppliers	GM Over 3,000	Toyota 300

Sources: Items 1–5 and 8 from Reports of Harbour & Associates, Detroit, 1982. Items 6, 7, 9 and 10 were computed by the author on the basis of industry data.

factories is related to the length of production runs; the Japanese have developed a manufacturing system that minimizes set-up time regardless of the length of production runs. While American factories separate quality-control functions from actual production (as is evident from the ubiquitous presence of quality inspectors in the plants), Japanese factories have almost eliminated quality inspectors by holding production workers responsible for quality. General Motors' inventory levels indicate that GM uses these inventories to cushion the uncertainties of market demand and the uncertainties in delivery and product quality from over 3,000 suppliers. Toyota has almost eliminated inventory by being flexible in its own production scheduling and in its 300 or so suppliers to cushion uncertainties in supply and market demand. As a corollary, Japanese manufacturing systems can be sustained only when factories keep employees' daily absentee and annual turnover rates to a bare minimum.

How do Japanese firms do it? We have pointed out elsewhere that corporate culture and its internal structure can be classified essentially into two models that we label A and J.[59] Model A firms are generally found in industries with mature technologies and markets, while model J firms refer primarily to industry involved in high technology, global competition, and rapid market growth.[60] Unlike model A, model J firms in both Japan and the United States share the internal characteristics of (1) management commitment to employee job security, (2) corporate goals widely shared from the top to the bottom of the firm, (3) free lateral and informal communication across divisional or functional boundaries of the organization, (4) long time horizons at all levels of the firm, and (5) management promotion from within (an internal labor market).

One should not overlook, however, one important attribute specific to the Japanese manufacturing system: the minute "division of tasks" among an industry's support groups. We have already described the *keiretsu* groupings of postwar Japan. In addition, each large firm has built up around it hundreds of support firms and subcontractors. For example, large manufacturing firms like Nippon Steel, Hitachi, Toyota, Nissan, Matsushita, Toshiba, and NEC have anywhere from 80 to 200 related firms that comprise an organic support system for the large central firm.[61] These firms are not necessarily subsidiaries. Over the years, each core manufacturing firm has cultivated a cluster of related supplier firms around it so that division of task could be exploited to the entire group's greatest advantage. By sharing long-term production goals and the necessary technical know-how between suppliers and customer plants, this mutually dependent group synchronizes production scheduling, as in the famed "just in time" delivery system (*kanban*) by which supplier plants deliver necessary supplies to appropriate sections of the customer plant as often as several times a day.[62] "Zero-defect" quality and timely delivery, rather than unit prices, are the two overriding criteria used by industrial customers in their selection of suppliers.

The superiority of this type of support system was first demonstrated by Japanese sewing-machine firms from 1947 to 1949. Fearing Singer's reentry into Japan after the war, Janome and three other leading sewing-machine companies together organized a supplier group of about 200 independent parts manufacturers and about 230 independent parts subcontractors. By standardizing the specifications of all parts, and by having each parts manufacturer and subcontractor specialize in one to three parts items, the large sewing-machine firms enabled their suppliers to reap production-cost and product-quality advantages that were derived from both static and dynamic economies of scale. In 1948, when Singer tried to reenter Japan, its Japanese competitors were ready to undercut Singer's price for comparable product quality. A typical Japanese parts manufacturer was producing over 500,000 units of the same part per month while Singer's largest production run of a single item at that time was estimated to be, at best, around 40,000 units per month.[63] By the late 1950s Japanese sewing-machine firms had captured over 30 percent of the U.S. market and went on to squeeze American and European sewing machines out of their home markets.

From the mid-1960s to the mid-1970s, when American competitors in consumer electronics and microelectronics were setting up offshore manufacturing subsidiaries in countries with lower wages, like Mexico, Korea, Taiwan, Singapore, and the Philippines, Japanese firms kept expanding and automating their own production facilities at home to exploit economies of scale.[64] When Japanese steel, textile, and consumer-appliance firms opened manufacturing subsidiaries in neighboring Asian countries and in Latin America, their operations were designed to assure continued exports of semifinished products from Japan rather than primarily to obtain cheap labor.

Unlike their American counterparts, Japanese steel firms sponsored the manufacture of products such as galvanized iron sheets and small construction items. In this way, the Japanese steel industry assured itself of continued sales of steel, iron sheets, and coils Toray, Teijin, and other synthetic resin and polymer producers were also actively involved overseas in setting up captive customers in the form of integrated textile mills for spinning, weaving, dyeing, and apparel making.

By 1982 Japanese makers of steel, microelectronics, automobiles, synthetic textiles, and industrial machinery had not only built up their own relative superiority in production processes and institutional techniques, but had also upgraded their innovative capabilities in R&D to produce new technologies. Many leading Japanese firms were thus better prepared than ever to ride international product cycles, from innovation to growth and eventually to the maturity stage in important world markets.

CONCLUSIONS: CONFLICT AND ACCOMMODATION

Table 3–6 compares two macroeconomic variables, the real growth rate of gross domestic product and the unemployment rate for the United States and Japan for two time periods. As the table shows, the oil crisis of 1973–1974 stalled both economies into negative real growth. However, Japan took less than a year to recover from this massive shock, while the U.S. economy did not recover for two years. The second oil crisis of 1979 again hit both economies hard, but the Japanese economy withstood this shock rather well while the U.S. economy suffered deepening economic ills. The U.S. unemployment rate soared as firm after firm resorted to the custom of laying off rank-and-file employees. After computing the relationship of production level unemployment for both countries, the United States was found to have a rate of -4.46, while the Japanese rate was zero. Thus, for every 1 percentage point decline in industrial production in the United States, the unem-

Table 3–6. Growth in Gross Domestic Product and Unemployment Rates for the United States and Japan, 1972–1982.

	JAPAN		UNITED STATES	
	GDP Real Growth Rate	Unemploy- ment Rate	GDP Real Growth Rate	Unemploy- ment Rate
1972	8.8%	1.1%	5.6%	5.5%
1973	8.8	1.1	5.5	4.9
1974	−1.0	1.9	−0.7	5.5
1975	2.3	2.0	−0.9	8.6
1979	5.5	2.1	2.8	5.8
1980	4.2	2.2	−0.2	7.2
1981	4.2	2.2	−1.0	8.1
1982[a]	3.5	2.2	−3.0	9.5

a. 1982 income was estimated by the author.
Source: Bank of Japan, *Comparative International Statistics* (Tokyo, 1974, 1976, and 1981).

ployment rate rose to 4 to 5 percent of the prevailing rate before production decline.[65]

In Japan the unemployment rate doubled (from 1.1 to 2.2 percent) between the two oil crises, but the system seemed to regain its ability to absorb external economic shocks without aggravating the social costs of carrying the unemployed. Behind this system lies the "Japanese income policy."[66] True to the model J type of corporate culture, the firm—the microcosm of the economy—adjusts quickly to sales declines through immediate reductions in salaries (from the top down) and in dividends cuts. Adjustment costs are thereby contained inside the firm. Government, business, and labor leaders informally agree to hold down salary and wage increases in order to protect real job security.

In short, the industrial and corporate management systems of postwar Japan turned out to be effective in temporarily absorbing even massive economic shocks as well as managing rapid industrial growth. The congruence of public and private benefits is related to Japanese firms' self-interest in survival and growth.

Since trade and investment conflicts between the United States and Japan are likely to be caused by differences in industrial and corporate management, no feasible accommodation between the two countries can be gained by preaching the notion of "reciprocity in trade and investment." Nor is it conducive to the maintenance of multilateral trade and investment throughout the world for the United States and Japan, two leading industrial powers, to conclude product-by-product or ad hoc bilateral trade restrictions. A better approach would be for the two countries to encourage cross-investments by contending Japanese and American firms in one another's home markets. Instead of fruitless and ideological debates over the government's role in industrial policies, the U.S. government should begin to link its fiscal and legal incentives to R&D growth, exports, employment stability, and management's acceptance of a quality-first approach to manufacturing operations.

NOTES

1. There are two opposing views of the role the Japanese government played in the economy. One view holds that the all-wise govern-

ment effectively guided the entire economy and that industrialists, fired by patriotism, contributed to the national goals. The second view contends that the government merely created the opportunity and the framework for development ad hoc bilateral trade restrictions. See Johannes Hirshmeier, *The Origins of Entrepreneurship in Meiji Japan* (Cambridge, Mass.: Harvard University Press, 1964); and Tsunehiko Yui, "The Personality and Career of Hikojiro Nakagawa, 1887–1901," *Business History Review* (Spring 1970).

2. Yoshi Tsurumi, "Japanese Efforts to Master Manufacturing Technology," in *Japanese Business* (New York: Praeger, 1978), ch. 1.
3. Yoshi Tsurumi, *The Japanese Are Coming* (Cambridge, Mass.: Ballinger, 1976), ch. 1.
4. Ibid., pp. 28–29.
5. Yoshi Tsurumi, *Sogoshosha: Engines of Export-based Growth*, (Brookfield, Vt.: Renouf, 1984).
6. Byron Marshall, *Capitalism and Nationalism in Prewar Japan: The Ideology of the Business Elite, 1868–1941* (Stanford: Stanford University Press, 1967), pp. 20–21.
7. Johannes Hirshmeier and Tsunehiko Yui, *The Development of Japanese Business,* 2nd edition (London: George Allen and Unwin, 1981), pp. 346–47; Yoshi Tsurumi, "Critical Choice for Japan," *Columbia Journal of World Business* (Spring 1977): 15–16.
8. For the origins of enterprise-based unions in Japan, see Robert Cole, "Enterprise Unions," and Solomon Levine, "Labor Conflicts," in Bradley and Ueda, eds., *Business and Society in Japan* (New York: Praeger, 1981), pp. 36–51.
9. Tsurumi, *The Japanese Are Coming,* pp. 12–13.
10. Ibid., pp. 16–18.
11. Caryl Callahan, *Business-Government Relations in Japan,* (Scarsdale, N.Y.: Pacific Center Foundation, 1980), pp. 6–8.
12. Yoshi Tsurumi, "The Case of Japan: Price Bargaining and Controls on Oil Products," *Journal of Comparative Economics,* no. 2 (1978): 128–30.
13. Ibid., p. 130.
14. "In the U.S., industrial structure is described and expressed statistically. In Japan, industrial structure is viewed as a system for setting and implementing goals." Quoted from Namiki Naito in Diane Tasca, ed., *U.S.-Japanese Economic Relations* (New York: Pergamon, 1980), p. 62.
15. Ryutaro Komiya, "Planning in Japan," in M. Bornstein, ed., *Economic Planning: East and West* (Cambridge, Mass.: Ballinger, 1975); Kanji Haitani, *How Japanese Economic Systems Work* (Lexington, Mass.: Lexington Books, 1976).

16. For interactions between Japan's industrial policies and corporate behavior, see William Rapp, "Japan: Its Industrial Policies and Corporate Behavior," *Columbia Journal of World Business* (Spring 1977): 38–48; Ira Magaziner and Thomas Hout, *Japanese Industrial Policy* (Berkeley: Institute of International Studies, University of California, Berkeley, 1980); Yoshi Tsurumi, *Technology Transfer and Foreign Trade: A Case of Japan, 1950–1965* (New York: Arno, 1980); and *U.S. Industrial Competitiveness: A Comparison of Steel, Electronics, and Automobiles,* Office of Technology Assessment, U.S. Congress, July 1971, 052–003–008–14–9 (Washington, D.C.: U.S. Government Printing Office, 1971).

17. Yoshio Suzuki, *Money and Banking in Contemporary Japan,* Part I (New Haven: Yale University Press, 1980).

18. Richardson Bradley, "The Contemporary Myth of Japanese Protectionism," in Bradley and Ueda, eds., *Business and Society in Japan* (New York: Praeger, 1981), pp. 115–17.

19. Rapp, "Japan," pp. 38–39.

20. Yoshi Tsurumi, "Japan," *Daedalus (Perspective in Oil Crisis),* (Fall 1975): 113–27; "The Case of Japan: Price Bargaining and Controls on Oil Products," *Journal of Comparative Economics,* no. 2 (1978): 138–39.

21. Yoshi Tsurumi, "How to Handle the Next Chrysler," *Fortune* (June 16, 1980): 87–88; "The U.S. vs. Japan: Business-Government Relations in the Automobile Industry," *Pacific Basin Quarterly,* no. 5 (Spring-Summer 1980): 10–12.

22. From 1950 to 1980, Japan imported about 25,000 identifiable technologies through licensing agreements with American and European firms. For annual data, see *White Paper on Science and Technology,* Science and Technology Agency, Tokyo, for appropriate years. For further treatment of Japan's "balance of trade" in technology, see Tsurumi, *The Japanese Are Coming,* ch. 7.

23. Tsurumi, *Technology Transfer and Foreign Trade,* pp. 203–54.

24. For example, see *White Paper on the Economic Situation, 1961* (Tokyo: Economic Planning Agency, 1962); Edward Denison and William Chung, "Economic Growth and Its Sources," in Hugh Patrick and Henry Rosovsky, eds., *Asia's New Giant: How the Japanese Economy Works* (Washington, D.C.: The Brookings Institution, 1976), pp. 83–138. For an econometric estimation method, see Hiroki Tsurumi and Yoshi Tsurumi, "A Bayesian Estimation of Macro and Micro CES Production Functions," *Journal of Econometrics,* no. 4 (1976): 1–25.

25. *United States-Japan Trade: Issues and Problems,* Report by the Comptroller General of the United States, ID-79–53 (September 21, 1979), pp. 164–65.

26. Yoshi Tsurumi, "R&D Factors and Exports of Manufactured Goods of Japan," in Louis Wells, ed., *The Product Life Cycle and International Trade* (Cambridge, Mass.: Harvard University Press, 1972), pp. 161–92.

27. Eleanor Hadley, *Japan's Export Competitiveness in Third World Markets*, Center for Strategic and International Studies, (Washington, D.C.: Georgetown University, 1981), pp. 49–78; Tsurumi, "R&D Factors," *op. cit.*, pp. 163–64.

28. Kimio Uno, "Beikokuni Semaru Nippon No Gizutsu Ryoku" (Japanese Technological Strength Catching up with U.S.), *Nihon Keizai Shimbun* (December 5, 1981), p. 12.

29. See Robert Reich, former director of policy planning at the Federal Trade Commission, "High-Tech Rivalry," *The New York Times,* November 20, 1981, Op. Ed. page.

30. During the 1970s alone, total cost overruns of Pentagon weapon procurements were estimated to be about $200 billion, enough to wipe out the projected budget deficits for 1982 and 1983.

31. Jack Barranson, *The Japanese Challenge to U.S. Industry* (Lexington, Mass.: Lexington Heath, 1980); and *High Technology and Japanese Industrial Policy*, Subcommittee Report on Trade, U.S. House of Representatives, Washington, D.C., 1980.

32. Tsurumi, *The Japanese Are Coming,* p. 17. In 1982 MITI approved applications fielded by six Japanese computer makers and two electrical manufacturers to set up the Institute for New Generation Computer Technology. The group invited U.S. firms to join, but no applications from the U.S. had been filed as of April 14, 1982. That the Japanese government decided to include foreign firms in its joint R&D efforts is a historical event.

33. Magaziner and Hout, *Japanese Industrial Policy,* p. 50.

34. Ibid.

35. Eleanor Hadley, *Antitrust in Japan* (Princeton, N.J.: Princeton University Press, 1970), pp. 61–106.

36. Rebecca Tsurumi, "The Origins of Japanese Productivity—Rejection of the Hawthorne Experiment," *Pacific Basin Quarterly,* no. 7 (Spring-Summer 1982).

37. Ibid.

38. In prewar days, four *zaibatsu* banks and combined (Mitsui Bank, Mitsubishi Bank, Yasuda Bank, and Sumitomo Bank) and held over 75 percent of Japan's total bank deposits. For intragroup markets of capital, technology, information, etc., see Tsurumi, *Sogoshosha,* ch. 6.

39. K. Bieda, *The Structure and Operation of the Japanese Economy* (Sydney, Australia: John Wiley, 1970), p. 217.

40. Eleanor Hadley, *Antitrust in Japan,* chs. 1–3; also W. W. Lockwood,

The Economic Development of Japan (Princeton N.J.: Princeton University Press, 1954), p. 215; and C. D. Edwards, "The Dissolution of Zaibatsu Combines," *Pacific Affairs* (September 1946): 213.

41. See, for example, "Just Like Old Days," *Time* (August 20, 1959): 10.

42. For the accounts of U.S. conglomerates, see Jess Markham, *Conglomerate Enterprise and Public Policy* (Boston, Mass.: Division of Research, Graduate School of Business Administration, Harvard University, 1973).

43. This observation was offered to the author by Professor Alfred D. Chandler, Jr. of Harvard University.

44. The terms "group capitalism," "financial capitalism," and "managerial capitalism" were first suggested to the author by Professor Alfred D. Chandler, Jr. For an account of managerial capitalism in the United States, see Chandler, *The Visible Hand: The Managerial Revolution in American Business* (Cambridge, Mass.: Harvard University Press, 1977).

45. The degree of corporate diversification can be measured by the breadth of a firm's product line as classified by the SIC three-digit industrial code. Under this classification, few large Japanese firms can be classified as "diversified."

46. For the theory of the product cycle of international trade and investment, see Raymond Vernon, "International Investment and International Trade in the Product Cycle," *Quarterly Journal of Economics* (May 1966): 190–207.

47. For the possibility of a follower nation riding the international product life cycle, see Yoshi Tsurumi, "Japanese Multinational Firms," *Journal of World Trade Law* (January-February 1973): 74–90; also *Multinational Management* (Cambridge, Mass.: 1977), ch. 1, pp. 1–16.

48. Videotape recorders (VTRs) or video cassette recorders (VCRs) were first commercially developed in 1956 by Ampex, a U.S. supplier of broadcasting firms. This industrial model cost $100,000. Both Sony and Matsushita obtained technical licenses for basic VTR technology from Ampex. It was Sony that first developed a $1,000 mass-produced consumer VTR model.

49. Tsurumi, *Japanese Business*, pp. 62–63. This account points out the close interplays among Toray, Mitsui (a trading firm), and the Japanese university community to monitor Du Pont's nylon technology and develop Toray's own product technology from 1938 to 1940.

50. *Chosa Geppo*, Research Monthly, Japan Long-Term Credit Bank, Tokyo, no. 192 (April 1982): 62–76.

51. Robert Hayes and William Abernathy, "Managing Our Way to Economic Decline," *Harvard Business Review* (July-August 1980).

52. This point was also recognized by Magaziner and Hout, *Japanese Industrial Policy,* pp. 12–13.
53. "U.S.-Japan Competition in Semiconductors," Parts I and II, *JEI Report,* nos. 41 and 42 (December 1979 and January 1980).
54. The Japanese willingness to borrow more heavily than their American competitors is partly the result of their banks' continued support and partly because of their banks' abilities to reduce loan risks by carefully screening their clients' investment projects and by closely monitoring their progress.
55. Richard Anderson, general manager of Hewlett-Packard, revealed the test results in March 1980 at a seminar on quality control sponsored by the Electronics Industry Association of Japan in Washington, D.C..
56. Kenneth Arrow, "The Economic Implications of Learning by Doing," *Review of Economic Studies,* no. 80 (June 1962): 155–73.
57. Magaziner and Hout, *Japanese Industrial Policy,* pp. 24–28. For a popular account, see, Walter Kiechel, "Playing the Global Game," *Fortune* (November 16, 1981): 111–24.
58. Yoshi Tsurumi, "Japanese Productivity," *The Dial* (September 1981): 48–49.
59. Yoshi Tsurumi, *The Japanese Are Coming,* ch. 9; "Two Models of Corporation and International Transfer of Technology," *Columbia Journal of World Business* (Summer 1979); *Multinational Management,* ch. 11 (Cambridge, Mass: Ballinger, 1983).
60. Yoshi Tsurumi, "The Productivity: Japanese Approach," *Pacific Basin Quarterly,* no. 6 (Summer 1981): 7–11.
61. Dodwell Marketing Consultants, *Industrial Grouping in Japan* (Tokyo, 1978), pp. 10–11.
62. Shigeru Saito, *Toyota Kanban Hoshiki nò Himitsu* (Secrets of Toyota's Kanban System) (Tokyo: Koshobo, 1978).
63. Tsurumi, *The Japanese Are Coming,* pp. 26–27.
64. For example, the Japanese steel industry reduced its production labor hours per one ton of crude steel from 0.75 in 1960 to 0.37 in 1973. The bulk of this improvement was recorded from 1960 to 1966. See Hiroki Tsurumi, "A Bayesian Test of the Product Cycle Hypothesis Applied to Japanese Crude Steel Production," *Journal of Econometrics,* no. 4 (1976): 389.
65. The high U.S. rate of production-level elasticity of unemployment owed to American firms pushing their own costs of economic adjustments onto society at large.
66. Tsurumi, *The Japanese Are Coming,* pp. 275–76.

4 DEVELOPMENT OF THE GERMAN ECONOMY AND NATIONAL ECONOMIC POLICY

Klaus Macharzina

In the Federal Republic of Germany there was until 1963 no official statement of economic objectives. At that time a "Council of Experts for the Evaluation of National Economic Development" was legally established,[1] which led four years later, on June 6, 1967, to the enactment of a "Law for the Advancement of Economic Stability and Growth."[2] The latter piece of legislation required decisionmakers to consider the overall objectives of a national economic equilibrium, that is, price stability, full employment, external equilibrium, and appropriate growth (the so-called magic quadrangle).

In order to measure West Germany's economic performance, we will investigate a number of indicators. It is common practice to measure economic development according to growth of the national product in real terms, either gross or net, minus depreciation. In the Federal Republic, an average annual growth rate of 4.5 percent has been officially regarded as appropriate. The Council of Experts, the Federal Bank, and the Department of Trade also use the nation's production capacity as a measure of growth in trade cycles, and capacity utilization as an indicator of economic development.

In order to measure price levels about twenty-five different indices are currently used. Chief among these are the consumer

81

price index (CPI), the wholesale price index, and the gross national product deflator (GNPD). The goal of price level stability does not imply stability of all prices; rather, there is a constant average price level of consumer goods that should vary only within a range of 2.3 to 1.8 percent. The level of employment as a rule, is measured by comparing the total number of jobs with the number of unemployed people (unemployment rate) and the absolute number of unemployed and short-time workers. Full employment has been defined as an unemployment rate of 0.7 to 1.2 percent. While there is no generally accepted definition for the term "external equilibrium," the Council of Experts defines it as a state wherein, given a constant exchange rate, receipts and payments are balanced without any additional transactions.[3] The federal government considers an export surplus of 1.5 to 2 percent of the GNP as a condition necessary for fulfillment of external obligations in foreign currencies.[4] Economic stability is, moreover, legally defined as the state in which the four overall economic objectives are simultaneously achieved, a state so far never attained.

GERMAN ECONOMIC DEVELOPMENT

The rapid economic growth of postwar West Germany is a well-known phenomenon that does not need to be illustrated by statistical evidence. But this development was not a steady one. There were, in fact, four major growth cycles during the periods 1950–1954, 1954–1958, 1958–1963, and 1963–1967. Each of these cycles was marked by a boom during the first two years and a subsequent decline in the following years, with average growth rates decreasing cycle by cycle. Notably, the recession periods worsened after each cycle until Germany experienced its most serious recession in 1967.

State Intervention

The economic crisis that ensued brought about a fundamental change of opinion regarding intervention by the state, and resulted in the introduction of the so-called national economic control defined in the "Stability Law" of 1967. The 1967 economic

crisis was precipitated by a number of factors: (1) the German
Federal Bank failed to react early and strongly enough; (2) there
was a conspicuous lack of coordination between credit and fiscal
policies, and between public and private institutions; (3) pre-1967
increases in production capacity did not adequately take into account long-term sales prospects; and (4) the recession happened
to coincide with a deep structural crisis in the mining industry, and
later in the iron and steel industries.[5] This law hoped to provide
trade-cycle control through the creation of a system that would
regulate competition and institute countercyclical economic controls. The primary institutions responsible for carrying out this
trade-cycle policy are the German Federal Bank (in the area of
monetary policy), and the public authorities (in the area of fiscal
policy). The federal government publishes annual forecasts of the
expected development in the achievement of economic objectives
for a period of one to four years. These forecasts act as an economic guide and as a quantitative measure of economic realities.[6]

Economic Development vis-a-vis National Economic Control

Economic development after 1967 was unstable despite national
controls and the active promotion of a cooperative industrial-rela-
tions climate between government, trade unions, and boards of
industries (which ended in 1979). The 1960s had been a period
that shifted from high growth, low unemployment, and relatively
high inflation rates to low (real) growth rates together with higher
unemployment and a relatively low rate of inflation. During the
early 1970s, these instabilities were coupled with a strong downward inflexibility of prices. It is for this reason that the inflation
base increased with each new upswing. This inflexibility of prices
during periods of recession has given a new dimension to instability commonly referred to as "stagflation," that is, the simultaneous
appearance of inflationary movements and stagnation of growth.
In the 1970s and 1980s additional forces have contributed toward
instability. These forces are due to external influences from foreign economies and were "imported" via fixed as well as flexible
exchange rates.[7]

Increasing instability has tested the concept of countercyclical national economic control, and it is unclear whether or not this concept comes to grips with the true origins of instability. Some argue that the recessions were aggravated by faulty decisionmaking on the part of those responsible for economic policy, as when the Deutschmark was revalued too late, considering the time lag with respect to trade-cycle policy effects and external influences. In particular, governmental policy has been accused of having stimulated procyclical movements, for instance in the years 1957–68 and 1971–72.[8]

Based on the period from 1974 to 1978, it may be said of national economic control that it was either too slow in curing the problems or that it was unsuccessful. From the government's standpoint, the failure of this concept was primarily due to extra-national effects, whereas critics argue it was due to ineffective application of fiscal policy.[9] In addition, increased market concentration and the tendency to increase public expenditures, which are typical of recession periods, are largely beyond the aegis of national economic control.

Economic Growth, Financial Stability, and Employment

From 1967 on the growth of the German GNP in constant Deutschmarks was slow if somewhat cyclical.[10] Structural changes in industrial production obviously influence growth, particularly with respect to productivity rates. In 1981 the real GNP growth was negative (-0.2 percent).[11] While the real average growth rate during the period 1967–1975 was still 3.3 percent, it was only 2.2 percent between 1975 and 1981. This development was, however, not uniform for the whole economy but varied for different sectors.

The goods-producing or secondary sector—mining, energy, manufacturing, and constuction—reacted more readily to cyclical fluctuations, with manufacturing, which comprises 75 percent of this sector, reacting the most dramatically. In the tertiary sector, however, trading and transport had lower than average reaction, while banking, insurance, and rental services showed a positive growth in the 1967 recession. During upswing and boom periods, manufacturing quickly enjoyed high growth rates considerably exceeding those of the secondary sector and those of the entire national value. High growth rates during upswing periods were also shown by trade and transportation, while services displayed smaller but more constant rates of growth.

The stability of real economic development was only marginally achieved in 1967–68. More recently, the decrease of growth rates has been accompanied by an increasing inflationary movement. Even in the recession period of 1974–75 inflation remained high, partly due to the hikes in world oil prices. The latter were also mainly responsible for the renewed increase of inflation after 1978. Increased prices for raw materials in 1980–81 (up 42 percent in one year) also contributed to inflation, partly due to the devaluation of the Deutschmark (DM). As a consequence, domestic prices climbed in all sectors, especially chemicals. Eventually, in 1981, drastic increases in imports led to an absorption of 5 billion DM of real private purchasing power which is thought to have caused a reduction in private consumption for the first time in postwar Germany.

Employment levels tend to follow growth rate trends, which explains why there are often employment problems during periods of reduced growth. After 1967, except for 1969 to 1973, the unemployment rate constantly exceeded the officially defined rate (0.7 to 1.2 percent) of full employment. This was especially true during the recession periods when the construction and automotive industries were severely hit.

If unemployment rates are adjusted for dependent workers, nonregistered unemployed, and foreign workers who left Germany, the official rates, 2.1 percent in 1967 and 4.6 percent in 1977, become 4.5 percent and 10 percent respectively.[12] Contrary to the previous boom phases, the job situation after 1975 did not improve noticeably, mainly due to increased productivity of labor.[13] Since 1980 the job situation has again suffered with an average unemployment rate of 5.3 percent in 1981, 7.5 percent in 1982, and 9.2 percent in April 1983.

Foreign Economic Involvement

The economic development of West Germany is clearly influenced by its foreign economic involvements. From 1972 to 1982, the value of exports and imports tripled to 428 billion DM, and 376 billion DM, respectively. Also, the make-up of real GNP showed an increasing growth rate of exports (+72 percent) and imports (+ 52 percent). Moreover, exports as well as imports have increased to more than 30 percent of the GNP. Thus, more than every third Deutschmark of the GNP has been earned outside West Germany, with export volume approximating one-quarter of total demand. On the other hand, nearly the same amount has been spent for foreign merchandise. During this period, except for 1980, exports have been consistently higher than imports—both in actual and constant DM.[14] Looking at annual growth rates, it is apparent that despite enormous growth, the development of imports is closely correlated with domestic demand, which in turn reflects domestic business cycles. Yet exports have grown even faster, functioning both as a major stimulus to growth and a stabilizing factor during economic crises. It is through this expansion of foreign trade and the utilization of the international division of labor that the Federal Republic has continued a growing dependency on the international economy.

In analyzing German foreign trade by regions, there is an increasing tendency to export to European Community (EEC) member states and to OPEC nations, and decreasing exports to developing countries and East Bloc countries. Combined with other industrialized countries (with a share of 6.7 percent to North America), the Western industrialized nations constitute about 77 percent of total German exports. Roughly 75 percent of Germany's imports come from Western industrialized countries, with North America accounting for 8.6 percent. With respect to the United States and Canada, there is a slight foreign trade deficit.[15]

In contrast to the regional pattern, striking differences exist between exports and imports with respect to manufactured products. Merchandise makes up about 83 percent of total exports and 51 percent of total imports (compared to 32 percent in 1960). Exported merchandise is clearly dominated by machinery, automotive manufacturing, and electrical equipment (51 percent), followed by primary extraction products, such as chemical, iron, steel, and metal products, and finally, consumer goods. Among imports, there is an increase in primary extraction products with a shift from coal and iron toward oil and gas. Imports of capital

Table 4–1. Regional Pattern of German Exports and Imports, 1982.

	Exports	Imports
EEC countries	46.9%	47.3%
Other industrialized countries	29.9	28.0
OPEC	9.0	10.2
Developing countries (without OPEC)	8.8	9.3
State-trading countries	4.9	5.2

goods, consumer goods, and products of basic goods industries have been stable in the 1970s. Trade surpluses occur mainly in the areas of machinery, automotive manufacturing, and chemical products, as well as electrical equipment, iron, steel, and metals. Major deficits in foreign trade may be attributed to oil, natural gas, mineral products, textiles, clothing, and food markets.

The volume of German foreign trade has grown spectacularly compared to world trade: foreign trade surpluses increased from 15 billion DM in 1970 to 50 billion DM in 1974. But this positive balance was clearly on the decline from 1975 to 1980 (37 billion DM in 1975 to 8.9 billion DM in 1980). Only in 1981 did the foreign trade balance again begin to rise to 27 billion DM. These surpluses were mainly due to the long-lasting undervaluation of the Deutschmark and to the differing goals of German economic policy in contrast to those of other countries. Because of a very restrictive trade-cycle policy designed to produce stability, German manufacturers had formerly been virtually forced to serve foreign markets. Then, due to the disruptive effects of rising oil prices and the balance of payments of Western countries, German exports began to drop. This tendency was finally aggravated by a speculation-fueled revaluation of the Deutschmark. Recent strong increases in exports are again due to an actual devaluation of the DM in the international context. This also led to a deficit on the current account for the first time since 1965. In 1981 there was a reversal of this trend because of large merchandise trade surpluses which in turn resulted in a lower balance of payments deficit. For the first time, in October 1981, there was a surplus in the current account of 2.9 billion DM.[16] Further high surpluses in the balance of trade led to a surplus in the current account of 8.1 billion DM in 1982.

In addition to foreign trade, direct investments have tightened the integration of Germany into the international economy. Except for 1974 and 1977, there have been net capital imports since 1970 (1981: 10 billion DM). This is the result of long-term capital transactions, and in particular, large public foreign borrowings. On the other hand, the private sector exported capital (1980: 14.5 billion DM) with 50 percent going to direct investment and land, and 50 percent to loans and portfolio investments.[17] German foreign direct investments increased 2.5 times to 12 billion DM between 1962 and 1967. Between 1967 and 1980, there was a further increase of about 62 billion DM to 74 billion DM, six times the value of 1967. Since 1978 there has been an upward trend from 6 billion to 9.9 billion DM in 1981, and 8.7 billion DM in 1982. Foreign direct investments in Germany have also risen from 14.7 billion DM in 1962 to 27.5 billion in 1967 with a further increase to 70.6 billion DM in 1980. Until 1973 there was a growth in foreign direct investment flow into Germany, but from 1974 onward a relative decline has occurred. In 1980 the stock of German foreign direct investment abroad exceeded foreign investment in Germany for the first time. This trend increased in the following years.[18]

The regional distribution of German foreign direct investments has followed a constant pattern over recent years. The overall picture shows an allocation of almost 70 percent to industrialized countries, about 30 percent to developing countries, and a small amount to OPEC states. Notably, almost one-third of the total amount was invested in EC countries. The pattern of key countries" has, however, changed since 1976, with the United States increasingly gaining the attention of German investors. Between 1976 and 1980, German investment in the United States rose from 5.4 to 15.7 billion DM. There were also high rates of growth (although much less than that in the U.S.) with respect to German investments in France, Belgium, and Luxenbourg. Table 4–2 illustrates the pattern of German foreign direct investment in 1980.

Investment in the United States was mainly in chemicals, iron and steel, machinery, automotive manufacturing, electrical equipment, and investment trusts. It is interesting to note that there was

Table 4–2. German Foreign Direct Investment, 1980.

	(percentage)	(billions DM)
United States	21.2%	15.664
Belgium/Luxembourg	9.8	7.276
France	9.2	6.807
Switzerland	7.9	5.833
Brazil	7.2	5.359
Canada	6.5	4.818
The Netherlands	5.9	4.403

a substantial increase in the amount of investment trusts, which rose by 1.255 billion DM alone in 1980.[19]

The primary foreign investors in Germany are listed in Table 4–3. Major industries that attract U.S. investors in Germany are petroleum refining, electrical engineering, mechanical engineering, and automotive manufacturing. Switzerland, for example, aims at mechanical engineering, Holland at iron and steel, and Great Britain at petroleum refining and chemicals.[20] Other foreign investors in Germany are attracted mainly by investment trusts.

THE INTERNATIONAL COMPETITIVE POSTURE OF THE GERMAN ECONOMY

The developments described above demonstrate the importance of external economic relations to West Germany's domestic economy. Because the Federal Republic is a country that produces more than it consumes, there is a force driving it toward world

Table 4–3. Primary Foreign Investors in Germany, (1980).

	(percentage)	(billions DM)
United States	35.3%	20.312
Switzerland	15.1	8.683
The Netherlands	12.6	7.240
Great Britain	11.7	6.764
France	5.9	3.421
Belgium/Luxembourg	5.7	3.264

markets. Due to the high current-account deficits of recent years, it was feared that the international competitive posture of the Federal Republic was unsatisfactory and that it would further deteriorate.[21]

In economic theory, comparative cost, exchange rates, and terms of trade are considered the key parameters of international competition. The problem, however, is that they do not seem to be able to explain adequately the efficiency of this competition. Traditionally, an improvement in international competitiveness, designed to overcome balance of payment problems, may be achieved by either of two ways. The first alternative is to reduce income claims, such as wages and profits. This may also be achieved indirectly by devaluing the currency, resulting in cheaper domestic goods relative to other countries. In the second alternative, a strategic planning approach points to other measures to improve competitiveness, for example, improved quality of products, the capacity and resources for innovation, the ability to recognize and develop market potential created by technological advances, and other factors that influence productivity and eventually per capita income.[22]

Competitiveness is not a one-dimensional concept, but rather an amalgam of factors, the effects of which may overlap or even complement one another. Analysis of a single parameter is possible by discriminating between environmentally oriented factors beyond corporate control and those directly controlled by corporate management. In their comparison of international competitiveness, the European Management Forum developed a framework for determining competitiveness. This consisted of 10 groupings containing 240 single criteria that measure a country's competitiveness. Criteria included dynamics of the economy, productivity, cost of production, dynamics of markets, earning power, human resources, role of the nation state, infrastructure, external orientation, future orientation, sociopolitical consensus, and stability.[23]

Development of German Competitiveness

In terms of the above criteria Germany ranks fourth in international competitiveness, behind Japan, Switzerland, and the United

States. There is, on the other hand, a significant distance between these leaders and their nearest competitors, Canada, Sweden, the Netherlands and France.[24] One of the most important parameters of international competitiveness is a country's external orientation. This is measured not only by a country's ability to invest and sell beyond national borders but also by its willingness to let in foreign products and investment. The importance of foreign trade to the Federal Republic is reflected in the ratio of its exports and imports to its GDP or GNP, in both cases a little more than 46 percent in 1980. Compared to the total worldwide volume of exports, Germany's exports increased until the beginning of the 1970s, but showed a decline afterward. In 1980 the German share in world exports was only about 10 percent. However, based on the heavy volume of exports in 1982 there are indications that it might well grow again. The major competitors, the United States and Japan, showed diverse trends, namely declines for the former and considerable increases in the case of Japan (see Table 1–2).

In the future, Japan can be expected to be a major competitor in the international marketplace where research and intensive capital goods are being traded—markets in which Germany has traditionally possessed its highest comparative advantage. This may lead to problems regarding the competitive position of German products in precision mechanics, optics, electrical equipment, automotive manufacturing, as well as machinery. Only Germany's position in chemicals remains relatively unchallenged in world markets.

One can also expect future reductions of market shares resulting from changes in the structure of German foreign economic relations. While OPEC states increased their imports more than sevenfold between 1972 and 1979, and imports by other developing countries increased four times over 1972, imports of industrialized countries increased only 3.5 times. Growth of German exports was, however, below average in the quickly expanding Third World markets. This becomes apparent from the regional structure of German foreign trade, which concentrates on the markets of industrial countries. The same is true of the regional pattern of foreign direct investment. It is only because of the relative weight of industrialized countries in world trade that the German decline has not, to date, been more severe. The major competitors of the

Federal Republic, Japan in particular, appear to have adopted a much broader focus in their international economic relations. Obviously, Japan is much better represented in the rapidly expanding Southeast Asia markets, as well as in the rest of the Third World, markets that are expected to expand much faster than industrial markets in the 1980s.[25]

The decline of German exports relative to world exports may also be due to the strong bias toward exports of manufactured goods, which seems to explain about 80 percent of the decrease for the period from 1972 to 1979. Compared to manufactured goods, oil prices increased at a faster average rate, and therefore the share of oil-exporting countries in world export markets has increased considerably. Certainly strong fluctuations of exchange rates have added to this trend. For example, the devaluation of the DM against the U.S. dollar led to a reduction in Germany's share of world exports, which again impaired its terms of trade. On the other hand, competitiveness improved through the devaluation, for well-known reasons.

In order to measure the global competitiveness of a country more accurately, it is necessary to factor out biases arising from exchange rate differences in international price or cost levels. The development of "real" exchange rates (adjusted for inflation) allows for a better judgment of whether a country has traded internationally at increasing or decreasing price or cost levels. In the German case, price-oriented competitiveness deteriorated in the 1970s, but it revived after the DM devaluation in 1978. This was particularly noticeable in 1981 when Germany's increase in export prices was below the international average and no revaluation of the Deutschmark was made.

There are also positive forecasts with respect to the development of export prices because German inflation rates are estimated to remain the lowest among the major industrialized countries until 1990—around 4 percent.[26] The modest increase in German export goods resulted from the Deutschmark being devalued by 50 percent beyond the nominal devaluation when measured in real terms. Accordingly, the foreign value of the Deutschmark decreased by an average 8 percent per annum in real terms from 1979 to 1981, which compensated for the overvaluation of the DM in the years from 1970 to 1978. This was also true of the valuation of the DM on a cost basis; with the turning point in 1978 the cost level of 1970 could be attained again. Therefore, German exporters took part in world trade with lower price and cost levels compared to the years before 1981. Despite the worldwide recession, they were able to increase their exports by a much higher percentage than the growth of total world trade in 1981 and 1982.

Among West Germany's main competitors, Japan shows a similar development. Japan's competitive position with respect to prices has worsened only for a short time because Japanese companies managed to compensate for the increase in costs by reducing their profit margins. Following the yen devaluation of 1978, Japan was able to improve its competitive position in terms of cost and price levels. Cost levels, however, were much higher in 1980 as compared to 1970. The revaluation of the yen after 1980 has neutralized this competitive advantage. Meanwhile, the United States experienced a constant devaluation over the period under consideration. The revaluation of the dollar combined with the increase in inflation stopped this trend, with the consequence that U.S. exporters will have to compete on the basis of increasing costs and prices for the first time since the 1960s.[27]

In terms of factor costs, Germany is among the leaders, which adversely affects its international competitiveness. In manufacturing, the wage level in 1980 was more than twice that of 1970. In 1981 the employment cost, that is, labor cost per hour (including fringe benefits that represented 72 percent of the employment cost in 1982) amounted to 26.08 DM, which placed Germany fifth among seventeen western countries after the United States.

A comparison (in equal units of account) shows that the United States underwent considerably a smaller increase in wages than Japan, which suffered from a higher increase in labor costs until

Table 4–4. Wages and Fringe Benefits—Manufacturing Industry (DM/working hour).

Year	Japan	United States	Federal Republic of Germany
1970	3.94	15.80	9.42
1975	8.29	16.10	15.95
1980	12.35	18.23	23.40
1981	16.69	24.97	25.03
1982	16.27	28.48	26.08

(See also Table 13–1.)

1980. The picture altered in 1981 because of changing exchange rates. The labor cost ratio between Germany and Japan has shifted from 2.4:1 in 1970 to about 1.5:1 in 1982. Generally, differences in cost levels may be compensated for by greater productivity. But obviously there have been no striking differences in productivity between these countries since the end of the 1970s. Differences in labor costs have thus become increasingly important in determining competitiveness between nations.

A comparatively unfavorable position is held by the Federal Republic with respect to annual standard and effective weekly working time. The weekly working time available to firms is twenty-seven hours in Germany, thirty-six in the United States, and thirty-eight in Japan.[28] On the other hand, the volume of social conflicts, measured by working days lost per 1,000 employees, places Germany in an internationally favorable position with an averge value of 5.9 over the years.[29] Nevertheless, a recent study placed West Germany ninth in the international order when socioeconomic consensus was applied as a measure of competitiveness. West Germany also ranked low with respect to human resources, state interventions, and the necessary infrastructure for industrial development; yet it ranks well in categories such as economic and market dynamics, and external and future orientation.[30] Further determinants of a country's attractiveness in the international marketplace include quality, reliability and flexibility of suppliers, and the degree of product innovation. However, the data are nearly absent regarding these parameters apart from measures of R&D expenditures. In the 1970s German R&D expenditures have increased at a higher rate than the increase of GDP, a factor that certainly contributed to safeguarding Germany's world market position. Compared to other countries, Germany is in a favorable situation in this respect.[31]

Prospects for the Immediate Future

In 1983 Germany had a much more difficult position in the international marketplace than ten years before. If, in 1982, international competitiveness did not seem to be threatened—mainly because of the DM devaluation—enormous cost pressures on the German economy will make it necessary to increase productivity further and systematically rationalize unprofitable areas in the years ahead. Wage policy must make sure that not all productivity benefits will be distributed via wages and profits. However, it would be dangerous to try to regain lost ground through exchange-rate maneuvers. This would be a step in the wrong direction because the resulting increase in competitiveness primarily affects products in markets where German suppliers must compete with foreign producers who are able to offer equivalent products at even lower prices due to lower labor costs. This would tend to neutralize any gain in competitiveness resulting from devaluation, and may in fact lead to further losses of market share for German suppliers.

Germany is more apt to maintain and secure its international competitiveness by developing new products. Germany will have to offer products that guarantee competitiveness not on the basis of price but on their high user advantage. Apart from this requirement, it will be necessary to seek higher investments, higher productivity, new markets, better products, less oil consumption, and economical use of natural resources. The decisionmakers in economic and wage policy must, therefore, be called upon to improve the conditions for innovation and investment in the Federal Republic in order to secure the traditionally good position of Germany in international competiion.[32]

NOTES

1. Bundesgesetzblatt 1963, Part I, p. 685.
2. Bundesgesetzblatt 1967, Part I, p. 582.
3. Sachverständigenrat zur Begutachtung der gesamtwirtschaftlichen Entwicklung, Jahresgutachten 1968/69, Alternativen ausenwirtschaftlicher Anpassung, Kohlhammer, Stuttgart-Mainz, 1968, fig. 193, p. 59.
4. Bundesregierung, Jahreswirtschaftsbericht 1971 der Bundesregierung, Bundestag-Drucksache VI 1976, fig. 139.
5. K. Neumann, *Konjunktur und Konjunkturpolitik,* 2nd ed. (Frankfurt: Europ. Verlagsanstalt, 1975), p. 48 ff.
6. H. Kock, E. Leifert, A. Schmid, and L. Stirnberg, *Konzepte der Konjunktursteuerung* (Koln: Bund, 1977), p. 15.
7. Ibid., p. 17 ff.
8. Ibid., p. 11 ff.

9. Memorandum von Wirtschaftswissenschaftlern, "Für eine wirksame und soziale Wirtschaftspolitik," *Blätter fur deutsche und international Politik* 20, no.11 (1975) : 1298 ff.

10. J. Krack and K. Neumann, *Konjunktur, Krise, Wirtschaftspolitik* (Koln-Frankfurt: Europ. Verlagsanstalt, 1978), p. 120 ff.
    R. Muller and W. Rock, *Konjunktur- und Stabilisierungspolitik,* 2nd ed. (Stuttgart-Mainz: Kolhammer, 1980), p. 133 ff.

11. Deutsches Institut für Wirtschaftsforschung, "Bundesrepublik Deutschland: Wirtschaftsentwicklung auch 1982 unbefriedigend," *Wochenbericht 1982* 49, no. 7 (January 1982) : 8 ff., 26.
    Sachverständigenrat zur Begutachtung der gesamtwirtschaftlichen Entwicklung, Jahresgutachten 1981/82, Investieren für mehr Beschäftigung (Stuttgart-Mainz: Kohlammer, 1981), pp. 70 ff., 255 ff.

12. Sachverständigenrat zur Begutachtung der gesamtwirtschaftlichen Entwicklung, Jahresgutachten 1977/78, Mehr Wachstum mehr Beschaftigung, Kohlhammer, Stuttgart-Mainz, 1977. fig. 116, p. 69.

13. Muller, R., Rock, W., op. cit., p. 134 ff.
    Deutsches Institut für Wirtschaftsforschung, Grundlinien der Wirtschaftsentwicklung 1983, Wochenbericht 1–2/83, Vol. 50, 6 January 1983, p. 21.
    Bundesministerium fur Wirtschaft, Die wirtschaftliche Lage in der Bundesrepublik Deutschland, Monatsberich 3'83.

14. Sachverstandigenrat . . . , Jahresgutachten 1982/83, Gegen

15. Glastetter, W., op. cit., p. 213 et seq., Voss, W., Die Bundesrepublik Deutschland, Kohlhammer, Stuttgart-Mainz, 1980, p. 204 ff.

16. Deutsche Bundesbank, Statistische Beihefte zu den Monatsberichten der Deutschen Bundesbank, Reihe 4, Saisonbereinigte Wirtschaftszahlen, no. 4, Frankfurt, April 1982, p. 25,

17. Sachverständigenrat . . . , Jahresgutachten 1981/82, op. cit., p. 310 et seq.

18. Institut der Deutschen Wirtschaft, p. 69.

19. Institut der Deutschen Wirtschaft, p. 69.

20. Institut der Deutschen Wirtschaft, p. 69.

21. Sachverstandigenrat . . . , Jahresgutachten 1981/82, p. 185.

22. Fels, G., Internationale Wettbewerbsfähigkeit—Japan, Vereinigte Staaten, Bundesrepublik—Fakten, Trends, Hypothesen, Zeitschrift für betriebswirtschaftliche Forschung, Vol. 34, No. 1, 1982, p. 8.

23. European Management Forum, Report on Industrial Competitiveness 1981, Cologne/Geneva, 1981, p. 15.

24. Ibid., p. 20.

25. Sachverständigenrat . . . , Jahresgutachten 1981/82, p. 187.

26. Author unknown, Prognos Prognose bis 1990, Basel, Blick durch die Wirtschaft, Vol. 24, 17 December 1981, p. 1.

27. Fels, G., op. cit., p. 16 ff.
28. Schiefer, F., Faktoren der internationalen Wettbewerbsfähigkeit
     —aufgezeigt am Vergleich USA, Japan, Deutschland.
29. Institut der Deutschen Wirtschaft, Internationale Wirtshaftszahlen
     1981/82, p. 7.
30. European Management Forum, op. cit., p. 11 et seq.
31. Sachverständigenrat . . . , Jahresgutachten 1981/82, p. 195 ff.
     Fels, G, op. cit., p. 22 ff.
32. Sachverständigenrat . . . , Jahresgutachten 1981/82, p. 191 ff.

5 THE UNITED KINGDOM AND THE CHANGING ECONOMIC WORLD ORDER

Neil Hood and Stephen Young

To imply that Britain has played anything more than a minor role in the challenging of U.S. economic power over the last decade or so might, at first glance, seem wholly inaccurate. Preoccupied with the problems of postwar reconstruction, declining overseas earnings, and increased competition in export markets in the first two decades after World War II, Britain was plagued with low growth, persistently high inflation, and massive industrial-restructuring demands in the 1970s. Yet in spite of the hostile domestic environment, and to some degree because of it, there are a number of areas in which both the industrial policies and the corporate strategies of major U.K. firms do impinge directly on the United States. These issues will be more understandable if we briefly consider some of the long-standing problems of the British economy.

THE U.K. ECONOMY IN THE POSTWAR PERIOD

Since World War II, the British economy has witnessed a dramatic decline in relation to its principal competitors. Although the British economy over the past three decades should have been treated as a sick patient, it has, unfortunately, always had more diagnosticians than physicians.[1] Among the symptoms have been both a low level of per capita income and low relative growth; and low levels of productivity; and persistent balance-of-payments and related exchange-rate crises, together with "stop-go" domestic policies. The 1970s merely added higher inflation, substantial intra-European industrial restructuring, and severe unemployment to that list.

According to most conventional economic indicators, the relative performance of the British economy has been poor even though, in terms of gross domestic product (GDP), the nation was economically healthier between 1948 and 1970 than in the inter-war years. Table 5–1 provides data on some of these indicators, and while they have to be treated cautiously in view of the well-established definitional problems associated with international comparisons, the picture of deteriorating British performance is clear. Moving from relative growth rates to relative levels, Britain again fares badly, as is indicated by figures on per capita GDP in Table 5–2. On both measures indicated in the table the U.K. position relative to the major countries in the European Economic Community (EEC) has clearly deteriorated. Similar patterns emerge from comparative studies on labor productivity in manufacturing, even when allowance is made for differences in capital.[2] Again U.K. innovative ability would appear to be relatively poor across quite a wide range of industries,[3] and although the gross investment rate in manufacturing does not compare too unfavorably with major competitors, the incremental output/capital ratio does.[4]

In matters of trade, marked changes have occurred in the British position—changes that reflect both trade liberalization and fundamental changes in competitive forces. As regards the geographical composition of U.K. trade, traditionally the bulk of trade was with the Commonwealth and overseas sterling-area countries. In 1955 some 40 percent of U.K. merchandise trade was still with that group, but by the late 1970s the figure was under 20 percent. Conversely, while total trade to the developed nations rose from 65 to over 75 percent during the same period, a marked shift came with an increase in the proportion of trade carried out with Western Europe, which now accounts for some 55 percent of U.K. merchandise trade. Closely related to this movement has been the changing structure of U.K. imports. Most significant is the increase

Table 5–1. Major Economic Indicators: Some International Comparisons for the Postwar Period (average annual growth rates).

Country	Industrial Production			Output per man hour in manufacturing			Consumer prices			Wage costs per unit of manufacturing output		
	1951–58	1958–69	1969–77	1951–58	1958–69	1969–77	1954–58	1958–69	1969–77	1954–58	1958–69	1969–77
Canada	4.19	5.98	3.79	—	—	3.69	1.84	2.40	7.51	—	—	7.04
France	5.60	5.72	3.72	5.66	5.94	4.87	5.06	4.02	8.51	2.05	2.00	8.54
Germany	8.65	6.50	2.66	4.39	5.85	4.46	2.07	2.35	5.35	1.38	2.04	4.90
Italy	7.00	8.00	3.20	1.53[a]	7.37	4.26	2.46	3.25	12.05	1.90	—	14.99[d]
Japan	11.78	15.61	4.69	—	9.53	7.28	0.47	4.93	10.25	0.0	1.89	9.33
Netherlands	4.87	7.72	4.25	—	—	7.29[c]	3.05	—	7.44	—	—	—
United Kingdom	2.18	3.52	0.60	1.67	3.85[b]	2.66	3.53	3.24	12.74	2.60	2.28	13.71
United States	1.96	5.64	2.65	2.52	3.47	3.42	1.84	2.18	6.48	0.0	0.33	3.79

Notes:
a. 1954–8 all industries
b. 1959–69
c. 1969–74
d. 1969–76
A dash indicates the absence of suitable data.
Source: Calculated from data provided in National Institute Economic Review (statistical appendices) in P.S. Johnson, ed., *The Structure of British Industry* (Granada, 1980).

Table 5-2. (A) GDP Per Head at Current Official Exchange Rates.[a]

EUR 9[b] = 100

	United Kingdom	Germany	France	Italy	Holland	Belgium	Luxembourg	Ireland	Denmark
1962	109.7	116.7	114.4	62.7	81.8	101.0	124.0	53.5	—
1967	103.9	108.2	120.0	68.7	92.2	103.8	115.9	54.3	130.2
1972	85.5	127.8	114.1	66.2	104.3	109.9	121.9	56.0	132.9
1977	71.7	138.0	117.7	57.0	126.0	129.4	127.8	48.3	148.2

(B) GDP Per Head at Current Purchasing Power Parities.[a]

(Index EUR 9[b] = 100)

	United Kingdom	Germany	France	Italy	Holland	Belgium	Luxembourg	Ireland	Denmark
1962	108.3	115.6	101.6	72.6	101.9	97.6	124.1	58.7	—
1967	105.1	111.7	106.0	75.1	104.4	99.2	117.6	59.1	122.4
1972	95.8	116.2	110.1	73.9	106.3	104.7	120.2	63.4	122.0
1977	91.8	118.5	113.5	72.2	107.7	108.9	110.1	62.3	118.8

Notes:
a. The estimates at current market prices are taken from National Accounts ESA–1960–1977 Aggregates published by Eurostat.
b. EUR 9 denotes the total of the nine countries of the European Community.

in the proportion of imports of finished manufactures, the share of which more than quadrupled (to around one-third of U.K. imports) by the late 1970s.

These data clearly indicate that the U.K. manufacturing industry has experienced and will continue to experience greater foreign competition in home and export markets. This trend is evidenced in Figure 5–1 for the 1970–1979 period. During this time the overseas trade performance of British manufacturing industry weakened. The rise in import penetration from 16 percent in 1970 to 26 percent in 1979 far outweighed the improvement in the proportion of exports to sales of manufacturers which rose from 18 to 24 percent in the same period. Indeed, in the two years 1977–1979, the volume of U.K. exports of manufactures rose by 3 percent; the volume of imports of manufactures rose ten times as fast—by 30 percent.

These internal indicators are mirrored in the case of British exports. The United Kingdom's share of manufactured exports by the major industrialized countries fell from around 20 percent in the mid-1950s to around 5 percent in 1983, a decline that occurred across a wide spectrum of industrial activity. The particularly serious aspect of this decline is that it took place when world trade was expanding fairly rapidly. Some researchers argue that these developments have been partially offset by the comparative advantage Britain has in services and that the declining manufacturing base is not as serious a problem as it might first appear. However, it has been reliably estimated that the United Kingdom's share in world exports of services would have to increase by one-third to compensate for a 1 percentage point fall in its share of world exports in manufactures.[5] All these data point to an alarming decline in the competitiveness of U.K. industry abroad, an issue of crucial importance to a country that still exports about a third of the net output of its manufacturing industry.

Until the mid-1970s, occasionally the various measures of U.K. trade competitiveness (such as relative export prices, relative wholesale prices, unit labor costs, and so on) moved in conflicting directions. Between 1978 and 1981, on the other hand, performance was disastrous by all measures. For example, on the basis of relative normal unit labor costs, 1978–1980 saw a decline of 30 percent in U.K. competitiveness. It is, of course, in this area that trade performance, inflation levels, and exchange rates become

Figure 5–1. Import Penetration and Export Shares in the United Kingdom (1970–1979).

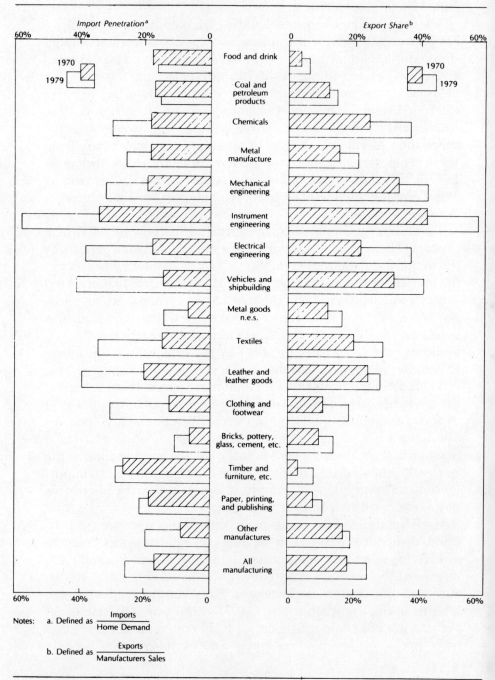

Notes: a. Defined as $\dfrac{\text{Imports}}{\text{Home Demand}}$

b. Defined as $\dfrac{\text{Exports}}{\text{Manufacturers Sales}}$

Source: *Economic Trends,* No. 320, Central Statistical Office, HMSO, June 1980.

completely intertwined. Thus, while much of the 1960s was dominated by exchange-rate crises stemming from persistent balance-of-payments deficits, the later 1970s witnessed this problem in a quite different guise. Other things being equal, many of the changes outlined in this section would normally have driven sterling rates down. The presence of oil and government policy, however, worked in the opposite direction. Therefore, the debate over whether Britain can have both North Sea oil (and subsequently an inflated exchange rate) and a U.K. manufacturing industry is a real one. Moreover, policies since 1977 have tended toward the use of high exchange rates to aid in the reduction of inflation. Similarly, high interest rates directed toward the same end encouraged capital flows and kept the exchange rate high. In short, manufacturing industry in the United Kingdom took a severe battering from all sides in the 1970s, with profound consequences.

Looking at the British economy approaching the mid-1980s, many of the fundamental economic problems still remained. In employment terms, especially, the position had deteriorated further, with 3 million people unemployed in 1983 against 1.2 million in 1979. In other ways, however, there were signs of improvement, with an inflation rate below the OECD average, and sharply improved productivity and corporate profitability. When taken together with modest wage settlements and a depreciating currency most of the loss of competitiveness which occurred at the end of the 1970s had been eliminated.

Before considering specific hostile aspects of the U.K. business environment, it is worth reflecting on the net in which the United Kingdom lies in the early 1980s. It is not a market on which major international companies can afford to depend heavily either in terms of domestic market growth or as an export base. Some U.S. companies have already paid the price for not arriving at that conclusion early enough. Many U.K. companies clearly arrived at that view during the last decade and have accelerated their direct investment abroad or shifted their asset distribution. Much of the British challenge to the United States over the past five to seven years has come from the outworking of these economic adjustment processes on business decisions, both in terms of foreign direct investment (FDI) in the United States and in the context of U.S. investment in Britain. This topic is developed more fully later in this chapter.

As a prelude to evaluating the attempts to tackle the industrial problems emerging from these profound changes, three U.K. industrial issues deserve special mention as they increasingly dominate discussion of the future of the industrial base: profitability,[6] innovation, and employment in manufacturing.

Profitability of U.K. Industry

All the measures of real profit shares and rates of return for the United Kingdom showed a downward trend between 1960 and the start of the 1980s, with a particular fall in profitability since 1973. This pattern is borne out by Figure 5-2. "Chronic excess capacity, pricing policies misguided by a reverence for historic cost accounting principles and unexpected increases in costs as inflation accelerated have probably been major influences depressing profitability. These difficulties have been compounded by the rise in real energy prices which directly squeezed profits, especially in manufacturing industry, and also added to inflationary pressures."[7] While the importance of these variables has been extensively debated, their long run effect on both the ability to invest and the incentive to invest is quite clear. Evidence suggests that environment might also be influencing the nature of the investment—toward replacement rather than expansion, with an emphasis on labor-saving investment where possible. Even more important in the context of this study is the relative position of the United Kingdom among other nations (see Table 5-3). While the comparisons are only approximate, the United Kingdom position is stark by this particular measure of profitability.

Innovation in U.K. Industry

Technical innovation is essential for competing successfully in world export markets. The problem in Britain, however, is one of emphasis rather than simply total amount of innovation. The U.K. performance in terms of per capita innovative activities and per capita exports, for example, falls well behind that of West Germany, Sweden, Switzerland, and the Netherlands in chemicals and

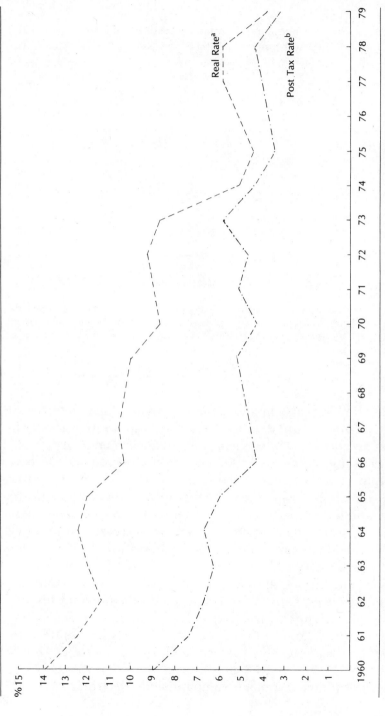

in United Kingdom (excluding North Sea activities).

a. Real rates of return defined as gross trading profit plus rent received (rent taken as zero for manufacturing) less stock appreciation, less capital consumption at replacement cost, as a percentage of net capital stock (fixed assets other than land) at replacement cost plus book value of stocks.

b. The basis of post-tax rates of return is as follows. Taxes, including those on dividends and interest in the hands of recipients, are deducted from earnings and the capital base is reduced to allow for the proportion financed by tax allowances etc. on investment. The backward looking measure computes tax allowances by reference to those in force when the capital was installed.

Source: *Bank of England Quarterly Bulletin* (various editions).

Table 5–3. International Comparisons of Profitability, 1955–1978 (net rate of return[a]: manufacturing industry).

	Canada	United States	West Germany	United Kingdom
	(Percentage)			
Average for years[b]				
1955–59	22	29	n.a.	17
1960–62	19	27	29	15
1963–67	18	36	21	14
1968–71	16	26	22	11
1972–75	17	22	16	7
1976–78	13	24	n.a.	5

Notes:

a. Defined as net operating surplus as percentage net capital stock of fixed assets (excluding land).

b. Apart from the first two and the last, which are governed by availability of data, the groupings of the years are related to the cycles in U.K. rates of return for industry plus transport, each starting in the year after a trough and ending in a trough year. Figures for other countries for the same years may cover more or less than a complete cycle and in this sense can only provide a broad comparison with United Kingdom.

Source: W.E. Martin, ed., *The Economics of the Profits Crisis* (London: HMSO, 1981).

capital goods. It is also below these nations and Japan in terms of household durable goods. Instead, Britain's innovative activity in the past decade or so has concentrated on nuclear energy, defense, and civil aviation. Between 1967 and 1975, the relative U.K. concentration in these areas actually increased, while for the same period, the United Kingdom was the only major country of the Organization for Economic Cooperation and Development (OECD) in which industry-financed R&D decreased in absolute terms. It would appear then that national priorities in R&D in the United Kingdom have been, and remain, very different from those of major competitors, and while centers of excellence continue, the emphasis is perhaps not in keeping with the need for broadly based improvements in technology and comparative advantage. More recently, following the report of the Alvey Committee, the government has launched a major initiative in microelectronics. Together with the ESPRIT program in the EEC, the aim is to enable the country to remain competitive in electronics.

Figure 5–3. Manufacturing and Nonmanufacturing Employees in Employment[a] (seasonally adjusted).

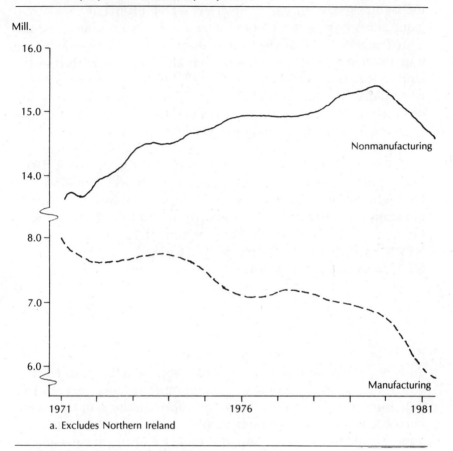

a. Excludes Northern Ireland

Source: *Department of Employment Gazette*, 90, 2 (February 1982).

Manufacturing Employment

Sharp reductions in manufacturing employment during the 1970s and the opposite path of nonmanufacturing jobs (as illustrated in Figure 5–3) point to a deindustrialization of Britain. This divergence has been the cause of extended controversy.[8] Certainly the ratio of nonindustrial to industrial employment grew much faster in the United Kingdom during the early 1960s than it did in other European nations or in the United States. A substantial part of this rise in nonindustrial employment was in government, particularly at the local level, and it has been argued that such expansions in the public sector, in effect, diverted scarce productive resources from industry at a crucial time in the nation's economic history.

The stark reality of the U.K. situation is that, since 1966, an unparalleled loss of 4 million industrial jobs has occurred in the United Kingdom (a 34 percent loss),[9] 3 million of which were in were in manufacturing alone. In sectoral terms, metal manufacture declined by 48 percent since 1961; since 1951, textiles declined by 67 percent and clothing and footwear by 55 percent. Even the least affected sectors, such as paper, printing, and chemicals, have recorded employment declines of around 20 percent. Since 1977, the decline has been even more pronounced: over 1 million jobs lost between June 1979 and June 1981 alone. Given the growth-inducing characteristics of manufacturing and the links between the growth of manufacturing output and GDP, this situation can only be reported as most serious (see Figure 5–4). (For comparable U.S. data see Table 1–4, ed.)

INDUSTRIAL POLICY IN BRITAIN

Britain's relative economic decline, as charted in the preceding discussion, has proved to be a nightmare for policymakers. The underlying causes of the country's economic problems are still not fully understood despite a range of interpretations and explanations and an equally wide offering policy solutions. A recent study puts the blame squarely on the low level of net investment in manufacturing industry.[10] This report rejects any suggestion that the trade unions are responsible. The alleged lack of entrepreneurship on the part of British management is also rejected. Instead, the author argues that the truth lies in the policies pursued by postwar British governments. Conservative and Labour governments alike have "concentrated first and foremost on symbolic figures and quantities, like prices, exchange rates and balances of payments, to the neglect of real quantities like goods and service produced and traded."[11] Politicians' preoccupation with the short-term view and a profound "contempt for production" are seen as the major explanations for the continuing decline in Britain's competitive position in world markets.

The divergent philosophies of the two major political parties in

Figure 5–4.   Unemployment and Vacancies in the United Kingdom (three-month moving average, seasonally adjusted).

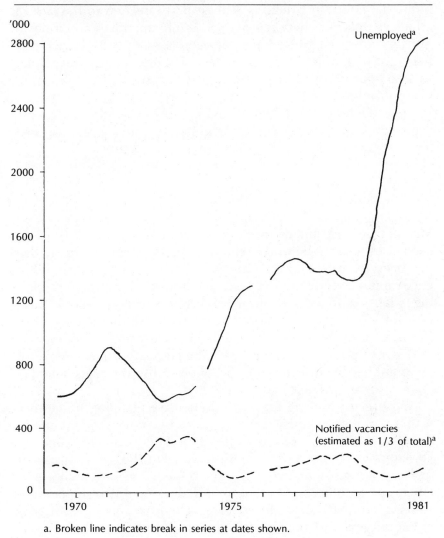

a. Broken line indicates break in series at dates shown.

Britain have done nothing to help the situation. The Conservative Party has traditionally concentrated on the macroeconomy with industrial policy taking something of a backseat (although this is less true of the Conservative government of the 1980s). By contrast, the Labour Party has assumed a more actively interventionist stance toward industrial policy. Even if the reality of what policy the parties actually follow is rather different from the political rhetoric, it is still true that the instability and ad hoc nature of industrial policy in Britain is at least partly related to the lack of a policy consensus between parties. While initiatives and innovations in industrial policy have not been lacking, these have rarely been given an opportunity to work and, consequently, have done little to improve productivity and competitiveness or to stem deindustrialization.

A consideration of British industrial policy over the last twenty years reveals a wide variety of measures directed at the national level, at the sectoral level, and at specific companies.

Policies Pursued at the National Level

Many of the instruments of policy in Britain are similar to those used elsewhere in the world regarding monopolies and restrictive practices, the use of tax allowances and investment grants to influence capital investment in industry, and manpower measures relating to labor mobility, industrial training, and market clearing. Support for industrial innovation is also handled at the national level through the National Research Development Corporation (NRDC),[12] although, in fact, by far the largest portion of government aid has been sector-specific, allocated to the space and aircraft industries or nuclear power.

An observer looking for a comprehensive planning framework within which such policy measures have been devised and implemented would be sorely disappointed. The National Economic Development Council (NEDC) was formed in 1961 and consists of high-level representatives of government, management, and labor; and an office was set up to help develop a British planning system. The NEDC produced comprehensive sets of both economic targets and policies for growth, but neither these documents nor the Department of Economic Affairs' National Plan of 1965 could be regarded as an industrial strategy. As one recent observer has noted: "Two decades later, it is fashionable to suppose that the planning movement which started in the early 1960s has been much ado about almost nothing."[13] Regarding the NEDC specifically, by the mid-1980s its role and influence were very limited.

Policies Pursued at the Sectoral Level

At the same time as the establishment of the NEDC, Economic Development Committees (EDCs) were set up for individual industries with a similar tripartite composition. In 1976 Sector Working Parties (SWPs) were also formed under NEDC to work toward the industrial strategy. SWPs covered a substantial part of U.K. private manufacturing industry in their efforts to chart the development of their respective sectors, identifying problems and priorities for both private and public action. In addition to establishing data on the health of industry and setting out guidelines for future performance, some SWPs have acted as effective pressure groups in tackling issues such as dumping (in industrial electrical equipment); pressing the case for uniform standards throughout Europe for military work (electronic components); and confronting government with the special needs of their sector. Perhaps the most serious limitation of the SWPs was in the lack of effective instruments for implementing their recommendations.

The second and more direct form of sectoral policy, which operated from 1973 to the early 1980s, has involved government financial support to improve the efficiency and competitiveness of sectors by encouraging product developments and investments in contemporary technology. These sectoral schemes were introduced for a limited period of time and with a specified budget, and the criteria by which industries were chosen have varied. The schemes have included overcapacity sectors (textiles, clothing, and machine tools); newer, developing technologies (microelectronics); sectors whose performance was influenced by EEC regulations (poultry); and those suffering severely from import penetration (footwear). The conservative government virtually ended new schemes in 1979, while allowing original schemes, all of which had been introduced for a limited time duration, to run their course. Paralleling this rundown, the activities of the EDCs and SWPs have been much reduced.

As of the mid-1980s policy emphasis was on support for innovation through national, cross-sectoral support schemes designed to improve manufacturing performance, develop new products and processes, and apply new technology.

Policies Pursued at the Company Level

One product of the National Plan was the establishment of the Industrial Reorganisation Corporation (IRC). The purpose of this body was to encourage concentration and rationalization in industry in order to promote increased efficiency and international competitiveness. The feeling was widespread in Europe at this time that enlarging the size of companies was necessary to allow for effective competition with American multinationals. With capital of £150 million, wide powers, and considerable freedom from government control, the IRC was active in promoting mergers. For example, BLMC (later British Leyland), Rowntree Mackintosh (formed after the U.S. corporation General Foods had put in a bid for Rowntrees), and RHP (Ransome, Hoffmann, Pollard) formed as a result of the IRC aim to create a major, British-owned ball-bearing company. The IRC's role in industrial policy was mainly on the company-specific level, and the same was true of its successor, the National Enterprise Board (NEB), created in 1975 when the Labour Government came back into power. The NEB was given more capital than the IRC (up to £1 billion) and a wider mandate to invest in British industry to improve efficiency. The NEB, however, became involved, on behalf of the government, as a holding company for a number of firms that had been taken into public ownership (as an alternative to their liquidation). By the end of 1978, two of these firms, British Leyland (BL) and Rolls Royce, accounted for 89 percent of the value of NEB shareholdings. Between 1975 and 1978, the NEB acquired thirty-eight companies (excluding the transferees BL and Rolls Royce) but in only eight of these cases did the acquisition cost in excess of £1 million.

When the Conservative Government came into power in 1979, responsibility for BL and Rolls Royce was transferred to the Industry Department; the overall scope of the NEB was reduced to include only high-technology projects, regional investments, and loans of up to £50,000 for small businesses. In 1981 the NEB was merged into a new organization known as the British Technolgy Group. The NEB's biggest investment was in Inmos, a company set up in 1977 to give Britain an indigenous stake in the microchip business. This company had government and NEB backing of £85 million, the latest tranche of which is being used to build a factory in South Wales to operate in cooperation with an Inmos facility at Colorado Springs, Colorado. The NEB tried to raise private investment for Inmos during 1980 but had to accept that the project then looked unattractive. However, in mid-1984 it successfully sold Inmos to Thorens EMI, a large British electronics and entertainment group.

Aside from government support to companies through institutions such as the IRC and NEB since 1968, the government passed an act enabling it to finance projects designed "to promote efficiency, to support technological advance, or to create, expand or sustain productive capacity."[14] This act was first applied in March 1968 to a government-initiated merger in the computer industry, out of which emerged International Computers Ltd. (ICL). Assistance was also given under the act to establish a major aluminium-smelting industry in Britain, as a project to conserve foreign exchange. Other controversial projects included the £100 million loan and credit-guarantee arrangement for the Concorde aircraft and loans for the construction of the Queen Elizabeth II cruise ship. In spite of a philosophical desire for "disengagement," the Conservative Government in the early 1970s also became locked in a series of support programs, beginning with the takeover of Rolls Royce after its spectacular collapse. The biggest rescue of all occurred in 1975 when British Leyland was taken into public ownership. Funds were committed as part of a long-term plan for the company, with hope of reaching profitability by 1984. The cost to the taxpayer has been staggering: between 1974 and 1980 the company had a cash deficit of £1.762 billion, which was financed by grants, borrowings guaranteed by government, and share issues subscribed by government. When this cost is coupled with the cash flow of at least £1.14 billion that the company projects it will need for 1981–1984, the total cash deficit over eleven years will have been on the order of £3 billion, and during that time, BL will have lost around 100,000 workers!

Although the government laid down criteria for the expenditure of money for rescue operations, in an attempt to introduce some logic and predictability into their responses, these criteria were actually set aside. As one observer has remarked, "In the last analysis, none of these interventions was a policy. They were reactions to events, sometimes vigorous or innovative, more often reluctant and despairing expedients, rather than policy."[15]

Large sums of money have also been spent in offsetting the financial deficits of the publicly owned British Shipbuilders and British Steel Corporation in recent years and in painful restructuring of these corporations. Four firms—BL, Rolls Royce, British Steel, and British Shipbuilders—consume half the Department of Industry's budget.[16] Another quarter has gone into regional development grants to subsidize investment in the economically depressed areas of the United Kingdom Thus only a limited portion of government funds is left to fulfill the principal aims of industrial policy since the 1960s, namely, improving efficiency and promoting technological development.

Despite the fact that during the 1970s Conservative governments were forced to retreat from their aim of disengagement, the Thatcher governments of the 1980s, have followed a much more consistent policy in attempting to reduce the size of the public sector. "Privatisation" became the theme, whether reflected in the return of traditionally nationalised industries to the private sector, or the sale of NEB (British Technology Group) holdings as soon as possible after the companies have attained viability. Aside from the sale of Inmos, the sell-off of Jaguar cars, a part of British Leyland is, for example, also planned soon. Moreover, severe limitations on company-specific aid have been imposed.

The discussion so far has concentrated on domestic industrial policy. In the area of international policy, the principle of liberalization in trade and direct investment has been a guiding British theme pursued by both political parties. There have been no policy moves, as there were in France toward "reconquering the home market," although it is fair to say that the debate on free trade is still going on. The view is strongly held in some quarters that the country that adopts free-trade policies is allowing its industrial structure to be determined by others. And the belief that protectionism would permit reflation of the British economy, regeneration of British manufacturing industry, and higher employment levels is now reflected in Labour Party policy. Suggestions have been made that inward investing corporations are producing only their relatively low value-added goods in Britain; moreover, there is some evidence that foreign multinational enterprises are operating in sectors in which the biggest deterioration in trade performance appears to have occurred during the 1970s. Such views are largely rejected by the Thatcher government, however, which is keen to reduce non-tariff barriers.

BRITISH INDUSTRIAL GIANTS AND THE OUTWARD INVESTMENT CHALLENGE

In spite of declining competitiveness and the shrinkage of its manufacturing base, Britain posseses a significant number of very large corporations that have been and will continue to be in a position to challenge their counterparts in the United States. For a variety of reasons, a big increase in industrial concentration took place in the United Kingdom from the 1930s to the end of the 1960s. By the end of the period, the degree of this concentration in British industry had become higher than in any other industrialized country. (The small-firm sector in Britain has grown less important than in other industrial countries—a situation some observers have claimed is responsible for at least part of the problems of the economy.)[17]

Given this level of concentration, it is not surprising that both foreign trade and FDI are heavily dominated by a small number of huge enterprises: in 1979, 57 enterprises with exports of over £100 million each were responsible for over half of the country's exports; the proportion rises to two-thirds if the largest 122 enterprises are considered. From a slightly different perspective, exports are not only dominated by large firms, they are dominated by international firms: in 1979, 83 percent of exports were made by enterprises with international connections—with British multinationals accounting for 50 percent and British subsidiaries and associates of foreign-owned multinationals for 33 percent of the total.[18]

By the same token, British outward investment is heavily concentrated. According to the 1978 Census of Overseas Assets, 1,891 U.K. enterprises had assets overseas (excluding oil companies, banks, and insurance companies).[19] However, of total net assets of £19.2 billion, thirty-eight percent was accounted for by 13 enterprises (with net assets of over £200 million each) and 60 percent was represented by 43 enterprises. These two categories, moreover, owned 1,547 and 3,815 overseas affiliates, respectively, out of the total of 14,193.

It is true, of course, that a good number of these British multinationals have been growing less rapidly than similar firms in other countries. One source indicated that British representation within the world's largest industrial companies (in terms of sales) had declined from thirteen in 1957 to nine in 1979.[22] On the other hand, the position had been stable for most of the 1970s, which fits in with other evidence, concerning the more aggressive strategies being pursued by many of the largest British industrial concerns in this period. As L. G. Franko has commented: "Against this mediocre, even bleak, background stand forth some of the world's most successful and profitable enterprises. . . . If one seeks a pattern to developments in the history of British industry, one finds that the industrial sector *per se* has not been the 'star', as it has tended to be in the United States, Germany and Japan. Rather the 'star' has been the British *company.* "[21]

In considering the challenge to the United States posed by these British multinational corporations, it is worth recalling developments in international investment activity over the past few years. After the recovery of the U.K. economy from World War II, British FDI was directed principally toward Commonwealth states, and by 1962, 60 percent of the U.K. stock of overseas investment was located in the Commonwealth. A reorientation of FDI began late in the 1960s and accelerated in the 1970s as firms belatedly recognized the need to build, develop, and hold their market positions within the largest, richest, and most advanced countries. In support of these trends, persistent low growth in the U.K. economy has led a number of corporations to declare publicly that their policy was to move their asset base away from the British market. To neglect the markets in developed countries in this reorientation, in favor of softer pickings in the Commonwealth, would only have left British enterprises more exposed in their home base than before.

By 1978 Western Europe and North America accounted, respectively, for 31 percent and 26.1 percent of the book value of British firms' net assets abroad (excluding oil companies, banks, and insurance companies). On a flow basis, the redirection was even more marked (see Table 5–4): from 1975 to 1979, 41 percent of net outward investment was directed to North America alone, and in the years 1978 to 1979, the proportion rose to 52.6 percent. (As footnote (b) to Table 5–4 shows, two-thirds of this investment in North America took the form of acquisitions.) The result was that by 1975, for the first time since 1960, there was more U.K. manufacturing investment in North America than North American manufacturing investment in the United Kingdom.[22]

Does British FDI in the United States pose a challenge to U.S.

Table 5–4. British Outward Direct Investment Stock and Flows.

	Book Value of Net Assets (excluding oil companies, banks, and insurance companies)				Total Net Investment (excluding oil)			
	1962		1978		1975–79		1978–79[b]	
	£million	%	£million	%	£million	%	£million	%
Western Europe	455.4	13.4	5,954.5	31.0	2,459.6	22.9	985.3	17.8
North America[a]	785.3	23.1	5,017.5	26.1	4,433.2	41.3	2,908.0	52.6
Other Developed Countries	922.9	27.1	4,446.2	23.1	1,637.8	15.3	579.7	10.5
Rest of the World	1,241.4	36.4	3,796.7	19.8	2,198.6	20.5	1,055.3	19.1
TOTAL	3,405.0	100.0	19,214.8	100.0	10,729.2	100.0	5,528.2	100.0

Notes:

a. The division between Canada and the United States is as follows (%):

	Book Value of Net Assets	
	1962	1978
Canada	14.2	6.5
US	8.9	19.6

b. The proportion of this net investment which took the form of the acquisition of overseas companies' share and loan capital was as follows (%):

Western Europe	North America	Other Developed Countries	Rest of the World
47.1	63.0	—	12.4

Sources: Business Monitor, MA4 (1978 Supplement), Table 2 for stock data; Business Monitor, MA4 (1979), Table 1.3 for flow data.

industry? A positive answer to this question would require various conditions to hold true. British FDI would need to be important within the overall inward flow of investment to the United States and, furthermore, to represent a significant level of penetration within the sectors involved. Additionally, there would need to be indications that British competitiveness was in some way being enhanced by the surge of investment into the United States. Although Britain is the largest single investing country in America in manufacturing industry, and the country is still ranked first in terms of number of firms operating in the United States, the fact remains that total FDI penetration in America is generally quite low.[23] So, except perhaps in isolated subsectors, British investment does not pose any great challenge in the United States.

The competitiveness question is thus difficult to address directly, but it is possible to look at British firms' motives and methods of entry into the United States and derive some inferences. The observation made earlier concerning entry methods for British companies can be confirmed: in 1979 and 1980 acquisitions accounted for 93 percent of investment outlays by British multinationals in the United States.[24] Consideration of intentions requires investigation of specific companies, however, which, given the concentration noted previously, is more relevant that aggregate figures. As to motives, British corporate investors seem to fall into four groups: technology acquirers, conglomerates, diversifiers, and base-business expanders.[25]

Among the most active U.K. investors, Racal and [British] General Electric serve as examples of companies acquiring access to U.S. technology in fields allied to their base businesses. General Electric (GEC) is a useful illustration of changes in strategy by a U.K. company that has traditionally been weak in the U.S. market (only $175 million of its 1978 total corporate sales of $4.4 billion came from this source). In effect, a substantial part of its diversification out of the slow-growth, industrial-equipment markets has involved purchases of U.S. companies in fields ranging from aerospace to office systems. In most cases, GEC has linked up with U.S. corporations whose businesses, are already closely related to its existing electronics operations in order to maximize the benefits of the acquired technology.

A broadly similar policy underlies the Racal approach. Racal built a substantial part of its business in Third World markets, essentially by selling simplified versions of its radio communications systems for military use. With revenues rising at a compound rate of around 33 percent per year for the last decade, Racal has been among the most expansive U.K. companies. In the United States the company has been planning to repeat its success in the radio communications market by expanding into data communications via the acquisition of U.S. technology. A number of other U.K. companies display some of the same characteristics as Racal, in that they have shown an interest in acquiring U.S. corporations that are relatively new and much smaller than themselves in order to pursue a process of internalizing the acquired knowledge within one of their own divisions.

Within the conglomerate group, one of the most interesting cases involves Thomas Tilling. With twelve acquisitions between 1977 and 1979, Tilling has been by far the most active U.K. company in the United States in spite of its late start. A large and highly diversified conglomerate, Tilling has strong internal consistency in its operations. In contrast to a number of other major U.K. companies, Tilling has not aimed at vast individual purchases, but rather has concentrated on smaller operations that can be managed within its own divisional structure. In spending around $300 million in U.S. expansion over a three-year period (largely financed through rights issues), Tilling has strongly emphasized the purchase of distribution networks and acquisitions within high-growth markets. These two objectives can often be combined in the same purchase.

Another interesting aspect of the Tilling approach has been its negotiation with large U.S. corporations for the purchase of divisions the latter were willing to divest. Three of the largest acquisitions have been of this type, including the purchase of a $100 million sales construction subsidiary from Ashland Oil of Superior Iron Works in Texas, and two divisions involved in the distribution of oilfield supplies and materials for industrial construction and maintenance. While Tilling is not the only U.K. company to use this approach, it has employed it most frequently and, in so doing, exploited its considerable knowledge of, and contacts in, the U.S. market. The size of Tilling and the fact that it is a conglomerate are also factors that aid in this type of negotiation since the company rarely poses a strong competitive threat to the base business of the seller. Some 25 percent of the company's profits are now from its U.S. interests.

The other groups of recently active U.K. companies are those with long-standing policies of diversification and those whose strategy is more specifically that of base-broadening. Among the former, not only are the strategic commitments to diversification substantial, the United States is only one of a number of market areas in which such policies have been pursued. Companies within this group include Rio Tinto Zinc, BAT Industries, Metal Box, BICC, and various food firms such as Cavenham, Dalgety, and United Biscuits.

Questions as to the ability of these various categories of British enterprises to assimilate the acquisitions, exploit the acquired technology, and so on remain. Some signs of success are evident. J.H. Dunning, analyzing outward direct-investment flows, comments that "in the last decade and a half, U.K. firms have been improving their performance relative to firms of other nationalities in world markets (and therefore), the greater part of the U.K.'s poor international performance must be laid at the door of the deterioration in the location advantages of the U.K. relative to those of other countries."[26] The British malaise is thus a function of factors specific to the U.K. economic environment, rather than general failings in management or technology. Outward FDI may lead to greater competitiveness. On the other hand, even if competitiveness is improving, it may have no great depth within British industry (given the high concentration levels quoted).

THE PROBLEMS OF AMERICAN MULTINATIONALS IN BRITAIN

It is possible that the British economic environment may have an adverse impact on all enterprises—British and foreign—operating within the United Kingdom, and there is evidence to support this conclusion with regard to U.S. multinational firms in Britain during the early 1970s.[27] This evidence is based on companies' dependence on the U.K. economy. The United Kingdom was commonly the country to which U.S. corporations were drawn in their initial internationalization, and many have continued to reinvest in the United Kingdom rather than spread their asset base throughout Europe. Singer, Goodyear, and Hoover are classic examples of this involvement: in 1978 U.K. employees of Hoover Ltd. accounted for 60 percent of total employment in the Hoover Company; when employees of Hoover Ltd.'s overseas subsidiaries and associated companies are added in, the figure rises to over 70 percent. In some years, Singer's plant at Clydebank in Scotland alone produced around 20 percent of the total Singer Company output. Examples could be extended to include Chrysler U.K., the major drain on the Chrysler Corporation in the mid-1970s. Even today, U.S. multinational affiliates are heavily, probably overly, committed to the British market. A recent study indicates that more than one-third of American companies have no European plants other than those in the United Kingdom and about 50 percent of sales of U.S. affiliates are consigned solely to the slow-growth British market.[28] Other evidence indicates that productivity levels in multinational subsidiaries in the United Kingdom are lower than in sister affiliates in other major industrial countries.[29]

For some U.S. companies, thus, the commitment to the low-growth British market has been a factor in their loss of competitiveness. On the other hand, Britain is now seen as the most attractive overseas location for U.S. firms in the electronics industry, with Britain being used as an export base. The research capability and capacity within British universities, the ability to recruit and retain scientists and technologists and technicians, government innovation assistance, the ability to operate non-union plants, etc. are all factors of importance in this regard.

THE CHALLENGE FROM THE U.K. FINANCIAL AND SERVICE SECTORS

London remains a major financial center, distinctly characterized more by its international emphasis than by its size relative to New York, Tokyo, or Zurich. For example, the trade value of the U.K. stockmarket was estimated in 1980 at $190 billion, making it the third most important stockmarket after the United States and Japan and accounting for around 8.5 percent of world equity-market capitalization. Of an estimated total world insurance-premiums business of $140 billion in 1980, $40 billion was insured outside the country of origin, with London handling around $7 billion or about 20 percent of the business requiring international capacity. Insurance reinsurance, brokerage, and commodity trade account for some 80 percent of London's foreign earnings. Although expanding by a factor of five between 1968 and 1978, these earnings have grown much more slowly since then, but continue to represent over one-third of the United Kingdom's net invisible income. The slippage reflects a drop in insurance and banking earnings, with foreign income for Eurocurrency transactions proving particularly vulnerable. It also reflects the emergence of other centers offering fiscal incentives and the opening up of new markets such as those in New York, Bermuda, and Singapore for insurance.

At the level of corporate strategy, the activities of the British banks are of particular importance. Major U.K. banks have been pursuing strategies of geographical and functional diversification that reflect the changing emphasis of U.K. trade. While the acquisition of major U.S. banks has attracted particular attention, it is but one part of the story. For instance, the 1979 takeover of Union Bank of California by Standard Chartered was a part of a changing asset emphasis. Comparing Standard Chartered's asset distribution in 1975 and 1980 illustrates the point: the United Kingdom and Europe represent 34 percent in 1975 versus 24 percent in 1980; the United States 5 percent versus 24; the Far East 20 percent versus 24; and Africa 47 percent versus 28.

Taking a somewhat broader view of the United Kingdom's relative position on invisible earnings reveals a number of different signals to be interpreted. The surplus on invisibles was a record £3.3 billion in 1981, compared to 1.9 billion in 1980. While some of this improvement came from increased overseas earnings from both direct and portfolio investment and from interest on U.K. bank's borrowing and lending in foreign currencies, much of it is accounted for by sterling depreciation during 1981. The United Kingdom still has a large surplus on invisibles from the private sector and public corporations, but this is substantialy eroded by deficits emerging from government transactions. Furthermore, in recent years, the surplus has been prone to strong influences from profits earned in the North Sea by foreign companies and contributions to the EEC budget.

Aside from these sources of variation, positive progress on the compensating build-up of foreign earnings has been made, but it is not spectacular when compared to the manufacturing deterioration noted earlier. The data in Table 5–5 provide one illustration of the problem in the matter of U.K. overseas technological royalty transactions. While a net surplus continues to be recorded, aggregate receipt and expenditure figures have been growing at similar rates, the latter at least in part because of the nature and problems of the U.K. economy. For example, licensing agreements with foreign companies are one way of offsetting U.K. technological lags. As far as the United States is concerned, the net deficit position remains large in spite of some substantial growth in receipts over recent years. Net surplus positions remain with Western Europe and especially Japan. None of the figures in Table 5–5 suggests a major upsurge of U.K. international activity to pose a serious overall challenge to any of its competitors, although, as noted earlier, more localized, corporate pressures may be strong.

Additional Areas of Potential Competitiveness

Set against the background of the U.K. economic decline described in this chapter, any economic challenges to the United States are likely to continue to be on narrow, specific fronts. It is worth touching, however, briefly on a number of areas that have not been discussed where a challenge might occur.

British initiatives in the computer and microelectronics business will almost certainly have to remain "company specific" in order to be effective, and they can be expected to have only limited impact on the United States and other advanced markets. The case of Inmos is an exception. Financed by the NEB, Inmos represents an interesting type of initiative to develop advanced microchip memory units from scratch through the hiring of experienced U.S. technologists and managers and by undertaking product development and initial production in the United States. The sum of money to be committed through the Alvey and ESPRIT programs, for example, is much too small to reach any other conclusion.

But the United Kingdom has been active in information technology in other ways. Through sustained support for International Computers Ltd., some potentially important new products have been developed—including their distribution array processing (DAP) system—which enable ICL to build very large computers at low prices. While this ability will certainly aid ICL's relative position, the company is in no real position to challenge the United States on an international basis.[30] Similar developments are evi-

Table 5-5. U.K. Overseas Technological Royalty Transactions, £ million.

	Receipts				Expenditure			
	1976	1977	1978	1979	1976	1977	1978	1979
Overseas technological royalty transactions—								
Analysis of returns received by area or country								
Western Europe[a]	61.18	63.55	64.58	70.58	50.04	48.15	49.33	45.54
European Community	43.77	45.31	44.37	49.19	28.45	26.90	32.24	27.33
of which Belgium/Luxembourg	5.73	6.13	5.97	..	..	..	1.54	..
France	12.00	12.79	11.59	12.34	9.73	10.97	14.39	8.90
West Germany	11.99	11.29	13.50	13.83	5.14	4.76	8.09	..
Italy	9.05	8.38	8.74	9.71	2.40	3.01	2.74	0.96
Netherlands	3.25	4.56	2.41	2.37	..	4.55	6.49	8.35
EFTA	8.27	9.35	9.81	11.40	21.02	21.02	15.86	18.06
of which Sweden	2.58	3.94	4.25	4.19	1.37	1.59	3.27	3.12
Switzerland	2.27	2.52	..	..	19.16	18.92	12.04	14.39
Australia	12.42	10.43	11.87	12.31	0.36	0.56	0.44	0.78
Canada	5.32	5.80	6.01	4.60	0.17	0.24	0.38	..
Japan	28.03	34.60	43.21	..	..	0.81	0.85	..
New Zealand	2.20	2.77	3.07	..	..	..	..	..
South Africa	10.22	10.31	11.81	11.55	..	..	0.12	..
USA	51.83	60.27	58.33	98.11	150.54	178.69	197.99	..
Rest of the World	55.44	63.30	65.13	55.28	4.59	5.61	9.21	2.22
of which Caribbean, Central and S. America	7.29	7.52	9.04	7.92	0.14	0.17	0.27	0.05
World technological and mineral rights	227.69	251.14	273.99	297.67	206.32	234.16	258.33	258.29

a. Including other Western European countries: Cyprus, Gibraltar, Greece, Malta, Spain, Turkey, and Western European countries not separately designated.

Source: Department of Trade; *Economic Trends*, no. 334 (August 1981).

denced in this field by the tie-up between the tiny but highly innovative Sinclair Electronics firm and Timex.[31] The high hopes associated with Inmos have, however, disappeared. Even though the firm was sold to a U.K. buyer it is certainly the case that any new developments will probably be focussed on U.S. rather than U.K. Inmos plants.

Although many aspects of the North Sea oil developments in the United Kingdom over the past ten to fifteen years have been dependent on external technology, there are grounds for believing that a number of British-based corporations have now built up a high level of expertise in this field which could pose a challenge to competitors in offshore technology in other parts of the world. The pace of development and the rigors of the physical environment have inevitably led to an acceleration of technological progress at a time when the worldwide search for oil is keen, if not hostile.

CONCLUSIONS

The reordering of world economic power has already had a dramatic effect on the British economy. The erosion of the industrial base has been unprecedented, and the speed of change in the recent past has been alarming. It is not difficult to conclude as did Pollard, that by the end of the century, in Europe, only Albania will be poorer than Britain.[32] The United Kingdom still retains comparative advantages on a limited number of fronts in specific companies, and this situation is likely to continue. In terms of the challenge to the United States, there is more to fear from these corporate entrepreneurs than from any industrial policy measures adopted so far. The speedy deterioration of domestic market conditions has clearly concentrated the mind in numerous boardrooms, and it has led to the adoption of more competitive and aggressive strategies directed against the United States. Further stategic developments in this vein are to be expected at a growing pace and involving ever smaller corporations.

The United Kingdom currently possseses vast idle resources of manpower, considerable excess industrial capacity, and low real wage costs. Given a stable political environment and the sustained application of industrial policy measures designed to enhance productivity growth, Britain still has the opportunity to rebuild competitive advantage across a broad range of industrial activity, but only if the opportunity for a new start is not frittered away.

NOTES

1. See R. E. Caves, *Britain's Economic Prospects* (Washington, D.C.: The Brookings Institution, 1968).
2. See, for example, M. Panic, ed., *The U.K. and West German* @ Manufacturing Industry 1954–72 (London: NEDO, 1976); C. F. Pratten, *Labour Productivity Differentials within International Companies,* University of Cambridge, Department of Applied Economics, Occasional Paper No. 50 (Cambridge: Cambridge University Press, 1976).
3. K. Pavitt, ed., *Technical Innovation and British Economic Performance* (London: Macmillan, 1980).
4. A. Mueller, "Industrial Efficiency and UK Government Policy," in C. Bowe, ed., *Industrial Efficiency and the Role of Government* (London: HMSO, 1977).
5. F. Blackaby, ed., *De-industrialisation* (London: Heinemann and Nier, 1979), p. 3.
6. This issue is exhaustively examined in W. E. Martin and M. O'Connor, "Profitability: A Background Paper" in W. E. Martin, ed., *The Economics of the Profits Crisis* (London: HMSO, 1981).
7. Ibid., p. 8.
8. As, for example, in R. Bacon and W. Ellis, *Britain's Economic Problem: Too Few Producers* (London: Macmillan, 1976).
9. A. P. Thirlwall, "Deindustrialisation in the United Kingdom," *Lloyds Bank Review,* no. 144 (April 1982).
10. S. Pollard, *The Wasting of the British Economy* (London: Croom Helm, 1982).
11. Ibid.
12. Originally through the National Research and Development Corporation. This is now, along with the National Enterprise Board, part of the British Technology Group.
13. J. Pinder, "Industrial Policy in Britain and the European Community," *Policy Studies* 2, part 4 (1982).
14. *Industrial Expansion,* Command 3509 (London: HMSO, 1968).
15. S. Golt, "Government Organization and Support for Private Industry: The United Kingdom Experience," in S. J. Warnecke, ed., *International Trade and Industrial Policies* (London: Macmillan, 1978).
16. *The Sunday Times,* London, March 21, 1982, p. 13.

17. S. J. Prais, *The Evolution of Giant Firms in Britain: A Study of the Growth of Concentrate in Manufacturing Industry in Britain, 1907–70,* National Institute of Economic and Social Research, Economic and Social Research Studies No. 30 (Cambridge: Cambridge University Press, 1976).
18. *Business Monitor,* MA4 (1979).
19. *Business Monitor,* MA4 (1978 Supplement), Table 12.
20. V. Droucopoulos, "The Non-American Challenge: A Report on the Size and Growth of the World's Largest Firms," *Capital and Class* (Summer 1981): 36–46.
21. L. G. Franko, "British Industry: The International Dimension," in C. L. Suzman, ed., *Foreign Direct Investment in the Southeast: West Germany, the United Kingdom and Japan,* Papers on International Issues No. 1, The Southern Center for International Studies, Atlanta, Ga. (August 1979).
22. J. H. Dunning, "The UK's International Direct Investment Position in the Mid-1970s," *Lloyds Bank Review,* no. 132 (April 1979).
23. E. Zupnick, *Foreign Investment in the US: Costs and Benefits* (Washington, D.C.: U.S. Government Printing Office, August 1981).
24. U.S. Department of Commerce, *Survey of Current Business,* Washington, D.C.: U.S. Government Printing Office, August 1981).
25. N. Hood and S. Young, "Recent Strategic Expansions by British Corporations in the United States," Strathclyde Business School Working Paper, no. 8109 (1981).
26. Dunning, "The UK's International Direct Investment Position in the Mid-1970s," p. 16.
27. R. A. Lincoln, *American Business in the U.K.* (London: Economist Intelligence Unit, 1974); J. H. Dunning, *US Industry in the U.K.* (London: Wilton House, 1976).
28. N. Hood and S. Young, *Multinational Investment Strategies in the British Isles,* report to the Department of Trade and Industry (London, HMSO, 1983). The study was based on a sample of 140 companies, 70 American and 70 continental. It is fair to comment that the results indicated a good deal of satisfaction with the performance of American companies in Britain.
29. C. F. Pratten, *Labour Productivity Differentials within International Companies,* University of Cambridge, Department of Applied Economics Occasional Paper No. 50 (Cambridge: Cambridge University Press, 1976).
30. *Fortune* (January 21, 1982.
31. *Fortune* (March 8, 1982): 84.
32. S. Pollard, *The Wasting of the British Economy.* op. cit.

6 THE RECENT PERFORMANCE AND FUTURE CHALLENGES OF NEWLY INDUSTRIALIZING COUNTRIES

Luciano Coutinho

In the late 1970s, amid the erosion of international trade and protectionist pressures from the advanced economies, a new economic category of countries appeared: the newly industrializing countries or NICs. The NICs were so baptized by an influential report of the Organization for Economic Cooperation and Development (OECD) published in 1979,[1] which defined NICs as middle-income countries (in terms of per capita income) with a fairly advanced industrial system, rapid growth of domestic demand for manufactures, increasing share of industrial employment, and impressive productivity growth. Four southern European countries (Greece, Portugal, Spain, and Yugoslavia), two Latin American (Brazil and Mexico), and four Southeast Asian (Hong Kong, Korea, Singapore, and Taiwan) were judged as meeting these criteria. Rapid growth of GDP and exports, although a significant feature of each country, does not adequately describe individual NICs in all their diversity. Nevertheless, certain generalizations can be made about the process of industrialization in "peripheral" economies in the post-World War II period.

131

THE PERIPHERY IN THE 1946–1973
INTERNATIONAL DIVISION OF LABOR

Successful industrialization on the periphery of the world economy was a limited and specific phenomenon. It was limited because only a handful of countries were able to overcome the difficult obstacles encountered in building up a modern industrial base. And it was specific because it took place in a particular period of rapid expansion of the world economy, in the context of extremely fast changes in the international division of labor and patterns of world hegemony.

To these late-latecomers, industrialization imposed formidable challenges. The dominant pattern of twentieth-century industrial development, characterized by rapid differentiation of durable consumer goods and mass consumption, required a large base of heavy industry (steel, electric power, basic chemicals), basic metal and chemical intermediate-input sectors, at least somewhat developed mechanical, electrical, and machinery sectors, as well as the existence of an extensive infrastructure. Building these complex, interdependent structures on a large scale in a very short time (in most cases concentrated between the mid-1950s and late 1960s) was extremely difficult. It also required extensive direct state participation, initiative, and unorthodox policies for planning, financing, and completing many of the large projects.

Attempts have been made to characterize the potentialities and limitations of the industrialization process and to relate the redefined role of the periphery to the changes that occurred in the postwar economy.[2] These findings may be summarized as follows:

1. The industrialization process, insofar as the construction of a *modern, integrated industrial system* is concerned, has been completed only in a few peripheral economies, and even in those cases, some structural constraints have hindered the development of a fully fledged capital-goods sector. Rapid industrial growth both demands and presupposes the continuous development of production capacity that uses the basic inputs for extensive production of industrial goods.
2. Nearly all the rest of developing peripheral economies are presently trying to establish this industrial production-goods

sector. They are industrialized nations *in process,* and their success and continuity depend, essentially, on the states' abilities to put together feasible financing (in the form of subsidies and credits), and on developing large public enterprises. The industrialization process will not be complete until the production-goods sector is built up enough to provide a technological base capable of allowing capital accumulation to proceed without the need to import basic inputs.

3   The level of development of the production-goods sector dictates the degree of "density" (the interrelationship of industries) and the degree of capital "deepening" (that is, the potential for penetration by and expansion of the subsidiaries of international enterprises) of an industrial system.

4.   The advance of industrialization (however incomplete) in important segments of peripheral economics has transformed some NICs into attractive investment fields for international industrial capital, thereby redefining the latter's role in the new international division of labor. On the other hand, affiliates or subsidiaries of big international corporations have significantly changed important segments of the periphery, thus playing an active role in the industrialization process.

5.   In many countries, market penetration by foreign corporations was followed or accompanied by an effort, mainly through direct state initiative, to encourage heavy industry. However, a direct causality between market penetration by foreign enterprises and the development of the production-goods sector cannot be firmly established. The creation of a vigorous production-goods sector demands the simultaneous, interconnected development of a number of main components, for example, steel and heavy metal-mechanical industries, heavy electrical goods and equipment, and a large basic chemical industry. Furthermore, this development requires a massive infrastructure based on social capital. Even the minimum investment capital needed to develop any of these sectors is quite large. The combined development of these blocks implies an advanced degree of capital concentration and centralization that is absent in peripheral economies, no matter how advanced their industrialization process might be. This financial constraint has been a hindrance for late industrializations.

6.   State intervention is, therefore, decisive. The state must work as a direct accumulator of capital (through taxation for financial means) and as a promoter of private "monopolization" within the national economy. It must create conditions, either directly (through public enterprises) or indirectly (as a supporter of certain business sectors) for the establishment of the production-goods sector. The extent to which the state is able to proceed in this task determines the degree of integration among sectors (density) and the possibilities for expansion and penetration by foreign international firms (deepening). The connection between subsidiaries of international corporations and the state defines both the areas for new investment and the "residual" areas, which national private capitalists can enter, thus shaping a particular structure of capitalist organization.[3]

7.   The state and industrialization in the periphery cannot be divorced. In fact, a state's policies and regulations mold the structure within which domestic private capital can operate. On the other hand, the state is is itself inextricably tied to the monopolist structure through its own public enterprises. Hence, industrialization in the periphery can only be accomplished with the simultaneous development of a specific form of state monopoly capitalism.

8.   Participation of foreign capital is different in each case, however, and depends on the particular role an NIC is playing in the world division of labor. If we consider, for instance, the group of NICs defined by the OECD criteria, striking differences among countries can be noted. Brazil's and Mexico's industrial systems are basically oriented toward internal markets, whereas those of Korea and Taiwan combine a strong export orientation with internal markets that are relatively larger. On the other hand, economies like Hong Kong and Singapore are actually export "platforms" for international corporations, with very specialized industrial bases. They can hardly even be considered as industrialized economies if a broad, integrated industrial system is taken as a criterion.

9.   Coexisting with the few recently industrialized countries and with a certain number of countries where industrialization is still an ongoing process are a large block of mostly poor, peripheral economies that remain dependent on some domi-

nant, primary good export sector. These primarily exporting economies also have some degree of manufacturing activity and growth, but the scope, size, and autonomy of their industrial growth is limited because it is subordinated to the cyclical performance of the dominant primary export sectors.

10. Within this latter block is a special subgroup, made up of oil-exporting countries, whose obvious uniqueness and exceptional situation has enabled some to attempt a shift toward industrialization that is not subordinated to the exporting sector.

The belated industrialization in the periphery has reached different degrees of development in different areas. The ability to sustain the expanding growth of a modern industrial system with internally generated inputs can only be assured by the existence of a constellation of basic industrial branches (a production-goods sector). The extent of development, integration, and relative weight of this sector is a crucial element in defining when countries have completed the process of industrialization and no longer need to depend on the (formerly) dominant export activities to sustain economic growth. Nor do they need to continue emphasizing import-substitution, which ceases to be the basis of industrialization precisely when the completion of a broadly integrated industrial base has been achieved. At this point industrial development becomes internally determined, and the economic cycle gains its own momentum. This does not mean, however, that the few advanced peripheral economies are able to provide all or most of their capital-formation needs from internally produced capital goods. Production of advanced machinery and equipment requires the mastering of high technology, a tradition of engineering skills, sophisticated research and development systems, a large and up-to-date scientific system, and so on.

The description of NICs thus far, although providing a consistent basis for classifying a true NIC, cannot differentiate among their individual characters and profiles. In each case the interplay of state, local, and international capital within the industrial structure and market organization is unique. Furthermore, all such interplays are related to the role of the NIC in the world economy, both through trade relationships and degree of foreign investment.

Moreover, even though recently industrialized peripheral countries may share a common technology with the advanced industrial economies (inasmuch as massive internationalization of production by transnational firms has contributed to a homogenization of basic technical processes throughout the world), substantial heterogeneity remains among them. The following section will highlight the distinctive features of two successful cases—Brazil and Mexico—of Latin American industrialization.

LATIN AMERICAN INDUSTRIALIZATION IN POSTWAR DYNAMICS

Latin America, a relatively advanced peripheral region, began its entry into the new international division of labor as a result of massive penetration by subsidiaries of international enterprises, and its integration in the world economy has grown sharply throughout the postwar expansion. Most of this region's economies are still struggling to expand since industrialization has been limited, incomplete, and unbalanced. Market penetration by foreign industrial subsidiaries was accomplished mainly through the manufacture of nondurable consumer goods which does not depend on vertically integrated and technologically advanced support structures for the provision of parts, components, and other basic inputs. In the more advanced economies of this group (Venezuela, Colombia, Chile, and Peru), significant progress in the production of simple, durable consumer goods has taken place. Final assembly of more complex durables was also introduced, which demanded a vertically integrated back-up structure. However, almost all basic inputs are still imported, and only technologically simple parts are produced domestically. In addition, wherever a vertically integrated structure developed, it did so with important participation by foreign subsidiaries, particularly for inputs, parts, and components in the light electrical, chemical, mechanical, and metal industries.

In these economies, however, several links in the chain of interindustry relations are still to be connected, and the productive base of some fundamental inputs remains insufficient and incomplete, thus limiting the density of industrial integration. The capital-goods sector is rather restricted and technologically backward.

While these shortcomings have not and do not now constitute an *absolute* restriction on industrial growth and market penetration by international enterprises, they impose serious limitations and obstacles. Import elasticities of inputs and capital goods tend to be very high during periods of fast growth. Hence, constrained capacity to import recurrently appears, shortening the length of accelerated-growth periods. Sustainable capital accumulation thus remains dependent on the performance of the export sectors (i.e., the well-known dilemma of the import-substituting process). In the less advanced group of countries (Ecuador, Bolivia, Uruguay, Paraguay, and those of Central America), these shortcomings are quite severe, and the predominance of the export sectors remains unchallenged.

Foreign direct investment flows into Latin America, despite having reached high average rates superior to those of the periphery as a whole, have varied considerably among countries during the postwar period. Stable inflows of risk capital require a solid prospect of economic expansion and confidence in a country's political stability, as well as economic policies favorable to the entry of foreign capital. In Argentina, a combination of these conditions occurred only during two periods of little more than two years each: during the Frondizi government (1959–1960) and in the beginning of General Ongania's "modernizing" authoritarian administration (1967–1968). Considering the lack of regular synchronization of economic cycles within the countries of Latin America and the overall political instability, it is not at all surprising that direct investment flows have shown erratic behavior.

Table 6–1 clearly illustrates the tendencies described above, and shows how the Argentine economy lost influence and importance for long periods of semistagnation while other countries experienced relatively high growth rates. The table also illustrates the dynamism of the Brazilian economy and the steadiness of Mexican growth.

Mexico's growth, in contrast to Argentina, was extremely stable from the mid-1950s up to the late 1960s—a phase already known as *desarollo estabilizador.* Mexican economic expansion cycles were relatively long, although moderate, and recessions were brief and few, coinciding with the short American economic recessions or with changes in presidential mandates. Throughout the postwar period, Mexican policy was favorable to foreign capital, while at

Table 6–1. A Comparison of the Percentage Distribution of the GDP with U.S. Foreign Direct Investment in Latin America.

	1955		1968		1973		1978	
	%US–FDI	GDP	%US–FDI	GDP	%US–FDI	GDP	%US–FDI	GDP
Argentina	20.0	28.0	20.0	19.0	13.0	10.0	8.5	6.0
Brazil	33.0	26.0	26.0	25.0	13.2	34.0	40.0	40.0
Mexico	21.0	22.0	27.0	25.0	28.0	24.3	25.0	23.7
Colombia	5.0	5.0	5.0	6.0	5.0	5.0	4.5	5.0
Chile	3.0	4.0	2.0	5.0	0.7	2.0	0.6	2.0
Venezuela	5.0	7.0	10.0	7.0	8.5	8.5	9.2	9.8
Peru	3.0	3.0	3.0	4.0	2.5	4.5	1.4	2.0
Other Latin America Countries	4.0	4.0	2.0	3.0	2.5	3.5	2.6	3.7
Central America and Caribbean	6.0	5.0	5.0	7.0	7.8	7.2	8.2	7.8
Total	100.0	100.0	100.0	100.0	100.0	100.0	100.0	100.0

Sources: US–FDI data from the Department of Commerce, *Survey of Current Business*; GDP data from ECLS's *Boletins Estatisticos* for 1955 and 1968 and the IMF's *International Financial Statistics* for the years 1973 and 1978.

the same time, it protected the market niches occupied or claimed by local capital. The state developed the basic infrastructure for industry and encouraged the production of industrial goods, in gradual phases when development was stronger than at other times.[4]

In the case of Brazil, the postwar expansion cycles were not only long but also extremely vigorous. Under the 1956–1961 Kubitschek government, the production-goods sector was built up through a concentrated investment effort, while the production capacity of durable consumer goods was rapidly differentiated and vertically integrated (under the leadership of foreign subsidiaries). Local capital was actively used by both buyers and suppliers of components. Foreign capital was also active in most branches of nondurable consumer goods, industrial inputs (chemicals, electric equipment and materials, metal processing, etc.), and capital goods (electric and nonelectric equipment). Local firms shared with international enterprises the new market segments that were created in the process.

Following the 1963–1967 crisis, when the whole state institutional apparatus was subjected to widespread reform (in the form of wage laws, taxes, banking, and financial reforms), the economy began to grow again. After absorbing the idle capacity that had resulted from two years of expansion, the economy again experienced a vigorous investment boom after 1970, when all the newly formed industrial and managerial structures expanded in size and number at very high rates. In the course of the amazing 1968–1974 expansion, the Brazilian economy consolidated and adjusted itself into a full-blown, large-scale industrial economy. During this period, the industrialization process was not only complete but probably reached the maximum possible limits of expansion within the potentialities opened up by the new international division of labor before the post-1973 world economic slowdown.

The integration of specifically Latin American industrial systems into the dominant expansion pattern of advanced capitalism has other distinctive features. Foreign subsidiaries' penetration into the consumer-goods sectors stimulated a precocious "transplant" to the periphery of the prevailing consumption patterns of the central or industrialized western economies: product differentiation, line segmentation by market layers, and so on. This trickle-down of sophisticated consumption patterns to the Latin American upper-middle classes accelerated the concentration of income in that class in all economies, and particularly in those where industrial growth was fast. In a similar carry-over, the industrial and household patterns of energy use of the advanced economies were also adopted.

THE ROLE OF THE NATIONAL CAPITALIST STATE

A fundamental aspect of late-latecomer industrialization in Latin America has been the rapid and concentrated development of state structures. The economic apparatus of the states has taken on new institutions and instruments (such as exchange rates, minimum wages, interest rates, and control of credit expansion) to regulate economic relations and establish a framework for capital accumulation. In addition, regulatory agencies and mechanisms have been developed to support weaker economic sectors; public enterprises and development banks have also been created in order to support the new projects required for industrial progress.

The build-up of these state instruments did not develop in a linear sequence; it was accomplished through advances and retreats, in the context of different political regimes. In the cases of Brazil and Mexico, the process has now reached an advanced stage: both countries now have what can be called a national capitalist state that is very advanced in terms of institutional apparatus and the scope of regulatory functions.

The centralized structures of Brazil's capitalist state began to take shape during the lengthy presidency of Vargas (1930–1945). After 1946, with the restoration of a constitutional democracy under Dutra (1946–1950), this movement was interrupted and appeared to recede, although only superficially. The return of Vargas during 1950–1954 provided a new and important impetus to the development of the state operational structure. This phase was crucial for it saw the initiation of the main policy instruments and plans that were subsequently employed by Kubitschek (1956–1960).

Pragmatic and less nationalist than Vargas, Kubitschek created an informal power locus for coordinating economic policies within the existing state structure, thereby circumventing bureaucratic resistance, in order to implement his ambitious *Programa de Metas.* At the end of this extraordinary expansion phase of 1956–1961, the huge public investment effort had completely drained the existing fiscal and financial capacity of the state. Moreover, the state's regulatory structure and operational organization had become too restrictive for the newly created, integrated industrial economy with its production-goods base and great potential for expansion. Aggravated by the post-1961 political and economic crisis, the debilitation of the state structure became pronounced and was one of the contributing factors to the general spread of the crisis.

The authoritarian military regime after 1964 initiated a series of reforms and the building of a new, advanced state structure. The moves were designed to reform and expand the tax system, the monetary and banking system, social security, wage laws, and so on. The entire public administration system (including public enterprises and authorities) was subjected to comprehensive reform between 1964 and 1967, which finally resulted in the present configuration of the Brazilian state.

The stability of the Mexican political regime after the 1910 revolution permitted construction of a central base for the national state. Since the second half of the 1920s, this state apparatus has grown relatively denser and become better equipped to foster economic development. Under President Calles's influence, and later during the 1930s with Cardenas's remarkable initiatives, the Mexican state developed a constellation of new institutions—a reorganized Bank of Mexico the Nacional Financeira, agrarian reform banks, the Foreign Trade Bank, Comision Federal de Electricidad, and PEMEX (the state oil monopoly). These basic structures continued to develop throughout the postwar period, with different degrees of intensity in each presidential term.

In the Aleman administration (1964–1952), significant developments took place in the central administrative apparatus. For example, river-basin development commissions and specific public authorities for certain agricultural products were created. New public enterprises were also founded, but the social apparatus continued to stagnate. In the following period, under Ruiz Cortines, initiatives were few. With Lopez-Mateos (1958–1964), however, the state apparatus once again developed rapidly. Existing agencies and structures were expanded or reformed, and new state secretaries were created. This trend continued at a slower pace under Diaz Ordaz (1964–1970) and accelerated during the Echeverria administration (1970–1976) when several public enterprises and special funds were created.

We have already noted that a distinctive characteristic of Latin American industrialization has been the establishment of unique monopoly structures. These structures are peculiar conjunctions, usually asymmetric, between the state and local and foreign capital. Once such a monopolist structure is established, as in the linking together of foreign subsidiaries, private national firms, and large public enterprises, the state must face the hard task of coping with the further evolution of this complex structure. A fundamental feature of this evolution is related to the specific manner in which the nation's economy is integrated into the new international division of labor.

The evolution and development of such complex state-capitalist structure is complicated by the absence of "national technological autonomy," that is, the inability of peripheral countries to generate significant technical progress through purely indigenous means. In recently industrialized peripheral economies, powerful obstacles exist that prevent the capital-goods sector and the production-goods sector from achieving a high degree of integration, which would promote technological exchange and development. To a large extent, this technological gap is related to the way in which large international enterprises function. Global corporations have a marked propensity to import capital goods from their home countries for assembly by foreign subsidiaries. Therefore, the *intrafirm* division of labor tends to reinforce the concentration of high technology and capital-goods production in the advanced industrial economies. The technological innovation generated by the advanced capital-goods corporations is usually conveyed to the rest of the world through monopolistic practices (international firms being particular agents of this process) which encourages the existing hierarchy in the international division of labor. This tendency does not impose an absolute restriction on technological development in the periphery, but it hinders the development of strongly integrated, interindustry linkages in the capital-goods sector. Hence, the capital-goods sector cannot achieve technical autonomy in the sense of being capable of a continuous renewal of its own technological base.

Table 6–2 shows how the production of capital goods is signifi-

Table 6–2. World Distribution of Industrial Value Added and of Value Added by the Capital-Goods Industry in 1970 in Market Economies (percent).

	Industrial Value Added (A)	Value Added in Capital Goods (B)	(B)/(A)
Advanced Capitalist Economies	86.70	95.20	1.10
of which			
United States	36.90	46.60	1.26
Japan	9.30	15.20	1.63
West Germany	9.80	10.30	1.05
France	6.30	5.80	0.92
United Kingdom	5.30	7.30	1.37
Developing Economies	13.30	4.80	0.36
of which			
Latin America	5.70	3.10	0.54
—Brazil	1.70	0.95	0.56
Asia	7.60	1.50	0.22
Africa		0.20	

Sources: Column A: OECD, *The Impact of the Newly Industrializing Countries* on Production and Trade in Manufacture (Pans: OECD, 1979), p. 18. Column B: OECD, *Facing the Future* (Paris: OECD, 1979), p. 347. Figures were recalculated to exclude the centrally planned economies.

cantly concentrated in the advanced economies. Comparisons of the world distribution of manufacturing value added and that of capital-goods production indicate that developing countries were significantly "underendowed" in terms of capital-goods production in 1970. On the other hand, the United States and Japan were not only the leading producers but also had higher relative participation in capital-goods production within total manufacturing. The same is true for the United Kingdom, which has a long tradition in capital-goods manufacture.

Lack of self-determination and technological autonomy by local capital thus determines the specific characteristics of the monopolist structure in developing countries. If the lower degree of financial centralization of domestic capital is also taken into account, it becomes evident that whenever new capital enters a country the relative position of local capital tends to be threatened. All new investment opportunities in high-technological production or those requiring a very large amount of initial capital tend to put international corporations in advantageous positions.

Thus, state intervention becomes necessary to mediate conflicting interests and to rearrange the division of markets and production capacity between national and international capital. In order to protect domestic capitalists and to change the monopolist structure, the state creates advanced forms of capitalist organizations, such as powerful public financial systems and large state enterprises. A concentration of these organizations and the expansion of the regulatory sphere of the state is, therefore, a structural characteristic of dynamic NICs—for example, Brazil, Yugoslavia, Spain, Mexico, and Korea.

LATIN AMERICAN NICS IN THE POST-1973 WORLD ECONOMY

The 1973 worldwide economic crisis gave rise to serious concern about the future of peripheral economies: on the one hand, "third worldism" and other ideological reactions with great political appeal and based on the concept of "North-South contradictions" sprouted up vigorously; on the other hand, more realistic reactions noted grave concern about the deleterious effects of inflation, about the constraining effects of the energy crisis, and more recently, about the ability of several peripheral economies to service their sizeable foreign debts. These serious and immediate problems have been the central concern of most recent studies and surveys. One important question that has been relatively ignored, and on which this section will focus, has to do with the post-1973 trend of foreign direct investment by international firms in periphery economies.

Growing Participation in World Industrial Production

The growing participation of NICs in world manufacturing has been remarkable, as Tables 6–3 and 6–4 clearly show. In the recent years of global economic slowdown, NICs' participation continued

Table 6–3. The Growing Participation of NICs in Global Manufacturing (percentage distribution of world industrial production).

	1963	1973	1977[b]
Newly Industrialized Countries [a]	5.40	7.60	9.28
of which			
Brazil	1.57	2.10	2.50
Mexico	1.04	1.30	1.46
Yugoslavia	1.14	1.31	1.62
Spain	0.88	1.37	1.56
Portugal	0.23	0.30	0.32
Greece	0.19	0.30	0.33
Korea	0.11	0.32	0.69
Hong Kong	0.08	0.18	1.24
Taiwan	0.11	0.34	0.46
Singapore	0.05	0.08	0.10
"Lagging" LDCs	8.98	9.65	9.80
of which			
India	1.21	1.03	1.19
Argentina	0.94	1.09	1.06
Advanced Economies	74.63	72.92	71.61
United States	40.25	36.59	36.90
Japan	5.48	9.74	9.14
West Germany	9.69	9.19	8.85
France	6.30	6.25	6.15
United Kingdom	6.46	4.78	4.16
Italy	3.44	3.29	3.33
Canada	3.01	3.08	3.08
World	100.00	100.00	100.00
Growth Rate of World			
Industrial Production		6.2	1.6
		(1963–73)	(1973–77)

Notes:
a. OECD definition.
b. See Table 1–2 for later trends.
Source: Extracted from OECD, *The Impact of the Newly Industrializing Countries on Production and Trade in Manufactures,* (Paris: OECD, 1978), p. 18, Table 1, with the author's estimates for the shares of Brazil and Hong Kong in 1977.

to increase because the average growth rates in GDP (in the 1974–1981 period) declined less markedly than in advanced industrial economies.

Faster relative growth resulted in narrowing the absolute differ-

Table 6–4. Comparative Post–1973 Growth Performances of Advanced Economies with NICs (GDP).

	Average Annual Rates (in percent)				
	1963–73	1974–75	1976–79	1980–81	1974–81
Seven Largest Industrial Economies	5.0	−0.2	4.5	1.5	2.4
United States	4.2	−0.9	4.7	0.6	2.1
Japan	10.4	0.6	6.0	4.6	4.3
Four Largest European Economies	4.6	0.5	3.3	0.9	1.9
Non-oil Developing Countries[a]	6.0	4.9	5.2	4.6	5.0
Net oil exporters[b]	6.2	5.7	5.2	6.8	5.7
Net oil importers	5.9	4.6	5.2	4.2	4.8
NICs[c]	8.4	4.9	5.8	4.7	5.3
Low income[d]	3.5	4.6	3.6	3.5	3.8
Oil Exporting Countries[a]	9.2	3.9	5.6	−1.1	3.5

Notes:

a. Oil Exporting and Non-oil Developing Countries were classified according to the IMF's criteria, based on World Bank data.

b. Comprises Bahrain, Bolivia, Congo, Ecuador, Egypt, Gabon, Malaysia, Mexico, Peru, Syria, Trinidad-Tobago, and Tunisia.

c. NICs, according to the IMF's definition, include Argentina, Brazil, Greece, Hong Kong, Israel, Korea, Portugal, Singapore, South Africa, Yugoslavia.

d. Low-income category comprises forty countries whose per capita income was below US $ 350.00 in 1978.

Sources: Based on IMF data from *World Economic Outlook* (September 1981), and World Bank data published in annual reports.

ences in GDP between the NICs and the advanced industrial countries. Table 6–5 compares the relative shares in manufacturing production and rankings of the fifteen largest industrial economies between 1963 and 1977. Note the spectacular advance of Japan and the significant decline of the United Kingdom among the

Table 6–5. Rank-Size of Manufacturing Production of Capitalist Economies (developed and newly industrialized in 1977 and 1963).

	1977		1963	
	Percent World Share	Rank	Percent World Share	Rank
United States	36.90	1st	40.25	1st
Japan	9.14	2nd	5.48	5th
West Germany	8.85	3rd	9.69	2nd
France	6.15	4th	6.30	4th
United Kingdom	4.16	5th	6.46	3rd
Italy	3.33	6th	3.44	6th
Canada	3.08	7th	3.01	7th
Brazil	2.50	8th	1.57	8th
Yugoslavia	1.62	9th	1.14	10th
Spain	1.56	10th	0.88	13th
Mexico	1.45	11th	1.04	11th
India	1.19	12th	1.21	9th
Argentina	1.06	13th	0.94	12th
South Korea	0.69	14th	0.11	16th[a]
Taiwan	0.46	15th	0.11	16th[a]

a. South Korea and Taiwan in 1963 were behind Portugal and Greece, which respectively held the 14th and 15th positions.
Source: Based on Table 6–3. .

advanced countries. The relative position of the United States also deteriorated, although not as steeply as the United Kingdom; Germany, France, Italy, and Canada lost shares only moderately. In the recently industrialized group, Brazil, Spain, Yugoslavia, Korea, and Taiwan grew rapidly and narrowed the gap between them and the advanced countries. Mexico also grew swiftly but at a slightly slower rate than the above group.

A closer look at Brazil's and Mexico's industrial weight, in proportion to the manufacturing sectors of a few selected advanced economies, is offered in Table 6–6. Brazil's share in world manufacturing, relative to the advanced economies, has increased sharply since the mid-1950s. In 1977 it represented approximately 80 percent of Canada's industrial production, 40 percent of France's, and 27 percent of Japan's. It is remarkable that Brazil

Table 6–6. Percentage Share of Brazil's and Mexico's Manufacturing Production Relative to the United States, Japan, France, and Canada in 1963 and 1977.

	U.S.		Japan		France		Canada	
	1963	1977	1963	1977	1963	1977	1963	1977
Brazil	3.9	6.8	28.0	27.0	25.0	41.0	52.0	81.0
Mexico	2.6	3.9	19.0	16.0	16.0	24.0	35.0	47.0

Source: Computed by the author with OECD data from previous tables in this chapter.

almost kept pace with the brilliant Japanese performance in the 1963–1977 period. Mexican industrial growth performance was also vigorous (although somewhat less than Brazil's), as the table illustrates. Argentina and India, on the other hand, exhibited much weaker growth trends, losing relative positions in the rankings. For the Far Eastern NICs, growth trends have been very dynamic. In these cases, however, growth has been more intimately related to rapid export expansion than in the Latin American NICs.

Growing Participation in World Trade

Increased participation in world trade of manufactures has also been a positive feature of NICs' recent performance. As Table 6–7 indicates, the group of countries defined as NICs by the OECD has consistently augmented its share of total OECD imports of manufactures since the early 1960s. It must be stressed that this trend has not decelerated substantially in recent years, as shown by Table 6–8.

The most spectacular performance has been that of the Far Eastern economies (Korea, Taiwan, Hong Kong, and Singapore), whose share jumped from a mere 1 percent of total OECD imports in 1963 to around 5.3 percent in 1979. The European NICs also experienced a strong growth trend, as well as Brazil and Mexico, whose combined share, however, is still rather small relative to their size. Table 1–2 of Chapter 1 depicts the above trends in greater detail.

Table 6–7. Total OECD Imports of Manufactures in Selected Years (current billion U.S.$ and distribution).

Imports from	1963 $	1963 %	1970 $	1970 %	1973 $	1973 %	1979 $	1979 %
United States	7.8	17.1	20.7	16.4	32.3	13.8	78.3	12.7
Japan	1.9	4.2	8.9	7.1	17.0	7.3	49.0	8.0
Germany	9.4	20.8	23.8	18.8	44.9	19.2	107.2	17.4
France	3.5	7.8	9.3	7.3	18.7	8.0	50.4	8.2
Italy	2.5	5.5	7.9	6.3	14.2	6.1	43.1	7.0
United Kingdom	4.7	10.5	10.3	8.1	16.2	6.9	41.6	6.8
Canada	1.8	4.0	7.5	6.0	11.5	4.9	25.0	4.1
Other OECD	10.3	22.7	27.2	21.4	51.6	22.1	121.7	19.8
Total NICs[a]	1.2	2.6	5.6	4.4	15.9	6.8	55.0	8.9
OECD NICs[b]	0.4	0.8	1.4	1.1	3.8	1.6	12.7	2.1
Brazil + Mexico	0.1	0.3	0.6	0.5	2.0	0.9	6.9	1.1
Far Eastern NICs[c]	0.5	1.2	3.1	2.5	9.0	3.8	32.6	5.3
DCs[d]	1.0	2.3	2.2	1.8	4.9	2.1	16.1	2.6
Other countries[e]	0.3	0.7	0.8	0.6	1.7	0.7	14.0	2.3
Socialist Bloc	0.8	1.8	2.2	1.8	4.8	2.1	13.9	2.3
World	45.3	100.0	126.4	100.0	233.6	100.0	615.3	100.0

Notes:
a. Total NICs: OECD NICs, Brazil and Mexico, Far-Eastern NICs, and Yugoslavia.
b. OECD NICs: Greece, Portugal, Spain.
c. Far Eastern NICs: Hong Kong, Singapore, Korea, Taiwan.
d. LDCs: include OPEC and all LDCs in Africa, Latin America, Southeast Asia, Oceania.
e. Other countries: South Africa, non-OPEC Middle East countries and unspecified.
Source: OECD, *The Impact of the Newly Industrializing Countries,* updating of selected tables from the 1979 Report (Paris: OECD, 1981).

So far as the advanced industrial countries are concerned, the well-known vigorous export performance of Japan is clearly illustrated in Table 6–7. France also exhibited a notable growth trend, strengthening its market position within the European Economic Community. Germany's relative position, although still dominant within Europe and generally strong elsewhere, has steadily diminished over time, apparently suggesting a continuous erosion of its export competitiveness. In the case of the United States, the loss of export competitiveness appears to be unquestionable for its relative share has consistently dwindled in the 1960s and 1970s,

Table 6–8. Average (Geometric) Growth Rates of Exports of Manufactures to the Developed Countries (OECD).

	1963–1973	1973–1979
United States	15.3	15.9
Japan	24.5	19.3
Germany	16.9	15.6
France	18.2	18.0
Italy	19.0	20.0
United Kingdom	13.2	17.0
Canada	20.4	13.8
Total NICs	29.5	23.0
OECD NICs	25.2	22.9
Brazil and Mexico	34.9	22.9
Far Eastern NICs	33.5	23.9
LDCs	17.2	21.9
Socialist Bloc	19.6	19.4
World	17.8	17.6

Source: Calculated by the author from Table 6–7.

as revealed in Table 6–7. The United Kingdom's global export share in manufacturing trade also markedly declined, although less steeply after 1973.

A closer look at the NICs' exports is provided by Table 6–9. This increased market penetration has not been confined to traditional product lines like clothing, footwear, textiles, wood, and cork manufactures. Export growth of these items seems to be tapering off, while participation has significantly increased in heavier, more mature technologies, such as steel, motor vehicles, shipbuilding, simpler machine-tools, and so on.

Fast expansion of less sophisticated consumer electric and electronic appliances has been another remarkable feature in the case of the Far Eastern exporters. Here, the role of international firms, particularly Japanese, has been predominant in the launching of these aggressive export platforms. The product-cycle hypothesis seems to fit the recent evolution of NICs' export capabilities very well since the content of their exports has changed according to the evaluation of their industrial structures.

One factor that has significantly helped the NICs to sustain rapid export expansion in the post-1973 period has been their

Table 6–9. NICs' Participation in World Exports of Manufactures in Selected Years (percentages).

	1963	1973	1979[b]
Latin American	0.23	1.20	1.27
Brazil	0.05	0.35	0.50
Mexico	0.17	0.64	0.60
Argentina	0.01	0.21	0.17
European NICs[a]	1.02	1.97	2.22
Far Eastern NICs	1.35	3.33	5.41
of which			
Korea	0.05	0.78	1.61
Taiwan	0.16	1.04	1.45
Export Platforms	1.14	1.51	2.35
(Hong Kong, Singapore)			

Notes:
a. Yugoslavia, Spain, Portugal, and Greece.
b. See Table 1–2 for later data.
Sources: Columns for 1963 and 1973 from OECD, *The Impact of the Newly Industrialized Countries on Production and Trade in Manufactures* (Paris: OECD, 1979). For 1979 shares were estimated by the author with the help of the updating of the OECD report.

successful penetration of the newly opened OPEC markets. This feature was highlighted in a well-known 1979 OECD report.[5] South-South trade flows by NICs had generally weakened up to 1973, as their exports were increasingly directed toward the advanced industrial economies of the North. After 1973, however, this trend reversed as NICs exports gained rising shares of the intensely competitive OPEC markets.

The rising importance of NICs as exporters of manufactures has been consistently offset by their growing imports. Thus, NICs have actually accumulated a rising deficit in manufactures vis-à-vis the industrialized countries. As Table 6–10 shows, the NICs' importance as a market for OECD exports of manufactures increased sharply between 1963 and 1973 and stabilized thereafter. The combined share of Brazil and Mexico has, however, remained roughly stable throughout the period, which means that their imports of manufactures did not grow above the world average. This outcome is perfectly consistent with the high-tariff protection policies adopted in the course of their import-substitution strategy.

Table 6–10.   Total OECD Exports of Investment Goods
(by country or area of destination).

Country or Region of Destination	Percentage Share [a]			Annual Growth Rates [b] 1973–1979
	1963	1973	1979	
Canada	5.3	5.6	4.4	0.0
United States	6.2	9.1	8.5	3.1
Japan	1.4	2.2	1.8	0.2
France	2.0	6.9	6.7	3.7
Germany	2.9	6.7	7.5	6.2
Italy	1.7	3.9	3.4	2.3
United Kingdom	4.7	6.4	5.7	2.0
Other OECD	20.5	22.3	19.0	−2.7
OECD NICs	3.2	3.8	2.9	2.0
Total OECD	48.0	66.9	60.0	2.3
Brazil and Mexico	3.2	3.7	3.4	3.0
Far Eastern NICs	0.5	4.0	5.3	9.3
Total NICs	7.8	12.7	13.1	3.7
Eastern Bloc	1.3	4.6	5.0	6.0
OPEP	2.0	5.4	10.5	16.4
Other Developing Countries	17.5	10.4	10.6	4.6
Other Countries	26.6	3.6	3.7	4.6
World Total	100.0	100.0	100.0	4.2

Notes:
a. Percentages were rounded up. They were based on current prices and exchange-rates
b. Geometric growth rates calculated by the author based on deflated OECD volume data
Source: OECD. *The Impact,* op. cit.

While the NICs' trade balance in manufactures with the advanced industrial economies has generally shown a deficit, its distribution is extremely interesting. Table 6–11 exhibits the percentage distribution of OECD export surplus with NICs in both pre- and post-crisis phases. It is quite clear that, whereas almost all industrial countries held surplus positions with NICs (in terms of manufacture trade), the Japanese trade surplus is not only the largest but has increased substantially in the recent period. The U.S. position is the major exception, for it shows an accumulated trade deficit with the NICs, especially in the recent phase, probably as a consequence of the weakening of U.S. manufactures' export competitiveness in relation to Japan and other advanced economies.

Table 6–11. Geographical Distribution of the OECD Export Trade Surplus (f.o.b.) in Manufactures with NICs (percentages and billion U.S.$).

Reporting country of origin	1963		1973		1979	
	World	Of which with NICs	World	Of which with NICs	World	Of which with NICs
Canada	−8.5	0.7	−11.0	−2.5	−5.1	−6.8
United States	31.2	23.9	−15.4	−9.4	0.7	−28.1
Japan	15.2	14.4	56.3	44.8	42.8	89.6
France	9.7	10.1	6.1	9.2	10.7	5.8
West Germany	35.2	18.9	61.2	25.5	29.0	17.3
Italy	3.4	8.4	15.3	11.6	18.2	12.1
United Kingdom	24.7	9.8	−4.2	2.6	4.0	−0.9
OECD NICs	−7.3	−0.4	−4.9	1.8	2.1	1.0
Other OECD	−3.5	14.0	−3.5	16.5	−2.5	10.0
Total OECD	100.0	100.0	100.0	100.0	100.0	100.0
(Total OECD billion $)	(0.8)	(4.3)	(33.8)	(9.6)	(—)	(10.7)

Increased Penetration by Foreign Direct Investment

Foreign direct investment (FDI) has become a crucial dimension of the international division of labor, especially for the NICs, where foreign subsidiaries generally operate as the leading firms. Nevertheless, the study of post-1973 changes and trends in FDI has been neglected. One important finding, however, is that the periphery kept absorbing foreign risk capital at still relatively high rates in the post-1973 phase, even though the pace was slower than during the 1950–1973 phase. The total outflow of risk capital exported from advanced economies to the periphery grew at a positive average annual rate of approximately 5 percent in the 1974–1976 period, despite the sharp recession in advanced capitalist economies.

Recent Japanese direct investments have been concentrated in Japan's immediate area of influence (Eastern Asia and the Pacific) but curtailed in Latin America. The "withdrawal" of Japanese investments from Latin America is an exception to the general tendency of advanced industrial countries to invest there, however. Recent investments by West German corporations in Latin America have continued at an accelerated pace. These investment flows to Brazil were particularly impressive, whereas the outflows directed to the rest of the periphery have increased at modest rates.

When one investigates recent capital outflows, by macrosectors from America and Japan (the only countries for which such disaggregated data are available), a few interesting points emerge: first, overall capital outflows from the United States indicate that, despite a sluggish economy, there was actually an acceleration in recent times. This striking acceleration is explained by a qualitative change in American capital exports, represented by the extremely fast foreign expansion in the areas of finance, services, and trade. Actually, this change is related to the recent extensive internationalization of large and medium-sized American banks.[6]

As one might have expected, U.S. capital outflows to manufacturing sectors decelerated sharply in the post-1973 period, because central economies were plagued by recession and capital accumulation came to a standstill. During this period, however, U.S. manufacturing FDI outflows to peripheral economies kept growing, particularly toward Latin America. Again, Brazil has been by far the most important recipient, accounting for some 40 percent of the total U.S. manufacturing investment in the region. The recent policy of "Mexicanization" during Echeverria's administration has probably moderated the outflows directed to Mexico.

In the case of Japan, the disaggregation of capital exports by macrosectors also indicates a shrinkage of manufacturing FDI outflows, whereas foreign investments in oil, mining, and raw material sectors continued to grow at relatively high rates. This growth is perfectly consistent both with the extreme dependence of the Japanese economy on imported energy and raw materials and with its traditional long-term investment strategy in those sectors, designed to guarantee orderly and safe sources of supply.

Judging by Table 6–12, where the stock of invested capital was taken as a basis (instead of the flows), one is led to conclude that overall foreign direct investment has not receded in the recent period,[7] but seems to have accelerated slightly. Besides the unreliability of such stock estimates, one must take into consideration that world rates of inflation accelerated sharply in the recent

Table 6–12. Growth Rates of the Stock of Capital Held Abroad (geometric annual rates).

	1967–1973	1973–1978
Total	10.7	12.3
United States	10.2	10.7
United Kingdom	7.4	8.8
West Germany	25.8	21.7
Japan	37.8	21.1
Switzerland	14.2	22.2
France	6.6	11.1
Canada	13.2	9.0
Netherlands	16.5	12.0
All other	7.6	12.0

Sources: UN–CTC data from *Transnational Corporations in World Development,* 1978, and from *Salient Features and Trends of Foreign Direct Investments,* October 1981, mimeo.

phase (from about 4.5 percent annually between 1963–1973, to 10.4 percent between 1974–1981). Thus, since the stocks and flows of FDI data are valued in current dollars, all the growth rates for the recent period are automatically overestimated. An attempt to deflate the FDI series in a study by the UN Center on Transnational Corporations[8] tends to support this interpretation.

The fact that FDI outflows kept growing even moderately (up to 1979) in the recent period of world economic slowdown deserves a tentative explanation. A few plausible hypotheses are listed below:

1. The subsidiaries of international enterprises have succeeded in maintaining significant positive rates of expansion in recent times, possibly through greater diversification of existing production lines[9];
2. In a few technologically advanced sectors, the movement of oligopolist internationalization was not sharply interrupted, since it was still going on at full-steam when the slowdown began;
3. The world crisis has created the necessity or the opportunity for internationalizing certain sectors, for instance, banking and other specialized services;

4. Finally, a differentiated and more advanced block of peripheral economies emerged as a fertile bed for FDI outflows, thus contributing to the moderately positive growth rates.

As Table 6–13 shows, gross private investment trends in all developed economies were very weak up to 1978. Hence, in light of the relative stagnation of investment frontiers in advanced economies, whatever big international corporations had to invest was more intensely directed toward the dynamic peripheral economies, whose growth rates had declined moderately. Between 1978–1980, however, when private investment picked up in advanced countries, cross-FDI outflows to these economies also revived.

Tables 6–14 and 6–15 also confirm the hypothesis that, in the present phase of world economic slowdown, the periphery has gained relative weight as a field for foreign direct investment. Between 1970–1973, during the preceding widespread boom in advanced economies, the periphery had lost relative weight even though its expansion rates were very high. The increased relative weight of peripheral economies as absorbers of FDI flows is certainly related to the growing importance of the NICs in world industrial production and international trade.

Recent information suggests that these more dynamic segments of the periphery succeeded in attracting foreign capital, and thus

Table 6–13. Gross Private Investment Growth Trends in Advanced Economies (residential construction excluded).

	Average Rate 1960–1973	Average Rate 1973–1978	Average Rate 1978–1980
Japan	14.3	0	8.0
West Germany	4.2	−0.2	6.6
France	7.2	0.2	2.3
England	4.0	3.5	−0.1
Italy	4.6	−1.2	
Canada	6.0	2.4	
United States	4.9	0.7	4.0

Sources: OECD, Economic Outlook, Paris: OECD, 1979; U.S. data based on BEA-Commerce Department publications; 1978–80 growth rates computed from OECD Country Survey.

Table 6–14. Growing Relative Importance of the Periphery as a Recipient of FDI (percent of the periphery in total FDI flows).

Origin	1961–1970	1971–1973	1974–1977
United States			
All sectors	20.9	19.8	22.7
Oil, mining, etc.	28.7	28.2	—
Manufacturing	20.0	21.8	23.0
Other sectors	18.6	32.2	50.6[a]
Japan			
All sectors	59.5	57.7	61.9
Manufacturing	←——59.1——→		62.2[b]
West Germany			
All sectors	23.5	27.0	30.1
England			
All sectors	22.4	14.4	22.0
Manufacturing	—	13.1	18.2

Notes:
a. U.S. data updated to 1978.
b. Percent refers to the 1974–1976 subperiod.
Source: Calculated by the author based on various tables from the Billerberck, K. and Yasugi, Y. Report.

reinforcing their rates of expansion, either because they function as important export platforms (such as Hong Kong, Singapore, Taiwan, and Korea) or because they have large and more promising home markets owing to their stable economic policies and to their advanced levels of industrialization (like Brazil and Mexico).[10]

Table 6–15. Average Percentage Participation of the Periphery in Total Flow of FDI from Advanced Economies.

Origin	1963–1970	1971–1973	1974	1975–1979
U.S. and Canada	23.6	18.3	−20.0	36.8
Western Europe	33.4	30.7	24.0	31.0
Japan	60.4	52.7	35.0	42.4
All countries	27.1	25.0	5.0	34.2

Source: UN Center on Transnational Corporations, *Salient Features and Trends in Foreign Direct Investments* (October 1981), mimeo.

Hard Challenges for the 1980s

The NICs' belated industrialization, begun during the 1950s and 1960s, followed a dominant world pattern that was destined to enter a period of exhaustion after 1973; this industrial pattern was still in process within the NICs when the global crisis arrived. While NICs pursued active policies to maintain their pace of development in spite of the world crisis, their debt ratios expanded vigorously in almost all cases. A handful of them (Brazil and Mexico at the top of the list) owed close to $350 billion to international banks by the end of 1981.

The second oil-price shock and escalating interest rates in the 1979–1982 period extracted further tolls on the NICs. Forced to decelerate their growth rates significantly (Brazil, for instance, plunged into the worst recession of its economic history since the 1930s), NICs had to face the inconsistencies and contradictions of their recent growth strategies.

Besides the grave external debt problem, which is bound to constrain economic policies in the future, NICs in 1983 were confronted with another perhaps harder challenge: the technological revolution. Advanced microelectronics and semiconductor technology will certainly bring major changes to many assembly-line production processes. These changes will affect many sectors in which NICs have important productive capacity, for example consumer electronics, apparel, machine tools and metal processing, motor vehicles, and so on. NICs' technological dependency is likely to be intensified in coming years, engendering radical changes in comparative advantages that might make certain newly developed sectors of the NICs prematurely obsolete.

In order to speculate on the extent and possible effects of this threat, let us clarify a few points about NICs' productive structures. One aspect, which has already been discussed in this chapter, has to do with the degree to which their respective industrial systems have advanced and the extent of their integration into world trade. If we define this "industrial aperture" to world trade as the ratio of a nation's share of world industrial exports to its share of world industrial production (or as industrial exports as a percentage of GDP), this aperture varies widely for NICs, as Table 6–16 shows. Hong Kong and Singapore clearly function as export platforms for

Table 6–16. Aggregate Degree of Industrial "Aperture" toward International Trade of the Newly Industrializing Countries in 1976.

	$\left(\begin{array}{c}\textit{Share} \\ \textit{in World} \\ \textit{Industrial} \\ \textit{Exports}\end{array}\right) \div \left(\begin{array}{c}\textit{Share} \\ \textit{in World} \\ \textit{Industrial} \\ \textit{Production}\end{array}\right)$	*Industrial Exports as a Percentage of Gross Output[b]*
Far Eastern NICs		
Korea	1.9	37.3
Taiwan	2.9	30.0
Export Platforms[a]		
Hong Kong	5.5	78.3
Singapore	5.8	77.2
European NICs		
Yugoslavia	0.4	12.6
Spain	0.7	10.4
Latin American NICs		
Brazil	0.16	4.7
Mexico	0.35	n.a.
Argentina	0.16	n.a.
India	0.4	n.a.

Notes:

a. Not considered as "true" NICs in this paper.

b. Data are for 1974 and *exclude* typically "domestic" sectors like food, beverages, tobacco, and nonferrous metals.

Source: Based on previous tables in this chapter.

Japanese and other international corporations, with minute internal markets with "biased" and incomplete industrial structures (heavily concentrated in a few sectors). NICs face the extremely serious risk of losing export competitiveness in the coming decade since their industrial base is heavily concentrated in sectors that are obvious candidates for rapid technological change (e.g., production and assembly of consumer electric and electronic appliances, clothing, and footwear).

The "true" NICs in Asia (Korea and Taiwan) might well be affected by these same factors since their industrial structures are also heavily specialized in export activities. On the other hand, inasmuch as they have reasonably broad and advanced industrial systems oriented to their domestic markets, it may be easier for them to protect themselves and prevent disruptive effects of rapid technological change. The close relationship between Korea and Taiwan and Japan might help to soften potentially adverse effects if they are willing to concede larger market shares and other advantages to Japanese corporations. These corporations have proven to be quite successful in keeping key innovations out of other Eastern Asian economies through tough licensing agreements and other restrictions.

For Brazil and Mexico the challenges are also difficult. High external debts (around $83 billion for Brazil and $80 billion for Mexico by the end of 1982) represent an uncomfortable constraint on their growth potential and put them in a very vulnerable position in negotiating economic and financial deals abroad. Furthermore, because international banks are increasingly reluctant to sustain the growing external debt of Third World countries, one must conclude that both Brazil and Mexico will continue to face serious difficulties in financing their high current-account deficits in the near future. The slowdown of international financing (which hit Brazil in 1980) has forced both countries into recessions through deficit financing. Brazil and Mexico must depend on a rapid recovery of the world economy (and on a simultaneous fall in interest rates) merely to escape from deeper and retrogressive recessions.

Because subsidiaries of international firms hold strategic positions in the industrial structures of Brazil and Mexico, while local capital remains unstable, the integration of their capital-goods sectors with the rest of the economy remains neither broad nor dynamic. The technological gap is thus an especially strong obstacle. On the other hand, the weakness of private capital is partially compensated for by a powerful state apparatus. These state structures have been weakened currently, however, in both countries by serious fiscal crises that hinder the coordination of economic activities.

To counter these obstacles, Brazil and Mexico need planned and resolute structural adjustment policies and institutional reforms—fiscal and financial reforms coupled with aggressive and selective industrial-technological policies geared to generate and assimilate innovations. Both Brazil's and Mexico's economies have quite broad, heavy manufacturing sectors (steel, metals, heavy machinery, chemical, etc.) and fairly advanced durable consumer-goods sectors that will not survive without continuous technical modernization just to keep afloat. But in order to do so, they need flexible and highly conscious policies in the areas of microelectronics and biotechnology if their technology is to avoid the risk of becoming obsolete in a few years. The technical basis of comparative advantage is changing and will keep changing with this new wave of technological progress. One cannot safely rely on old patterns of exporting labor-intensive goods or raw materials. Unfortunately, the external debt constraint has greatly reduced these countries' ability to implement such policies.

After three years under tough austerity programs supervised by the IMF this contradiction is increasingly grievous. The leaders of the developed countries and the international financial community must devise new conditions for the world monetary and financial system that will enable the developing countries to grow again.

NOTES

1. OECD, *The Impact of the Newly Industrializing Countries on Production and Trade in Manufactures* (Paris: OECD, 1979).
2. See L. Coutinho, "Mundancas na Divisāo Internacional do Trabalho," *Revista Contexto,* n. 2; (Sao Paulo: 1977); and L. Coutinho and Luis G. Belluzzo, "O Desenvolvimento do Capitalismo Avancado e a Reorganizacao da Economia Mundial no Pos-Guerra," *Estudos CEBRAP,* n. 23 (Sao Paulo: 1979).
3. By "monopolies" we mean a particular conjunction of production functions, market areas, sectorial profiles, division of labor, and pattern of capital concentration and control among state, local, and international capital.
4. After the first initiatives and big projects of the Cardenas administration (1934–1940) and the initiatives undertaken during the war phase with Avila Camacho (development of the Mexican Altos Hornos Steel Mill in 1942), more projects and public enterprises were introduced during the postwar period, which established a base for a production-goods sector, although in a rather disorganized way. A concentrated investment effort in heavy industry and in the electric sector was undertaken during the Lopez Mateos administration (1958–1964) with the nationalization of foreign distributors and the reinforcement of the Comision Federal de Electricidad. Priority was given to the steel sector, and its vertical and horizontal connections

were more consistently planned than previously. This attempt to put together the basic production sectors continued throughout the Diaz-Ordaz presidency. Production of basic inputs for generalized industrial use, essential for a modern, integrated manufacturing structure, was gradually developed and finally consolidated by the late 1960s.

5. OECD, *The Impact of the Newly Industrializing Countries,* pp. 53–54.
6. American banks represent about one-third of international financial transactions in the Eurocurrency market. In 1975 no more than 25 U.S. international banks operated a network of approximately 1,300 branches abroad, according to the UN Center on Transnational Corporations (New York, 1981).
7. By definition, growth rates of capital stocks should be equal to the rates of capital accumulation. However, accounting problems with the correct valuation of all the components of the capital "stock" invalidate the possibility of interpreting these growth rates as true capital accumulation rates.
8. UN Center on Transnational Corporations, *Salient Features and Trends in Foreign Direct Investments* (October 1981), mimeo.
9. Raymond Vernon, "The Product-Cycle Hypothesis in a New International Environment," Harvard University (1979), mimeo.
10. See OECD, *The Impact of Newly Industralizing Countries,* and Daniel Chudnovsky, "The Present Economic Crisis and the Role of the Periphery for the Advanced Capitalist Economies," UN-CTC (October 1978), mimeo.

7 FRANCE

Bernard Cazes

In the past quarter of a century, France has witnessed the creation, almost *ex nihilo,* of an urban civilization, with a high degree of technology, which appears to be capable of an economic growth far superior than past history might lead one to believe. The first phenomenon one might mention that has affected the economy is demography. France, like the other industrialized countries, had a baby boom that began in 1942 and continued until the 1960s. From 1945 to 1970, the population of France grew by 25 percent.[1] The population also grew younger. The decrease in the fertility rate that occurred after 1965 ended this trend. The proportion of those less than 20 years old, after peaking in 1968, fell in 1981, while the greater-than-65 age group rose that year. The consequences of this change were intensified because the birthrate necessary to insure the renewal of population (2.1 children per woman of child-bearing age) was not maintained after 1975.

The increase in population plus an increase in the standard of living (discussed later) triggered a renewal in urban growth which had been rather slow during the early twentieth century even negative between the two wars. The rapid increase of immigration from rural areas to the cities at one time even led to the fear that a "French desert" might be created outside of Paris. In fact, however, the threshold of 2,000 inhabitants that serves as the dividing line between urban and rural areas is probably out of date, and if

163

one were to adopt a more modern criterion, 15,000 inhabitants, for example, one could conclude that the rural population has hardly changed since the end of World War II.

This more numerous and younger population also experienced a rapid augmentation of its "human capital" during the last quarter of the century. Better educated on the average, the French work force has also seen its sociological and professional make-up profoundly changed. The most characteristic change consists of a sharp decline in the proportion of agricultural workers (from 26 to 10 percent between 1954 and 1975) and an increase in managerial and professional occupations (which grew from 9 from 20 percent in the same period).

The most visible evidence of the emergence of an industrial and urban civilization is without a doubt the impressive change in private consumption both as far as total consumption is concerned and as to its make-up. The changes in the make-up of consumption do not appear to be unique to France and seem to conform to trends observed in all industrialized countries: a continuing decrease in spending for food and clothing and an equally regular increase for lodging, health and personal care, transportation and communications, and culture and recreation. One can also note an equally rapid increase in the amount of durable goods owned by families. In 1950, 14 out of 100 families owned an automobile, 3 a refrigerator, 2.5 a washing machine; television was practically nonexistent and the dishwasher totally unknown. In 1979 the percentages had reached 68 percent for automobiles, 95 percent for refrigerators, 78 percent for washing machines, 93 percent for television, and 14 percent for dishwashers.

Let me add that although this increase in private consumption was considered by some gloomy minds to be an (unfortunate) sign of Americanization, some specifically French cultural aspects remain, which might be measured by how people allocate their time. Whether it is the time spent in the kitchen or at a meal or the average length of vacations that are taken, substantial differences still exist between lifestyles on different sides of the Atlantic.

Changes in private consumption are not the only signs of a modern way of life that we find in this retrospective. The spectacular technological progress that has occurred in France since the war should also be mentioned, not only because of the role it has played in economic development but because it also has important symbolic value. Under the Fourth Republic, the large hydroelectric dams, the accelerated electrification of the railroads, the new steel mills, the Caravelle jet transport plane, the 1958 decision to construct the atomic bomb—all expressed what one psychoanalyst has called a "technological survival complex" in reaction to the near historic past, when technological inadequacy of the country was seen as having disastrous consequences.[2] Under the Fifth Republic, this symbolic value of progress was equally strong, and perhaps had something to do with the complex mentioned above.[3] But the big difference between the times was the expression of the symbol in a unique spokesman, General DeGaulle, who made constant efforts, sometimes successful, to Gallicize all the major technologies—nuclear, space, aircraft, electronics—which rightly or wrongly were seen as the keys to national independence and prosperity. No matter what the causes, this tenacious drive for technological self-reliance was in no way influenced by the publication of *The American Challenge* which was not published until 1967, about the time that the productivity curves in the United States began to move downward.

Since we are, more now than in the time of Edmond Burke, in an era of "sophisters, economists and calculators," we must finish this broad brushing of the background by mentioning economic growth trends. In an earlier period, from 1949 to 1960, growth in the production of goods and services was strong but irregular, since it oscillated between a minimum of 2.3 percent and a maximum of 7.9 percent around an average annual rate of 5 percent. From 1961 to 1973 the average annual rate was a little higher (5.6 percent), but the amplitude of the variations was strikingly smaller. What is remarkable is that, in this period the low (4.3 percent) was 1968 while the peak occurred in 1969 with 7 percent. The "happenings" of May 1968 were indeed not good for the economy (compared to the average for that period, naturally), but the French, who had given the impression of wanting to turn their backs completely on growth, managed to catch up again only one year later. With these results, France found itself in a relatively good position as compared to other industrialized market-economy nations: For the period 1969–1973 the growth rate of 5.6 percent put France behind Japan (10 percent), Spain (7 percent), and Canada (5.8 percent) but ahead of Italy (5 percent), West Germany (5.4 percent), the United States (4.2 percent), and Great Britain (3 percent), and was above the average for all the Organization for Economic Cooperation and Development (OECD) nations (5 percent).

It would without doubt be going too far to blame the slow-down in economic growth that occurred in France (as well as elsewhere) after 1973 solely the oil crisis, for certain signs that appeared before then had already suggested that the economic machine was beginning to malfunction. The unemployment rate began to increase in France in 1967; inflation, which at the beginning of the 1960s was only about 3 percent in the OECD countries, had more than doubled by 1973; finally, the international monetary system began to unravel beginning in 1971 and continuing through the first oil crisis.

Nonetheless, it was after 1973 that a true break occurred in the rhythm of economic growth in the industrialized countries. Certainly growth did not disappear entirely, but one can say that it was only half as strong as during 1961–1973. Between 1973 and 1980, the gross domestic product (GDP) in France grew only at the rate of 2.8 percent per year, which was still greater than the average rate for France for the period 1913–1961 and the OECD growth rate after 1973—2.1 percent per year in both cases. Even Japan was affected. Though it remained the leading developed nation in the world so far as growth was concerned, Japan's annual growth rate was only 3.7 percent.

As a result, public opinion in the western world was obliged to undergo a radical change of thinking. In the past we had been asked to believe, as with Servan-Schreiber in 1969, that economic growth would remain high but would thereafter be increasingly unequally distributed to the benefit of "American Multinationals in Europe," or in as 1972 with the Club of Rome, that economic expansion was grinding to a halt due to the depletion of natural resources. Now the public must get used to a world within which economic expansion might remain positive but weak, and in which the principal differences between nations will be their respective rates of inflation and unemployment and in which American dominance has at least temporarily been superceded by Japan.

FRENCH INTERNATIONAL TRADE

To understand the evolution of France's position in international trade let us turn back to the year 1958, the year in which both the Common Market and the Fifth Republic were inaugurated. At that time France was still economically introverted. If we measure the ratios of French exports or imports to the value added in the production of traded goods (and disregard trade with French overseas possessions), we find that in 1958 the ratio of exports to value added was 12 percent and the ratio of imports 15.2 percent. These figures were somewhat higher than those in the United States, but they were much lower than those in West Germany (30.2 and 25.5 percent), Italy (20.7 and 25.8 percent), and the United Kingdom (37.1 and 43.8 percent).[4]

The founding of the European Economic Community (EEC) permanently opened France to foreign trade and effectively ended the extreme protectionist policies that had long been a national characteristic. As a result, the two previously cited ratios began to grow: 17.5 for exports and 19.3 percent for imports in 1963, 21.3 percent and 21.2 percent in 1968, 31 percent and 33.1 percent in 1973. At this point France was almost on a level with West Germany, with ratios that were almost double those of the United States. The slow-down in economic growth and international trade that occurred after 1973 did not stop this trend, and in 1976 these ratios for France were 44.3 percent for exports and 51.9 percent for imports.

If we look at a more conventionally used indicator, the ratio of exports to GDP (see Table 7–1), we see a particularly strong increase in the proportion of GDP exported between 1969 and 1973. This phenomenon is probably related to the end of the start-up phase of the Common Market, to the reduction in EEC tariffs under the General Agreement on Tariffs and Trade (GATT), and to the devaluation of the franc in 1969. France's heightened openness to the outside world, which led to its becoming the fourth largest exporting nation in the world, did not, however, change the rank order of the five countries in Table 7–1. Aside from the temporary drop in 1969, France in 1982, as in 1961, was three points above the OECD average.

In the make-up of the current balance over the period from 1959 to 1982, we notice a marked difference between the "invisible" balance and the trade balance. The former has evolved quite favorably since 1973, whether viewed in absolute values or compared to France's principal trading partners. As far as invisibles are concerned, France in the early 1980s had become the second largest exporter in the world, behind the United States and equal to Great

Table 7–1. *Ratio of Exports to GDP*

	1961	1969	1973	1979	1982
France	14.5	14.6	18.2	22.0	23.2
West Germany	18.1	21.7	21.9	25.5	31.0
Britain	20.8	22.6	24.2	29.2	27.0
United States	5.0	5.2	6.9	9.1	8.6
Japan	9.3	10.6	10.0	11.8	15.3
OECD Total	11.5	12.7	15.4	19.0	19.9

Ratio of Imports to GDP

	1961	1969	1973	1979	1982
France	12.6	15.2	17.6	21.8	25.5
West Germany	15.8	18.8	18.9	24.9	28.6
Britain	21.0	22.1	26.7	29.0	24.8
United States	4.2	4.8	6.8	10.4	9.6
Japan	10.9	9.0	10.0	14.6	14.3
OECD Total	11.0	12.4	15.1	19.6	20.5

Source: OECD National Accounts.

Britain, while France's market share had grown by 3 percentage points from the beginning of the 1970s.

France enjoyed a favorable trade balance position in 1959, thanks largely to the 1958 devaluation. Thereafter, the trade balance began to deteriorate until it became a deficit in 1964. Then followed successive improvements and relapses, until the devaluation of 1969 resulted in a series of positive trade balances which, in turn, ended with the oil crisis.

The trade balance in agricultural products steadily improved from the creation of the Common Market until 1974. The subsequent deficit years 1976–1978 were compensated for by a vigorous improvement in 1979 and 1980. However, it must be mentioned that the items in this category yielding a positive trade balance (cereals, wines, dairy products, sugar, and flour) are all included in the Common Agricultural Policy of the EEC, and therefore such balances are very dependent on the continuation of this policy. Moreover, France's European partners in the EEC are strong competitors for those products in which the balance is negative (pork, fruits, vegetables, and fish). In addition, the percentage of processed foods exported remains small, which some observers ascribe to the large proportion of multinational subsidiaries involved in the French processed-foods sector.

The situation is complicated by the fact that the trade balance has improved substantially since the oil crisis thanks to healthy sales of industrial products to developing countries and regular increases in the positive balance for automobiles and aircraft, which compensated for the deterioration in consumer goods. Since 1978, however, a deterioration in the balance for industrial goods suggests that this compensatory process is no longer operating. Another structural characteristic concerning France's foreign trade in industrial goods is that "French trade is largely in deficit as far as (its) relations with the OECD countries are concerned and positive with the countries outside the OECD."[5] This positive balance outside the OECD is largely the result of major engineering service contracts, which are often tied directly to French governmental support.[6]

Three Constraints

The fact that foreign trade comprises almost one-fourth of the GDP has had profound consequences for the French economy. These consequences, in turn, exercise external pressures on France's short- and medium-range economic policies in the form of energy, commercial, and financial constraints.

The energy constraint has been the most obvious and also the most recent. In 1973 France's net oil bill was 1.5 percent of GDP; in 1981 the figure had risen to 5.2 percent. The heavy increase in the oil bill, though strongly affected by changes in the price per barrel of oil, masks two important phenomena. First is the growing efficiency with which energy is being used. From 1960 to 1973, the consumption of energy increased at an average annual rate (5.7 percent) roughly equal to that of the GDP (5.9 percent). From 1973 to 1980, however, we note a significant reduction in this ratio: an average annual rate of increase of 2.9 percent in GDP required only 1 percent more primary energy each year. The second phenomenon has been the steady implementation of the French nuclear power program, which has raised the portion of nuclear energy to the whole of primary energy supply from 2 percent in 1977 to 11 percent in 1981. The 1981–1983 Interim

Plan projected that by 1990 nuclear electrical energy would provide 30 percent of the total energy supply (see Table 7–2).[7]

This loosening of the energy constraint will clearly permit some increase in growth. Using an average elasticity rate for imports to GDP and taking into account that energy imports represent about 30 percent of total imports (c.i.f.), we can say that 7 percentage points economized on energy imports correspond to a reduction of 2 percent in total imports or about 1 percentage point of the GDP.[8] Moreover, the use of a nuclear energy source whose costs are lower than for the equivalent amount of oil, gas, or coal cannot but encourage the competitiveness of French firms.

The commercial constraint consists of trade flows on the one hand and direct investment on the other. Foreign trade plays an essential role in a large number of sectors in France, either because imports are indispensable to that sector's production (for example, nonferrous ores and metals, basic chemicals, synthetic fibers, mechanical engineering, household equipment), or the sectors depend on foreign customers for their exports (automobiles, aerospace products, and armaments). The trade surplus is also spread over a large number of customers. France has a positive balance in excess of a billion francs with only three developed countries (Britain, Switzerland, and Italy), while the major part of its surplus is the result of trade with developing countries and countries of the Eastern bloc.

Deficits, on the other hand, are characterized by a double concentration. As far as industrial goods are concerned, a French deficit exists with five trading partners (West Germany, the United States, Japan, the Benelux countries, and Italy) with a resulting

Table 7–2. French Sources of Energy (in equivalent million metric tons of oil).

	1973	1981	1990
Coal	30.5	33.5	35–40
Oil	117.3	93.0	70–45
Gas	15.0	24.6	31–40
Water Power	9.8	15.0	14–15
"Soft" Energies	2.5	3.4	10–14
Nuclear	3.1	19.5	60–66

1980 deficit approximately the same size as the one France had with the OPEC countries. The other concentration is in terms of industrial equipment, precision instruments, machine tools, and communication equipment. Moreover, within these categories, each country that had a surplus in trade with France obtained it on a limited number of items. For example, nearly 90 percent of France's deficit with Japan was the result of imports of photographic and optical equipment, office machines, and equipment for sound recording and reproduction.

With respect to foreign direct investment (FDI), France was late in recognizing the importance of improving its access to raw materials or increasing market penetration abroad. For the period 1971–1979, the net outflow of FDI increased threefold, but because industry was late in starting, France ranked only seventh among the industrialized countries.[9] At the same time, FDI into France has increased rapidly due to the existence of the Common Market. The penetration of FDI in France, principally from fellow members of the EEC, has been particularly strong in high- and medium-technology intensive sectors"[10] (see Table 7–3). Presumably this penetration has not been entirely beneficial for the

Table 7–3. Principal Sectors of French Industry Penetrated by FDI (1982).[a]

	percent
Information Technology	75.6
Oil and Gas	51.4
Agricultural Machinery	55.8
Chemical and Allied Products	54.1
Iron Ores	20.6
Pharmaceuticals	43.9
Consumer and Industrial Electronics	31.6
Materials Handling Equipment	36.9
Rubber Industry	22.8
Precision Instruments	36.6
Oils and Fats Processing	34.6
Basic Chemicals	33.9

a. Estimates based on percentage of sales of foreign manufacturing firms to total sector sales (both net of taxes).

Source: Ministry of Industry, Industrial Statistics Unit.

French economy since foreign-owned firms export a smaller percentage of their output than do French-owned firms. Moreover, the latter appear to sell low-technology products while importing a substantial amount of high-technology products.

The financial constraint is evidenced in the area of exports and in foreign-exchange market operations. Bank financing is concentrated mainly on exports to developing countries (about two-thirds) and the East Bloc countries (about one-fourth). Enjoying attractive interest rates as a result of government guarantees, these loans have the advantage of opening up markets in those countries with limited financial resources, although no official authority has been able to offer convincing arguments for the preferential credits accorded the Soviet Union by France (and by its partners in the West). The French economy is also very sensitive to international capital movements. As a result, monetary authorities have periodically prodded private and public firms to borrow in foreign financial markets to finance their investments. Additionally, the actions of foreign-exchange traders with respect to the franc have had a decisive impact on the rate of exchange, with all of the well-known consequences this trading has on the terms of trade. Quite naturally this variable is difficult to manipulate (as is devaluation), for the lower import costs due to the appreciation of the franc are compensated for by the additional handicap to exporters, whose customers must then pay higher prices in terms of their own currencies.

Some Controversial Questions

The creation of the Common Market raised numerous fears, although mistrust vis-à-vis the European Defense Community weighed more heavily than the apparently rational argument against the Common Market, which held that the national economy was not yet ready to emerge victorious in this kind of international competition. On the other hand, some politicians favored the idea of building Europe and stressed the positive impact the Common Market would have on the modernization of the French economy. The business community believed—or said they believed—that "to create a common market before we have eliminated all of the disadvantages must certainly lead to catastrophic consequences and a final disaster."[11] Actual events have belied the prophets of gloom: not only has the French economy not stagnated as a result of the Common Market, but beginning in 1958, it has experienced unprecedented prosperity. Nevertheless, one has the impression that, deep in the collective psyche of France, anxiety still exits over the economic threats posed by foreign competition.

The eruption into the world marketplace of the newly industrialized countries has likewise given birth to a number of misgivings. These have been tempered somewhat by a 1978 report of the Commissariat General du Plan, entitled *The Economic Challenge of the Third World,* which demonstrated that the increase in trade between the developing countries and France had in fact resulted in a net increase in employment for the latter.

Japan's spectacular economic success, together with the realization that the U. S. competitive strength was not particularly affected by the "American Disease" which sociologist Michel Crozier diagnosed in 1980, again triggered concern about the ability of French industry to succeed in an environment of stagflation and increased competition. Moreover, the 1981 accession to power of a very different political administration resulted in a reexamination of past economic results with a critical eye, if only to convince public opinion that there was a heavy economic burden from the past that needed correcting.

These misgivings are perceived in two different ways. The first consists of believing that the state can and should provide the appropriate answers. Thus, we will examine the way in which the state has intervened in the economy and, more specifically, in industry. The second viewpoint, less "state-centered," consists of asking if, when all is said and done, it isn't the *société civile* itself that is the real source of strengths and weaknesses of the French economy. Since Hobbes, Rousseau, and Hegel the "civil society" has been seen as consisting of a combination of institutional forces (families, businesses, voluntary groups, etc.) together with the cultural forces (values, attitudes, lifestyles), none of which are part of the state itself. The state, after all, is but one of many interacting elements that together, in the long run, determine the international competitiveness of the economy.

A GLASS HALF EMPTY AND HALF FULL

It is difficult for an impartial observer to understand the strengths of French businesses because of the wide diversity of opinion that has been expressed on the subject. In 1980 an article in *Business Week* stated that "13 years after J. J. Servan-Schreiber prodded France . . . to bridge the technology gap, French industry seems to be doing just that—and launching an independent challenge of its own."[12] On a less lyrical note, Professor Balassa of the World Bank took issue with the pessimistic views of economists Alain Cotta and Christian Stoffaes, who viewed French industry as suffering from serious structural weaknesses (such as exports poorly adapted to world demand and an abnormally high income elasticity of imports).[13] Balassa pointed out that, in fact, France compares quite favorably with West Germany in the areas of overall export-demand growth rate, the export thrust of the economy, and import elasticity to income.[14] Michel Develle has stated that French businesses have remained competitive in foreign markets for the more recent years. But he qualified this assessment in a major way by stressing that firms have attained their competitiveness by holding down their export prices, which they counterbalanced with price increases in the domestic market. This practice, however, provoked a notable increase in imports. "In a word, we have paid for our external competitiveness at the price of internal competitiveness."[15]

France's moderately satisfactory performance has been the subject of many researchers. A 1982 study by the Institute for Business Research of Lyons on the quality of French marketing of industrial goods, and based on a questionnaire sent to English, West German, Italian, and Swedish customers, for example, concluded that France was distinctly outdistanced in such marketing by Sweden and West Germany, but that it was slightly better than the Italians and substantially better than the British.[16] The Commission du Bilan, established after the 1981 elections to assess the economic and social situation in France, likewise concluded that French industry was in an "intermediate situation" among the developed economies. The commission added that the policies pursued by the previous government were not conducive to improving the situation.[17] A more extreme range of opinions, however, is advanced by Cotta and Stoffaes. Although written prior to 1981 by economists who were not socialists, the works of Cotta and Stoffaes call for changes in the industrial structure through selective governmental intervention.[18]

It is, of course, quite natural that the Mitterand government, newly arrived in power and desiring a show of initiative, would want to state its concern over the competitiveness of national industries. Rather alarming assessments are, as a matter of fact, found in the short-term plan for 1982–1983. While admitting that the "intermediate situation" for France's industry is satisfactory, the plan forcefully deplores the lead gained by France's principal industrial competitors, the reduction of private investment since 1974, excessive dependence on imports "in those industrial sectors where an economic upturn increases domestic demand," and the rapid penetration by foreign industrial goods, which is creating a "veritable state of subordination vis-à-vis those countries which dominate the world industries (i.e., Japan, the United States, and West Germany), and that the situation was particularly disquieting as far as technology was concerned."[19]

Faced with this presumably serious deterioration of the industrial fabric, the logical conclusion seemed to be to strengthen the economic role of the state by widening and extending the public sector and by providing government assistance within the framework of sectoral plans for such sectors as textiles, machine tools, and electronic components.

At this point we may question how the state has stimulated industrial performance.

CAN THE STATE REALLY DO ANY GOOD?

Let's begin with a pseudo-Tocquevillian generalization. Were Americans to wonder whether economic intervention by they state had been effective, they would probably be surprised if the answer were affirmative, and in the event of a negative answer, they would conclude that the state should not have intervened in the first place. Should Frenchmen ask the same question, they are not likely to expect a negative response at all, and if they get one, their conclusion would be that the state should nevertheless have intervened—but in a different fashion. The French are generally surprised to see that there are things that work well *without* the state involving itself!

In an effort to answer the questions surrounding the value of state intervention, we can distinguish several typical situations in which the state plays a role.[20]

1. To begin, the state is led to play an active role involving those firms that it legally owns because they are, in effect, nationalized (e.g., electricity, gas, coal, railroads), and if the state is the de facto owner, it shoulders a significant part of the financial investment, as in the case of the steel industry until 1981. But as far as the steel industry is concerned, the results have on the whole been negative. The relationships established between the state and the steel industry have demonstrated two characteristics that are profoundly regrettable.

First, the approach to the problems was excessively dominated by nonrational considerations; as a result, the industry was treated by all of the players in the "steel complex" game as a symbol of power and modern technology. Everybody saw the maximization of production (and of corresponding investments) as an essential national goal, the necessity of which no one was permitted to question.

Second, the respective roles of public decisionmakers and private managers have never been clearly defined; government officials have acted as if they were responsible for the profit-and-loss statements of the steel firms, and the businessmen have acted as if their mission were the accomplishment of a task in the national interest. A most frustrating game resulted for all the participants, since the former were disappointed to see the financial situation of the firms deteriorate despite all the money spent by the state, whereas the latter were unhappy at being treated as scapegoats for the poor results while all they had done was execute the governmental decisions (with which, of course, they were in full agreement).[21]

The outcomes in the truly nationalized sectors were far more successful than those in the steel industry, especially when compared with Italy or Great Britain. It is nevertheless necessary to distinguish between those nationalized firms that were monopolies and those that functioned in a competitive sector, for only the latter have any significance in estimating the chances of success of the recent nationalizations, which consist of firms in this category.

There have been undeniable successes—Renault being the most obvious—but these successes appear to have depended on an almost miraculous joining of some very specific conditions.[22] These conditions consisted of a set of "safeguards," such as a great sense of moral responsibility and a high degree of managerial competence, a spontaneous harmony between the managers' way of looking at the business and the objectives of the state, as well as the discipline of an existing complete immersion in the world market.

2. The state also has a role to play vis-à-vis those activities in which it is an important client (weapons, nuclear power plants, telecommunications). Public purchases appear to constitute efficient instruments for industrial development, although the results are sometimes less constructive from a purely technological point of view. For example, though the French nuclear industry developed a successful graphite-gas reactor, the government was forced to abandon the original French technology in favor of American technology.

As a means of intervention, public procurement poses another difficulty since it can only be used by those public agencies that have something to buy, which is not the case for the two principal ministries responsible for French industrial policy, Finance and Industry. Furthermore, certain rules concerning government contracts limit the discretionary power of the responsible agencies; as a result, this means of intervention is less attractive than subsidies, which allow those agencies that distribute funds the opportunity to examine in great detail the investment projects of the subsidy-seeking firms.

3. The third case is one in which state intervention is considered by all countries as a self-evident need to help businesses in difficulty. The Interministerial Committee for Reordering of Industrial Structures (CIASI) was created in 1975 for the specific purpose of ensuring the survival of firms in difficulty that could not be permitted to disappear or (more rarely) those that were felt to have some chance of being rejuvenated. It is difficult to pass a clear judgment here because, as Le Franc explains so well,[23] this "anomalous agency," given the mission inside a market economy to counteract the very forces of that economy, should never have been created, since it absorbs resources that might better be used by private firms in the creation of new and viable enterprises. At the same time, it is difficult to envision abolishing this kind of agency, given

that from time to time such rescue operations are seen as necessary in democratic systems. Such political exigencies are inevitable, and the virtue of a CIASI is that it requires a certain discipline in rescue operations.

4. For reasons at once political and economic, French officials have recently discovered small business and have created an Inter-ministerial Committee for the Industrial Development and Support of Employment (CIDISE), whose objective is to help the growth of "thriving small businesses or those that can become thriving but are handicapped because of inadequate risk capital." The mission here is not one of rescuing deteriorating industries but of helping future "winners." The experience of CIDISE has been too limited to judge, but Le Franc believes that financial assistance given as a result of an examination by a committee of requests from businesses and not by means of well-defined and predetermined criteria poses serious difficulties. These problems are, on the one hand, a blurring of roles (government officials deciding in committee tend to substitute themselves for the chief executive), and on the other hand, the treatment of symptoms instead of the treatment of causes. If promising small businesses are having difficulty increasing their capital, this may be due to structural factors (such as the low propensity of the French to invest their savings in industry), which no piecemeal interventions will change.

5. The most difficult category of intervention to conceptualize involves the so-called strategic industries. This term has often been used in an extremely loose and pompous fashion to characterize any sort of economic activity deemed important to the national interest, even if it is not very profitable. In the French administrative connotation of the term, one can nevertheless discern a pragmatic interpretation that ties it to specific markets. These industries are not closely related to the independence or sovereignty of the country, but in them the risk of industrial competition by foreign firms is high (even if this risk is not in the near future). In them also exists the solid presumption that French-based firms could, in a reasonable time, reach world ranking. It is this interpretation that seems to have justified the creation of the Committee for the Development of Strategic Industries (CODIS) in 1979 to encourage "that kind of production for which it is

desirable to undertake vigorous action," such as automated office equipment, biotechnologies, robotics, consumer electronics, the offshore oil industry, energy-saving devices, and the textile industry. As in the case of CIDISE, CODIS was too recently formed to allow for a balanced evaluation, but its dedication to selectivity, its reliance on audits by independent experts, and the educational role it has played for business executives suggest that, on the whole, its results have been positive.

It is necessary to underline the fact that the industrial policies of the preceding administration continue to be applied by its socialist successor, for the latter is faced with comparable problems. The increased size of the nationalized sector will not reduce pressure on the government to use the nationalized sector for short-term safeguarding of employment. Small businesses need attention and will no doubt benefit from the recently inaugurated territorial decentralization of permitting local contracts between government officials and business executives (a benefit, however, that always carries with it the risk of political patronage). But the government must fight the climate of distrust so prevalent in small-business circles, which tend to be suspicious of any socialist government. Finally, official concern over the rejuvenation of the industrial fabric is not in and of itself sufficient to define a coherent industrial policy, a policy that, for the time being, consists of the vague slogan to "reconquer the domestic market" and to replace "market niches" with "vertical chains."[24]

In summary, the role of the French indicative-planning system for the period we are considering cannot be judged in terms of either black or white. To use a term already mentioned here, the results appear to have been "intermediate." In those areas where the Commissariat was authorized to give guidance, it appears in general to have made sense, not because it is made up of individuals with high IQs, but because its position is a bit away from the center of actual government policy making. A sort of "marginality near the center" guards it against being seduced by the stereotype thinking of the day. The Plan has been able to have a significant impact in those cases where it acted to promote positive trends (e.g., the nuclear energy program), but it has lacked sufficient influence to cause poorly conceived policies to be changed (e.g. supersonic transport, the French computer program).[25] The plan-

ners were just as slow as other government officials to admit that
the mass of the French people really wanted automobiles, their
own private housing, and telephones.

COMPETITIVENESS, STRUCTURAL RIGIDITIES, AND THE EMPLOYMENT/INCOME DILEMMA

Submerged for so long by the omnipresence and omnipotence of
the state, the French seem to have only recently discovered the
existence of the *société civile*. The works of sociologists describing
France as a "stalemate society" (*société bloquée*) have certainly has-
tened this discovery, but the economic progress of West Germany
and of Japan, where state/civil society relationships are quite different from France, have also contributed to this enlightenment. The
rather late recognition that sociocultural factors influence development has led to a fresh look at the roots of pre-1973 competitiveness. And it is quite likely that this recognition will play an
increasingly important role in the on-going debate on the post-
1973 version of the competition problem.

The problem of competitiveness, as understood prior to the
early 1970s, is simply the Schumpeterian idea of economic growth
as a process of "creative destruction"—that is, the disruption of
vested interests, which then permits sufficient growth for a positive-sum game to develop. From a state-centered point of view,
competitiveness is positively correlated with the degree of state
intervention. This implies that any "technology gap" will be all the
more rapidly closed the quicker one dispenses with a laissez-faire
attitude on the part of the state. But the approach to the problem
from the viewpoint of the civil society leads to a different way of
thinking, because it emphasizes the actions of nonstate forces that
affect the adaptability of the economic structure and its capacity to
take advantage of new opportunities as they appear. Such a viewpoint actually amounts to a true rediscovery of the working of the
market economy as a self-regulating system in which different ac-
tors pursue their individual goals without attempting to reach an
agreed-on set of a priori objectives.

According to this view, a country will be competitive to the
degree that it evidences the double flexibility described by T.
Scitovski. "The first concerns the different economic forces them-

selves, the flexibility of consumers to change the make-up of their expenditures, of producers to modify their production methods and to use those factor inputs that become more plentiful, and finally that the providers of productive services furnish those services that are in greatest demand. The second kind of flexibility is the ability of the system as a whole to modify the way in which it uses the different economic forces in order to take advantage of those that have become more suitable for the changing situation while reducing the role of those forces or factors which are no longer suitable or cannot be made suitable."[26]

The following question then arises: If this flexibility or adaptability is decreasing worldwide, for reasons inherent in the development of the welfare state, are there certain countries that are in greater danger of "sclerosis" than others? Since a comprehensive index for such a menace, a sort of a GNS (Gross National Sclerosis) that would allow us to measure the different economies by a common yardstick does not exist, we are forced to rely on fragmentary evidence. The evidence that exists in France can be traced to three criticisms concerning certain structural rigidities, one expounded by the "right" and two by the "left."

The attack on structural rigidity that one distinguishes as coming from the right can be summarized in two points. First, as a political observer recently put it, France is, economically speaking, "psychologically backward and remains dominated by a way of thinking that is to a large degree pre-industrial. (France) considers that competition is an intolerable aggression, that to undergo the risks of the market place is to undertake a perverse adventure, that making a profit is almost presumed to be embezzlement."[27] The second point asserts that the French constitute a society that subtly combines meritocracy with class and privilege.[28] Advantages and privileges are earned by means of a diploma or any other form of entitlement sanctioned by the state, and once obtained, these privileges become untouchable and must be preserved, again by the state. They thus form a series of inviolate rights vigorously defended by the wage-earners who have attained them. Public administration belongs to the bureaucrats; religion, to the clergy; health, to doctors; education, to teachers; intelligence, to the intellectuals; and presidencies to the "Polytechniciens."[29]

In the language of the traditional left concerning the French rigidities, we find the same factors that we have just identified but with two essential differences. Those with a preindustrial mentality and caste spirit are seen as protecting their private interests. These traits concern only those segments of society that are very small in number even though they are, regrettably, influential. The existence of these minor rigidities justifies intervention by the state in order to ensure that the general interest of all prevails over the abuse of private power. According to this perspective, the reallocation of wealth and power to the detriment of nonlegitimate *and* malthusian interests is a positive-sum game, since it costs the wage-earners nothing while it supposedly eliminates the obstacles to a reallocation of resources that would be at once more efficient and more just.

In order to be even-handed, mention must be made of a line of thought somewhat more original than these leftist ideas, which, for want of a better word, can be called "the new left" line of thought. Similar in certain respects to the right's way of thinking in that it refuses to close its eyes to the contribution of the wage-earners to the creation of structural rigidities, it is differentiated by its tendency to consider the state as a possible means for achieving reforms (e.g., through a system of collective negotiations) which would benefit everyone because these reforms would open up deadlocked situations.

It is impossible to estimate the chances of one or the other of these three lines of thought being translated into reforms. The first line of thought, which seems fundamentally sound, is handicapped in the context of French politics, first, by its rightist label and, second, by the inability of political parties adhering to this line of thought to use it in anything but speeches. The second line of thought amounts to little more than denying that any problem exists and can only encourage perpetuation of the problem until the economic situation deteriorates sufficiently to lead to electoral reactions of the kind that benefited Prime Minister Thatcher in Great Britain. The third line of thought is more credible because it is less monolithic. However, its supporters must demonstrate that it does not suffer from the same weaknesses as the right's line of thought and that it can be transformed from rhetoric into publicly acceptable policy.

In the traditional approach to the problem of competitiveness, the fundamental question was to determine what countries would be the most capable of escaping from apparently irresistible and increasing structural rigidities, and whether France would or would not find itself in this group of a "happy few." It now seems that since 1973 the problem has changed considerably. With economic growth slower than in the past, the search for competitiveness, and the economies in labor inputs that this inevitably implies, has resulted in increased difficulty for displaced labor to find other employment. Hence the dilemma of employment/income, which is at least as formidable, if not more so, as the dilemma of efficiency/equity. Rejecting the prerequisites for competitiveness may well preserve employment, but it prevents an increase in the standard of living; accepting the prerequisites of competitiveness may increase the standard of living, but it prevents increased employment. How do the three lines of thought described above react to this dilemma?

The right opts for income, which is not surprising. It believes that the most urgent priority is to place the economy on a sound footing (that is, to get rid of the undermining structural rigidities), for then and only then will the economy be able to provide durable employment. Will there be sufficient jobs? That question is not really addressed, probably because the right counts on unemployment to overcome the resistance to necessary structural change. It also probably vaguely hopes that, for one reason or another (the launching of a "Marshall Plan" for the Third World or the welcome arrival of a new upward phase of the Kondratieff cycle), the ensuing growth will reach a level permitting full employment once the "cheating" unemployed, who are encouraged by the financial laxity of the welfare state, have disappeared. The opponents of this line of thought claim that if the right does not take a definite position concerning the future of unemployment, it is because they count on a solution that is difficult to avow publicly—a dual economy in which two categories of individuals would exist. In one category would be those employees working for pay in activities that enter into the make-up of the GNP; in the other, those in a so-called informal economy, where they would live by their own means, by barter, by private or (more rarely) public transfers, and by "underground" work.

The left's line of thought on the dilemma of employment/income refuses to decide between the two. It believes that progress depends on a mixed strategy combining the search for more self-reliant growth (read: protectionism) with exploitation of the latent reserves of productivity that the regimes of the right were incapable of mobilizing, with the obligatory reduction of working hours (misnomered as "work-sharing," whereas it consists simply of producing the same output with more labor input). It is difficult to say whether denying the existence of the dilemma really amounts to sacrificing, without saying so, income to employment or if there is a loss on both sides of the ledger.

The ideal type of new left thought admits the existence of the dilemma, as does the right, but it opts for employment while hoping to minimize sacrifices in earnings. It relies for that purpose on two levers. For the short and medium term, this consists of an appeal for solidarity (a theoretically powerful argument in any leftist line of thought) that consists basically of pleading for a true sharing of work[30]—that is, a sharing of wages among a larger number of participants, and hence, in the short term, a lower income per capita. In the longer term, the new left gambles on a change in the public mind concerning the relative balance between paid working time and nonpaid free time. The hope, of course, is that the choice will progressively tend toward the latter, which in the long run would lead to a "dual economy," but the dualism would *be inherent to each individual.*[31]

The new left's appeal for solidarity is a search for a "good" that is unfortunately rare. The classic left is not particularly inclined this way and has a great deal of difficulty resigning itself to the need to moderate the rapid expansion of the welfare state. If this expansion does continue its course, due to the aging of the population and the consequent increased financial burden, the feeble reserves of solidarity that remain in society will be sorely tried. Second, even if the wager on "postmaterialist" values is revealed to be justified, it may be necessary to wish that the approach will at least partially fail, for the new man that it postulates, "this man that is finally free, well rooted and protected, will he not be the easy prey of the rebel of the Third World or the regimented man of the Soviet empire?"[32]

CONCLUSION

From the foregoing discussion, we are tempted to draw some tentative conclusions concerning the focus of this whole book, the apparent reversal of "American challenge" to "challenged America." While the former phrase is definitely obsolete, the latter goes too far. True, there is no more American challenge, no dominant national economy keeping other countries under economic vassalage. All Western nations are currently confronted with the same series of intractable problems of stagflation, oil dependence, and all-out economic competition. Moreover, one cannot say that the United States is more "challenged" than its partners. Things would be simpler if that were true, if one country were uniquely weak, and could thus serve as an example of what should *not* be done.

With the Reagan and Mitterrand elections, one might have anticipated a resumption of the confrontational mood of the 1960s in France. But while admittedly a confrontation of sorts does exist, it has nothing to do with French nationalism, French socialism, or U.S. multinational investments. What we have, in fact, is a serious divergence of views between Americans and Europeans, which stems from conflicting views and interests along the East-West geopolitical dimension.

Finally, perhaps the most crucial aspect of this discussion is that, while during the 1960s the main issue in international economics was the rather straightforward one of running faster than one's competitors on an upward-moving escalator, now the escalator is almost level and even threatening to go downward. The best hope is to minimize one's losses in inflation or unemployment terms, even if that strategy is detrimental to one's trading partners. "Challenged West," one might say, except that "South" and "East" are not faring any better.

NOTES

1. The increase in immigration has certainly played a role in the population increase, but its final effect was only to bring the percentage of immigrants in 1968 up to the level that France knew in 1911 (a little more than 7 percent).
2. P. Trouillas, "Psychologie française, technologie et progrés social," *La Société française et la technologie* (Paris: La Documentation Francaise, 1980.)
3. Nor should we forget the celebrated appeal of June 18, 1940, by

General DeGaulle in which he stated: "Struck down today by the power of mechanical strength, we will be able to win in the future through a mechanical strength even higher."

4. B. Balassa, "L'economie française sous la Ve Republique," *Revue Economique,* no. 6 (1979).

5. J. Mistral and M. Dolle, "Le commerce extérieur," in vol. I of Appendices to the Rapport de la Commission du Bilan, *La France en mai 1981* (Paris: La Documentation Française, 1982), p. 254.

6. It is estimated that these large contracts amount to about 10 percent of exports and absorb 95 percent of government assistance to foreign trade (Mistral and Dolle, "Le commerce extérieur," p. 263).

7. Taking into account the total of domestic energy resources, the degree of dependence in 1990 will be on the order of 50 percent (against 76 percent in 1973 and 68 percent in 1981).

8. M. Develle and N. Drancourt, *Economie et Entreprises: 1981–1982* (Paris: Institut de l'Entreprise, 1982), p. 59.

9. Banque de Paris et des Pays-Bas, *Bulletin de conjoncture* (June 1981).

10. Ibid.

11. *Bulletin du Conseil National du Patronat Français,* cited in Balassa, "L'économie française," p. 948.

12. "The New French Connection," *Business Week* (May 19, 1980).

13. Alain Cotta, *La France et l'impératif mondial* (Paris: Presses Universitaires de France, 1979); and Christian Stoffaes, *La grande menace industrielle* (Paris: Calman-Levy, 1978).

14. Balassa, "L'économie française," pp. 956–59.

15. Develle and Drancourt, *Economie et Enterprises,* p. 60.

16. *Le Nouveau Journal,* May 5, 1982.

17. Commission du Bilan, *La France en mai 1981.*

18. Cotta, *La France et l'impératif mondial;* Stoffaes, *La grande menace industrielle.*

19. *Plan Intérimaire 1982–1983,* (Paris: Flammarian, 1982), pp. 149–150.

20. J. Le Franc, *Industrie: Le Péril Français* (Paris: Le Seuil, 1983).

21. J. Padioleau, *Quand la France s'enferre* (Paris: Presses Universitaires de France, 1981).

22. Telesis, *Les entreprises publiques du secteur concurrentiel,* A study for the Commissariat General du Plan (1982), mimeo.

23. Le Franc, *Industrie: Le Peril Français.*

24. A market niche (*creneau*) is defined as a narrowly limited market opportunity that is viewed on its own merits. A "vertical chain" (*filière*) includes the links that unite a specific product to the and user subsectors, i.e., a vertically integrated chain. To master the whole of a *filière* (e.g., forestry-sawmill-furniture) is currently con-

sidered economically more rational than capturing a series of disjointed market niches. All of this cannot help but recall the arguments of fifteen years ago about "disjointed incrementalism" versus Planning, Programming and Budgeting Systems (PPBS).

25. It was not even able to get published the Hannoun report on government aid to industry, which criticized the heavy concentration
of such aid to a small number of industrial groups (many of which
have since been nationalized) and the mediocre effectiveness of the
aid.

26. T. Scitovsky, "Can Capitalism Survive?", *American Economic Review*
(May 1980).

27. A. Duhamel, *La Republique de M. Mitterrand* (Paris: Grasset, 1982),
p. 109.

28. I have termed this "Corporatisme Meritocratique d'Etat" (CME) in
"The Role of the Market in the West: The Case of France," *Il
Politico,* no. 4 (1979). The initials CME constitute a parody of an
acronym much in vogue in certain French intellectual circles where
it means Capitalisme Monopoliste d'Etat.

29. A. Peyrefitte, *Le mal français* (Paris: Plon, 1996), p. 319.

30. This idea, developed since 1975, is found in Michel Albert and J.
Ferniot, *Les Vaches Maigres* (Paris: Gallimard, 1975).

31. G. Aznar, *Tous a mi-temps—le scenario bleu* (Paris: Le Seuil, 1981); and
M. Albert, *Le Pari français* (Paris: Le Seuil, 1982).

32. J. Lesourne, *Les mille sentiers de l'avenir* (Paris: Seghers, 1981), p. 236.

BIBLIOGRAPHY

Albert, M. *Le Pari français,* Paris: Le Seuil, 1981.
Aznar, G. *Tous a mi-temps —le Scenario bleu.* Paris: Le Seuil, 1981.
Balassa, B. "L'economie française sous la Ve Republique." *Revue Econo-
mique,* no. 6 (1979).
Banque de Paris et des Pays-Bas. *Bulletin de conjoncture* (June 1981).
Business Week "The New French Connection," May 19, 1980.
Cazes, B. "The Role of the Market in the West: the Case of France" *Il
Politico,* no. 4 (1979).
Commission du Bilan. *La France en mai 1981.* Paris: Documentation Fran-
çaise, 1982.
Develle, M. et Drancourt, M. *Economie et Entreprises 1981–1982.* Paris:
Institut de l'Entreprise, 1982.
Duhamel, A. *La Republique de M. Mitterrand.* Paris: Grasset, 1982.
Lafay, G. "La nouvelle specialisation des grands pays industriels." *Econo-
mie Prospective Internationale,* no. 1 (1980).

Le Franc, J.-D. "Quelques reflexions sur la politique industrielle," Commissariat General du Plan, 1981. (Mimeo.)

Lesourne, J. *Les mille sentiers de l'avenir.* Paris: Seghers, 1981.

Ministere de l'Industrie *La Competitivité internationale des industries françaises au seuil des années 1980.* Paris: La Documentation Française, 1981.

Mistral, J. et Dolle, M. "Le Commerce exterieur," in Appendices to the Rapport de la Commission du Bilan, vol. I. Paris: La Documentation Française, 1982.

Padioleau, J. *Quand la France s'enferre.* Paris: Presses Universitaires de France, 1981.

Peyrefitte, A. *Le Mal français.* Paris: Plon, 1976.

Scitovsky, T. "Can Capitalism survive?" *American Economic Review* (May, 1980). French translation, *Chroniques d'actualité SEDEIS* (November 15, 1980).

TELESIS *Les Entreprises publiques du secteur concurrentiel,* a study for the Commissariat General du Plan, 1982. (Mimeo.) Trouillas, P. "Psychologie française, technologie et progres social." In *La Societé française et la technologie.* Paris, La Documentation Française, 1980.

8 AUTOMOBILES
Shifts in International Competitiveness

Yves Doz

For more than fifty years, from the early 1900s until the 1960s, the automobile industry was the leader of industrial growth in the United States. As late as 1959, U.S. auto manufacturers held an 85 percent world market share. By 1979, however, their share had dropped to 49 percent, while foreign manufacturers, mostly European and Japanese, captured a 51 percent worldwide share. Since 1980, Japanese unit production has exceeded U.S. automobile production, excluding the production of U.S.- or Japanese-owned subsidiaries abroad. In 1982 imported Japanese cars captured 23 percent of the U.S. market. While exporters in 1981 increased their profits from U.S. sales by 25 percent over the previous year, U.S. car industry losses totalled about $2 billion, following $4.2 billion in losses in 1980. U.S. domestic sales in 1981 fell back to their 1959 level, and in the course of this unprecedented volume and profit crisis, the third largest U.S. car manufacturer, Chrysler, avoided bankruptcy only with the assistance of the U.S. government. Ford's future seemed to depend on the success of a whole raft of new products to be introduced between 1982 and 1985. American Motors' losses were putting to the test the strength of its French partner's commitment to the U.S. market. Even General Motors' position was weak following the lackluster market performance of its 1981 models. In 1983–84 the U.S. situation im-

189

proved due to the strong recovery and, above all, the imposition of import quotas on Japanese exports to the United States which blunted the Japanese attack.

Some of the U.S. auto industry's problems were of a broad economic nature. Years of high inflation, high unemployment, and high interest rates combined to depress the domestic car market. The rate of scrappage of old vehicles reached record low levels in 1982; meanwhile U.S. real car prices were increasing rapidly. Driven by the false hope of breaking even on new, reduced volumes, U.S. car makers had priced their new front-wheel-drive cars much higher than the models they replaced. With the economy still weak, price hikes in 1982 cut into sales volume even more. Consequently, by that year U.S. manufacturers no longer generated the cash flows needed to complete the new investments and launch the new products in which they saw as their only hope of competing successfully against the Japanese. Only the strong economic recovery of 1983–84 allowed U.S. producers to break out of the vicious circle of higher prices, lower demand, higher costs, shrinking cash flows, and reduced investments. Moreover, several structural factors exacerbated the erosion in the competitiveness of the U.S. auto industry with the result that the landed U.S. cost advantage of Japanese cars was usually estimated at $1,200 to $1,600 per unit in 1982 and around $1,000 in early 1985.

This chapter is an attempt to summarize and synthesize the factors that transformed the auto industry from being the stalwart of the U.S. economy to a sector relying on protectionism for survival in the early 1980s. How did the early U.S. lead in the car industry dissolve? And why? Why and how did the so-called Japanese challenge come about? Why didn't the Europeans capitalize on U.S. weaknesses? And finally, what are the issues on which future competition between the U.S. auto industry and its foreign rivals will hinge?

LOSS OF THE EARLY U.S. LEAD

The U.S. auto industry enjoyed its early global lead for a number of reasons.[1] A potential mass market for cars developed earlier in the United States than elsewhere, and Henry Ford's "Model T" was the right product to elicit mass demand. Ford's pioneering of new production methods allowed low-cost mass manufacture on an unprecedented scale.[2] When, by the 1920s, the public was ready for a somewhat better vehicle at a somewhat higher price, Chevrolet filled the gap at the expense of the "Model T."[3] At the same time, European auto makers' devotion to powerful, stylish, hand-crafted vehicles for the wealthy few left a gap in their markets that Ford and GM quickly filled, so that by 1920, 16 percent of U.S. car production was being exported. When Europeans reacted to the trade imbalance, U.S. manufacturers jumped the newly erected tariff barriers by investing in Europe. Ford, already present in Ireland and the United Kingdom, developed operations on the continent, and GM bought a German car producer, Adam Opel.[4] These moves started a long stream of investments that World War II interrupted.

The depression of the 1930s and World War II, however, had delayed the emergence of a mass market in Europe. Not until the mid-1950s did standards of living begin to rise rapidly throughout Europe. Yet, the U.S. automakers did not fully capitalize on this opportunity for several reasons. Although GM and Ford resumed some investing in Europe after World War II, in the United Kingdom, West Germany, and Belgium, they did not move heavily into southern Europe until later (France in the 1960s and early 1970s, then Spain in the later 1970s). Chrysler, in turn, started investing in Europe only in the 1960s by taking equity positions in existing small manufacturers (Rootes in the United Kingdom, Simca in France, Barreiros in Spain).[5]

In addition, the mass market developed in Europe began at the very low end of the product range, in keeping with Europe's moderate personal incomes, poor highway infrastructure, and high gas prices. Shorter trip distances in Europe also created different needs for car space and comfort than in the United States. Thus, a gap developed between European demands and U.S. automotive products.

To meet the European market demand, West German, French, and Italian producers quickly started to manufacture small, low-powered vehicles that were cheap to produce. Britain was slower; its Austin "mini" appeared only in 1959. These various European cars quickly became the dominant designs in their home countries. Mass production, basic designs, slim profit margins, and government price controls contributed to keeping the prices of these

Figure 8–1.   Japan and U.S. Automobile Production (overall).

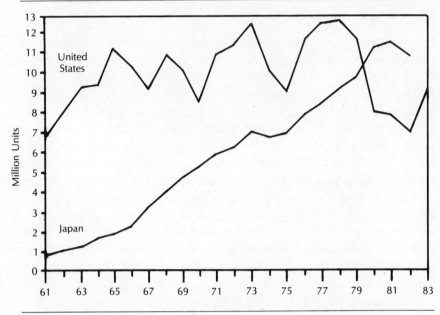

Source: "Automobile Monthly Statistic Report." Japan Automobile Manufacturers' Association (January 1981).

small cars low.[6] European subsidiaries of U.S. manufacturers concentrated their efforts on the middle to upper end of the market, where competition dealt more on features and distribution than on price, which yielded much higher profit margins.[7]

The Japanese market developed as the European market had, but later. Furthermore, Japan's hilly terrain, poor highways, and urban congestion resulted in Japan having fewer cars per 100 inhabitants than most other countries with similar levels of gross national product. After some early postwar hesitations about the appropriateness of developing an indigenous car industry, the Japanese government started to support the industry by restricting imports and encouraging exports.[8] In 1951 it also began to help with investments. When, in the late 1940s, both Nissan and Toyota were wracked by extreme labor disruptions and violent strikes, their managers coaxed employees into a permanent employment system negotiated with the unions,[9] and government assistance saved both companies from bankruptcy. The Industrial Bank of Japan funded Nissan, and government loans helped Toyota. Government support did not limit competition in the Japanese domestic market, however, as a number of manufacturers vied for dominance of the booming market for "people's cars."

Active competition among a half dozen manufacturers led to intense price wars in the late 1950s and 1960s. Real prices fell rapidly, generating a surge in demand. Rapid growth in overall GNP also contributed to a surge in demand in the late 1960s (see Figures 8–1 and 8–2). As a result, the Ministry of International Trade and Industry (MITI) did try to limit the number of entries into the car industry (by preventing potential entrants from acquiring foreign technology via licenses) and to encourage mergers among existing producers. The most tangible result was the 1966 merger of Prince and Nissan, which was financed by the government's Japan Development Bank. Toyota also "linked up" with smaller producers in the 1960s, in particular, Hino and Daihatsu. More successful were government plans to consolidate the component sector of the auto industry into a few, large, and diversified component makers enjoying long-term affiliations with the major car assemblers.[10]

Figure 8–2. Japan and U.S. Automobile Production (by company).

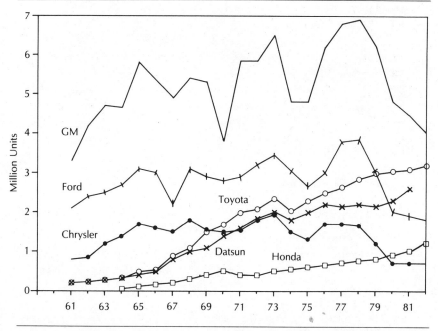

Sources: "Automobile Monthly Statistic Report." Japan Automobile Manufacturers' Association (January 1981; news reports).

The rapidly increasing demand and intense price competition during this period created both the opportunity and the need for major productivity gains in the Japanese industry. It also made feasible the addition of new capacity, which allowed the use of the most effective plant layouts and equipment. Most of the Japanese passenger-car plants, with the exception of Honda's, were built in the 1960s. Market share gains by the largest two competitors, Nissan and Toyota, added further cost pressures for the smaller producers. Active cooperation between management and labor, and between automakers and component-makers, made the search for productivity gains more all-encompassing and more pronounced than might otherwise have been the case. Capital intensity and labor productivity rose rapidly from the mid-1960s onward (Figures 8–3 and 8–4). At the same time, labor shortages, together with the availability of relatively cheap financing, further encouraged major auto manufacturers to invest in efficiency in-

Figure 8–3. Japan and U.S. Automobile Productivity (valued added per employee).

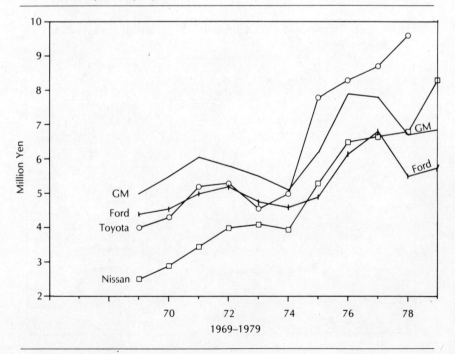

Source: Financial statements from each company. Added value = current profit + financial revenue + depreciation + salary and wages.

Figure 8–4. Japan and U.S. Auto Capital Intensity (fixed assets per employee).

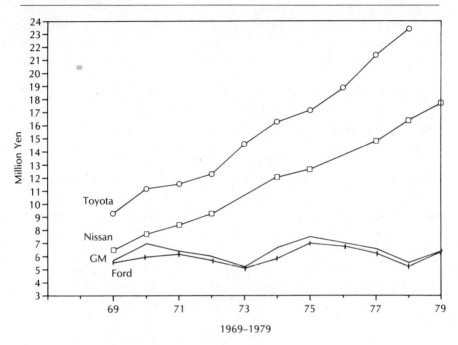

Source: Financial statements from each company. Added value = current profit + financial revenue + depreciation + salary and wages.

creases in their existing plants. Material costs also decreased rapidly as the productivity of other sectors, such as steel, rose.[11]

The dynamics of the domestic Japanese market, exploited by active manufacturers protected and supported by the government, combined to push the Japanese auto industry from relative backwardness into the position of major international competitor in hardly more than a decade, from 1958 to 1970. Even though the United States still accounted for the largest share of the world's car production in 1970, that dominance had already been undermined.

THE JAPANESE SUCCESS: STRATEGY OR LUCK?

In the decade from 1967 to 1978, Japan's share of world car exports increased from 5.3 percent to 18.9 percent, mainly at the expense of the United Kingdom and the United States. As British car exports dwindled from the leading position they had held right after World War II, the U.S. relative export share also declined.

In the U.S. domestic market, Japanese car imports grew initially at the expense of West German imports. In 1970 Japanese imports had only 3.9 percent of the U.S. market, 14.5 percent in 1979, 21 percent in 1980, and 23 percent in 1982. Meanwhile, the West German share of the U.S. market fell from 9.1 percent in 1970 and to 3.1 percent in 1979 and to less than 2 percent in 1983. U.S. makers controlled 76 percent of their home markets in 1970 but 72 percent in 1979–1982.

In the early 1970s, Volkswagen, unable to replace its venerable "Beetle" quickly enough, found itself with an unattractive product line. For little more money, substantially better cars than the "Beetle" were available with more interior space and better accessibility —the Datsun 210 and the Toyota Corolla. Revaluations of the Deutschmark also made successful competition more difficult for Volkswagen. When a new product, the Rabbit, was finally introduced in 1975, its price was substantially higher, and its reliability much lower, than the comparable products of Japanese competitors. Having lost its early preeminence, Volkswagen was unable to recapture its share in the American small-car market.

U.S. makers' early entries at the low end of the market were not fully competitive with Japanese cars. Ford's Pinto did not match the practicality or reliability of its Japanese competitors, nor did GM's captive imports from West Germany. The Japanese manufacturing cost advantage also made it difficult for U.S. manufacturers to price their models competitively and still make a profit, whether the cars were produced in the United States or in Western Europe. Ford, for example, lost substantial amounts on its captive imports of Fiestas.

The 1973 oil crisis allowed Japanese car manufacturers to capitalize fully on the temporary weakness of Volkswagen's product range and on U.S. manufacturers' inability to match Japanese product offerings quickly and profitably. Although some European car manufacturers, such as Fiat and Renault, had the small products that the oil crisis made so appealing, they lacked the distribution networks, the financial means, or the corporate willingness to compete strongly in the U.S. market. With so little competition, the Japanese were able to push exports even more when sales in the Japanese domestic market fell 20 percent in 1974. Japanese exports rose from 1.45 million units in 1973 to 2.54 million units in 1976.

Only two years after the first oil crisis, an oil price decline led to a resurgence of big-car demand, which gave mixed signals to the U.S. industry and further delayed its competitive response to small-car makers. Whereas to U.S. manufacturers the demand trends lacked clarity,[12] Japanese importers perceived a structural change toward smaller cars. General Motors did commit massive resources to "downsizing" its whole product range and introduced a new small car, the Chevette, but its sales performance was disappointing. The Chevette was a mixed blessing: it provided GM's dealers with a small-car entry, but at the same time made it difficult for GM dealers to take on important Japanese franchises. (With U.S. car sales in steep decline, dealers were all too willing to take on Japanese franchises to fill out their lines or even to switch completely to Japanese suppliers. The quality and density of Japanese car distributorships thus increased rapidly.)

No sooner had U.S. production recovered in 1977–1978 than the Iranian revolution triggered a second oil crisis, with major price increases. Retail gasoline prices of over $1 per gallon in the United States sent the demand for small cars soaring again while that for big cars collapsed. Japanese production set new records, and imports to the United States reached 1.77 million units by 1979, while U.S. production dropped to its lowest level since 1961.

Among imports, the Volkswagen share had continued to deteriorate. In 1981 five Japanese car manufacturers topped the list of importers into the United States, followed at a distance by Volkswagen, Volvo, Mercedes, and other European companies. In addition to Japanese imports under their own brands, Chrysler imported large numbers of Mitsubishi cars that they sold under Chrysler brand names.

As can be seen from this summary, Japanese success in international markets, and in the United States in particular, stems more from a succession of fortuitous and highly propitious events than from a deliberate grand strategy to dominate the world's car market.[13] The rapid development of the Japanese domestic market, combined with and helped by intense price competition, led the Japanese car industry to install large new plants in the 1960s and 1970s and to engineer them for low-cost manufacture. Favorable relationships between labor and management allowed the potential productivity gains of these installations to be exploited to the fullest in the 1970s. One deliberate choice, that of relying on scarce, increasingly well-paid and well-trained Japanese labor rather than importing guest workers, as European countries had chosen to do, created further pressures to improve productivity and working conditions. The Japanese also emphasized quality, at first mainly to satisfy the demands of Japanese car buyers. The fortuitous effect abroad, however, was a reversal of the previous shoddy image of Japanese imports.

As noted earlier, the initial Japanese push into the United States was greatly facilitated by Volkswagen's problems with product line and pricing structure, and by the neglect by U.S. auto manufacturers of the allegedly unprofitable small-car market. By 1973 Japanese manufacturers had the distribution channels in place to take full advantage of the shift in U.S. demand. Japanese manufacturers had also established a sizable presence in the markets of Europe's fringe countries—Ireland, Finland, Portugal—as well as in the more central Benelux countries and Switzerland. Finally, they had launched car sales and assembly in a broad range of developing countries.

SOURCES OF JAPANESE COMPETITIVE ADVANTAGE

The Japanese competitive advantage has been variously assessed and explained, but the studies that depend on comparing statistical data for Japan with data for other countries are often marred because of differences in industry structures, accounting and financial practices, product mix, degree of vertical integration, plant age, and labor relations. Studies that have developed conclusions from actual observation of shop floor and management practices, rather than from aggregate statistics, are probably more accurate.[14] Estimates of the sources of the cost advantage in manufacturing from the most detailed of these studies are presented in Table 8–1.

Before discussing the results of these studies, some popular myths about the Japanese challenge that are not borne out by the data must be set to rest. First, the work pace is not much higher

Table 8–1. Two Detailed Studies on the Sources of the Japanese Cost Advantages.

	Study "A"	Study "B"
Plant Engineering		
Process Yield	40%	28%
Quality Control	9%	5%
Technologies		
Automation	10%	6%
Product Engineering	7%	6%
Human Resources		
Absenteeism	12%	18%
Broader Job Classifications and Lesser Supervision	18%	23%
Production Rates	4%	6%
Unallocated	—	8%
	100%	100%

Source: See note 14

in Japan than in the United States. The image of a Japanese worker as an ant rushing at top speed from one task to the next is an illusion that bears no relation to reality. In fact, Japanese machines and plants work more slowly than elsewhere. Slow, relaxed, but continuous, work is typical of Japanese automobile factories.

Second, automation is not a decisive factor. Statistics cite a high robot population in Japan, but Japanese automats would not be counted as robots elsewhere.[15] The presence of robots in the auto industry in Japan is not greatly different from that in Europe or the United States. Automation accounts for 10 percent or less of the cost differential between the United States and Japan. Generally, the manufacturing technology of Japanese industry is no more advanced than that of European and American manufacturers.[16] Third, product engineering for ease of manufacture does contribute to a productivity difference, but only as a minor factor.

The decisive factor, first and foremost, is really a combination of factors that can be called process yield—a term that is obviously somewhat broad and requires more detailed examination. Process yield begins with the relationships among affiliated companies that minimize inventories of parts and work in process via the *kanban* or "just-in-time" system.[17] Frequent deliveries of parts from subcontractors directly through the plant gate and onto the assembly line permits the plant to hold very low material inventories. Coupled with tight, well-planned production scheduling, *kanban* requires minimal in-process inventories and therefore greatly reduces working-capital requirements.

Second, the elimination of buffer inventories calls for an extremely careful balancing of machine cycles and processing speeds throughout plants for smooth continuous operations. Less work in process inventory allows a high machine density and requires less plant space for a given production capacity, further lowering investment needs. Smooth functioning of plants is also attributable to the *jidoka* system of plant operations that allows single workers to supervise groups of machines, and delegates considerable autonomy to small work groups.[18] Quality control by the workers themselves, motivated by group pride, avoids both numerous and costly quality inspections and the extremely costly and difficult repair of defective vehicles at the end of the assembly line. Toyota, for instance, finds defects in only 5 percent of its vehicles, whereas comparable figures in Europe are 25 to 30 percent. Most Japanese plants also operate on only two shifts, which leaves more time for major maintenance, machine setting, and die or tool changes during the night. Minor maintenance is performed by the workers themselves. This sharing of maintenance minimizes unforeseen breakdowns and assures continual high quality when the plant is in operation.

Note that it is not so much any particular feature of the Japanese manufacturing system that provides a decisive advantage in car manufacture as it is the interaction between various factors. This interaction depends on a cooperative relationship between management and labor. Since the initial cooperation of unions with management in the early 1950s, a number of features have contributed to the continuous viability of this relationship. First, Japan is a culturally homogeneous society when compared to Europe and, to a lesser extent, the United States. This homogeneity carries over into the automobile plants. Second, workers have high and uniform educational backgrounds. Toyota and Nissan recruit only high-school graduates from the national education system based on yearly competitive exams. Since working for a large reputable corporation is quite prestigious, the companies have little difficulty attracting some of the best graduates and obtaining their commitment to the firm. Third, this commitment is fostered by intensive training and indoctrination in the first year of employment. Japanese companies believe in the concept that human capital must be valued and developed to its maximum potential. Such intensive training continues throughout an employee's life in the company. Furthermore, thanks to the shelter and cushion provided by affiliated subcontractors, major automakers have an extremely high number of lifetime employees—up to 95 percent at Toyota— whereas in Japan's total working population lifetime employees account for little more than 10 percent. The emphasis on human capital development is reinforced by sharing the firm's wealth among its active members, in addition to its owners, and by the relatively low income differentials between blue-collar and white-collar employees.

The organization of workers into small groups and their long-term commitment to the firm's success provide the basis for an efficient working system of quality improvement, meaningful programs, and job enrichment. These, in turn, contribute to workers' satisfaction and decrease absenteeism.

Labor costs have always been significantly lower in Japan than in the U.S. auto industry. Various sources quote somewhat different figures, but the approximate ratio remains a two to one advantage in favor of Japan: about $10 to $20 per hour in 1983. As long as the U.S. automobile remained an intrinsically simple and cheap product with little import competition, wage increases could be passed on to willing customers, and U.S. unions gained tremendous wage and fringe benefit concessions. With wages based on security and in the framework of a much lower national wage structure, the Japanese auto industry took advantage of the low wages earned by comparatively young employees (about 30 years old on average). Rapid growth kept the average age of the workforce relatively low.

THE AMERICAN RESPONSE

To counter the growing trade imbalance with Japan and the corresponding rise in unemployment, the initial American response was of a legal nature. The United Autoworkers Union (UAW) and some automakers, after failing to trigger a formal action from the

International Trade Commission, went to Congress to request bills that would limit auto imports.[19] The UAW leadership hoped that limiting imports would prompt Japanese companies to invest in the United States and hire some of the unemployed autoworkers. The concentration of about 300,000 unemployed autoworkers in a few states helped convince legislators of a need to intervene.

Before the legal process came to a close, however, the new Reagan administration urged informal restraints on Japanese exporters. Negotiations with MITI led to a proposal to reduce U.S. auto imports from Japan by 7 percent (in units) during fiscal year 1981 (compared to 1980) with slight increases permitted for subsequent years, provided the U.S. market grew. Japanese automakers were not easily convinced by MITI, however. They viewed selling cars as a strictly commercial matter that should not be turned into a domestic or diplomatic political issue.[20] After trying to avoid any restraints, they yielded to MITI's proposal in the late spring of 1981, but only when faced with the realization that the alternative would be much stronger restrictions imposed by a whole range of countries.

Limits on numbers of imports did not, however, put an end to Japanese competition in the United States or worldwide. First, Japanese marketing and pricing strategies in the United States shifted. Toyota and Nissan both put more emphasis in their advertising and sales mix on mid-size cars such as the Datsun 810 and Toyota Celica. These models attack the middle and upper segments of the U.S. market and have higher profit margins than the smaller cars. The Japanese companies also increased their prices (and profitability) in the small-car segments where they were dominant.

Second, Japanese manufacturers continued to exercise strong price pressures against their U.S. competitors. Full lines of options were included in the base price. When GM tried to follow this as a competitive response with its "J" cars, the company almost priced itself out of the market. The result of the Japanese strategy has been that exports to the United States are becoming increasingly profitable to Japanese firms, although the volume is limited. (Due to intense competition, Japanese sales in their domestic market are not very profitable.)

Third, Japanese manufacturers have increased their efforts to capture newly opening geographic markets. Saudi Arabia became in 1979 the second largest export destination for Japanese cars. Already during the 1970s, Japanese car exports began to supplant European exports to a number of countries (see Table 8–2). This trend further accelerated in the early 1980s.

Fourth, partly as intended by the trade restriction measures, Japanese manufacturers have started establishing plants in foreign markets. Nissan and Honda took the lead, while Toyota kept its facilities concentrated in one region within Japan. Nissan is developing operations in Spain, Italy, Mexico, the United States (pickup trucks), and possibly in Taiwan and Europe, beyond its smaller scale assembly operations in a number of developing countries. Honda is also investing in a U.S. plant. More recently Toyota launched its joint venture with General Motors in California.

Investments and Management

Beyond the short-term stop-gap measures of trade restriction, the U.S. auto industry engaged in a major long-term renewal of its product range and production facilities. The American product range is evolving rapidly from big, rear-wheel-drive vehicles to smaller, front-wheel-drive ones. By 1982 Chrysler had substantially completed this transition, General Motors had converted most of its product lines, and Ford is to complete the change in 1984–85. The new vehicles offer roomier interiors, lower weights, better aerodynamics, and much improved fuel economies.

In the process of revising their product line, U.S. automakers have had to develop new management skills. To speed up the introduction of new models, both Ford and GM drew on the engineering and design competence of their foreign affiliates.[21] GM

Table 8–2. Japanese and EEC Car Exports.

		S. Africa	Australia	Malaysia	Iran
1970	Exports To	146.813	144.944	27.341	33.915
	EEC % Share	81.0%	54.6%	59.0%	98.7%
	Japan % Share	13.2%	43.3%	37.0%	0.4%
1978	Exports To	158.369	237.310	74.886	162.872
	EEC % Share	56.1%	13.7%	30.0%	79.1%
	Japan % Share	43.9%	83.9%	60.0%	14.4%

developed a flexible "project center" approach to combine the competence and inputs from several U.S. divisions and foreign subsidiaries into a single, temporary, coordinated structure. While the approach was rather successful for individual components, results of the first complete joint efforts were mixed.

The new "J" cars were very successful in Europe, but less so in the United States, maybe because of the excessive price of the well-appointed models.[22] Furthermore, the close similarity between the product lines of GM's various divisions blurred their identity in the customers' eyes and probably reduced their success in the market.[23] GM executives had mixed feelings about whether the management difficulties surrounding the development and introduction of the "J" cars should be seen as learning costs or whether to question the whole concept of "world cars" developed jointly by domestic and foreign divisions.

Ford relied on the experience of its successful European management team and moved most of the team to the United States in the late 1970s in order to turn around its ailing North American car operations. The new "Escort" car was primarily a European project. It met with outstanding success in the United States and in Europe, but needed a yearly worldwide production volume of about 1 million units to break even. That production volume may have been reached in 1982 for the first time.

Even Chrysler relied largely on foreign capabilities for its new line. Its initial entry in the small, front-wheel-drive car segment was, by and large, of French design from its ex-subsidiary Simca. Furthermore, Chrysler models use engines and mechanical components from West German, French, and Japanese sources. Chrysler also distributes Mitsubishi cars in the United States.

Massive new plant investments were needed and will continue to be necessary to achieve the transition to small, efficient, front-wheel-drive vehicles. The total investment required in the domestic U.S. auto industry between 1980 and 1985 has been estimated at about $60 billion. As part of this major investment effort, U.S. automakers are increasing the automation of their plants. GM plans, for example, to install more than 14,000 robots by 1990 for painting, welding, and other tasks.[24] Ford, Chrysler, and American Motors have similar plans to automate their operations, but they are somewhat less advanced than GM in designing robots for their own uses and may take longer incorporating them.

The outcome of these massive rejuvenation efforts remains unclear. On the one hand, the U.S. industry will acquire more appealing and more competitive products, as well as modern plants. On the other hand, it will be burdened by massive financial charges and huge, unamortized investments. Modern plants and a renewed product line will not restore the success of the U.S. auto industry unless they are accompanied by measures to attack deeper, long-festering causes of the industry's loss of international competitiveness. Two of these difficulties involve the adversarial relationship between labor and management, and between management and the federal government.

Changing U.S. Labor Relations

After World War II, labor relations in the U.S. auto industry settled into a stable pattern. The strong UAW won, over time, major concessions from the auto companies regarding wages and fringe benefits. Wages were increased yearly via packages containing cost of living adjustments (COLA) and 3 percent annual improvement factor (AIF) in productivity agreements. The COLA and AIF formulas, first adopted in 1948, survived unchanged until 1980.

Fringe-benefit increases were much more important than wage gains, however. Full medical coverage and additional "personal" holidays were won over the years, so that, whereas the perhour assembly worker's wage has only followed the average nationwide increases in inflation and productivity, the total hourly compensation cost to the auto companies has increased by 300 percent in real terms since 1948. Fringe benefits added 12.5 percent to wages in 1948 and over 76 percent in 1981.[25] The contract negotiating procedures, and the formulas used, divorced wage settlements from other aspects of labor relations such as productivity gains or the quality of work-life.

In 1982 some hopeful signs could be seen, however, that the labor-management relationship might be changing. First, the new contracts at GM and Ford put an end to automatic wage increases. Reductions in personal holidays cut real wages in 1982 and 1983. More importantly, some link was established between corporate performance and wage levels, thereby relating wages to productivity. More union participation in quality of work-life programs (in which GM took the initiative) as well as in employee involvement in quality and process improvement (in which Ford took an early lead) is being achieved.

Beyond these current labor contracts, however, there are few signs that labor and management are able or willing to work together in restoring the competitiveness of the U.S. industry. The modern automated production equipment now being put in place in the United States will only partly close the cost gap with Japan unless overall labor relations are deeply modified. But new cooperation would require financial sacrifices from workers and a sharing of power on the part of management that neither side seems willing to accept.

Labor relations have also created problems for U.S. auto companies with regard to the broader strategic context of industry location. The main bargaining strength of the companies was their ability—and threat—to move manufacturing outside the United States to overcome the compensation differential between U.S. workers and workers abroad. The number of cars made in the United States has been decreasing, first with AMC's and Chrysler's reliance on foreign suppliers for engines and other mechanical components, and then with the globalization and integration of Ford's and GM's manufacturing networks, which put foreign manufacturing sites in competition with U.S. domestic sites.[26] The UAW's response has been to renew its efforts to promote bills that would mandate a certain level of national content for all cars sold in the United States. Such bills would effectively block increases in car imports and also limit the relocation of U.S.-owned plants in lower labor-cost areas of the world.

Improved Government Relation

Adversary relations between the auto industry and the U.S. federal government seem to have prevailed since the early 1960s. Initial foot-dragging by major manufacturers in carrying out relatively obvious safety measures created distrust between Congress and the auto industry. At the same time, the strident voicing of safety issues by Ralph Nader and his followers extended this feeling of distrust to the general public. Then, the fragmented nature of the U.S. regulatory apparatus and its rapid institutional evolution (e.g., the creation of the Environmental Protection Agency and the extremely tight deadlines under which it had to provide pollution-level objectives) also made the development of a coherent national policy toward the auto industry impossible. As a result, uncoordinated regulations were imposed on the auto industry with little concern on the regulators' part for the maintenance of the industry's long-term competitiveness. On top of this problem, antitrust regulations hampered—or made more costly than necessary—compliance with the new environmental regulations, in particular by preventing companies from entering joint research and development programs for pollution control, fuel economy, and safety. Altogether, these adversary relationships have made it impossible for a national consensus to emerge between government and management on coherent policy choices for the auto industry.

Management Changes

Unable to control federal policy on union attitudes, car manufacturers have resorted to a piecemeal approach to improving their situation by using the factors they could directly control: new products, new production equipment, better and more flexible shopfloor practices, and relocation of production to foreign sites. Of particular importance was reduction in overhead costs. By the 1980s, U.S. automakers had begun to question the multiple layering of management and staffs. Ford cut almost $4 billion out of its overhead, mainly by reducing its salaried staff in the United States by 25 percent. Chrysler reduced white-collar employment by half, and GM eliminated managerial and staff employment substantially. Part of the reason for these cuts was the realization that Japanese manufacturers were achieving their success with fewer layers of management than U.S. companies and much simpler organizations.

If You Can't Beat 'Em, Join 'Em

American automakers have also tried to tap into Japanese efficiency by developing cooperative relationships with Japanese companies; this trend has been going on since 1969, when Japan liberalized foreign investment in its auto industry at the request of Mitsubishi and U.S. automakers developed links with their Japanese counterparts. In 1971 Chrysler obtained a 15 percent equity position in Mitsubishi, and GM a 34.2 percent stake in Isuzu. In the late 1970s, following the difficulties of Toyo Kogyo in 1975, Ford took a 25 percent equity interest in that company and attained access to Toyo Kogyo's manufacturing technology and design expertise. Ford's intensive study of Japanese auto manufacturers has inspired a broader, very successful productivity improvement program at Ford of Europe. The program is called, significantly, "After Japan."

In addition to process and management technology, Japanese manufacturers also provide products to their U.S. partners. Toyo Kogyo's vehicles are sold in some countries by Ford dealers under the Ford brand, as Chrysler does for Mitsubishi's cars in the United States. For instance, the new Toyo Kogyo's Mazda 323 Familia is sold under the Ford brand as the "Laser" in Australia. GM has integrated Isuzu into its worldwide manufacturing network, and Isuzu sells and manufactures in Japan derivatives of Opel-designed cars. In 1981 GM also took a small equity interest in Suzuki, from which it will buy mini-cars for resale in the United States. (Suzuki is also going to manufacture cars in India in a joint-venture with a local public company.)[27]

More far-reaching than these ventures is agreement between Japanese and American companies to coproduce vehicles in the United States. Following unsuccessful talks with Ford, Toyota signed the previously mentioned joint-venture agreement in 1983 with GM to manufacture a Toyota-designed model in a closed California GM plant for sale under the GM brand.

The future stability of many of these agreements can be, however, questioned. The equity participation and distribution agreements merely reflect the relative weakness of the second-tier Japanese automakers, particularly in distribution and, sometimes, in their finances. Relative strength between the partners changes over time, however, and Mitsubishi, for instance, is establishing its own distribution network in the United States because of its concern with the poor performance and shaky structure of its Chrysler partner (Chrysler's shrinking dealer network reduced Mitsubishi's U.S. sales in 1981). Mitsubishi has planned to sell in the United States models that compete directly against part of Chrysler's product line.[28]

The GM-Toyota link-up may have been borne out of GM's temporary weakness in small to medium cars and out of Toyota's desire to make a gesture of goodwill by producing autos in the United States without making the major financial, human, and organizational commitments necessary for manufacturing outside Japan. The agreement would, therefore, serve both partners' short-term needs well, but it offers little hope of long-term convergence unless the overall world view of Toyota's management changes considerably.

CONCLUSION

Industry experts predict that the current efforts of U.S. auto manufacturers can reduce the cost gap between the United States and Japan by $600 per unit, narrowing it to between $600 to $900 by 1985. It is unlikely, however, that the U.S. industry can fully close the gap through the 1980s. A continued brightening of the economic doldrums would obviously be quite beneficial to the U.S. auto industry, particularly since the population hardest hit by the recession is that which traditionally buys American auto products. With a brighter economy, scrappage rates of old vehicles would presumably rise.

Even with much larger volumes, and a market mix favoring larger cars, however, the U.S. industry probably still cannot fully regain competitiveness with Japan. In the long run, the most difficult challenge to the United States is that of technological evolution in products and processes. By the mid-1980s, U.S. automakers will have large amounts of essentially new manufacturing capacity carrying high depreciation charges. That capacity, by and large, represents 1970-vintage process technology, with a few notable exceptions such as GM's automated paint shops and some new manufacturing techniques. Most of Japan's capacity was put in place in the late 1960s and early 1970s, and a good part of it will soon be amortized. It will be easier, therefore, for Japan to undertake major manufacturing process changes in the 1980s and replace existing capacity. Financially, Japanese automakers have the potential for a quantum jump in competitive strength. Toyota could afford massive new investments, as could most other Japanese manufacturers. Whether technological evolution would justify, for instance, major further efforts in automation, or whether the social structure of Japanese firms would allow it, are unclear, however. Product research does not seem to be very advanced in

Japan, and early successes like the Honda CVCC have not resulted in any major breakthroughs in new products.

How the U.S. companies can respond in the long run is obviously a difficult question. In the short run, though, U.S. auto manufacturers are likely to continue along the main lines they already are following: automation and process improvement, relocation of productive capacity in Japan or in developing countries, sourcing of components and subassemblies from foreign manufacturers, and more efficient shopfloor labor relations. But a leaner, shrunken domestic industry would result with imports—captive and otherwise—taking an even higher share of the U.S. market than at present.

The kinds of adjustments described above have been characteristic of a number of maturing consumer goods industries in the machinery, electrical, and electronic sectors. Yet, its sheer size makes the car industry different. The number of workers, the dependent communities, the resources involved, the power of the unions—all these forces make a major readjustment unlikely. The alternative to a shrunken domestic industry would mean continued protectionism. Most developed countries have clearly signaled a commitment to the protection of their domestic auto industries. Some protectionism may create the basis for a compromise between Japan and the West that would lead to smoother future adjustments and to shifts in the relative competitiveness of the national industries involved. The danger, however, is for protectionist forces to succeed in removing international competitive pressures from the U.S. industry, particularly since a national consensus on such an issue would be extremely difficult to create in the United States. Even though the most appropriate course of action would probably lie somewhere between protectionism and unconstrained corporate adjustment to international competition, the United States may not be able to maintain such a compromise in the long run.

NOTES

1. Myra Wilkins, *The Maturing of Multinational Enterprise: American Business Abroad from 1914 to 1970* (Cambridge, Mass.: Harvard University Press, 1974), pp. 72–76.

2. Allan Nevin and Frank Ernest Hall, *Ford: The Times, the Man and the Company* (New York: Scribners, 1954).
3. Alfred P. Sloan, *My Years with General Motors* (London: Sidgwick and Jackson, 1965), chs. 4 and 9; and Carl Kaysen, "Alfred Sloan's Success Story," *The New Republic* (February 20, 1964).
4. George Maxcy, *The Multinational Motor Industry* (London: Croom Helm, 1981), chs. 4 and 5, pp. 69–89; and Louis T. Wells, "Automobiles," in R. Vernon, ed., *Big Business and the State* (Cambridge, Mass.: Harvard University Press, 1974).
5. Stephen Young and Neil Hood, *Chrysler U.K.: A Corporation in Transition* (New York: Praeger, 1977).
6. Wells, "Automobiles," and Myra Wilkins, "Multinational Automobile Enterprises and Regulation: An historical overview," in William J. Abernathy and Douglas Ginsburg, eds., *Government, Technology and the Automobile Industry* (New York: McGraw Hill, 1980). See also Mark Fuller "Intervention in Industry," Harvard Graduate School of Business Administration, 1981. (Unpublished.)
7. See "Ford Bobcat A1," (Harvard Business School Case Study No. 4-380-093).
8. Masaru Udagawa, "Historical Development of the Japanese Automobile Industry, 1917–1971 Business and Government," in P. Fridenson, ed., *The Global Automobile Industry and its Environment* (Cambridge: Cambridge University Press, 1982).
9. Koichi Shinokawa, "Product and Labor Strategies in the Contemporary Japanese Automobile Industry," (mimeo, 1984).
10. See Fuller, "Intervention in Industry," and Fumihiko Adachi, Keinosuke Ono, and Konosuke Odaka, "Ancillary Firm Development in the Japanese Automobile Industry—Selected Case Studies II," Hitotsubashi University, Institute of Economic Research Discussion Paper No. 41, March 1981); and Ono and Odaka, "Ancillary Firm Development in the Japanese Automobile Industry—Case Studies I (in process).
11. Hiroya Ueno and Hiromichi Muto, "The Automobile Industry of Japan, in Sate, ed., *Industry and Business in Japan* (New York: Sharpe, 1980).
12. Based on Yoshihiro Tsurumi's interviews with Japanese automobile exporters into the U.S. market and author's interviews with U.S. auto manufacturers in 1977–1980.
13. Yves L. Doz and Jean Pierre Lehmann, "Improving the Strategic Management Process: The Japanese Example," *Strategic Management Journal,* forthcoming.
14. Many western auto manufacturers have carried out such studies: some of the most detailed were made by Ford in the United States

and Peugeot in France. Published cost differential assessments based on some of these studies can be found in William Abernathy and Kim Clark in *Harvard Business Review.*

15. Author's interviews with Japanese and U.S. auto manufacturers.

16. Ibid.

17. Y. Sugimori, K. Kusunoki, F. Cho, and S. Uchikawa, "Toyota Production System and Kanban System—Materialisation of Just-in-Time and Respect-for-Human System," Proceedings of the 4th International Conference on Production Research in Tokyo (London: Taylor and Francis Ltd., forthcoming).

18. Ibid.

19. See Mark B. Fuller and Malcolm S. Salter, "Ford Motor Company (B): The Automobile Crisis and Ford's Political Strategy," (Harvard Business School Case Study).

20. Author's interviews at the Japanese Automobile Manufacturers' Association and Japanese auto manufacturers.

21. Author's interviews at Ford and General Motors. See also Y. Doz, "General Motors' Overseas Operations," and "Ford Bobcat E.," Harvard Business School Case Studies, forthcoming.

22. "Why Detroit Still Can't Get Going," *Business Week* (November 9, 1981): 72–76.

23. "GM's Next Move Is to Restore Division Identities," *Business Week* (October 4, 1982): 79.

24. "GM's Path With Robots: From User to Maker?" *Business Week* (June 15, 1981): 79.

25. Harry C. Katz, "SMR Forum: Assessing the New Auto Labor Agreement," *Sloan Management Review* (Summer 1982): 57–63. Also, U.S. Department of Labor, Bureau of Labor Statistics, unpublished data, December 1982.

26. Yves Doz, "The Evolution of the Organisational Structures and Management Processes of Multinational Car Manufacturers"; Fridenson, *The Global Automobile Industry;* and US Department of Transportation, *The US Automobile Industry 1980* (Washington, DC: Department of Transportation, January 1981).

27. "India Puts Japan behind the Wheel," *The Economist* (April 24, 1982): 97.

28. "Mitsubishi Revs Up to Go Solo," *Business Week* (May 3, 1982): 88–89.

9 THE CHANGING U.S. POSITION IN THE INTERNATIONAL STEEL MARKET
Output, Trade, and Performance

Hans Mueller

During the first six decades of this century, the steel industry of the United States enjoyed a position of world leadership. The availability of cheap raw materials, a skilled labor force, an already large and expanding market permitting large-scale production methods, access to the world's largest and most organized capital market, and the benefits derived from a continuous stream of innovations made by other sectors of the economy led to America's preeminence in the steel industry.

There were disturbing signs in the early postwar period, however, that this era of supremacy was drawing to an end. One was the failure by large American steel producers to reform their outdated plants so as to achieve productivity increases commensurate with the ambitious expansion and modernization programs of the 1950s. Another factor was the sharp rise in steelworkers' total employment costs relative to the average employment cost of all manufacturing industries. These two factors caused steel prices in the United States to climb nearly three times as fast as industrial prices generally during this period.[1] A third development foreboding problems for the U.S. steel industry was the rapidly growing competition from the rebuilt European and Japanese steel industries, which was given further impetus by the Korean War. These

213

industries were joined by steel exporters from Canada and eventually (in the 1970s) by steel firms from a number of new steel-producing nations, among them Spain, South Korea, Brazil, and South Africa.

The American steel industry responded in several ways to these problems. Initially it launched an extensive modernization program. Because this effort was not accompanied by long overdue structural reform, especially in the form of closures of poorly located and laid-out plants, little progress was made toward improving the industry's position relative to its major foreign competitors. Perhaps lacking faith in their own modernization efforts, several large American producers began to hedge their bets by channeling large amounts of money into the acquisition of non-steel enterprises.[2] This diversification movement, which began in the mid-1960s, was highlighted in 1982 by the U.S. Steel Corporation's acquisition of the Marathon Oil Company.

The mid-1960s also marked the start of a political response by the large American steel producers to the increasing presence of foreign competition in their home markets. For this purpose, U.S. producers arranged a truce with their traditional adversary, the United Steelworkers union (USW), and enlisted its support in vigorous publicity and lobbying campaigns against imported steel. These and subsequent efforts had considerable success in obtaining government intervention in the quantities and prices of steel brought into the United States. As a consequence, the U.S. steel market became in some degree insulated from the rigors of international competition, and, in most years, domestic steel prices have remained above those prevailing in the world market during periods of weak demand.[3]

While trade intervention shielded domestic prices against erosion by low bids from foreign exporters, it did little for the profitability of American steel producers. One reason was that the latter kept postponing decisions concerning the restructuring of their obsolescent plant structure. Only toward the end of the 1970s did some companies begin closing marginal plants and eliminating unprofitable product lines. It appears that the easing of competitive pressures by means of government-negotiated or imposed trade measures had clearly reduced the pressures on managers to pursue drastic, and often highly unpopular, avenues for improving efficiency and trimming costs. Another reason for the relatively low profitability of the U.S. steel industry was related to the apparent obligation of management to "repay" the USW for lending its political support to the companies' campaign against imported steel and for a 1973 agreement putting a stop to (import-inducing) nationwide strikes. Steel wage costs rose from 30 percent above the average for all U.S. manufacturing wage costs in the late 1960s to 94 percent in 1982,[4] decreasing to 77 percent above the average in 1983 after intense pressure on the United Steelworkers union.

Absence of such political success might have induced the industry to undertake a more vigorous restructuring effort and to put up greater resistance to union demands. The industry might thus have found itself in a better competitive position than it did in the early 1980s. Furthermore, by raising domestic steel prices, this protectionist policy has impaired the international competitiveness of many American steel-fabricating firms and contributed to the deteriorating American trade balance in steel-containing goods.

The following sections of this chapter will focus on the changing fortunes of major world steel industries and, especially, on the causes of these changes, including shifts in demand, pricing and investment policies, the effect of management decisions and workers' attitudes on productivity and innovation, as well as the role played by governments. At the center of the discussion will be the interactions between the large U.S. steel producers with their foreign rivals and with a new breed of steel producers, the so-called minimills.

STEEL PRODUCTION, TRADE, AND COMPETITION

World steel output rose from 41 million net tons (mnt) in 1900, to 212 mnt in 1950, and to an all-time high of 824 mnt in 1979. World output fell to 732 mnt in 1983. Trade in steel products amounted to less than 5 percent of total production before World War II. It rose to 10.7 percent in 1950, 17.2 percent in 1965, and 24.8 percent in 1980. Expressed in raw steel equivalent, the total amount of steel exported (or imported) in 1979 amounted to 137 mnt (excluding intra-EEC and Comecon trade).[5]

Table 9–1. World Raw Steel Output, 1960 and 1983, by Major Region (in million net tons and in percent).

	1960	%	1983	%	Change in %	Growth Rate
Western World	265.7	(69.6)	446.9	(61.2)	68.2	2.29
Industrialized Countries	256.2	(67.1)	377.0	(51.6)	47.2	1.69
EEC (10)	108.0	(28.2)	120.6	(16.5)	11.7	0.48
United States	99.3	(26.4)	83.4	(11.4)	−16.0	−0.76
Japan	24.4	(6.4)	107.1	(14.7)	338.9	6.64
Developing Countries	9.6	(2.5)	69.9	(9.6)	628.1	9.02
Communist Countries	115.9	(30.4)	283.6	(38.8)	144.7	3.97
USSR	72.0	(18.9)	167.6	(22.9)	132.8	3.74
Eastern Europe	22.8	(6.0)	65.1	(8.9)	185.5	4.67
China & N. Korea	21.0	(5.5)	50.9	(6.8)	142.4	3.92
World	381.6	(100.0)	730.5	(100.0)	91.4	2.86

Source: International Iron and Steel Institute, *Steel: Statistical Yearbook,* various years.

Size of Steel Industries

In the first four decades of this century, the two towering giants of world steel production were Western Europe and the United States. Because of the war damage suffered by Europe's industries, American steel producers accounted for an overwhelming share of world steel output after World War II. This share exceeded 50 percent until 1948, but as other nations rebuilt their steel industries it gradually fell to about one-third by 1958. The large European steel industries began to surpass their prewar records in the mid-1950s, and in 1960 Western Europe as a whole was out-producing the United States. Japan's steel production in 1960 was three times as large as its wartime record, but it was still below that of England or Germany and less than a quarter of American steel output.

To an observer familiar with the world steel industry of 1960 it might have seemed that, except for the gradual increase in the shares of world steel production held by Eastern Europe and Japan, the future constellation of major steel industries would not differ greatly from that of the past. No one could foresee at that time the magnitude and speed of the changes that were to take place in the next two decades. First, there was the astounding growth of the Japanese steel industry: it took only six years, from 1960 to 1966, for Japanese raw steel output to double. By 1970 it had nearly doubled again, and by 1973 it had increased more than fivefold from its 1960 level. Second, several European nations— among them Spain, Yugoslavia, Rumania, Finland, and Turkey— as well as South Africa expanded their steelmaking capacity at very fast rates. Third, it would hardly have been possible to foresee the rapid increase of steel production in the Third World—from less than 10 million tons in 1960 to 70 million tons in 1983, with the number of developing nations possessing steel plants rising from nineteen to fifty. Fourth, few observers anticipated the prolonged stagnation that has characterized the steel markets of the advanced Western countries from 1975 to the early 1980s.

Table 9–1 and Figure 9–1 illustrate the changes in steel production that have taken place from 1960 to 1983. The figures cited conceal the fact, however, that for many nations growth turned to stagnation or even decline after 1974 (see Figure 9–2; pg. 219). It is noteworthy that the decline in the U.S. share of global production was considerably greater than the fall in the U.S. share of global consumption due to a significant deterioration of the American steel trade balance since 1960.

The Changing Line-Up of the Largest Steel Firms

In 1960 the leading U.S. firms were still far ahead of their foreign competitors in size. The capacity of the U.S. Steel Corporation was then 42 million net tons and that of Bethlehem was 23 mnt. At that time, the large foreign firms—Thyssen in Germany and Yawata in Japan with 8.5 mnt each, and several other European and Japanese firms, with sizes varying from 6 mnt to 7 mnt— reached only the size of the fourth- to sixth-ranking American firms.[6]

Figure 9–1. World Raw Steel Output 1960 (in italics) and 1983 (in million net tons).

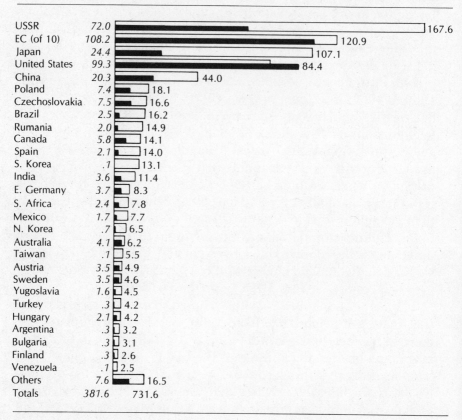

	1960	1983
USSR	72.0	167.6
EC (of 10)	108.2	120.9
Japan	24.4	107.1
United States	99.3	84.4
China	20.3	44.0
Poland	7.4	18.1
Czechoslovakia	7.5	16.6
Brazil	2.5	16.2
Rumania	2.0	14.9
Canada	5.8	14.1
Spain	2.1	14.0
S. Korea	.1	13.1
India	3.6	11.4
E. Germany	3.7	8.3
S. Africa	2.4	7.8
Mexico	1.7	7.7
N. Korea	.7	6.5
Australia	4.1	6.2
Taiwan	.1	5.5
Austria	3.5	4.9
Sweden	3.5	4.6
Yugoslavia	1.6	4.5
Turkey	.3	4.2
Hungary	2.1	4.2
Argentina	.3	3.2
Bulgaria	.3	3.1
Finland	.3	2.6
Venezuela	.1	2.5
Others	7.6	16.5
Totals	381.6	731.6

Source: International Iron and Steel Institute, *Steel: Statistical Yearbook,* various years.

In 1983 the capacity list was led by Nippon Steel, which in 1969 had been formed from a merger of two Japanese steel companies (Yawata and Fuji). As shown in Table 9–2 (see pg. 220), the U.S. Steel Corporation had dropped to second position, followed by Nippon Kokan, Finsider, Kawasaki, Sumitomo, British Steel Corporation, Bethlehem, Thyssen, and Usinor. Farther down the list, in the 8–13 mnt category, one finds a fairly large number of firms. Among the Third World producers, only Siderbras of Brazil, Posco of South Korea, Steel Authority of India, and Iscor of South Africa are in this category. However, in contrast to many large producers in the advanced nations, Third World steel producers have grown at a rapid rate and are still expanding, or intend to expand, their capacity.

Figure 9–2.   Apparent Steel Consumption Index by Region[a]
(1973 = 100).

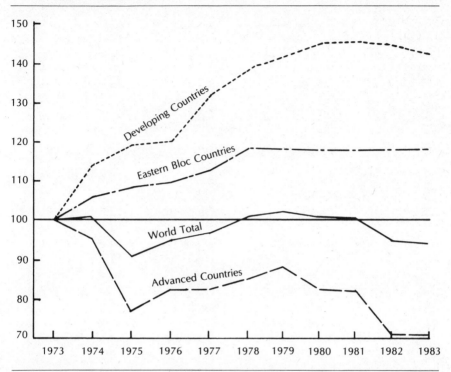

a. Eastern Bloc Countries include North Korea and China.

Source: International Iron and Steel Institute (IISI), *Steel: Statistical Yearbook, 1981*, pp. 32–33; and IISI, *World Steel in Figures, 1983*, p. 21.

International Competition and Trade

In the 1920s and 1930s, Europeans dominated the world market for steel, accounting for more than 80 percent of all international steel trade. American steel exports did not attain a position of preeminence until the 1940s and the early 1950s. Toward the end of the 1950s, however, steel producers in Europe and Japan gained a cost advantage with respect to many non-flat products. In the following decade this advantage spread to plate and sheet products.

For a while, the Europeans managed to reassert their dominance of the international steel market. By 1960 European steel exporters accounted for about 80 percent of all steel trade (exclud-

Table 9–2.   Output and Capacity of the Largest Steel Firms in the Noncommunist World, 1983 (in million net tons of raw steel equivalent).

Ranking (by capacity)	Company	Country	Capacity	Output
1	Nippon Steel	Japan	34.0	29.6
2	U.S. Steel	U.S.	27.0	14.8
3	Nippon Kokan	Japan	22.0	12.6
4	Finsider	Italy	20.7	13.4
5	Kawasaki	Japan	20.0	11.4
6	Sumitomo	Japan	20.0	11.4
7	BSC	Britain	19.0	14.0
8	Bethlehem	U.S.	16.8	10.7
9	Thyssen	Germany	15.6	10.4
10	Usinor	France	12.8	9.4
11	Siderbras	Brazil	12.6	10.1
12	Jones & Laughlin	U.S.	11.8	7.6
13	SAIL	India	10.4	6.8
14	Republic	U.S.	10.4	6.3
15	Cockerill-Sambre	Belgium	10.0	5.2
16	Kobe	Japan	9.8	6.7
17	Posco	S. Korea	9.4	9.3
18	Inland	U.S.	9.3	6.3
19	Sacilor	France	9.3	7.6
20	BHP	Australia	8.2	6.1
21	Armco	U.S.	8.1	5.8
22	Iscor	S. Africa	8.0	6.0

Sources: Capacities are author's estimates; output data are from *Metal Bulletin Monthly,* April 1984, p. 67.

ing intra-EC and Comecon trade), with the largest portion of this share going to the European Economic Community. But by 1970 Japan had conquered a world market share of 30 percent, while the European Community's share had declined to 32 percent (see Table 9–3). In 1976 the Japanese share reached 42 percent while that of the EC dropped to 22 percent, although by 1980 these percentages had nearly reverted to their 1970 position.

The strikingly rapid expansion of the Japanese steel industry and the determination of European steel exporters to defend their large share of the world market led to spirited competition be-

Table 9–3. Shares of World Exports and Imports (excluding intra-EC and intra-Comecon trade).

	Exports			
	1950	*1960*	*1970*	*1980*
United States	20.2%	10.2%	10.8%	3.8%
EC (9)	65.9	57.5	31.8	29.6
Japan	4.3	8.4	29.5	30.3
Other Western Europe	2.3	9.5	7.7	12.4
Comecon	5.0	8.3	11.1	8.2
All Others	2.3	6.1	9.0	15.7
Total Exports (in million net tons)	14.1	29.3	65.6	109.1

	Imports			
	1950	*1960*	*1970*	*1980*
United States	8.7%	10.3%	19.9%	14.0%
EC (9)	2.9	9.5	14.9	11.1
Other Western Europe	18.0	18.6	18.0	13.0
Comecon	2.1	11.3	6.0	8.1
Latin America	16.8	11.4	5.6	8.1
Africa and Middle East	17.3	12.8	10.5	15.2
Asia	14.6	15.7	14.4	22.6
All Others	19.5	10.4	10.7	7.9
Total Imports (in million net tons)	14.1	29.3	65.6	109.1

Sources: International Iron and Steel Institute, *Steel: Statistical Yearbook, 1981,* pp. 26–29; American Iron and Steel Institute, *Annual Statistical Report,* various issues.

tween these two groups in the 1960s. Before World War II, the Europeans, in collaboration with U.S. steel producers, had averted such confrontations in the international market through cartel agreements.[7] With the formation of the European Coal and Steel Community in 1952 and its strict code concerning such combinations, quota arrangements with outsiders became difficult. During the 1960s, the competitive climate within the community itself became as severe as that reigning in the world market. Among the reasons were the rapid capacity build-up by each national industry, recessions in the steel market, the diversity in managerial background and temperament (which made tacit collusion and price discipline difficult), and a redirection of marketing efforts by the steel industries of Belgium and Luxembourg from the world market—where Japanese competition was stiffening—to the home markets of other community members.[8]

In the 1970s competition in the world market further intensified following the construction of modern steel mills in several newly industrializing countries as well as in such nations as Spain, Canada, Australia, and South Africa. Furthermore, exports from Eastern Europe—especially Poland, Czechoslovakia, and Rumania—were growing in volume. The situation was aggravated by a prolonged recession that, beginning in the mid-1970s, at first affected primarily the industrialized nations of the noncommunist world, but eventually spread to the developing countries. As home-market demand declined in many steel-producing nations, more production was channeled into the world market with devastating effects on the international price structure and losses were incurred even by relatively efficient steel producers.[9] Many privately owned firms turned to their governments for financial assistance, with the largest steel companies in France and Belgium eventually going into public receivership.

The result was an increasing tendency by the governments of the major industrialized nations, including the United States, to restrict steel imports. The United States, which had put into effect "voluntary" quotas on carbon steels from 1969 to 1974, imposed a quota on specialty steels from 1976 to 1980, a system of price controls on imported carbon steels from 1978 to March 1980 and again from October to January 1982, a quota arrangement on carbon steel imports from the EC in October 1982 (to be effective until the end of 1985) and a mixture of quotas and higher tariffs on specialty steels in July 1983.[10] The European Community instituted trade measures in 1977 that impose controls on both the quantities and prices of imported steel. Meanwhile, the governments of many developing nations have redoubled their efforts to achieve self-sufficiency in steel while taking strong measures to protect their new steel industries from international competition.

One might expect that a consequence of this rising level of interference by governments would be a decline in the volume of steel exports and imports during this period. In fact, there has been an almost constant increase in steel trade in the last two decades, a trend that asserted itself during both boom and recession periods.

Causes Behind the Rising Steel Trade

The rising volume of steel trade reflects in part an ever greater specialization of the international steel market with respect to products and regions. Output and trade figures conceal the shift that has taken place over time toward new types of steel products and toward products of higher quality. In addition, due to the regional concentration of production facilities, steel users in some nations find that shipping costs from domestic producers exceed those of foreign suppliers. Product specialization is in some degree attributable to the high cost of investing in plant and equipment to turn out new steel products. It is becoming increasingly difficult for national steel industries to be all things to all customers. Moreover, differences in the age of steel plants, especially of the rolling mills, have a considerable impact on the product quality these industries are able to supply. Although such quality differences are usually of limited duration in the case of individual products, they may in their totality account for a significant volume of trade in any year.

Before cyclical changes in demand became synchronized among the major steel-producing regions of the noncommunist world in the early 1970s, the international exchange of steel products was in some degree also the result of supply deficits occurring in some parts of the world while others experienced a surplus, often because of differences in the timing of major expansion projects.[11]

It should be noted that the various types of specialization by product, region, or over time, do not necessarily require that one industry possess an ex-mill cost advantage relative to any of its rivals. In other words, the volume of steel trade is a function of international specialization as well as of relative cost differentials.

The Changing U.S. Position in the International Steel Market

As previously mentioned, by the 1960s the U.S. industry's competitiveness had weakened considerably, and the U.S. balance of trade for steel products shifted from a moderately positive to a highly negative position (Table 9–4 and 9–5). In the 1970s steel imports into the United States, as a percentage of consumption, fluctuated widely, averaging in the vicinity of 15.5 percent over the decade.

A long strike in 1959 by the United Steelworkers triggered the first large wave of steel imports. In the following period, imports surged each time a labor contract with the United Steelworkers union was up for renegotiation, especially in 1965 and in 1968. In between, the volume of imports either remained at high levels or continued to rise. While potential supply disruptions were the ostensible cause of these rising imports, it is doubtful that events would have turned out fundamentally different in the absence of these strike threats. In the first place, the decline in the relative cost of ocean shipping, in conjunction with the regional concentration of the American steel industry in a few Northeastern states, invited competition by foreign producers in Western, Southwestern, and in parts of the Southern regions of the United States. Second, a number of American steel users, with memories of having been put on allocation during a period of tight demand in the 1950s and occasional dissatisfaction with customer service of the large domestic firms, turned to imports for part of their requirements. Third, a certain amount of steel was imported because delivery periods lengthened abnormally during business upswings or because the new foreign mills could observe better tolerances and guarantee greater product uniformity. Finally, beginning with the early 1960s, an increasing number of foreign competitors gained a sufficient cost advantage to underprice the large U.S. producers in some or all of the latters' home markets even after absorbing freight and exporting costs.

The first three points listed above are related to industry specialization by region and product. Such specialization is a normal and even desirable outcome of economic development. All the major steel-producing nations of the world, in recent years including even Japan, import considerable amounts of steel. A high degree of specialization exists in the European Community, where nearly 30 percent of all the steel produced is traded among member countries. As already noted, the volume of steel trade is by no means exclusively a function of ex-mill production costs plus freight and tariffs (i.e., of comparative advantage in an abstract setting).

Table 9–4. The Changing International Position of the U.S. Steel Industry.

	United States			European Community			Japan			World Output
	Output[a]	Percent of World Total	Net[b] Exports	Output[a]	Percent of World Total	Net[b] Exports	Output[a]	Percent of World Total	Net[b] Exports	
1870	1.8	16.2%	—	7.5	69.2%	1.2	—	—	—	10.8
1900	14.6	35.4	—	20.3	49.4	5.0	—	—	—	41.1
1920	49.2	58.9	2.2	27.8	33.7	8.0	.9	1.1%	—	82.3
1950	96.8	52.9	1.6	53.2	25.6	9.0	5.3	2.6	.4	200.0
1960	99.3	27.8	-.2	107.8	29.6	9.7	24.4	6.7	2.5	360.3
1970	131.5	21.1	-6.3	151.6	23.8	7.4	102.9	16.1	22.3	637.8
1980	112.1	14.4	-11.4	140.0	20.0	15.0	122.8	14.0	34.7	802.0

Notes:

a. In net (or short) tons of raw steel.

b. Exports minus imports, in net tons of steel products.

Sources: American Iron and Steel Institute, *Annual Statistical Report*, various years; Eurostat, *Iron and Steel, Yearbook*, various years; *Tekko Nenkan*, various years.

226   REVITALIZING AMERICAN INDUSTRY

Table 9–5.   United States Foreign Trade in Steel Mill Products (in thousands of net tons).

	Net Shipments by U.S. Steel Producers	Exports	Imports	Apparent Consumption	Imports as a Percentage of Apparent Consumption
1958	59,900	2,823	1,707	58,800	2.9%
1961	66,126	1,990	3,163	67,299	4.7
1964	84,945	3,442	6,440	87,943	7.3
1967	83,897	1,685	11,455	93,667	12.2
1970	90,798	7,062	13,364	97,100	13.8
1973	111,430	4,052	15,150	122,528	12.4
1976	89,447	2,654	14,285	101,078	14.1
1979	100,262	2,818	17,518	114,962	15.2
1982	61,567	1,842	16,663	76,388	21.8
1983	67,584	1,199	17,070	83,455	20.5

Source: American Iron and Steel Institute, *Annual Statistical Report,* various years.

Nevertheless, emerging cost differentials were an important cause of rising U.S. steel imports in the 1960s. According to a study undertaken by the Federal Trade Commission, Japanese steel producers had gained an advantage in the cost of major inputs that amounted to $32 per net ton of steel products in 1960 and rose to $120 by 1976.[12] For the first half of the 1970s, European Community steelmakers seemed quite capable of matching the Japanese. However, they proved less successful in coping with rapidly rising labor and energy costs and the rising value of their currencies in the second half of the decade. Only after 1980 did they regain their cost competitiveness in the U.S. market, in large part due to the strengthening of the U.S. dollar.

A glance at the bottom of Table 9–6 (see pgs. 228-229) reveals that a significant change has taken place since 1960 in the source of U.S. steel imports. Whereas the share of the European Community of total U.S. imports fell from 62.4 percent in 1960 to 24.1 percent in 1983, Japanese, Canadian, and Third World countries' shares rose considerably.[13] To a large extent, this change in import shares closely reflects a shift in the relative cost advantages of national steel industries.

It must be pointed out that only the integrated domestic steel firms, and not the entire American steel industry, fell behind in international competitiveness. One segment of the industry—the so-called minimills—remains competitive, as will be explained below. Some factors that were partly responsible for rising imports —the increasingly poor location with respect to markets of some of the integrated plants and high production costs—also encouraged the growth of the domestic minimills. In 1960 both imports and minimills commanded a share of less than 5 percent of the U.S. market. By 1983 both groups had increased their respective shares to about 20 percent.

At this point it may be useful to sum up the principal causes of the U.S. industry's lack of competitiveness: (1) an investment policy that put too little emphasis on creating modern, large-scale, well-located, and specialized integrated plants, (2) unduly high employment costs resulting from a combination of high wages and benefits and restrictive work rules, (3) lagging adoption of technological advancements, and (4) the loss of the American advantage in the cost of coking coal and iron ore due to the opening of rich mineral sources in many parts of the world and the decline in freight charges for these bulk materials. It is the first of these points that, by locking the structure of some of the integrated firms into the wrong mold, presents the greatest obstacle to future modernization efforts.

Intensifying Competition Among Domestic Producers

The traditional steel producers of the United States have increasingly been forced to compete in their own backyard. At the bottom of this development have been technological and locational factors. Traditionally, steel was produced in large-scale, so-called integrated plants consisting of ore-preparation facilities, coke ovens, blast furnaces, one or several steelshops, ingot or continuous casting shops, and a variety of rolling mills, especially mills that roll flat products such as plates and sheets. Integrated mills rely on iron ore and coking coal as primary raw-material inputs. The scale economies of three stages in the process—blast furnaces, steelshops, and hot-strip mills—grew to such an extent by

Table 9–6. Some Data Relevant to the U.S. Steel Market.

	Output[a] (in million of steel products)	Capacity[b]	Operating Rates	Number of[c] Employees (thousands)	Hours Worked[c] (millions)
1983	67.9	98	69.3	242.7	475
1982	58.5	104	56.3	289.4	526
1981	89.0	105	84.8	390.9	753
1980	81.8	103	79.4	398.8	758
1979	99.6	103	96.7	453.2	894
1978	99.9	104	96.1	449.2	892
1977	90.1	104	86.6	452.4	876
1976	91.4	103	88.7	454.1	877
1975	83.4	103	81.0	457.2	855
1971	83.0	100	83.0	487.3	932
1968	90.5	100	90.5	551.6	1,095
1965	91.0	99	91.9	583.9	1,158
1960	70.7	94	75.2	571.6	1,087

	Import Volume (million tons of steel products)					Shares of Total U.S. Steel Import (%)				Import Share of U.S. Market
	Japan	EEC	Canada	Others	Total	Japan	EC	Canada	Others	
1983	4.2	4.1	2.4	6.3	17.1	24.8	24.1	13.9	37.1	20.5
1982	5.2	5.6	1.8	4.0	16.7	31.1	33.6	11.1	24.2	22.3
1981	6.2	6.5	2.9	4.3	19.9	31.3	32.6	14.6	21.6	19.1
1980	6.0	3.9	2.4	3.2	15.5	38.8	25.1	15.3	20.9	16.3
1979	6.3	5.4	2.4	3.4	17.5	36.2	30.9	13.4	19.5	15.2
1978	6.5	7.5	2.4	4.8	21.1	30.7	35.3	11.2	22.8	18.1
1977	7.8	6.8	1.9	2.8	19.3	40.5	35.4	9.8	14.3	17.8
1976	8.0	3.2	1.3	1.8	14.3	55.9	22.3	9.1	12.7	14.1
1975	5.8	4.1	1.0	1.0	12.0	48.6	34.3	8.4	8.7	13.5
1971	6.9	8.5	1.3	1.6	18.3	37.7	46.5	7.0	8.8	17.9
1968	7.3	8.4	1.2	1.0	18.0	40.6	46.8	6.9	5.7	16.8
1965	4.4	4.9	.6	.4	10.3	42.5	47.3	6.2	4.0	10.3
1960	.6	2.1	.2	.4	3.4	17.9	62.4	6.3	13.4	4.7

Notes:

a. Output data were estimated by adjusting reported shipment figures for changes in producer inventories (the adjustments were made on the basis of Charles A. Bradford, Steel Industry Quarterly. Merrill Lynch March 1984, p. 21, and U.S. Senate, Steel Imports, December 19, 1967, p. 358).

b. Capacity that can be fully utilized for at least one full year, allowing for output-restraining events that can normally be expected to occur in any given year (such as harsh weather conditions).

c. Refers to all employees (both wage and salary recipients).

Sources: Shipping capacities are own estimates. Output data estimated from shipments and inventory changes (see note). All other data are from American Iron and Steel Institute, Annual Statistical Report, various years.

the late 1960s that, in order to exploit them properly, a steel plant would require a minimum annual capacity of 4 million tons of raw steel and cost several billion dollars to construct. Such huge amounts of capital constituted a major obstacle to the entry of new competitors into the steel market, a factor that used to facilitate the maintenance of stable prices in the U.S. market.

The new competitors, called minimills or market mills, are based on electric furnaces that use scrap as their primary raw-material input. With a minimum quantity of only 200,000 to 400,-000 tons of annual raw-steel output, they have been constructed for as little as $30 million in recent years, or less than 1 percent of the investment required for a new integrated mill. Because they are often located near large cities, which serve as a source of scrap and also as a market for their products, transportation costs for raw materials and finished products are usually lower than for integrated mills. Minimills can now be found in every major region of the United States while the bulk of integrated steel capacity remains concentrated in the Chicago-Pittsburgh areas. They are also widespread abroad and supplied some 14 percent of global consumption in 1982.

Competitive processes have yet to be perfected for rolling high-quality sheet products on equipment that fits the scale of minimills. The product mix of these firms is, therefore, limited to light, non-flat products such as wire rods, reinforcement bars, and small shapes.

Plant and Equipment Suppliers to the Steel Industry

Historically, one of the points that favored the competitiveness of the U.S. steel industry was the presence of a large and innovative equipment sector.[14] During the two decades following World War II, American equipment makers benefited considerably from the expansion of steel capacity in the United States, Europe, and Japan. By the late 1960s, however, European and Japanese firms had accumulated sufficient know-how and experience to offer stiff competition in overseas markets, especially in Third World countries. Their success was due in part to lower labor costs, relative to their American competitors, and to an overvalued dollar; but it can also be attributed to a more rapid rate of product innovation and to aggressive marketing strategies.

Until the late 1970s, American equipment firms continued to enjoy the loyalty of domestic steel producers. This was of relatively little help, however, because the latter undertook few major projects after 1970. In recent years, American steel producers have increasingly turned to foreign suppliers for their equipment needs as well as for technical assistance.[15] Possibly as a result, several domestic equipment suppliers have entered into licensing agreements or merged with foreign suppliers.

Longer prospects for the American equipment industry appear to be more encouraging. The market for steelmaking plants and equipment is likely to revive in the near future for several reasons. First, the market for steel is widely expected to stage a significant recovery by the mid-1980s. Second, rising quality demands of steel users will require a fundamental upgrading of rolling, and annealing, and coating facilities. Third, many of the large American steel producers have a considerable backlog of technologically obsolete equipment. Further incentives to the large-scale replacement of steelmaking equipment will result from new capital recovery rules and from labor concessions with respect to wages, fringe benefits, and work rules.

FACTORS AFFECTING COMPETITIVENESS OR COMPARATIVE ADVANTAGE

The U.S. industry's quandary is essentially due to deficiencies in four areas: equipment and process technology, the scale of major production stages and entire plants, plant layout, and plant location. To some extent, the problems in these areas are interwoven. For example, the installation of equipment embodying new technology may require a number of second-best solutions in an existing plant due to scale and layout constraints.

Technology

That innovation does not always "pay" was recognized long ago by one of the founders of the U.S. Steel Corporation, Andrew

Carnegie.[16] A similarly cautious attitude toward the swift adoption of new technology was exhibited by most of the large American steel companies until the late 1970s when, goaded by their Japanese competitors, they began to reassess their past policies toward innovation.

The two new major processes in steelmaking technology of the last thirty years are the oxygen furnace and the continuous caster. Both increase the productivity of three major inputs: capital, labor, and energy resources. Other major developments include the bell-less blast-furnace top that raises the efficiency of the smelting process, and the computerization of rolling mills that permits finer tolerances and, hence, the production of higher-quality material. Another noteworthy innovation is the direct reduction (DR) of iron ore into pellets or lumps used primarily by minimill operators as a substitute for steel scrap. But steep increases in the cost of natural gas have inhibited the application of this technology and confined its expansion to regions with abundant supplies of cheap natural gas.[17]

The adoption rates of several process innovations and the indicators of efficiency for a number of steel industries are shown in Table 9–7. Figure 9–3 illustrates the rates at which the oxgyen furnace and continuous-casting processes were adopted over time by steel industries in advanced and developing countries. In nearly all instances, Japan occupies the leading position followed usually by the Europeans. It should be added that gaps in the adoption of modern technology pertain exclusively to the integrated segment of the U.S. steel industry. American minimills, as a rule, operate highly modern electric furnaces linked to continuous casters. In fact, if minimills were left out of the comparison, the adoption rate of continuous casters by American steel producers would be even more unfavorable compared to their foreign competitors.

While information is available concerning the adoption rates of some of these methods, many other aspects of innovation by steel companies are more difficult to evaluate and compare. There are, however, several indirect indicators that can be used to compare the overall efficiency of steel industries. These indicators consist of labor and energy productivity, measured in terms of hourly units or Btu's per ton of steel products shipped, as well as the yield achieved, that is, the amount of finished output (see Table 9–7).

Technological achievement is closely related to the average vin-

Table 9–7. A Comparison of Technology and Performance.

	U.S.	EEC	Germany	Japan	Canada	Mexico	Brazil	S. Korea
Bell-less systems, 1983, in % (best practice: 100%)	12	46	41	23	51	62	37	20
Fuel Rate, 1980 (best practice: .460–.480)	.596	.538	.540	.466	.546	na	.506	na
Steel Melting, 1983, in %								
BOF	62.4	74.1	80.5	71.6	66.2	43.1	69.7	70.9
Electric Furnace	30.4	25.9	19.5	28.4	26.6	45.0	24.5	29.1
Obsolete (OH)	7.1	—	—	—	7.2	11.9	5.8	—
Continuous Casting, in % (best practice 90%)	31.2	60.4	71.8	86.3	37.4	36.1	44.4	56.6
Yield Estimates, 1982, in % (Finished steel per net ton of raw steel, adjusted for product mix)	74	78	77	86	77	76	76	83
Energy Use, 1978, per net ton Finished steel, in mill. Btu's	29.98	24.9	25.0	20.4	24.8	na	25.6	na
Scrap ratios (the greater the use of scrap, the less should be the energy use)	51.5	43.8	58.3	31.9	47.4	na	42.2	na
Labor Productivity, 1982 Man-Hours per net ton of finished steel (incl. both white and blue-collar employees as well as contract workers)	10.3	10.1	9.7	8.3	9.4e	24.0e	20.0	14.0

Sources: International Iron and Steel Institute (IISI), *World Steel in Figures*, 1984; IISI, *Statistical Yearbook Steel*, 1983; Bureau of Labor Statistics, U.S. Department of Commerce, "International Comparisons of Productivity and Labor Costs in the Steel Industry, January 1984; *Siderurgia Latinoamericana*, February 1983, pp. 2–5; Information obtained from the Brazilian Steel Institute, Hylsa, Mexico. The Co., and the Paul Wurth Co., Luxembourg.

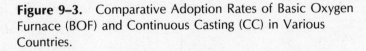

Figure 9–3. Comparative Adoption Rates of Basic Oxygen Furnace (BOF) and Continuous Casting (CC) in Various Countries.

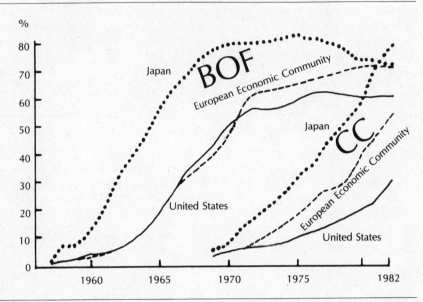

Sources: International Iron and Steel Institute (IISI), *Steel: Statistical Yearbook,* various years; IISI, *World Steel in Figures, 1983,* pp. 7–8; German Iron and Steel Federation, *Statistical Yearbook,* various years.

tage of plant and equipment. As shown in Table 9–8 integrated U.S. steel firms have fallen behind in the replacement of coking capacity while, with respect to rolling capacity, a significant age gap exists only vis-à-vis the Japanese industry. It goes without saying that much of the equipment in the developing countries is relatively new, given the rapid growth rate of Third World steelmaking capacity in the last two decades. This does not necessarily mean superior overall efficiency, however.

Economies of Scale

As Table 9–9 reveals, in 1960 the American steel industry was still ahead of Japan and the European Community regarding the size of plants. By 1980 it had fallen to third place: the average annual capacity of the ten largest American steel plants was 5.9 million net tons compared to 11.2 million tons in Japan and 8.3 million tons in the European Community.

Table 9–8. Differences in the Equipment Vintage of Major Steel Industries.

		U.S.	EEC (9)	Japan
Proportion of 1974 capacity installed before 1960		36%	26%	0%
Age of coke ovens:	older than 10 years	84	67	32
	older than 20 years	57	37	2
Cold-rolling mills:	older than 10 years	89	83	66
	older than 20 years	56	42	11
Plate mills:	older than 10 years	83	84	66
	older than 20 years	55	46	13

Sources: For coke-ovens: Lenhard J. Holschuh, *Annual Report,* 13th IISI Annual Conference, Sidney, Australia, Oct. 1979, pp. 7–8; for other data, K. Kawahito, *Issues of World Steel Production and Trade in the 1980s,* Monograph No. 26, Business and Economic Research Center (Murfreesboro: Middle Tennessee State University, December 1980), pp. 60, 63.

At the beginning of 1983, the average capacity of all the U.S. integrated plants was only 2.9 million tons. In fact, of the thirty-two integrated plants in this country, twenty-four had an annual raw-steel capacity of less than four million tons—the capacity generally considered to be the minimum efficient scale for a plant with a narrow product range. The optimum scale for integrated plants

Table 9–9. Changes in Plant Size.

Plant Size	1948 U.S.	1952 EC	1952 Japan	1960 U.S.	1960 EC	1960 Japan	1980 U.S.	1980 EC	1980 Japan
above 6 mnt	—	—	—	3	—	—	4	8	12
4 to 6 mnt	4	—	—	6	—	—	7	7	2
2 to 4 mnt	7	—	—	18	4	3	18	13	3
1 to 2 mnt	20	7	2	23	16	6	14	19	1

Sources: William Haller, "Technological Change in Primary Steelmaking in the United States, 1947–64," Hearings, Subcommittee on Antitrust and Monopoly, Committee on the Judiciary, September–October 1967, pp. 3,186–97; Louis Lister, *Europe's Coal and Steel Community* (New York: Twentieth Century Fund, 1960), Appendix E; Eurostat, *Iron and Steel, Yearbook 1970,* Table 11–8; Institute for Iron and Steel Studies, *Commentary* (January–February 1979 and January 1981); IISS, *Steel Industry in Brief, Japan (1977),* "The Steel Industry of Western Europe" (map).

with a wide product range is considerably larger, probably in excess of 8 million tons annual capacity.[18]

Plant size does not necessarily reflect scale economies at the level of individual production stages. There appears to exist, however, a fairly good correlation between the average scale of plants and that of major installations. With respect to equipment scale, the difference between the U.S., EC, and Japanese steel industries are especially pronounced for such expensive items as blast furnaces, strip mills, and plate mills, as shown in Table 9–10. The steel industry of Japan has evidently put considerably greater emphasis on the development of large blast furnaces and rolling mills. Oxygen steel converters are of similar size in each industry, but steelshops, in which several converters work in teams, are larger in the EEC and in Japan.

Japan also leads the world in the amount of integrated capacity built in the postwar period.[19] However, because such mills are usually constructed in several phases and only become profitable after completion of the second or third phase, it is extremely important that demand keep expanding while the project is underway. The large Japanese steel firms managed to complete the majority of their big plants prior to the onset of a prolonged recession in the mid-1970s. Several European producers (in England, France, and Spain) were caught by the recession with half-completed mills, which had devastating effects on company profits.

Achievement of scale economies is an even greater problem for the steel industries of Third World countries. Not only are their domestic markets small relative to the minimum efficiency size of an integrated steel mill, modest consumption growth, in absolute terms, delays construction of new plants or of additional phases of a single plant, even when growth of domestic consumption is high. One solution to this problem, which has been adopted in South Korea, Taiwan, and Venezuela, is to build a single large plant of a size that, initially at least, exceeds the absorptive capacity of the entire home market. But this strategy also risks technical problems or strikes that may leave the country virtually without any supply of flat-rolled steel (the type of product in which most integrated mills specialize).

Mexico, Brazil, and India have each built several integrated mills, some of them begun by regional factions in a rather haphazard manner.[20] In these cases, the loss of scale economies is to some

Table 9–10. Plant and Equipment Economics of Scale, 1979.

		United States	EEC	Japan
Plants	Capacity of the 5 largest plants, in maximum raw steel production potential	36	52	68
	Capacity of the largest 10 plants	59	83	112
	Number of plants with a raw steel capacity in excess of 6 million NT	4	8	12
Blast Furnaces	No. of blast furnaces with an inner volume in excess of 70,629 cubic feet (2,000 cubic meters)	6	19	39
Steelshops	No. of oxygen converters 220 NT or larger (charge weight)	31	39	32
	Average annual capacity of oxygen steelshops, mill net tons	2.4	2.8	3.5
	Capacity-weighted average converter size	225	240	218
Hot Wide Strip Mills	No. of mills a. fully continuous	23	11	9
	b. semi-continuous	14	14	8
	Average rated annual capacity, million net tons	2.3	3.1	3.5
Plate Mills	No. of mills (only heavy and medium reversing, except two and three high)	18	34	16
	Average total annual capacity, million net tons	.67	.62	1.68

Sources: Institute for Iron and Steel Studies, *Commentary*, January 1983; Metal Bulletin, *Iron and Steelworks of the World*, 1983; Japan Iron and Steel Federation, *Japan Steel Bulletin*, June 1979; Jonathan Aylen, "Innovation in the British Steel Industry", in *Technical Innovation and British Economic Performance* Keith Pavitt (ed.), (London: Macmillan, 1980), pp. 211, pp. 213, 218, and 220.

extent offset by freight cost reductions for shipments of steel to nearby consumers.

Plant Layout

A faulty layout, usually the consequence of frequent rounding out and piecemeal expansion, results in higher internal transfer costs of raw materials and semifinished products. In some plants, the existing layout makes it impossible to install new processes, such as continous casting, in a manner that yields maximum economies. The chief problem with a less than efficient layout is that, short of rebuilding a large portion of the plant, it is virtually impossible to eradicate flaws. Both energy and labor rates, and hence operating costs, will remain higher than those of recently designed plants.

Most large Japanese plants were conceived from the beginning for a terminal size ranging from l0 to 17 million tons of raw-steel output per year. Raw materials are delivered by bulk carriers (up to 250,000 tons) on one side of the plant and, under the guidance of computers, processed straight through the blast furnaces, the steel shops, continuous casters, and finishing facilities, to be shipped out at the other end.[21]

In many integrated plants in the United States, the transfer of materials often follows zigzag patterns as a result of frequent layout modifications and the grafting of new technology onto old. In addition, large installations sometimes have been custom-designed or shoehorned into plant sites hemmed in by hill slopes and urban growth. Most steel plants in Europe and in Third World countries were either built or completely rebuilt after World War II.[22] They have, therefore, fewer layout problems than the majority of integrated steel plants in the United States.

Plant Location

Steelmaking in the United States has traditionally been concentrated in the Chicago and Pittsburgh-Youngstown regions but the geographical market for steel products has shifted in the postwar period to new markets in the West, Southwest, and South.[23] The large companies seem to be content with expanding their mills in areas that they had previously acquired through mergers or purchased from the U.S. government after World War II.

Plant location has played a significant part in the competition between minimills and the traditional integrated mills. The former for the most part embody the latest technology and have been well-located with respect to both raw materials and markets, and, in many cases, employ non-union workers. The integrated mills in California, Utah, and Alabama had to haul their raw materials over considerable distances. They were also plagued with problems of scale and layout and burdened by rising employment costs resulting from high union pay scales and rigid work rules. Because no new integrated large-capacity mills were built in the West, Southwest, and South during the six-year reprieve from import pressures (in the form of the 1969–1974 voluntary restraint agreements), one can only infer that the large U.S. steel producers were in some degree abandoning those markets to foreign exporters.

All of the large Japanese steelworks are on sites with deep-channel harbors.[24] Nearly all raw materials as well as all exports and a sizable portion of domestic shipments are transported by sea; still, the long distances over which raw materials must be brought in and exported product shipped out makes the Japanese steel industry vulnerable to rising ocean freight rates.[25] To counter this threat, the industry has already begun a drive to develop more fuel-efficient ships.

The integrated European mills vary widely as far as the economic efficiency of their location is concerned. Several mills in France, Italy, the Netherlands, England, and Belgium are well situated for receiving low-cost materials and for exporting overseas areas but are less so for supplying the European manufacturing centers. The plants in the Ruhr strike a compromise, with higher freight costs for raw materials and exports but lower shipping costs to their customers. On the other hand, there are several plants in Lorraine, Belgium, and the German Saar region that, in part due to locational problems, have found it difficult to remain competitive.

The majority of integrated steel plants in the Third World were constructed for the purpose of import substitution.[26] While this does not interfere with the exporting costs of the tidewater plants in South Korea and Taiwan, it does present a problem for the international competitiveness of the inland-located plants in Brazil, India, Mexico, and elsewhere. In addition, since some of these plants were originally designed for a much smaller terminal size, they now suffer from inadequate rail and road systems, power supplies, and training facilities for skilled labor.

The Effect of Structure on Industry Performance

Industry performance—as reflected by indicators of efficiency and productivity, production costs, and, ultimately, profitability—depends on the quality of the capital stock that employees must work with. Capital stock is a function of the amounts invested and especially the caliber of the investment decisions made by management in the past. Inadequate supplies of investment funds have not been a fundamental problem for the large American steel producers. In the period from 1960 to 1980, the American steel industry invested a larger amount, per ton of capacity added or replaced, than its European and Japanese rivals.[27] American depreciation laws, the cost of compliance with environmental rules, and government intervention do not seem to have presented greater impediments to American steel producers than to the majority of foreign competitors.[28] The problems of American steel-company managers as regards the quality of their investment decisions, it would seem, grew rather out of the noncompetitive environment in which these decisions were made during the first six decades of this century. A premium had been placed on creating a stable, predictable, and almost serene environment for the companies, with the U.S. Steel Corporation assuming the role of the price leader and ceding part of its market share whenever the smaller companies expanded at a faster pace than the rate of market growth.

While such an environment may have ensured steady profitability, it hardly compelled the companies to tidy up the empires formed through a long series of mergers. In a more competitive atmosphere, many of their antiquated plants—some of them designed according to efficiency standards of the nineteenth century —would not have lasted as long as they did. Except for several steelworks built by the government during World War II, few wholly new plants were added. Most capacity expansion took place via the piecemeal expansion of existing plants that, due to geographic shifts of manufacturing industries, were often no longer convenient to growing steel markets. In addition, as mines were exhausted, iron ore had to be hauled over increasingly longer distances and transshipped from one mode of transportation to another.

Although the plants were periodically modernized, the splicing of new facilities onto old layouts did not permit sufficient scale economies in internal material flows or equipment that new plants could have achieved. Not only did this lead to imbalances within plants concerning the work speed or size of successive, vertically linked production stages, it also resulted in the unnecessary duplication of expensive, large-scale equipment, such as hot-strip mills,[29] and product runs of inadequate length. As a consequence, capital costs per ton of capacity added were exceedingly high.

Cost Factors

Only the cost of the principal factors entering into the production of steel—major raw materials, energy resources, labor, and capital charges—will be considered below. Others, such as spare parts and the services of outside contractors, are not included in the discussion because of the difficulty of obtaining data for these items. In the case of Japan, hourly employment costs are an estimated average of the cost of both regular and contract workers.

Raw Materials.   Among the inputs used in steel production, raw materials used by the integrated mills are the least likely at the present time to tip the balance for or against a national steel industry. Iron ore and coking coal are accessible to most integrated producers at similar shipping-point prices. Cost differentials arise, however, by the time these materials are unloaded at the blast furnace. Delivered costs are lowest for integrated steelworks with deep harbors able to accommodate ships of 150,000 tons or more displacement.[30] Delivered raw-material costs are somewhat higher for a plant located on inland waterways, as are many plants in the United States and Europe. Costs are even higher for landlocked plants, except for those located in the vicinity of ore and coal mines.

Many steel companies in the United States operate their own

iron-ore and coal mines. However, largely because of high wage costs, this has ceased to be an advantage in the case of iron ore. Large mines of iron-rich ore have been opened in Australia, Latin America, and Africa, and ocean freight costs have been significantly reduced through the use of very large bulk carriers. The advantage derived from the ownership of captive coal-mining operations is, in the early 1980s, still intact, but it has narrowed considerably due to high wages and the impact of safety and health regulations.[31]

Input consumption rates for iron ore and coal are primarily a function of the technology employed, that is, the vintage and scale of the blast furnaces in use. The Japanese industry has achieved the lowest iron ore and fuel rates per ton of hot metal as well as the lowest energy rates per ton of finished steel products. The EC industry, with a fair number of modern blast furnaces, is second among the major industries of the noncommunist world.[32]

Scrap, the chief input of minimills, is generally cheaper in the older industrialized countries—England, Germany, and the United States—than in Japan, Italy, Spain, or the Third World. However, in countries with cheap energy resources—such as Mexico, Venezuela, Trinidad, Saudi Arabia, and Indonesia—minimills are being operated with iron pellets reduced directly by means of natural gas.

Energy.   Major international differences exist in the cost of energy resources (other than coal) due sometimes to national or regional regulation of prices but in many cases because of differences in the relative scarcity of such resources. Integrated steel producers are frequently able to work around the rising cost of a particular energy input, such as heavy heating oil or natural gas, via input substitution and are thus less dependent on purchased electricity. In contrast, for the nonintegrated and direct-reduction (DR) mills the costs of electricity and natural gas, respectively, are crucial for economic survival. It is not surprising, therefore, that in the last ten years more nonintegrated steelmaking capacity has been constructed in the United States than elsewhere due to reasonable scrap and electricity costs in this country; DR-based mills have been springing up for the most part in regions where natural gas was being flared off, as in several Latin American and Asian countries.[33]

Labor. Hourly employment costs for steelworkers differ widely among the steel-producing nations of the world. Whereas in 1982 these costs were about $23 in the United States, they were only $10 in Japan, and $12.50 in the European Economic Community (see Table 9–11) In Third World nations, they varied from less than $2 to $5.[34] But in the case of many developing countries this advantage in labor costs is in large degree, or even entirely, offset by lower labor productivity and considerably higher investment costs per ton of capacity.

It is the excess of hourly employment costs in steel over the average in the manufacturing sector as a whole that, unaccompanied by increased labor productivity, has an adverse effect on the international competitiveness of particular national steel industries. This excess has reached 80 percent in the United States, much higher than in Japan or Europe. Furthermore, in contrast to the other major steel-producing countries, productivity in the United States has risen at a slower rate.

Total employment costs per ton of steel shipped, or unit labor costs, are the product of hourly employment costs and the input rate of labor, that is, man-hours per ton of steel. The American steel industry had the lowest such input rates of labor until 1973, when it was passed by the Japanese steel industry.[35] By 1979 it was temporarily (until 1983) also overtaken by the industries of Ger-

Table 9–11. An International Comparison of Employment Costs.

	Hourly Employment Costs		Hours per Net Ton of Steel Shipped		Unit Labor Cost	
	1960	1982	1960	1982	1960	1982
U.S.	$3.95	$22.74	17	10.3	$67	$234
EC	1.16	11.20	21	10.1	24	113
Japan	.54	10.18	51	8.3	28	85
Brazil	.60	4.00	n.a.	20.0	n.a.	80
South Korea	n.a.	2.65	n.a.	14.0	n.a.	37

Sources: Bureau of Labor Statistics, unpublished data; AISI, *Annual Statistical Report,* various issues; *Steel Employment News* (January 11, 1983); Eurostat, *Wages and Incomes,* various issues; Ministry of Labor, Japan, *Monthly Survey of Labor Statistics;* NRI (a consulting firm), Tokyo; *Siderurgia Latinoamericana* (June 1981) 7.

many, Italy, and the Netherlands.[36] The developing nations, except for South Korea and Taiwan, use considerably more labor per ton of steel than the advanced nations.

Capital.   The cost of raising capital was lower in the United States than in most foreign countries during most of the 1950s and 1960s. More recently, however, it has actually been greater in this country than in Europe and Japan. In the Third World, the situation has been complicated by high inflation rates and frequent government interference in credit markets. In several European and in nearly all Third World countries, the largest steel companies are government-controlled and have benefited from public loans, often at reduced interest rates, and equity capital (causing U.S. steel producers to resort to trade litigation).[37]

We have already mentioned that the efficiency of capital investments in steelmaking capacity has been lower in the United States than in Europe or Japan, that is, per dollar invested, the U.S. steel industry added or replaced considerably less capacity than its European and Japanese competitors. In most developing countries, however, capital productivity is below that achieved in the United States because the poorly developed industrial infrastructure of those countries often requires the setting up of extensive repair facilities at plant sites. Exceptions are the modern integrated steelworks in South Korea and Taiwan which apparently were constructed at less than the estimated cost of equivalent plants in the United States.[38]

Historical capital costs of major U.S. steel firms, consisting of depreciation and interest, appear to be lower than those of foreign integrated producers. This can be attributed to the traditionally lower debt leverage of American companies.[39] Depreciation and interest charges for American integrated producers ranged from $35 to $45, per ton shipped in 1982. For the German and Dutch steel firms, charges were from $40 to $55, but for other European steel firms and several of the large Japanese steel producers these costs were closer to $80 per ton.[40]

Recent plant construction and infrastructure problems have caused the burden of capital costs to be considerably higher for most steel firms in the developing world than for producers in advanced countries. In all likelihood, they vary from $90 per ton shipped for the integrated producers of South Korea and Taiwan,

to $120 for those of Brazil, and to $150 or $160 for newly con-
structed plants in Mexico and Venezuela.[41] For several plants
under construction in Brazil, Pakistan, and Nigeria capital costs
will be far higher, possibly reaching $300 per ton for simple carbon
steel products.

Total Production Costs.   In Table 9–12 various unit costs of major
operating inputs are compared for several steel industries from
advanced and developing countries. The data refer to the third
quarter of 1982. It is evident that employment costs account for
most of the advantage commanded by foreign industries. This
result will not change significantly when the remaining operating
costs, including scrap, are added to the list. It will be affected to
a considerable extent, however, when capital costs are likewise
taken into account. This is true, in particular, for integrated steel
production in the Third World.

These estimates should only be regarded as rough approximations. In the first place, the cost figures for foreign industries
fluctuate with exchange rates. A weakening of the dollar would
reduce the foreign producers' cost advantage with respect to in-

Table 9–12.   An International Comparison of Major Input Costs,
1982.

	Labor	Coking Coal & Iron Ore	Energy	Total	Difference from U.S. Cost
U.S.	234	103	72	409	zero
EEC	113	100	62	275	− 134
Japan	85	90	64	239	− 170
Brazil	80	95	65	240	− 169
S. Korea	37	90	66	193	− 216

Sources: Employment costs were calculated from hourly rates given in Table 9–11 and input
rates estimated from AISI, *Annual Statistical Report,* various years; Bureau of Labor Statistics,
unpublished data; Tekko Roren, *Rodo Handbook* (1981); and information obtained from the
Instituto Brasileiro de Siderurgia and the Grupo Industrial Alfa, Mexico.

Coking-coal and Iron-ore rates and costs were estimated from the standard industry sources;
rates per ton of hot metal were then transformed by the use of hot metal/raw steel and raw
steel/finished steel ratios estimated from IISI, *World Steel in Figures, 1983,* and German Steel
Federation, *Statistisches Jahrbuch, 1983,* p. 308.

Energy costs: author's estimates and Peter F. Marcus and Karlis M. Kirsis, *The Steel Strategist,*
Paine Webber Mitchell Hutchins, February 1984, Table 19.

puts that are not purchased at dollar-denominated prices in the world market, especially employment costs. Second, the data themselves are in some cases only approximations because reliable information is not publicly available for many inputs used in the steelmaking process. The information gap is especially large for the steel industries of the Third World. Third, there are substantial differences in the value of the product mix turned out by the various industries whose costs are being compared. Thus, the product mix of the U.S. steel industry is more valuable, probably by 2 to 3 percent, than those of the European and Japanese industries and somewhat more in relation to Third World industries.[42] Fourth, unit costs are computed with reference to the tonnage shipped in a given period. These costs are higher at low rates of capacity utilization, a recovery of the market and rise in utilization rates would thus result in lower unit costs.

Despite the foregoing reservations, total unit costs of the integrated U.S. producers substantially exceed those of their principal foreign competitors. Furthermore, because of the deficient structure and technological lag of many integrated U.S. steel plants and the continuing burden of high wage costs, there are no immediate prospects of a narrowing of these gaps short of a dramatic weakening of the dollar in international markets.

Other Factors Influencing Competitiveness.   In 1980 the International Trade Commission made a number of surveys, in connection with a major investigation of alleged dumping by European steel producers, to investigate why some American steel buyers had turned to foreign suppliers. The surveys covered the years 1977–1979. The reasons given by the buyers for switching sales from domestic sources to imports included the following: price, quality, alternative source of supply, and availability. Interestingly, lower price was not the foremost reason for the success of imported steel. Instead, it was availability, very likely because domestic sources were too remote from the purchaser or because delivery periods for domestic steel had become unduly long when temporary supply bottlenecks occurred in 1978 and the first half of 1979. Quality was also given as a reason in many instances, especially in the case of hot- and cold-rolled sheets. Only with respect to "angles, shapes, and sections," the category in which domestic minimills have become aggressive competitors, did lower prices account for more than 50 percent of the responses.

These findings were backed up by another survey, also conducted in 1980. The General Accounting Office, after contacting more than 100 domestic steel users, found that

> decisions to purchase foreign steel not only depend upon price considerations but also on quality, supply protection and marketing services and attitudes. In cases where consumers bought foreign steel, it was frequently because foreign mills performed better in many or all of these areas. . . . Most companies who criticized domestic steel quality pointed to Japanese steel as exemplary. The officials, however, identified high quality steel purchased from mills in 14 other countries. As a rule, the high quality was derived from more modern plants regardless of the country in which located.[43]

Foreign suppliers were said to be more responsive than the large domestic mills to customers' needs for new types of steel, and they delivered more consistently on time. Domestic minimills were also given high marks for excellent customer service.

GOVERNMENT-INDUSTRY RELATIONS

Most governments consider steel a strategic material. While they have demonstrated concern for an adequate and assured availability of steel products at all times, they have also imposed pricing controls on steel firms in order to reduce inflationary pressures. Moreover, because the steel industry is such a major employer in some regions, many governments have obliged firms to keep unneeded employees on and in return provided financial subsidies and protection from imports.[44]

There would be little to worry about if all interventions and support measures were of short duration. In fact, however, they are often retained longer than needed to deal with immediate problems, thus introducing lasting distortions into the working of the international market. If steel were a final good, the burden of intervention would fall primarily on the consumer. But steel is an intermediate good that is widely used in the manufacturing sector. Trade measures that raise the cost of steel impair the ability of steel-using firms (e.g., automobile producers) to compete in domestic and foreign markets. Long-term protection of steel industries is thus likely to impose a heavy cost burden on a country's metal-processing sector. In most nations, this sector adds more value and generates far more employment than the steel industry. Any policy that for a considerable period keeps the level of domestic steel prices significantly above the prices prevailing elsewhere will inevitably affect the international competitiveness of many manufacturing firms.[45] It may even lead to a shrinkage of domestic steel consumption by forcing steel consumers to close down their operations or to relocate them in countries where steel is consistently available at lower prices.

The various trade measures introduced in the United States— beginning with the late 1960s—were, as a rule, stop-gaps that failed to take into account the long-term consequences for the American steel-consuming sector and even on the steel industry itself. In particular, the "voluntary" restraint agreements with European and Japanese steel exporters (in effect from 1969 to 1974), the trigger-price mechanism (which during most of the period from 1978 to the beginning of 1982 put a de-facto price floor under most imports of carbon steel products), and the steel import quota of 1982 negotiated with the European Economic Community have caused steel prices in the United States to be above those prevailing in foreign steel markets.[46] These measures are in part responsible for the poor state of the U.S. balance of indirect steel trade, that is, trade in steel-containing goods.

In Europe several governments gave financial assistance to steel companies that were pushed to the brink of bankruptcy by the prolonged recession and the resulting severity of price competition in both home and export markets. However, because this assistance was not tied in a sufficiently resolute manner to the closure of surplus capacity, ruinous price competition and, hence, the companies' financial plight and need for further aid continued unabated.[47] In 1982 the EEC sought to resolve this problem by imposing mandatory production quotas and price controls on its industries.

It must be acknowledged, however, that the circumstances after 1974 during which several of those measures were taken, can only be called unique considering the length and depth of the recession that followed. Little will be gained, therefore, by explaining those events with the help of concepts and terms—such as fair or unfair methods of competition—that were conceived against the background of more normal conditions. The dispute that has arisen between American and foreign steel producers originates from differences in conduct during market downturns. Prior to the "internationalization" of the U.S. market, large American steel producers had been able to adhere to cost-plus pricing through good times and bad. They were abetted in this policy by social and economic conventions, that, unlike most other steel-producing countries, permit the massive layoff of workers during a recession. Among the foreign competitors, it has primarily been the various national steel industries of the EEC that—due to the diversity in managerial traditions and political institution—have often been unable to maintain price stability.[48]

As the number of countries exporting steel increased, market prices became extremely unstable. This price weakness spilled over into the U.S. market after imports developed a strong presence there, beginning in the mid-1960s. In 1968 and, again, in 1977 and 1982–1984, the time-honored pricing discipline among the large American producers broke down, in each case leading to a dramatic drop in profits and, soon afterward, demands for trade protection.

One might ask whether there is a need to protect U.S. steel producers from the vagaries and instability of the world steel market. There is, after all, little evidence that the industry took advantage of partial isolation from world market competition in the past to streamline its inefficient plant structure and invest in new technology. Indeed, after it obtained quota protection in 1969, the industry responded by greatly reducing its investment rate and by stepping up its diversification efforts. And the United Steelworkers saw in the trade protection only a further reason to stiffen their demands for wages and benefits without yielding ground in the area of work rules.[49]

If the public does respond favorably to pleas for protection from industry and labor, it should have the right to ascertain that the objectives of the policy are attained or, at least, approached. It has been suggested, for example, that public support for the steel industry should have been tied to a quid pro quo from the industry and the union in the areas of investments and productivity improvements.[50]

One reason favoring some degree of protection of a national steel industry (aside from defense considerations) is that steel is such an essential material for a large number of industries that a complete disruption of steel supplies could create havoc for the entire economy. The steel shortages during war periods and in the early 1970s, as well as the price gyrations in the international steel market, were sufficient justification for many developing countries to establish at least a core of steelmaking capacity, even at the cost of government assistance.

However, the infrequency with which supply bottlenecks have actually occurred in the world steel market speaks against the maintenance of uneconomic steelmaking capacity by means of protection or financial assistance. Reducing exposure to foreign competition would lower the incentive for management to modernize capacity and for labor to moderate demands for high wages and costly work rules. Such a policy would only cause those industries to fall further behind international norms of efficiency. In the final analysis, it is at least questionable whether the high (and rising) cost of protection or subsidization, to be borne by steel users or tax-payers, can be justified by the benefit of avoiding tight steel supplies during one year out of ten or perhaps only fifteen. An alternative and less expensive method for assuring stable steel supplies over the longer term might be a publicly supported program to stockpile semifinished products (billets, blooms, and slabs) and to retain excess rolling-mill capacity, that might otherwise be dismantled, for use during shortage periods.

CONCLUSION AND OUTLOOK FOR THE FUTURE

In most advanced countries, the steel market has been in a recession since the fall of 1974. The recession was preceded by three decades of almost uninterrupted expansion of steel capacity and output. Although considerable competition existed during much of this period, the market was strong enough to permit the survival of even relatively inefficient producers in the United States and Europe. The larger companies postponed major restructuring of their capital stock, and labor unions paid little attention to the effect their demands had on the companies' competitive position in the international market. When foreign competition became a major problem, the response was not an accelerated program of modernization and restraint by the unions but pleas for import controls (as in the United States) and for public financial assistance (as in several member countries of the EEC). Procrastination continued in the first years of the long recession, in part, because there were repeated signs—as in 1976 and again in 1978 and 1979—of an upturn in demand. A series of permanent plant closures took place in the late 1970s and early 1980s in the United States and and Europe. But a fundamental reassessment of the role of management, labor, and, in some cases, the public authorities occurred only in the 1980s.

The Japanese steel industry entered the recession with an excellent, although oversized, capital stock. There has been some retrenchment of capacity, but industry continues to invest heavily to achieve further productivity gains and improvements in product quality. In the Third World, steel consumption began to stagnate in 1982. But because many of the newly industrializing countries still depended heavily on foreign steel, they were able to increase steel production in their new mills by restricting imports. Eventually several of them became substantial exporters of steel but soon met with defensive trade restrictions, in the form of antidumping and countervailing duty litigation, in the United States, Europe, and elsewhere.

The U.S. steel industry appears to have lost its comparative advantage vis-à-vis the more efficient producers in Europe and Japan by the early or mid-1960s. Except for several years when the dollar was extremely weak, as from 1977 to 1980, the advantageous competitive position of European and Japanese producers remained fairly stable over nearly two decades. More recently, several steel firms from the developing world also gained a comparative advantage over the integrated U.S. producers, at least with respect to a few basic products.

What, then, are the chances for the integrated U.S. producers to improve their competitive position during the remainder of the 1980s? The integrated U.S. steel firms face a number of problems that can only be resolved by heavy investment expenditures. Given the companies' poor cash flow, the necessary investments would require more long-term borrowing. But the prospect of continuing high employment costs, a weak markets, and aggressive foreign competition as well as awareness of certain intransigent, almost ineradicable structural problems have acted (one should hope only temporarily) as a brake on the willingness of management to commit large sums to the revitalization of steel plants.

With or without intensive foreign competition, deep-seated structural problems will remain an Achilles heel for the integrated American steel companies. Geographical clustering of much integrated-steelmaking capacity in a few regions of the country has lowered the threshold foreign competitors need to overcome to penetrate U.S. markets. Thus, with total exporting costs (freight, tariff, interest, and harbor fees) to the Gulf coast amounting to, say, $70 per ton and shipping of steel from Pittsburgh or Chicago to the Gulf costing $40, foreign suppliers with coastal plants would need a cost advantage of only $30 to compete with the U.S. mills. By the same token, Japanese producers could compete on the Pacific coast of the United States even if their production costs were slightly higher than those of American firms located in the Pittsburgh-Chicago area.

But the lagging economic performance of the large American steel producers is not entirely a consequence of structural inadequacies. It is also attributable to management and labor attitudes that had become ingrained during the industry's earlier, prosperous era. Under pressure from the severe recession, these attitudes have undergone a certain amount of change. Management is more resolute than before in screening out unprofitable product lines and less reluctant in seeking technical assistance from outsiders, including foreign competitors. A new generation of managers did not hesitate to close down operations that could not be made profitable or press for concessions from labor regarding wages, fringe benefits, and work rules.

There is no reason why—with the appropriate commitment of owners and workers—the majority of integrated U.S. steel firms should not be fully competitive in their regional markets and in their chief product lines. But that will require a renewed investment effort as well as intensive cooperation by management and labor in the areas of productivity, costs, and product quality.

A policy of controlling foreign competition over the longer term is not likely to have salutary consequences for the U.S. economy or even the steel industry itself. By raising domestic steel prices above the prices prevailing elsewhere it would eventually jeopardize the growth, or even the survival, of metalworking firms that compete with foreign producers in domestic and foreign markets. The consequence would be an increasing deficit in the trade of steel-containing goods, the so called indirect steel trade. Politically, such a policy of isolating the domestic steel industry from foreign competition would trigger a chain reaction of claims for protection by metal-using industries, beginning with industrial fasteners, forgings, and steel-wire ropes and eventually spreading to steel containers, electricity towers, drilling platforms, and the like.[51] Such a policy may, therefore, not only lead to considerable distortions of this country's trade patterns, but it may ultimately reduce the domestic steel market to a greater extent than would occur if the market remained exposed to unrestricted foreign competition.

Any discussion of the future international competitiveness of American steel firms must also take into account the fortunes of foreign rivals. The latter are certain not to stand still while the domestic producers attempt to put their house in order. Needless to say, fluctuating exchange rates and unpredictable government policies here and abroad make it difficult to assess the expected competitive position of foreign steel producers in the world market.

The European steel industry possesses a number of highly efficient facilities. But it is also handicapped by the continued presence of obsolete and poorly located steelworks that, in part for political reasons, have not yet been closed down. Furthermore, by Japanese standards, many European mills are overstaffed, again, often for political reasons.

Under pressure from the supranational authority, the steel firms of the EEC are making considerable efforts to modernize their plants and trim off marginal facilities. They are likely to maintain a moderate technological lead over the integrated American steel firms. Nevertheless, in order to compete successfully with efficient steel producers from Japan and several developing countries, they must continue to modernize their capacity and thereby raise the productivity of their workforce.

The Japanese steel industry has managed so far to defend its superior competitive position in the world market against most of its foreign rivals, although the industry's advantage has varied with the rise and fall of the yen-dollar ratio.[52] Continued high annual investment outlays, aimed at achieving improved energy efficiency and product quality (as contrasted with the reduced investments by the EC and U.S. steel industries in recent years), are likely to fortify this position in the foreseeable future. Nevertheless, Japanese producers will remain under pressure to improve their performance as old competitors try to catch up and efficient new rivals vie for a greater share of the world market.

Statements about a comparative advantage of steel production in several developing countries—South Korea, Taiwan, and Brazil, in particular—must be interpreted with some caution. Although a number of mills in these countries can produce crude steel at a lower cost than many steel producers in the industrialized world, their advantage at the finishing level is limited to a few basic plate and sheet products. Moreover, they are considerably more modern than the integrated plants in other developing countries and therefore not representative of the state of steelmaking efficiency in the Third World. A number of steel mills in Asia and Latin America are poorly equipped, of suboptimal scale, and not capable of supplying the product quality demanded in advanced economies. When they are exporting significant quantities of steel, it is often because domestic price controls cause even low world-market prices to be attractive to them or because rigid employment policies discourage production cutbacks in a recession. In some instances, exports have been a method to utilize newly added capacity that, for reasons of economies of scale, temporarily exceeds domestic demand. In the immediate future, few major steel projects are likely to be started in the Third World. Many newly industrializing nations face severe adjustment problems due to excessive foreign indebtedness, while OPEC members suffer from stagnant or declining oil revenues.

Over the longer term more developing countries can be expected to gain a cost advantage over the industrialized nations with respect to some steel products. However, predictions of a massive shift of the comparative advantage in the production of carbon steels is shifting from the industrialized to the developing world will probably not be borne out.[53] What is likely to happen, instead, is that the circle of two-way trade in steel products will widen to include more and more Third World countries. The newly industrializing nations that developed an export capability in some products will continue to experience a need for other steel items that cannot yet be manufactured competitively by domestic producers.

The integrated segment of the U.S. steel industry will continue to be burdened by structural inefficiencies. But its fate is by no means sealed since many foreign rivals also fate problems that keep their performance below best-practice standards. Besides, with steel demand moving in the direction of more sophisticated, higher-quality products, the competitive position of national steel industries will tend to depend increasingly on innovative management and a skilled, dedicated workforce. Government policy of any description is likely to play a subordinate role in determining the outcome of international competition in the steel market.

NOTES

1. Council of Economic Advisors, *Report to the President on Steel Prices* (Washington, D.C.: U.S. Government Printing Office, April 1965), pp. 8–9; U.S. Senate, *Steel Imports*, 90th Congress, 1st Session (1967), p. 357.

2. William T. Hogan, *The 1970s: Critical Years for Steel* (Toronto: Lexington Books, 1972), pp. 11–32.

3. Walter Adams and Hans Mueller, "The Steel Industry," *The Structure of American Industry* (New York: Macmillan, 1982), pp. 103–109; Peter F. Marcus and Karlis M. Kirsis, *International Steel Price Analysis and Forecast*, Core Report S (New York: Paine Webber Mitchell Hutchins, December 1981).

4. Bureau of Labor Statistics, "Hourly Compensation Costs for Production Workers in Iron and Steel Manufacturing, 18 Countries, 1975–1982" (Unpublished Data, 1983).

5. Eurostat (Statistical Office of the European Community), *Iron and Yearbook 1976*, Tables 3 and II-2; International Iron and Steel Institute, *Steel: Statistical Yearbook, 1981*, pp. 2 and 23–24.

6. For capacities of the largest steel companies in 1960 see American Iron and Steel Institute, *Directory of Iron and Steel Works of the United States and Canada, 1960*, pp. 449–52; Louis Lister, *Europe's Coal and Steel Community* (New York: Twentieth Century Fund, 1960), pp. 151–52; Eurostat, *Iron and Steel, Yearbook 1960*, p. 10.
   For other characteristics of the largest steel companies in 1960 (output, employment, sales, profits, etc.) see *International Monetary Fund, The Largest Steel Companies in the Free World*, IMF Secretariat's Report to the Steelworkers' Conference in Duisburg, Germany, May 3–6, 1962.

7. Ervin Hexner, *The International Steel Cartel* (Chapel Hill: University of North Carolina Press, 1946), pp. 201–204, and George W. Stocking and Myron W. Watkins, *Cartels in Action* (New York: Twentieth Century Fund, 1946), p. 201.

8. Klaus Stegemann, *Price Competition and Output Adjustment in the European Steel Market* (Tubingen, Germany: Mohr, 1977), pp. 67–106; Henri Rieben, *La Bataille de l'Acier-L'Europe Siderurgique au Defi* (Lausanne: Centre de Recherches Europeenes, 1977), ch. V.

9. Peter M. Marcus, *Financial Analysis of International Steelmakers* (New York: Paine Webber Mitchell Hutchins, September 16, 1981), p. 9.

10. For a description of the agreement and an evaluation of its potential effects on the American steel market, see Hans Mueller and Hans van der Ven, "Perils in the Brussels-Washington Steel Pact of 1982," *The World Economy* 5, no. 3 (November 1982): 259–78.

11. In 1969 and 1970, for example, steel exports from the United States rose precipitously, especially to Western Europe where the supply situation had become very tight (OECD, *The Iron and Steel Industry in 1970 and Trends in 1971,* pp. 20, 80–81, and Eurostat, *Iron and Steel Yearbook,* 1976, pp. 138–42).
   On the nonsynchronization of international steel cycles during certain periods in the 1950s and 1960s, see Lennart Friden, *Instability in the International Steel Market* (Stockholm: Beckmans, 1972), pp. 180–82.

12. Federal Trade Commission, *The United States Steel Industry and Its International Rivals,* Washington, D.C., 1977, Chapter 3. For another comparative cost analysis also focusing on the 1960–1976 period, see Hans Mueller and Kiyoshi Kawahito, *Steel Industry Economics* (New York: Japan Steel Information Center, 1978), Ch. 3. For a cost analysis dealing with the years 1970–1976, see Council on Wage and Price Stability, *Report to the President on Prices and Costs in the United States Steel Industry* (Oct. 1977), pp. 140–42.

13. In 1983, the shares of some other countries of total U.S. steel imports were as follows: South Korea (10.1 percent), Brazil (7.4 percent), Spain (3.6 percent), South Africa (3.3 percent), and Argentina (1.7 percent).

14. High Authority, European Coal and Steel Community, *ECSC Factfinding Mission to U.S.A.—March-April 1957,* pp. 80–82.

15. *Business Week* (October 25, 1982), pp. 114–18.

16. Henry W. Broude, *Steel Decisions and the National Economy* (New Haven: Yale University Press, 1963), p. 165.

17. The rising cost of natural gas has led to the closure of nearly all direct-reduction plants in the United States. A large-scale merchant DR plant in Germany was shut down shortly after it went into production, while another new plant in Scotland was never started up.
   Total output of DR iron in 1982 was 8.2 million net tons (or less than 2 percent of the quantity of pig iron produced in blast fur-

naces). Of this amount, about 25 percent was produced in the industrialized nations. Venezuela and Mexico together accounted for 42 percent of the total.

18. Office of Technology Assessment (OTA), *Technology and Steel Industry Competitiveness* (June 1980), p. 290.
19. The capacity of integrated American steel plants is listed in Institute for Iron and Steel Studies (IISS), *Commentary* (January 1983), pp. 2–19.
   For a theoretical discussion of the minimum efficient size of integrated steel plants, see A. Cockerill, *The Steel Industry—International Comparisons of Industrial Structure and Performance* (London: Cambridge University Press, 1974), ch. VII.
20. Werner Baer, *The Development of the Brazilian Steel Industry* (Nashville: Vanderbilt University Press, 1969), pp. 79–83; William E. Cole, *Steel and Economic Growth in Mexico* (Austin: Texas University Press, 1967), pp. 7–22; and William A. Johnson, *The Steel Industry of India* (Cambridge, Mass.: Harvard University Press, 1966), pp. 188–89, 213, 303–304.
21. Norman Robins, "Steel Industry Research and Technology," *American Steel Industry Economics Journal* (April 1979): 49–58.
   Detailed accounts of the growth strategy followed by the Japanese steel industry can be found in Kiyoshi Kawahito, *The Japanese Steel Industry* (New York: Praeger, 1972); E. Kaplan, *Japan, The Government-Business Relationship* (Washington, D.C.: U.S. Department of Commerce, 1972), pp. 34–38 and 141; Luc Kiers, *The American Steel Industry: Problems, Challenges, Perspectives* (Boulder, Colo.: Westview Press, 1980), ch. 2 and Hogan, *The 1970s: Critical Years for Steel,* ch. 4.
22. Kenneth Warren, *World Steel* (New York: Crane, 1975), pp. 150–98.
23. *Ibid.*, pp. 228–42; Richard Boyce and Charles Ludolf, "The Structure of Steel Markets in the United States," U.S. Department of Commerce (October 1979). (Unpublished.)
24. Institute For Iron and Steel Studies, *Steel Industry in Brief: Japan* (Green Brook, N.J.: IISS, 1977), pp. 24–80. This study contains detailed descriptions, complete with location and layout maps, of all the large Japanese steelworks.
25. Despite the long haul of raw materials, Japanese steel producers enjoy far lower transport costs than most integrated U.S. steelmakers. The hauling distance for iron ore is almost three times greater for the Japanese, but because the ore can be shipped by sea in giant carriers of up to 250,000 tons, shipping costs to the blast furnaces were less than one-half of American freight costs, per ton of iron ore, in 1982.

26. Interviews by the author with government officials and steel executives from Brazil, Mexico, Venezuela, and Peru. See also Baer, *Brazilian Steel Industry,* pp. 68–69 and 91–92; Cole, *Steel and Economic Growth in Mexico,* pp. 26–27 and 148–50; Johnson, *The Steel Industry of India,* pp. 123–25; and Carl Liedholm, *The India Iron and Steel Industry* (East Lansing: Michigan State University, 1972), pp. 9–12 and 136.

27. From 1960 through 1980, the U.S. steel industry invested about $44.8 billion. Reducing this figure by a total of 35 percent to adjust for the higher wages of construction workers in the United States relative to Europe and Japan, and to account for larger U.S. investments in nonsteel operations as well as in coal and iron ore mines, leaves $26.9 billion in current dollars, or approximately $46.5 billion in constant 1978 dollars. Dividing the combined expansion and replacement tonnages into the (constant) dollar investment expenditures yields a figure of $517 per ton of capacity added or replaced for the U.S. industry. For the EC industry the figure is $443 and for that of Japan $476. (Annual investment data from United Nations, Economic Commission for Europe, *The Steel Market,* various years; for investments of the U.S. steel industry, 1950–1978, in 1978 dollars, less environmental and nonsteel expenditures, see OTA Report, *Technology and Steel Industry Competitiveness,* p. 123; the conversion of current values into constant 1978 dollar values was based on the European Community index for iron and steel capital-goods prices, reproduced in *European Coal and Steel Community, Investment in the Community Coalmining and Iron and Steel Industries* [Luxembourg] for the years 1965, 1975, and 1981.)

28. In 1980 periods allowing for cost recovery were very similar in the United States, Japan, and Germany (OTA Report, *Technology and Steel Industry Competitiveness,* p. 59). Since the 1981 changes in U.S. tax laws, this period is now shorter in this country than in Japan and in most countries of the European Community.

Concerning investments for environmental control, complete data are available only for the United States and Japan. From 1971 through 1983, U.S. steel producers spent $4,651 million dollars for this purpose. Japanese steel producers spent $4,982 million dollars during the same period (AISI, *Annual Statistical Report, 1983,* p. 10; and Japan Iron and Steel Federation, *Tekko Tokei Yoran,* various years). However, these totals conceal the fact that environmental expenditures by the U.S. steel industry have remained at the high level they attained in the mid-1970s, whereas Japanese expenditures fell greatly after the completion of the last major new plant in 1976.

29. Hogan, *The 1970s: Critical Years for Steel*, p. 34.

30. Annual Report of the Belgian Steel Federation, *La Sidcerurgie Belge en 1980*, p. 38. For example, in 1981 the freight charges for iron ore from Brazil to Antwerp or Rotterdam were $13.20 per metric ton for ships of 80,000 tons to 85,000 tons displacement, $8.40 for ships of 120,000 to 125,000 tons and only $6.60 for the largest ships of 200,000 to 250,000 tons. See also *Metal Bulletin*, "Freight Market," July 3, 1981, p. 33, and October 23, 1981, p. 35.

31. Peter F. Marcus and Karlis M. Kirsis, *Major Country Carbon Steel Price/Cost Assessments: 1969–1990*, Preliminary Core Report Q (New York: Paine Webber Mitchell Hutchins, September 198), 2–2, 3–2, and 4–2.

32. International Iron and Steel Institute, *Steel: Statistical Yearbook, 1980*, pp. 38, 41, and 42–43.

33. For a list of the Free World's minimills and a detailed description of many such mills see, "Mini-mill monographs," *A Supplement to Metal Bulletin Monthly* (December 1981).

34. Bureau of Labor Statistics, U.S. Department of Labor, "Hourly Compensation Costs for Production Workers in Iron and Steel Manufacturing, 17 Countries, 1975–1982", (Unpublished Data, 1982); American Iron and Steel Institute, *Steel Employment News*, (January 11, 1983).

35. The labor input rates for the Japanese steel industry include the workers of independent contractors. Japanese steel producers assign many tasks connected with maintenance, repairs, and the operation of ancillary facilities to such firms. In 1960 the number of workers employed by these contractors amounted to 36 percent of the steel industry's total number (both blue and white collar) of regular employees. This ratio increased to 48 percent in the mid-1970s and to 49 percent by 1980 (Tekko Roren, *Rodo Handbook*, various years). Steel firms cannot dismiss contract workers, they can only terminate the services of contracting firms.
Steel firms in the United States also contract out certain maintenance and repair jobs, but on a much smaller scale. Union leaders have put the number of "lost" jobs at 10 percent, a figure disputed by management as too high. The author's estimates of labor productivity in the U.S. steel industry in 1982 (see tables 9–7 and 9–11) are based on the assumption that the number of contract workers is 5 percent of the regular workforce. The number of contract workers in European steel plants seems to be negligible.

36. Bureau of Labor Statistics, U.S. Department of Labor, "International Comparisons of Productivity and Labor Costs in the Steel Industry; United States, Japan, France, Germany, United Kingdom,

1964 and 1972–82 (January 1984); Eurostat, *Iron and Steel Yearbook, 1983,* pp. 14, 70. Estimates for 1983 labor productivity in the U.S. and European steel industries were made by the author.

37. Federal Trade Commission, op. cit., ch. 6; British Iron and Steel Consumers' Council, *Cost Competitiveness in the ECSC Steel Industries, The Effects of Government Policies* (Richmond, England, 1981), pp. 2–10; and U.S. Department of Commerce, "Affirmative Counter-vailing Duty Determinations", vol. 47 *Federal Register* (September 7, 1982): 39303–95.

38. The lowest cost per ton of integrated capacity built in a developing nation seems to have been in South Korea with less than $600 (in 1980 dollars). This amount is similar to the cost of the Ogishima plant built in Japan in the mid-1970s. Other Japanese carbon steel plants cost less than $500 per capacity ton. A new plant in Brazil to produce semifinished products will cost $1,000 per capacity ton; if it were built to produce finished products, it would cost $1,600 to $1,700 per ton. Another Brazilian plant, Acominas, is likely to cost more than $2,500 per capacity ton by the time it is completed, as are several integrated plants being constructed in Nigeria, Algeria, and Lybia. See *Metal Bulletin,* November 20, 1979, p. 37, June 17, 1980, p. 37, January 9, 1981, p. 37, February 6, 1981, p. 29, and February 18, 1983, p. 27; *Siderurgia Latinoamericana,* November 1981, p. 20, December 1981, p. 19.

39. Putnam, Hayes, and Bartlett, *Economics of International Steel Trade.* A report prepared for the AISI (May 1977), Appendix, Exhibits A-11 and A-12; Marcus and Kirsis, *Major Country Carbon Steel Price/Cost Assessments,* pp. 2–2, 3–2, and 4–2.

40. Annual reports of major steel firms; and Peter F. Marcus and Karlis M. Kirsis, *Financial Dynamics of 52 International Steelmakers* (New York: Paine Webber Mitchell Hutchins, November 1982).

41. Calculated from the volume of total outstanding debt and current interest rates.

42. The U.S. steel industry produces far more tinplate, a relatively high-value and lower-yield product, than the European and Japanese industries. Furthermore, for the U.S. industry only shipment data are available for finished products. Unlike the production data reported by foreign industries, the American data contain several fabricated, and hence, lower-yield categories, such as finished wire products.

43. Comptroller General, Report to the Congress, *New Strategy Required for Aiding Distressed Steel Industry* (January 1981), pp. 3–1 and 3–6.

44. For accounts of public policy toward the steel industry and the steel market see Comptroller General, *New Strategy,* chs. 5, 6, and 7; OTA

Report, *Technology and Steel Industry Competitiveness,* ch. 2; Federal Trade Commission, Ch. 6; Adams and Mueller, "The Steel Industry," pp. 128–33; and J.E.S. Hayward, "Steel", in Raymond Vernon, ed., *Big Business and the State—Changing Relations in Western Europe* (Cambridge, Mass.: Harvard University Press, 1974), pp. 255–71.

45. See Robert W. Crandall, *The U.S. Steel Industry in Recurrent Crisis* (Washington, D.C.: Brookings, 1981), pp. 148–50; and Joel B. Dirlam and Hans Mueller, "Import Restraints and Reindustrialization: The Case of the U.S. Steel Industry," *Case Western Reserve Journal of International Law* 14, 3 (Summer 1982): 419–45.

46. It was only during the 1973–1974 worldwide steel boom that flexible international steel prices rose above the prices charged by U.S. steel firms that, until the spring of 1974, were subject to price controls imposed by the Nixon administration (Adams and Mueller, "The Steel Industry," pp. 105–109; and Peter F. Marcus and Karlis M. Kirsis, *Steel Pricing* [New York: Paine Webber Mitchell Hutchins, November 1979], pp. A3–41 to A3–53).

47. For an account of the recession in the EC steel market and the various supranational and national emergency measures to assist steel producers, see Etienne Davignon, "The Future of the European Steel Industry," *Annals of Public and Co-operative Economy* 51, no. 4 (December 1980): 507–19; David Dale Martin, "The Davignon Plan: Whither Competition Policy in the ECSC," *Antitrust Bulletin* XXIV (Winter 1979): 837–87; and William T. Hogan, *World Steel in the 1980s* (Lexington, Mass.: Lexington Books, 1983), pp. 47–49, 120, 130.

48. Hans Mueller, "The Policy of the European Coal and Steel Community toward Mergers and Agreements by Steel Companies," *Antitrust Bulletin* XIV (Summer 1969): 413–48; Adams and Mueller, "The Steel Industry," pp. 91–105; Stegemann, *Price Competition,* pp. 92–111; and Hayward, "Steel," ch. 12.

49. Investment outlays by the U.S. steel industry averaged $2,135 million in the three years (1966–1968) before the Voluntary Restraint Agreement (VRA) went into effect. In the years 1971 to 1973, that is, after the pact had been in force for some time, the average had dropped to $1,333 million (AISI, *Annual Statistical Report,* 1975, p. 9). The diversification movement among the integrated U.S. steel firms went into high gear in 1969, the year when the first VRA became effective. The history of this acquisition movement is described by William T. Hogan, *The 1970s: Critical Years for Steel* (Lexington, Mass.: Lexington Books, 1972), pp. 12–16.

50. Comptroller General, *New Strategy,* pp. 8–4 to 8–7, and Appendix

III; and OTA Report, *Technology and Steel Industry Competitiveness,* pp. 27–28.

51. *Iron Age,* July 17, 1978, pp. 24–30; *American Metal Market,* April 15, 1981, p. 1, and November 17, 1981, p. 1; Robert W. Crandall, "Steel Industry Productivity and Public Policy," in Walter H. Goldberg, ed., *Positive Adjustment to Structural Change: The Case of the Steel Industry* (Berlin: International Institute of Management, April 1982), pp. 136–37.

52. Nearly 35 percent of Japan's steelmaking costs are priced in terms of U.S. dollars (principally iron ore, coking coal, fuel oil, and some ferro alloys). This dampens the impact that exchange rate fluctuations have on Japanese production costs measured in dollars.

53. The view that the comparative advantage in carbon-steel production is shifting from industrialized to developing countries is expressed by Frank Wolter, "Perspectives for the International Location of the Steel Industry," Working Paper No. 60, World Trade Institute of Kiel University, Germany (October 1977), especially pages 19–21, and Robert W. Crandall, *The U.S. Steel Industry in Recurrent Crisis,* p. 151.

10 THE U.S. TEXTILE INDUSTRY International Challenges and Strategies

Jeffrey S. Arpan
Brian Toyne

Although a general weakening in the international competitiveness of several U.S. industries spans several decades, the situation became particularly evident and critical in the 1970s. Just as the previously discussed auto and steel industries, apparel, chemicals, electronics, and textiles are but a few of the sectors that have seen their domestic and international competitive positions erode.

The principal reasons put forward to explain this deterioration in competitiveness reflect the complexity of the problems confronting U.S. industries. They include charges of "unfair competition"; the restructuring of entire industries as a result of government intervention; declines in the quality of U.S. products, productivity, and technological innovativeness; escalations in the cost of energy; lack of an international orientation and awareness among the ranks of U.S. management and a bias toward short-term profits and goals at the expense of long-term objectives; and inconsistencies in the domestic and foreign commercial policies of the U.S. government.

This essay identifies ways to increase the future international competitiveness of the U.S. textile industry. In the course of our

The authors wish to acknowledge the other principal members of the team which conducted the research project on which this chapter was based: David Ricks and Terence Shimp of the University of South Carolina, and Andy Barnett of Auburn University.

study, we have analyzed (1) critical changes that directly and indirectly affect the global and domestic competitive environments of the industry; (2) strategies that U.S. and foreign competitors and their governments are using or developing; (3) future strengths and weaknesses of the U.S. textile industry with regard to international competitiveness; and (4) policy changes the U.S. government should consider implementing to encourage the participation of the United States in the world textile market.

The major focus of our investigation was directed at European, Asia Pacific, and U.S. textile manufacturers because these industries and the intervention policies of their governments have shaped the competitive environment of the global market for several decades. Particular attention was given to the economic, political, technological, and competitive adjustments undertaken by the industries of West Germany, France, Italy, the Netherlands, United Kingdom, Taiwan, and Japan. The Taiwanese and Japanese industries were chosen for study because their adjustment strategies differ substantially from one another and from those of the European and U.S. industries. In addition, they are unlike the industries of most other Asia Pacific countries in that they can be classified as mature, technologically advanced, and highly sophisticated in their international operations. They also pose a considerable competitive threat to U.S. textiles.

The European industries were selected for onsite investigation because they have had to make more rapid competitive adjustments than most other national industries. Consequently, the strategic adjustments these industries have made and the political options implemented by their governments can be used as guidelines for the United States and can provide information on what policies and strategies have and have not been successful, and why.

THE TEXTILE COMPLEX

The textile complex is involved in the production of natural and man-made fibers and their conversion into apparel, home furnishings, and industrial goods. (See Figure 10–1.) Natural and man-made fibers, chemicals, and textile machinery are essential inputs in the making of textile products. These inputs are produced by other industrial complexes, which often have specialized segments

Figure 10-1. The Textile Complex.

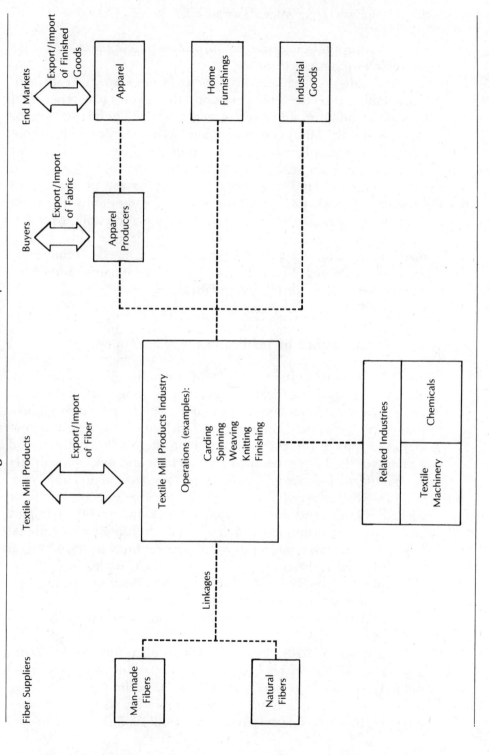

dependent upon the textile mill products and apparel industries for their economic prosperity.

The textile mill segment manufactures the yarns, threads, and fabrics and is directly dependent upon the apparel (the other chief employer)and home-furnishings, and industrial-goods sectors for their prosperity. Many countries manufacture textile products, but most lack the supply and demand conditions necessary to support entire textile complexes. In addition, not all countries are endowed with the land or climate required for the production of agricultural goods such as cotton and wool; some countries do not have the indigenous technological or financial capabilities to develop and support chemical complexes capable of producing man-made fibers; others lack the necessary internal markets required to achieve economies of scale in the production of man-made fibers, chemicals, and "mature" textile fabrics.

Importance of Textiles to the U.S. Economy

As of 1981 there were over 25,000 firms in the U.S. textile complex, with at least one located in every state. Together, these firms employ over 2.2 million workers, making textiles the largest industrial employer in the United States. One out of every eight manufacturing jobs in the United States is in the textile complex, and it is one of the largest employers of women and minority workers in manufacturing. In addition, it has been estimated that over 925,000 workers *outside* the textile complex are dependent on it for their livelihood, and that the capital expenditures by the complex and its principal suppliers require tens of thousands of additional jobs—a total additional employment generation of nearly 1 million workers. Finally, the combined output of the complex in 1980 was $114 billion, roughly one-half of which was delivered to final demand and intermediate demand *outside* the complex. Thus the direct and indirect impact of the textile complex on the U.S. economy is substantial.

Since the mid-1970s, the textile mill products industry has annually spent $7 billion on building materials and machines, $900 million on chemicals and dyestuffs, $500 million on paper products, and $100 million on warehousing and transportation. During the 1970s, this sector invested a total of $11 billion in new plants and equipment. Capital expenditures in 1980 alone amounted to $1.5 billion.

Figure 10–1 depicts the major linkages among key segments of the textile complex. In the case of the United States, the manmade fiber industry is dependent on sales to the textile mill and apparel industries for 99 percent of its output and cotton producers for 53.6 percent of their output. In terms of total fiber (natural and manmade) consumed, apparel absorbs more than 40 percent, home furnishings over 32 percent, industrial goods about 23 percent, and exports about 4 percent. While this ratio has been declining for apparel in recent years, the ratios for home furnishings, industrial goods, and exports have increased (though exports began declining in the early 1980s).

Vulnerability of Industry's End-Use Markets to Foreign Competition

Of the three major end-use markets supplied by the U.S. textile industry, the apparel market is the largest, yet most vulnerable. As shown in Figure 10–1, the home-furnishings and industrial-goods markets are supplied directly by the industry. Perhaps surprisingly, these markets are not as seriously threatened by foreign competition because of their rather unique features. For example, the U.S. textile mill products industry has led the world in turning the home-furnishings market into a fashion market, and in 1982 had a cost advantage in long production runs.

On the other hand, the apparel market is indirectly supplied by the industry, being directly dependent upon an apparel industry that has experienced considerable and increasing direct competition from low-cost Asian apparel producers and indirect competition from large retailers who have been purchasing apparel from contracted foreign apparel producers.

Between 1974 and 1979, the value of apparel imports increased by more than 140 percent, while domestic shipments increased by only 50 percent. In addition, foreign penetration into the U.S. apparel market has not been uniform. The compounded annual growth rate of imports in the 1974–1979 period for men's and boys' shirts and nightwear was 26 percent, for women's and misses' suits and coats 25 percent, for men's and boys' trousers 21 percent, and for women's and misses' blouses and shirts 20 percent.[1]

A recent study of the U.S. apparel industry identified several reasons for the industry's inability to compete successfully with foreign competitors, and including the following points:

1. The U.S. apparel industry is highly labor-intensive and is primarily made up of a large number of small and privately held firms (about 15,000) with limited management skills, resources and low profits. Although somewhat protected by tariffs and quotas, the U.S. apparel industry must compete with the low-wage industries of other, primarily Asian, countries, and the more marketing-oriented industries of Europe.

2. There has been considerably less replacement of labor with capital in apparel manufacture than in other industries. This is partly the result of the size of the firms in the industry (resources and profits), and partly the lack of technological innovation (virtually no R&D is undertaken by the industry).

3. Most smaller firms are managed by persons with experience in production or engineering. As a result, these managers are more production- oriented (inward-looking) than marketing-oriented (outward-looking). Because success in the apparel business is significantly dependent on good market judgment, this inward, production orientation has often proved to be a serious handicap.[2]

This inability of the U.S. apparel industry to modernize and remain internationally competitive seriously threatens the future growth of domestic apparel fabric sales. One alternative for the U.S. textile mill products industry is to encourage and assist apparel manufactures in modernizing their operations. However, the extent to which the U.S. textile industry can be of assistance is limited because of the structural characteristics of the U.S. apparel industry and government regulations.

Another possibility is for the U.S. textile mill products industry to increase its export activities. But this strategy is hindered by the industry's lack of an export orientation and inadequate management and marketing expertise necessary for success in foreign markets. The industry is also hampered by U.S. tariff and quota regulations that penalize apparel fabrics sold to overseas apparel producers for eventual sale in the U.S. market (e.g., uncut cloth is not covered by Item 807 of the U.S. Tariff Schedules which permits duty-free reentry).

STRATEGIC ADJUSTMENT IN TEXTILE MILL PRODUCTS INDUSTRIES

The competitive environment for textile mill products in both industrialized and developing countries has undergone considerable adjustment since World War II. Resultant pressures for industry adjustment in Europe and the United States are due to five major forces: (1) the formation of the European Economic Community in the late 1950s and the dismantling of trade barriers among member nations; (2) the trade liberalization movement of the 1960s and 1970s (e.g., Dillon, Kennedy, and Tokyo tariff rounds) that not only stimulated textile trade among industrialized countries, but also stimulated textile trade from low-wage countries; (3) the increasingly more sophisticated competition from these low-wage countries, particularly in high volume, low-cost textiles and apparel; (4) the slow-down in the growth of textile consumption in industrialized countries and the increase in the growth of textile consumption in other regions of the world; and (5) the competition for labor from other industries that offered higher wages and better working conditions.

Japanese and Taiwanese textile industries were also pressured into adjustment as they matured by stiffening market barriers imposed first by the United States and then by the European countries.[3] They were also challenged by other, even lower-cost developing countries, such as the Philippines and Indonesia, that were pursuing their own industrialization and economic goals. And like European industries they had to increasingly compete with other sectors for labor.

The Major Adjustment Strategies Adopted by Textile Mill Products Industries

As a result of these post-World War II pressures, the textile industries in both industrialized and developing countries experienced

270 REVITALIZING AMERICAN INDUSTRY

growing pressure for structural adjustment, technological change, political action, and competitive response. These structural and political changes and the competitive options adopted by the various national industries have had an impact on their international competitiveness and are partially reflected in the international trade patterns for textiles.

Adjustments appear to have been based on several major strategic options: tariff and nontariff protection measures; minimization of production costs through modernization of equipment and plants or the exploitation of international wage differences (e.g., foreign manufacturing); product specialization; increased emphasis on marketing; unplanned and planned industry restructuring; and internationalization (e.g., foreign direct investments and contractual arrangements). National industries eventually pursued a combination of strategies. However, national conditions such as domestic market size, international perspective, and stage of industrialization imposed limitations on the single and combined effectiveness of these options.

Unlike the U.S. textile industry, which has large, diverse, and high-consumption domestic markets for apparel, home furnishings, and industrial goods, the economic success of most other textile industries are highly dependent on their abilities to compete for a market share in regional or world markets. Consequently, they are generally "outward-looking," aggressive, and committed to enhancing their international competitiveness. They view foreign markets as natural extensions of their domestic markets and do not hesitate taking the competitive steps necessary to maintain or increase their shares in these markets. On the other hand, the U.S. textile mill products industry has traditionally been more concerned with its domestic market and the competition that prevails there. Most initiatives undertaken by the majority of U.S. textile companies have been designed to enhance domestic, not international, competitiveness.

The next section briefly traces and evaluates the evolving competitive strategies of eight national industries during the 1960s and 1970s. We will focus on the identification of environmental trends and strategy responses that have implications for the future international competitiveness of the U.S. industry and that need to be considered when developing strategy recommendations for this industry.

West Germany

With the formation of the European Economic Community (EEC), the West German textile and apparel industries were faced with heightened intracommunity competition but were protected from low-cost imports from developing countries. Germany reacted to this competition in the early 1960s by consolidating vertically and horizontally to exploit economies of scale and achieve market power. Major investments were made to intensify capital and larger firms adopted an undifferentiated strategy[4] by concentrating on the production of standardized fabric and clothing.

During the late 1970s, the larger textile firms switched from an undifferentiated to a differentiated strategy. This has resulted in smaller production units, more flexible production, substantial exports, and an emphasis on modern technology. The industry also supports industrial research encouraged by the federal and land governments. Offshore manufacturing, usually in Eastern European countries, is used extensively. The success of this more recent differentiated strategy is noteworthy.

The West German textile industry continues to be a strong supporter of free-market principles (except for imports from Hong Kong, Taiwan, Korea, and Brazil) and does not believe that the federal government (or any government) should subsidize the industry. However, survival probably has been helped by free-trade oriented trade unions that the industry regards as enlightened and cooperative, by an economy that was able to absorb a large number of redundant textile and apparel workers,[5] by local government assistance, and by banks.

Italy

Throughout the 1960s, Italy's textile industry was the principal beneficiary of the rapid growth in demand for textiles within the EEC. Italy's competitive success was the result of the development of a concentrated strategy and unique structural development in the private sector that fostered the development of a cooperative "cottage industry" structure for production and eventually marketing.

The development of cooperative, small-scale production units was the result of political conditions in Italy, the presence of a strong trade-union movement to preserve employment regardless of the cost involved, and certain peculiarities in the Italian labor market that resulted in the extensive use of low-cost, "underground" labor.

The reorganization of vertically integrated operations into small-scale production units started in the 1950s in response to surplus capacity and trade unions. The union movement pressured the government and large firms to preserve employment but with two contradictory results. The public sector's response was the nationalization of large textile firms at great public expense,[6] while the private sector's decentralized operations and employed "underground" workers.

The worldwide recession in the mid-1970s actually accelerated the restructuring process started earlier. The Italian industry is now an aggressive international competitor in quality synthetics and high-fashion designs. It is supported by highly specialized, yet vertically cooperative production units that benefit from their ability to make product changes quickly and to upgrade technology without greatly affecting production.

France

The French textile industry's adjustment to the competitive changes of the 1960s and 1970s was not as successful as those of West Germany and Italy. The French government has been a persistent supporter of the industry's demands for heavy protection against extra-EEC, low-cost imports. It pushed hard for the renewal of the Multi-Fiber Arrangement and the strengthening of its restrictive clauses. In order to justify this position on extra-EEC competition, the government argued that its textile industry was scattered and antiquated, modernization was only starting, and the industry needed protection until this process was completed.

The industry also went through a process of mergers that had the backing of the French government. It was thought that larger firms would be more capable of upgrading the industry's technology and thereby increase its competitiveness. Although the process of consolidation has resulted in a high degree of concentration, it is lopsided. While a small number of large and powerful groups have emerged that are technologically advanced, much of the industry remains fragmented and technologically backward. In addition, the large French firms often lack the flexibility to keep abreast of rapidly changing market conditions. This is in sharp contrast to the more even, technologically advanced, and flexible West German industry, and the highly specialized, efficient, and market responsive Italian industry.

The French textile industry concentrated on technological superiority and on improving production at the expense of developing marketing-based strategies similar to those of West Germany and Italy. France is also dependent upon a distribution system that is increasingly prone to imported textiles, while preserving its initiative in design and marketing.

United Kingdom

The lackluster performance of the British textile industry relative to other EEC countries during the 1960s and 1970s can be traced to the strategic option initially selected and the method used for its implementation: development of an undifferentiated strategy concentrating on standard cotton fabrics protected from low-cost imports.

The undifferentiated strategy pursued by Courtaulds and other large textile groups formed in the 1960s required vertical and horizontal integration and modernization. The goal was to displace low-cost Commonwealth suppliers who had been gaining an increasing share of the cotton markets since before 1960. It was believed that the economies of scale and market power achieved as a result of consolidation and modernization would reduce costs sufficiently to make domestically produced textiles competitive with imports in an open market.

However, by the early 1970s it became clear that the strategy was not a complete success. Although some mass-produced, standardized textiles were competing with low-cost imports domestically and in other EEC markets, a Commonwealth tariff was introduced in the early 1970s and extended to include manmade fibers in the mid-1970s.

Currently, the British industry has well-developed, technically advanced, competitive sectors that cover all aspects of textile manufacturing. It is strongly influenced by vertically and horizontally integrated firms that operate in many sectors: one manmade fiber producer (Courtaulds) and two textile mill companies (Tootals and Carrington) have integrated forward into retailing.

The Netherlands

Severe decline of the Dutch textile and apparel industries led to the adjustment strategies implemented by firms and the government in the 1960s and 1970s. Between 1973 and 1978, for example, employment in the textile industry declined by 40 percent, or from 58,700 to 35,200 workers; in the apparel industry, the labor force dropped from 40,200 to 19,800 persons. Over the same period, the number of apparel firms decreased from 446 to 349.[7]

The differentiated strategy pursued by textile companies and supported by government programs designed to aid displaced workers was based on free- market principles, comparative advantage, and a minimum of artificial supports. Inefficient firms were allowed to disappear or be taken over by stronger ones. The survivors are now helped by the Dutch government to improve planning and efficiency and to upgrade the range of production. Market research is also provided by the government together with certain policies aimed at encouraging exports.

Taiwan

The development of the Taiwan textile complex is typical of of policies by other newly industrialized countries (NICs): first, development of an apparel industry initially designed to replace imports, then the setting-up of a closely linked textile fabric industry, and finally the establishment of a manmade fiber industry. In the case of Taiwan, this development process was initiated by the government in the early 1950s and later aided by Japanese foreign investments and transfers of technology.

An undifferentiated strategy was pursued during the 1950s to the late 1970s in high-volume, low- to medium-priced apparel and textiles for local and foreign markets. Exports expanded rapidly in the 1960s as Japanese textiles and apparel lost competitiveness. By 1980, Taiwanese exports amounted to $100 million in fibers, $1.8 billion in yarns and fabrics, and $2.4 billion in apparel.[8] The United States was the most important foreign market for apparel, and Hong Kong, Japan, an Singapore for yarns and fibers.

To succeed, this strategy depended on three critical factors, two of which changed considerably between the 1950s and 1970s, and the third of which failed to materialize: (1) the continued expansion of export markets; (2) the availability of low-cost labor; and (3) the willingness of small Chinese apparel and textile firms to merge into larger groups.

In reaction to these strategies, and the reluctance of Chinese firms to merge into vertically integrated groups, the Taiwanese government's Council for Economic Planning and Development adopted a differentiated strategy and announced plans in 1980 to (1) consolidate the industry into larger groups as a result of new incentives; (2) increase productivity; (3) upgrade the quality and value-added of apparel and textile exports; and (4) diversify into higher-growth markets. Large investments in labor-saving machinery were also planned to replace departing workers.

Japan

Shortly after World War II, the Japanese textile industry adopted an undifferentiated strategy and emerged as the first major Asian source for high-volume, low- to medium-priced apparel and textiles. Although the initial development of the Japanese textile complex was similar to the process described for the Taiwanese complex, several important differences emerged that influenced subsequent adjustment strategies. First, the sequential development of apparel, then textiles, and finally fibers resulted in a dualistic complex dominated by a few totally linked (ownership and contractual) textile groups (e.g., Toray, Teijin). Second, Japan experienced labor shortages and resulting wage increases long before other Asia Pacific countries. Third, Taiwan, Thailand, and South Korea, and more recently mainland China embarked on the sequential development of textile complexes that threatened to displace Japanese exports to those countries and erode its competitiveness in European and U.S. markets. Finally, the U.S.-Japan textile agreement of 1971 severely restricted Japanese exports to the United States, and the system of preferential tariffs enacted by Europe about the same time gave developing countries other than Japan relatively easier access to the markets of industrialized countries.

Unlike the industrialized countries of Europe and the United States, Japan could not react defensively by imposing additional quota restrictions (although non-tariff barriers increased substantially). Also, the markets up on which Japan depended were the same markets being penetrated by its Asia Pacific competitors. To counter this problem, several of the major Japanese textile groups embarked on a strategy of internationalization through foreign direct investments (FDI) in Asia Pacific countries that threatened its export markets.[9]

These investments, combined with Japan's extensive network of contractual arrangements, are an important force in the development and growth of textile complexes in the Asia Pacific region. For example, the manufacture of synthetic fabrics in many Asia Pacific countries was initiated as a result of Japanese investments and technological transfers. Also, Japan's joint ventures still control most of the synthetic fiber sector of the entire region.

In addition to adopting an internationalization strategy to maintain markets in the Asia Pacific region and to gain better access to industrialized countries, the Japanese industry also undertook strategies to assure its regional superiority in technology and the production of synthetic and blended fabrics and apparel. Japan also adopted or adapted new forms of business operation, including the management of overseas production and international logistics, and more recently, marketing research and design.

Japan's current approach appears to be twofold: (1) improve the technologies of apparel and textile production in order to increase productivity and fabric quality, and decrease its dependency on labor, and (2) emphasize high value-added apparel and textiles through marketing research and the development of the Asia Pacific area as a fashion center.

Thus there has been a marked shift by Japanese textile companies away from an undifferentiated to a differentiated strategy. To gain comparative strength in segmented markets, Japanese firms are emphasizing the substitution of capital for labor and superior process technology. They are also aided by the forward integration of fiber companies into fabrics and contractual arrangements with other fabric and apparel companies. Along with their recent emphasis on sophisticated fibers and fabrics developed to meet the demands of domestic and foreign consumers, these strategies are providing Japan with competitive advantages over smaller and less market-oriented firms.

The United States

Compared to the adjustment responses of textile industries in Europe and the Asia Pacific area between 1960 and 1980, the U.S. industry's response has been less marked and more gradual. The only government involvement in the adjustment has been in the form of high tariffs to protect U.S. textiles from the imports of industrialized countries, and a combination of tariffs and increasingly stiff quotas to protect it from the low-cost imports of developing countries and Japan.

Unlike the European industries, American firms have not been forced to make the types of adjustments required by a redefinition of competition arising from the formation of the Common Market. Nor have they been faced as extensively with the kinds of competitive threats that the newly emerging textile industries of developing countries posed for the maturing Taiwanese and Japanese industries, due primarily to the vast size of the U.S. market. The United States has a very large and diverse domestic market that consumes about 20 percent of the world's textile output. It was also the leader in the introduction of manmade fibers and apparel. As a result of these factors, the U.S. industry has been comparatively insulated from international developments, and its adjustments were primarily due to internal changes in the domestic competitive environment.

Although the U.S. market's tastes are sophisticated, a high degree of product standardization is possible because of the market's size. The U.S. industry was thus able to concentrate on an undifferentiated strategy in the 1950s and early 1960s, resulting in horizontal and vertical integration within the textile mill sector. Mills became larger, highly rationalized, and emphasized the economics of long production runs of a relatively limited number of fabrics.

This undifferentiated strategy of the 1960s and early 1970s gradually gave way to a strategy that combined the cost-reducing, undifferentiated approach with a proliferated strategy. The industry led the world in promoting synthetic and blended fabrics in the 1960s and 1970s and turned home furnishings into a fashion market in the 1970s. There are also signs that the industry is shifting from large, fully integrated mills to smaller, more flexible, and more specialized mills as a result of this new strategy.

Cross-National Comparison of Adjustment Strategies

Clearly there are many elements common to the adjustment strategies undertaken by European, Asia Pacific, and U.S. textiles industries. Some of the more significant and easily discernible points of comparison include:

1. All countries have used protectionistic measures (tariff and nontariff restrictions) against imports;
2. All countries, industrialized and developing, have sought to reduce the impact of wage increases with productivity increases and strategies that minimized wage increases (e.g., use of immigrant labor in the European Community, and offshore investments by Japan and increasingly by South Korea);
3. All industrialized and maturing developing countries have sought some degree of specialization at the company or national levels (proliferation or differentiated strategies);
4. All countries have sought to vertically and/or horizontally integrate or link (through contractual arrangements, communications) their textile complexes, except for the Netherlands and the United States;
5. All countries have sought to upgrade their technologies and their manufacturing processes.

The results, however, have been quite mixed when measured in terms of performance and international competitiveness. Of the European countries, West Germany and Italy emerged as the most successful at the close of the 1970s, and France and the United Kingdom as the least successful. Taiwan and Japan[10] emerged as highly successful international competitors in terms of productivity and costs in certain product areas.

The reasons for this variation in industry performance and international competitiveness are many and complex. The more significant ones include: (1) the international scope of each industry's competitive environment; (2) the speed at which change occurred in this environment; (3) the adjustment strategy or strategies selected to cope with this change; and (4) the emphasis placed on particular elements of the selected adjustment strategies.

The next section addresses these major differences in order to identify underlying trends that may have significant implications for the international competitiveness of the U.S. textile industry in the 1980s.

IMPLICATIONS FOR THE U.S. TEXTILE MILL PRODUCTS INDUSTRY

America's textile industry, insulated from the relatively more dynamic international competitive environment, adjusted more slowly to competitive change than did European and mature Asia Pacific industries. However, the domestic market was large, competitive, and diverse enough, and textile mill companies strong and numerous enough to ensure that its adjustment was in the same direction as that of other textile industries: that is, favoring greater productivity and the replacing labor with capital. The U.S. industry entered the 1980s as a recognized world leader in productivity and the lowest-cost producer of textiles among industrialized countries (although this lead was eroding in the first years of the decade),[11] but it is not clear whether this superiority is sufficient to make it a leading international competitor in the future. There are several reasons for this concern:

1. The domestic rate of growth of textile demand, particularly in apparel fabrics, has declined considerably in recent years, yet the rate of growth of apparel imports has increased. This trend will increase pressures for further adjustment, probably through even greater specialization and heightened protection.
2. The successful European and Asia Pacific industries have already adopted strategies that emphasize specialization in

fibers and fabrics. This is not the case for U.S. industry: specialization is still overshadowed by an undifferentiated strategy. This suggests that the U.S. industry will be faced with foreign competition in domestic and overseas markets that are increasingly more specialized and narrow, yet highly sophisticated in meeting the demands of many market segments.

3. Capital expenditures by the U.S. textile industry, while increasing rapidly in absolute terms, continue to fall behind the capital expenditures of all U.S. manufacturing, and behind the capital expenditures of other textile industries (measured in terms of output). A possible outcome of this trend, if it continues, is a relative decline in the productivity of the industry. As Table 10-1 shows, labor productivity in the textile industries of other countries has increased considerably vis-à-vis the United States.

4. The declining value of the U.S. dollar, which aided the U.S. textile industry during the 1970s, was a lengthy adjustment to the over-valued dollar of the 1950s and 1960s. Dollar ex-

Table 10–1. Wage, Productivity, and Labor Costs Indices for Textiles: 1962, 1969, 1979 (1969 = 100).

	Wages (U.S. $)		Labor Productivity[a]		Unit-Labor Costs (U.S.$)	
	1962	1979	1962	1979	1962	1979
European Economic Community	55	500	70	200	75	250
United Kingdom	70	350	80	140	75	250
United States	70	200	90	140	80	140
Japan	35	700	70	190	50	350
South Korea	90	400	60	200	150	200

a. *American Textile Mfrs. Institute and U.S. Bureau of Labor* data indicate that U.S. productivity increased 49 percent between 1969 and 1979. The discrepancy is probably due to the different data bases used. The indices shown in the table are based on OECD and Int Labor Org. data, and were used to reduce problems normally encountered when comparing national statistics. It is just as conceivable that the productivity increases for the other countries are also understated.

Source: Geoffrey Shephard, *Textile Industry Adjustment in Developed Countries,* Thames Essay No. 30, Trade Policy Research Centre (London, 1981), Table 3.2.

change rates cannot be expected to favor the U.S. industry to the same extent during the 1980s.

5. Finally, foreign industries are well along in the process of rationalization of the worldwide production of textiles,[12] a process that U.S. industry has not participated in. The formation of the European Community forced European textile industries to rationalize, and the emergence of new, low-cost industries in Latin America and the Asia Pacific area has done the same for Taiwan, Japan, South Korea, and other NICs.

Much can be learned from the adjustment strategies of other industries that should be of value to the United States in meeting the challenges of the 1980s. These strategies are shown in Table 10–2.

The undifferentiated strategy (production of standardized fabrics) followed by West Germany and Japan in the 1960s, the United Kingdom and Taiwan from 1960 to 1980, and France in the 1970s failed to provide these industries with international viability. America's undifferentiated strategy succeeded in both decades primarily because of the size of its domestic market.

The reasons for failure of the undifferentiated strategy included: (1) an inadequate market base; (2) inherent inflexibility; and (3) the continued emergence of lower-cost industries. The United Kingdom failed in this strategy because of a wrongly focused emphasis on domestically displacing low-cost imports by developing countries of the Commonwealth. The combination of low U.K. wages (about two-thirds of those of other EEC countries) and an emphasis on the production-oriented use of technology were not sufficient to offset the favorable wage differential enjoyed by developing countries.

The earlier strategies adopted by West Germany, and eventually France, failed because they depended for success on large and stable markets. The European situation in the 1960s and 1970s required flexibility in production, something that the mass-market strategy inherently lacks, in order to adjust simultaneously to the mounting pressures for rationalizing the EEC textile industry and to the rapid changes occurring in manmade fiber and blended fabrics.

The concentrated and differentiated strategies—based on finding or creating market segments—provided those industries

Table 10–2. Adjustment Strategies of Textile Industries in the 1960s and 1970s.

Strategies of the 1960s		Strategies of the 1970s	
Homogeneous Market Undifferentiated	*Heterogeneous Market Concentrated*	*Homogeneous Market Undifferentiated*	*Heterogeneous Market Concentrated*
Japan Taiwan United Kingdom (largest firms) United States West Germany (majority of larger firms)	Italy (many firms were shifting to this strategy and away from proliferated or differentiated strategies)	France (larger firms) Japan (through foreign direct investment) Taiwan (plans to shift to a differentiated strategy in the 1980s) United Kingdom (larger firms)	Italy (high value segment)
Proliferated United Kingdom France[a]	*Differentiated* Netherlands West Germany (minority of larger firms)	*Proliferated* United States (still overshadowed to some extent by an undifferentiated strategy)	*Differentiated* Japan (many segments) Netherlands (few segments) West Germany United Kingdom (recent shift to a low value-segment strategy)

a. In the 1960s, France pursued a strategy that emphasized technological superiority.

that adopted them with international viability. The differentiated strategies of West Germany in the 1970s, Italy in the 1960s and 1970s, and Taiwan for the 1980s emphasized productive flexibility, advanced technology, a marketing orientation, and a strong export orientation. Italy and Taiwan also emphasized the development of linkages (cooperative or ownership) with their fiber and end-market sectors. The Japanese textile industry was unique in its development of an approach that combined the undifferentiated and differentiated strategies through an internationalization process that emphasized the rationalization of production.

The United States was the only industrial country to emerge from the 1970s with a successful undifferentiated strategy with regard to textiles. Yet, it increasingly adopted a new strategy in the late 1970s as a result of domestic competition. Unlike foreign industries that increasingly viewed markets as heterogeneous and therefore catered to specific market segment needs or requirements, the U.S. textile industry adopted a proliferated strategy that assumes market homogeneity. While this strategy inherently emphasizes productivity, flexibility, and advanced technology, it lacks a market orientation, a reason for linkage with other textile sectors, and an export orientation.

COMPONENTS OF THE ADJUSTMENT STRATEGIES

The four strategy alternatives outlined above place differing emphasis on various strategy components, and this difference in emphasis directly affects the international competitiveness. The components and the type of emphasis placed on them are shown in Table 10–3, and are discussed in the following section in terms of America's international competitiveness.

Technology

The four strategies all place considerable emphasis on technology, but for different reasons. The undifferentiated and proliferated strategies emphasize modern and advanced technology in order to increase productivity, fabric quality, and the replacement of in-

Table 10–3. Major Strategy Components of Textile Mill Firms and the Influence of Strategy Alternatives.

Strategy Component	Homogeneous Market		Heterogeneous Market	
	Undifferentiated Strategy	Proliferated Strategy	Concentrated Strategy	Differentiated Strategy
Technology	Technological improvements that reduce costs and/or increase fabric and yarn quality are emphasized: productivity, fabric and yarn defects, and the replacement of labor with capital.		Although the same technological improvements are sought for these strategies, greater emphasis is placed on productive versatility and product diversity in order to be responsive to changes in the needs and/or requirements of market segments.	
Production	Tendency is for textile mills to be large and integrated to gain economies of scale from long production runs.	Tendency for textile mills to be smaller (shorter runs) and have productive versatility.	Tendency is for textile mills and companies to be smaller. The mills are basically emphasizing the production of highly specialized yarns and fabrics of shorter production runs. Diseconomies of scale are generally offset by charging premium prices for products designed to meet specific needs and/or wants. Productive versatility is stressed.	

Marketing & Linkage	Major emphasis is placed on price and quality. Market research is used to identify short and intermediate demand changes and trends in competitors' product offering(s). Little, or no, emphasis is placed on developing relationships with other sectors of the textile complex except as buyers and sellers.	Although price and quality are important, emphasis is on nonprice factors. Both market and marketing research are used. Marketing research becomes increasingly more important as the market segment becomes a higher value-added segment. Also, direct linkage with other sectors of the textile complex is important to ensure an adequate knowledge of the market segment is gained, and the firm's ability to satisfy specific needs and/or requirements are enhanced.
Strategic Planning	Long-term planning is not emphasized. Since demand tends to be stable over time and broad-based, major emphasis is on correcting production for short-term or intermediate-term variations resulting from economic changes or technological changes associated with production. Thus, the planning activity of firms pursuing undifferentiated or proliferated strategies involve short or intermediate time horizons.	Long-term planning is emphasized. Since product offerings cater to specific end-market needs and/or requirements of market segments, a major emphasis is placed on predicting long-term trends in factors that affect these needs and/or requirements and the firm's ability to satisfy them (e.g., demographic changes, end-user technologies, market segment size, competitors' offerings, distribution channels, suppliers). The narrower market-base of concentrated and differentiated strategies necessitates a long-term planning horizon to offset the inherently higher risks associated with these strategies.

creasingly costly labor in the production of standardized or undifferentiated fabrics. Since economies of scale are important in
the production of undifferentiated products, mills tend to be large,
relatively inflexible, dependent on large orders, and relatively
unresponsive to market changes. Also, textile mill companies pursuing such strategies need not have strong ties with textile machinery manufacturers, since their products tend to be stable over time.

The concentrated and differentiated strategies, while seeking
the same technological advantages of the mass-market strategy,
place considerably more emphasis on productive flexibility and
versatility and on the development of new fibers. Because the
fabrics are differentiated and, of necessity, are developed to meet
specific demands, shorter and more varied production runs result.
Hence, smaller mills can be used (diseconomies of scale of these
shorter runs are generally offset by premium prices). In addition,
much closer ties are required between textile mill companies pursuing such strategies, textile machinery manufacturers, manmade
fiber producers, and end-markets.

For example, the increasing dependency of the U.S. textile industry on foreign textile machinery manufacturers is probably due
to its later and relatively weaker market-oriented proliferated strategy. Since the textile machinery industries of West Germany,
Japan, and Switzerland are the major U.S. sources for advanced
technology, it can be construed that these industries were responding directly to their indigenous textile industries' earlier
adoption of concentrated and differentiated strategies. This is further supported in the Japanese case because of the close ties that
exist as a result of the overriding influence of Japanese trading
companies. These trading companies are directly involved in marketing textile machinery, textiles, and apparel, and act as catalysts
in the development of new fibers, fabrics, apparel, and textile
machinery. The closer links that exist between other textile industries and their fiber producers and textile machinery manufacturers, especially Japan in both areas, and Italy and Taiwan in fibers,
provide these industries with distinct competitive advantages.

Production

The potential decline in American textile industry's status as a
low-cost producer relative to other major industries pursuing

highly market-oriented strategies suggests that the latter have greater international viability. The viability arises from the need to invest more heavily not only in modern and advanced technology, but also in manufacturing techniques related to process flexibility and product diversity. This approach also appears to stress small- to medium-sized firms that, even in the United States, tend to be better performers.

Marketing

The international marketplace is increasingly being divided into two distinct markets. The first market is for undifferentiated yarns and fabrics, which can only be satisfied with an undifferentiated or mass-market strategy. Yet the comparative advantage is increasingly being reduced by new competition from emerging countries with their large pools of low-wage labor and ready access to modern production technologies. The only way that this advantage can be exploited by the high-labor-cost industries of Europe, Asia Pacific, and the United States is through an internationalization strategy similar to the one adopted by Japan,[13] or by increased protection of domestic markets.

The second market is for differentiated yarns and fabrics. It has grown substantially since World War II and is the direct result of textile mills seeking to become dominant in particular market segments by satisfying the specific needs of these market segments (concentrated or differentiated strategies). However, unlike the homogeneous market approaches of the first market, the requirements for success in approaching the second market include: (1) sophisticated marketing research capable of identifying the changing needs of end-users (apparel, home furnishings, and industrial); (2) in-house forecasting of future demand (market reserach); and (3) a cooperative (if not direct) relationship with manmade fiber producers attuned to end-users needs.

At the present time, the European and mature Asia Pacific industries have a distinct advantage over U.S. industry in this second market. First, their industries are committed to heterogeneous market strategies. The U.S. industry's reaction has been a continued persistence in viewing their markets as homogeneous. Second, the European and Asia Pacific industries have been involved in developing their market-oriented strategies for much longer than the United States. This is particularly true of West Germany, Italy, and Japan. Third, they have developed cooperative or direct links with their fiber producers and their apparel manufacturers. This has resulted in a greater sensitivity to the needs of their end-users. For example, the Japanese trading companies have not only played a significant role in expanding and diversifying the market bases of Japanese textile firms, they have also provided an impetus for a stronger marketing orientation. In contrast, U.S. textile mill companies devote little of their resources to developing such an orientation.

Strategic Planning

Long-range strategic planning (5 to 10 years) is not practiced by most U.S. textile mill companies. Nor has the U.S. government displayed any interest in developing industry-specific development plans or an industrial policy, as have other countries.

The limited planning cycles of most U.S. textile mill companies reflect the homogeneous marketing philosophy (i.e., production orientation) that still dominates the industry. These firms apparently depend on industry forecasts, adjusting only to short or intermediate term economic and competitive international conditions. No formal or systematic attention seems to be paid to long-term trends in competitive international conditions.

With an increased emphasis on marketing-oriented strategies, the need for long-term, formal, and systematic planning is increased. The inherently higher risks associated with such strategies increase the need to be aware of long-term domestic and international trends in specific market segments, and how these trends may affect the short- and intermediate-term plans and objectives of the firm.

CONCLUSIONS AND RECOMMENDATIONS

The size and diversity of the U.S. textile market and the structure of the U.S. textile industry resulted in a gradual shift away from an undifferentiated strategy and toward a proliferated strategy. However, this shift was not as dramatic or as profound as those experienced by European industries and planned for by Asia Pacific industries. The European and Asia Pacific companies not only became more specialized in their offerings, they now view their markets as heterogeneous. The U.S. industry, on the other hand, continues to view its market as homogeneous.

A central question that must be answered is whether more rapid and profound adjustment is required of the U.S. industry. The answer appears to be yes if the United States is interested in enhancing its international competitiveness among textile manufacturers. While its superiority in productivity is yet to be surpassed by other countries, its low-cost producer status is in jeopardy because of international and domestic developments that will (1) directly affect dollar exchange rates adversely; (2) affect the price of manmade fibers adversely; and (3) reduce the impact that long production runs have had on overall costs of U.S. textiles. America's ability to compete in foreign markets is also questionable for other reasons. Because the U.S. textile industry lacks a strong export orientation, it has failed to develop needed skills in international management and marketing. And because of its particular way of perceiving its markets, the U.S. industry has also failed to develop as quickly as foreign textile industries the marketing research and strategic planning skills required to be successful in increasingly competitive markets. Finally, it has failed to develop the necessary linkages with fiber producers, textile machinery manufacturers, and apparel manufacturers.

The key question, then, is how can the U.S. textile industry increase its international competitiveness in the 1980s and beyond. The following recommendations concentrate primarily on company strategies, though industry-wide and government actions considered supportive of the company strategies are also reviewed.

1. *Reevaluate apparel fabric offerings more frequently using end-market research and market position techniques.* Domestic apparel output, and hence fabric purchases, will continue to grow, but more slowly than for industrial and home-furnishings uses. Also, apparel imports will continue to take a larger share of the domestic market. Competition in apparel fabrics is therefore expected to increase, and success will depend on sound market-oriented decisions.

2. *Increase corporate focus on foreign markets and operations.* The greatest future growth in demand for apparel fabrics (and perhaps all fabrics) is expected to occur *outside* the United States.

3. *Increase effort on reducing production costs or enhancing product features.* The reduction of production costs as a result of new production technology or the use of foreign investments in lower-cost countries is necessary to compete with the textile industries of developing countries. On the other hand, the enhancement of product features (e.g., fabric quality, cleanability, durability), allows the firm to compete in areas other than mere price, and in specialized submarkets (a strategy increasingly being pursued by European and mature Asia Pacific industries).

4. *Increase investment in human capital and working conditions.* Investment in new plants and equipment will not likely prove successful by itself, but greater productivity and the ability to attract competent workers require attention to the machine-operator interface.

5. *Significantly increase the resources (time, money, and personnel) devoted to marketing research.* The dynamics of competition in end-use markets are growing in complexity. New applications for existing fabrics, new fiber combinations, new production technologies, new competitors, and changing consumer needs and preferences are constantly opening up new markets and closing others. U.S. producers of textile mill products must anticipate such changes if they are to increase their competitiveness, especially if they adopt an exporting orientation.

6. *Increase emphasis on customer service.* A major competitive advantage a firm can possess, particularly over foreign firms in domestic markets, is better customer service. This includes presale and postsale services.

7. *Initiate joint-technology and marketing research efforts with suppliers and customers.* Closer cooperation among firms in the major segments of the U.S. textile complex would prove mutually beneficial, particularly in the R&D and marketing research areas where U.S. firms could reap the greatest returns in international competition.

8. *Implement strategic planning and management.* Virtually everything discussed in this chapter has shown the need for a strengthening of strategic planning and management and that most U.S. textile mill firms devote insufficient attention to them.

If the government wants to help the U.S. textile industry enhance its international competitiveness, the following recommendations should be considered:

1. Seek trade-barrier reductions in other countries for U.S. exports of textile mill products and products made from textile fabrics.
2. Provide funds or tax relief for cooperative R&D and marketing research in the textile mill products industry.
3. Provide additional funds for worker training (skill upgrading within the industry).
4. Establish regional centers for disseminating information and conducting programs on ways firms in the area can increase their international competitiveness.
5. Reexamine existing government regulations to see more precisely how they affect the international competitiveness of the textile industry.
6. Continue to examine the feasibility of providing support for (and removing impediments to) the establishment of large-scale trading companies similar to those in Japan.
7. Modify the restrictive clauses of Item 807 of the Tariff Schedules of the United States to include uncut fabrics.

NOTES

1. U.S. Department of Commerce, Bureau of Economic Analysis and Office of Textiles reports, various years.
2. J. Arpan, et al. *The U.S. Apparel Industry: International Challenge, Domestic Response* (Atlanta: Georgia State University 1982).
3. Examples of these barriers include the Long Term Arrangement (covering primarily cotton textiles) and the Multifiber Arrangement (MFA), both of which sought to establish greater control over textile and apparel imports into developed countries—a form of "orderly market" arrangements. Such arrangements establish "permissable" levels of import growth via quota levels.
4. An "undifferentiated" strategy is one of four generic strategies used by the authors to classify corporate strategies. Undifferentiated means the firm views the market as homogeneous and manufactures a single product (e.g., denim). A "proliferated" strategy has the same homogeneous market perspective, but the firm produces several products (e.g., denim, corduroy, linen). A "differentiated"

strategy means the firm perceives a heterogeneous market (market niches within the larger market) and produces several products for several market subgroups. A "concentrated" strategy is when a firm produces a single product for a specific market niche.

5. Between 1973 and 1977, only 10.5 percent of the 172,000 workers lost to these industries were added to the industries' registered unemployed. In Germany, workers are classified by the industries in which they work since the industries are required by law to help their unemployed.

6. Although government intervention directed at maintaining employment has resulted in the nationalization of some ailing textile firms, these public firms only represent about 5 percent of official textile employment and are inefficient and uncompetitive.

7. See J. Arpan et al., *The U.S. Apparel Industry,* ch. 5.

8. *The Economist,* (December 12, 1981): 77.

9. Individual Japanese firms often had little influence because of the number of firms involved in the internationalization process. Individual firms were generally only involved in a limited number of projects, many of which were small in scale. Ownership in joint ventures was minor, and a large number of foreign investment projects were undertaken by groups of Japanese firms (e.g., fiber firms, spinners, and trading companies).

10. Trade data on Japan's international competitiveness in the 1970s is somewhat misleading since it does not include data on its activities in other Asia Pacific and Latin American markets.

11. Admittedly, international comparisons of productivity and production costs are fraught with difficulties. However, data available from *Textile World* and Werner Associates, Inc. (New York and Brussels), among others, consistently showed a United States lead in textile productivity and lowest total manufacturing cost in spinning and weaving.

12. The European industries' adjustments in the 1960s and 1970s led them to become specialized in those sectors of the textile industry in which they had comparative advantages. The result has been an EEC textile industry with efficient subparts. The Taiwanese and Japanese industries are undergoing a similar process.

13. This strategy is becoming increasingly attractive since the high growth markets for textile products have shifted to planned and developing economies that are protective of their markets.

11 THE INFORMATION TECHNOLOGY SECTOR

William Davidson

The information technology sector consists of a number of related but distinct industries, including microelectronics, computers, and communications equipment. A rising level of integration of these industries, however, is occurring in each of the three principal market regions. In the United States, IBM, AT&T and others are extending their operations to develop a full range of information technology activities. In Japan, the same six firms that dominate the computer industry also dominate the components and communications industries. Information technology in France will exhibit an even greater level of integration following reorganization of nationalized firms by the Mitterrand government.

The structure of this evolving information technology sector could become increasingly concentrated over the next decade. In one scenario that has been advanced, a relatively small number of global competitors offering integrated information-processing systems will capture market share from smaller national producers. Many firms operating primarily within individual segments of the sector would be forced to merge or collaborate to attain the scale and scope necessary to compete under this scenario.

Although current trends support this scenario, certain factors suggest an alternative. The information technology sector, particularly in the United States, has been a fertile ground for innovation

293

and entrepreneurship, and new competitors will continue to emerge. These companies will invariably be niche-oriented, but it has generally been possible for specialists to attach their new products to existing systems, either by marketing directly or acting as suppliers to original equipment manufacturers (OEMs). This pattern is likely to continue. Competition between firms selling systems and companies offering system components will intensify, however.

Competition between global and national firms will also continue, but national firms will likely operate at distinct disadvantage. Only massive government support will permit a firm with operations in a single market to survive. National firms will be forced to expand abroad or lose competitiveness relative to larger global enterprises. Any middle ground will disappear as world markets converge and grow. The structure of this industry can thus be projected to include two broad categories of competitors in 1990: one set of firms selling integrated information-processing systems on a global basis, and another selling system components to end-users or OEMs on a global basis.

All system suppliers will rely on formal or informal collaborative agreements to meet technology and marketing requirements. At one end of the spectrum are those ten or so firms that possess internally most of the resources needed to support a systems-oriented strategy. At the other end are value-added resellers, who depend entirely on independent manufacturers for hardware. In the middle are firms relying on agreements with independent companies for major products or technologies. Honeywell, in agreements with NEC (mainframes), L.M. Ericsson (private branch exchanges or PBXs), Machine-Bull (European marketing), Convergent Technologies (workstations), and Control Data (peripherals), is one example among a large subset of companies operating in this mode.

In addition to system suppliers, a second group of firms will sell one or more parts of a full information-processing system to end-users or to OEM system assemblers. Firms selling everything from discrete electronic components to subsystems such as central processing units (CPUs), PBXs, and software will be active in this mode. This group of companies will provide a breeding ground for new technologies and for emergence of new systems-oriented competitors.

Relations within and across these two sets of firms will be complex. Within the system-component group, one set of firms will sell primarily to end-users in competition with systems-oriented suppliers. Another set will serve both of these competing groups as suppliers. Vertically integrated systems suppliers, particularly the Japanese, will operate in all three modes.

Competition and interaction within the information technology sector will be complicated by international activity. Foreign sourcing is common in this industry, through both internal and external channels. While sourcing relationships are expanding rapidly, international activity will be dominated by competition, not cooperation, between U.S., Japanese, and European suppliers. Intense competition between Japan and the United States, in particular, could be the principal force driving the future evolution of information technology markets. This issue is most apparent at present in the microelectronics industry.

MICROELECTRONICS

The microelectronics industry consists primarily of semiconductor-based products. New technologies, involving bioengineering and optoelectronics, are emerging, but semiconductor producers will continue to dominate this area for the foreseeable future. Semiconductors are used in a broad range of consumer, industrial, and military products, but their use in information-processing equipment is the most widespread. In 1982 computer and communications applications accounted for 45 percent of worldwide chip sales. These applications were estimated at 55 percent of industry shipments in 1984.[1]

The leading semiconductor producers appear in Table 11–1. These firms accounted for over three-quarters of total world semiconductor sales in 1983. It is important to note, however, that two of the largest producers of semiconductors do not appear on the list: IBM, the world's largest chip producer, and Western Electric. These firms, in addition to General Motors, General Electric, and others produce entirely for internal use. Captive producers shipped about one-fifth of the total volume sold in the merchant market in 1983.[2]

Several of the firms in Table 11–1 also produce chips for inter-

Table 11–1. *Leading Semiconductor Companies' Sales,* 1982 (in $ millions).

Motorola	$1,310
Texas Instruments	1,227
NEC	1,223
Hitachi	1,033
Toshiba	833
National Semiconductor	690
Intel	610
Fujitsu	505
Philips[a]	500
Matsushita	450
Fairchild	410
Mitsubishi	366
Signetics (Philips)	360
Advanced Micro Devices	315
Mostek	235
Siemens[a]	180
Sharp	135

a. Not including interests in Signetics (Philips) and Advanced Micro Devices (Siemens).
Sources: Annual company reports.

nal usage. Texas Instruments has made several attempts to add value to its chip output by integrating forward into the watch, calculator, and computer industries. Philips and Siemens both incorporate a significant percentage of their chip output in consumer and information-processing products. The Japanese producers all exhibit a significant level of internal chip usage, as illustrated in Table 11–2.

Industry Segments

The microelectronics industry can be divided into four basic segments: discrete components, integrated circuits for processing, control, and logic purposes, semiconductor memories, and microprocessors. While demand for discrete components (largely, transistors and diodes) accounts for over 25 percent of total semiconductor sales, microelectronic functions are increasingly performed

Table 11–2. Internal Sales for Japanese Semiconductors, (1981) (percent of total production).

NEC	16.9 %
Hitachi	18.5
Toshiba	19.6
Matsushita	n.a.
Fujitsu	39.1
Mitsubishi	20.0
Sharp	42.4
Oki	28.0

Source: Author's questionnaire.

by integrated circuits (ICs). The IC segment of the industry promises to have the greatest impact on the future evolution of not only the broader information technology sector but on virtually all areas of industrial activity. Within the IC sector, three distinct products and three distinct technologies can be identified.

The Integrated-Circuit Market

The first and largest segment of the IC market is in logic chips. Logic chips are silicon-based circuits that perform a vast range of functions in electronic applications. Standard logic chips include ICs that operate as amplifiers, converters, switches, timers, comparators, and regulators. Custom logic chips function according to the unique specification of the system they support.

Logic chips accounted for over 60 percent of the value of all ICs shipped in 1983.[3] The greatest users of logic chips are the data-processing and communications industries, which together consume almost half of total world output. Consumer products, principally the audio, video, watch, calculator, appliance, and automobile sectors, currently account for approximately one-third of total chip usage. The remainder of the market is devoted to industrial and military equipment.

The second major segment of the IC market is in memory products, which account for about one-third of the total IC market. This area can be further segmented according to the types of process technology employed in creating memory products. Three main types deserve discussion, as they are also the three processes used to produce logic chips. These techniques are known as bipolar, MOS (metal-oxide semiconductor), and complementary-MOS (C-MOS). The bipolar technique is the original process used to produce adjacent positively and negatively charged areas in a silicon substrate.[4] Current flow from a positive "source" to a negative "drain," or vice versa, activates semiconductor elements for logic or memory purposes. The MOS approach differs in the use of a "gate" between a positively and negatively charged area. When the current flow under the gate reaches threshold levels, the circuit switches on or off. If the circuit is a memory device, a gate that is on will be read as a "one"; a closed circuit is read as a "zero". All computer operations are based on binary digits (zero or one readings) or "bits."

MOS devices are superior in terms of density and power requirements, two critical performance criteria for semiconductors. MOS technology dominates the memory area, accounting for about 75 percent of all memory devices. Bipolar technology accounts for most of the remainder although C-MOS products are emerging. C-MOS technology permits the use of a singly charged area as both the source of one circuit and the drain for another, thus dramatically reducing the power usage of the chip. C-MOS is a rapidly growing technology with sales growth from $275 million in 1980 to over $1 billion in 1983.

The semiconductor memory market originated in 1971 when Intel introduced its one-thousand bit (1k), random access memory (RAM) chip. A RAM differs from a ROM (read-only memory), the other principal memory product, in that its contents can be written, and thus changed, by the user. The market for semiconductor memories has grown quickly since their introduction. Four successive generations of RAM memory products have appeared in the last decade, each exhibiting dramatic reductions in cost per bit and each surpassing its predecessor in sales (see Table 11–3).

The 64k RAM segment has been widely publicized because of Japanese activities in this area. Although IBM began mass-production of 64k chips for internal use in 1978, Fujitsu was the first firm to offer this product commercially in 1979. Aggressive expansion of the chip capacity has taken place since that time. In 1983 nineteen firms in the United States, Japan, and Europe produced 64k RAMs. The most aggressive firms in this segment have been Japa-

Table 11–3. Unit Sales of Semiconductor RAM Memories, (1972–82) (millions).

RAM Type	1972	1973	1974	1975	1976	1977	1978	1979	1980	1981	1982
1k	2.5	7.0	11.5	19.0	14.5	7.0	6.0	4.0	0.0	0.0	0.0
4k	0.0	0.0	0.0	1.5	0.0	40.0	65.0	78.0	65.0	26.0	18.0
16k	0.0	0.0	0.0	0.0	0.0	1.0	6.5	24.0	79.0	252.0	220.0
64k	0.0	0.0	0.0	0.0	0.0	0.0	0.0	0.0	0.2	9.0	61.0

Source: Dataquest Market Survey (1982)

nese, but Motorola, Mostek, Texas Instruments, and other U.S. producers have also been expanding capacity at a rapid rate (Table 11–4). One result of rapid capacity expansion has been sharp reductions in 64k prices. The average selling price for a 64k RAM in early 1981 was about $30 per unit. By early 1983 the price had fallen to about $5.00 per unit.

Acceleration of technology cycles can also be expected to continue in the memory field because of competitive pressures. Nippon Electric and Hitachi initiated mass-production of 256k RAMs in the fall of 1983, and Japanese pressure on prices, capacity, and technology cycles will continue to be a dominant force in this industry for the foreseeable future.

The fastest growing segment of the integrated-circuit market involves the microprocessor. Like the semiconductor memory chip, the microprocessor was first introduced by Intel in 1971 for a now defunct Japanese calculator company, Busicom Inc.[5] This product was seen as a potential standard replacement for a set of customized, complex logic chips. Shortly thereafter, the potential of the microprocessor was greatly enhanced by two developments. The invention of the EPROM (erasable-programmable read-only memory) permitted the user to customize and change microprocessor logic structures. Second, the development of the second-generation microprocessor, the Intel 8008, allowed processing of 8-bit units, the length of a standard "byte" in most data-

Table 11–4. Estimated 64k D-RAM Shipments in 1982 (millions of units).

Producer	To U.S.	To Other	Total	Share
Hitachi	6	6	12	20%
Motorola	7	3	10	16
TI	7	3	10	16
Fujitsu	4	4	8	13
Mitsubishi	2	3	5	8
NED	2	3	5	8
Oki	3	1	4	7
Mostek	2	1	3	5
Intel	1	1	2	3
Others	1	1	2	3
Total	35	36	61	100%

Source: Rosen Electronics Letter

processing systems. Four-bit units continued to be applied in games, appliances, and other less sophisticated products, but the bulk of the market by 1983 was utilizing 8-bit units. The 16-bit segment grew rapidly from $105 million in 1980 to $211 million in 1982 (see Table 11–5). In addition, a new generation of 32-bit microprocessors was introduced in 1981, and the power of these microprocessors far surpasses that of the previous generation. The new Intel APX432, one of the first 32-bit microprocessors, has, for example, a processing capacity of 2 million instructions per second, equivalent to the power of an IBM 370 mainframe computer.

The manufacture of microprocessors is largely dominated by American producers, although Japanese firms are very active in the segment for consumer applications. Japanese microprocessors are so far either licensed from U.S. producers or derivatives of American models. American makers determine the standards, and Japanese and European producers serve as "second-sources" for U.S. products. This practice, widespread in the industry, provides security to end-users and also aids in international marketing efforts.

Microprocessors have been subject to the same relentless reduction in prices and improvements in performance that mark the memory market. Prices for the first generation 16-bit microprocessors (8088, 6800, Z80) fell more than 50 percent between January of 1980 and January of 1982. As a result, unit volume was expected to grow from about 24 million units in 1981 to 550 million units in 1984.

Geographic Markets

Both the United States and Japan are largely self-sufficient in terms of local production of semiconductors, with a bilateral trade

Table 11–5. Sales of Microprocessors ($ million).

	1980	1981	1982 (estimates)	1984 (estimates)
4–bit	.73	.72	.73	.74
8–bit	358.80	426.60	480.10	596.30
16–bit	105.50	196.60	211.50	422.80
32–bit	0.00	0.00	5.00	200.00

Source: Dataquest Market Survey (1982)

flow that slightly favors Japan. Japan experienced a trade surplus of almost $200 million in semiconductor trade with the United States in 1983. Europe, in contrast, imports over half of its semi-conductors, an import market almost entirely dominated by American producers (see Table 11–6). These American firms are currently increasing their production capacity within the European Economic Community. Texas Instruments, for example, operates a total of six plants in England, France, Germany, Portugal, and Italy. In addition, several dozen U.S. electronics firms have estab-lished facilities in Ireland and Scotland under the industrial devel-opment assistance programs in those countries.

Japanese firms have also begun to initiate production within the European market. Fujitsu and NEC both produce semicon-ductors in Ireland, and Hitachi has chip facilities in Germany and England. In addition, Japanese producers, such as NEC, Hitachi, Mitsubishi, Oki, and Fujitsu, have invested heavily in U.S. chip-production facilities within wholly owned affiliates. Partially in re-sponse to potential import restrictions, each of these firms initi-ated production of 64k RAMs in the United States by the end of 1984.

The current wave of foreign investment in foreign assembly and production plants is largely occurring in cross-flows between the U.S., Europe and Japan. Philips and Siemens have each acquired U.S. chip producers in recent years, while U.S. investment is rising in Japan as well as Europe. Texas Instruments has a large chip facility in Japan, and other America producers, including IBM,

Table 11–6.   Estimated European Semiconductor Sales of American-based Companies, 1981 ($ million).

Texas Instruments	$395
Motorola	270
National Semiconductor	205
ITT	197
Intel	168
Fairchild	125
Signetics	108
Other	350
Total	$1,836

Source: Rosen Electronics Report

Motorola and Intel are operating or building facilities there in 1984. The first wave of foreign investment in assembly facilities in low-wage locations such as Mexico, Taiwan, Singapore, and Malaysia is largely over. In some cases, assembly operations are reverting to the home country because of increasingly efficient capital equipment. Wire-bonding, for example, can now be done with fully automated equipment, rather than through the traditional method of hand-wiring under microscopes.

The Role of Government

Government involvement to protect and promote domestic semiconductor industries is widespread (see Table 11–7). In Europe, direct government financial support has been extensive. Britain's efforts to develop a national semiconductor producer, for example, have focused on INMOS Ltd., a producer of RAM memory chips which lost over $25 million in 1982. The Alvey Project, a $400 million microelectronics effort, represents Britain's current thrust in this industry. In France, state support for semiconductor firms has had a longer history than in Britain,[6] and continued expansion of the French semiconductor industry can be expected given the $1.1 billion in government expenditures to support the industry over the next four years.[7] In addition, France will participate in the European Commission's $1.3 billion ESPRIT Project to develop new information techniques. Other European governments and companies will participate in ESPRIT's microelectronics efforts, but individual national efforts, such as the U.K.'s $500 million Alvey Project, are also underway.

Table 11–7.   Government Semiconductor Funding, 1979–81 ($ million).

United Kingdom	$330
Germany	300
France	250
Japan	250
United States	120
Italy	90

Source: *Rosen Electronics Letter* (April 28, 1982): 10.

Government activities in the United States to promote the semi-conductor industry have been focused on defense-related R&D and procurement contracts. Recently, the Defense Department has increased its role by supporting the Very-High-Speed-Integrated-Circuit (VHSIC) Project initiated in 1980 with funds amounting to $300 million.[8] This project, designed to produce the next genera-tion of IC technology, includes over a dozen major U.S. electronics companies. Defense purchases of ICs are also rising rapidly. Pro-jected defense budgets include a 33.4 percent increase in hardware purchases for 1983, in addition to a 21.3 percent increase in fund-ing for development, testing, and evaluation.[9]

Japanese support of the IC industry has also had a long history, but the recently completed Very-Large-Scale-Integration (VLSI) Project marked a major achievement in the development of Japan's semiconductor industry. This $300 million project involving six major semiconductor producers is largely responsible for bringing Japanese producers to their present position in the world industry. Additional government-backed programs are currently active in the areas of very-high-speed and optoelectronic circuits. Signifi-cant semiconductor projects are also incorporated in the present fifth-generation and supercomputer programs.

Current Trends in Industry Structure

The semiconductor industry has experienced a wave of acquisi-tions in recent years. Large, capital-rich companies such as Exxon, United Technologies, and Schlumberger have acquired major pro-ducers of semiconductors, and other IC makers have been ac-quired by firms in related industries, such as Intel (IBM), Intersil (Northern Telecom), Synertech (Honeywell), and MOS Technolo-gies (Commodore). Much of this acquisition activity in the industry has been stimulating by rising capital requirements due to increas-ing capital intensity in manufacturing, soaring chip design costs, accelerated technology cycles, and pricing pressures. At this point, many of the smaller producers will find it difficult to continue their activities without the support of a wealthy and benign parent cor-poration or government patron. Acquisition activity can also be expected to continue. Other means of meeting capital require-ments, such as cooperative research and development agreements and technology exchanges, are growing in popularity. In the United States, the Microelectronics and Computer Technology Center in Austin, Texas and the Semiconductor Industry Association Consortium in San Jose, California are the most prominent examples.[10]

Another likely trend in industry structure is an increase in vertical integration. Pure semiconductor components producers will find it difficult to compete with vertically integrated competitors who can add value to semiconductor components. Many semiconductor companies may seek to become competitors in the computer and peripheral equipment markets. Efforts to migrate into these markets, however, may be thwarted by severe competitive pressures. Texas Instruments' failure in the home computer market is but one example of the difficulty in migrating downstream.[11]

Many of the forces at work in the components area also operate in the computer industry. Corporate strategies and the broader industry structure are driven by four primary forces. Prices and margins are dropping faster than ever before due to growing competitive pressures, resulting, in many cases, in a reduction of cash flows. Second, rising competitive pressures are reflected in an increasingly dynamic technological environment. Product life cycles are shortening, further reducing cash flows for vendors. Third, while cash flows are drying up, capital requirements are growing rapidly. Research costs are soaring and the pace of R&D activity is quickening. At the same time, massive investments in automated plants and equipment are needed to realize scale economies, reduce costs, and maintain margins. Finally, the market appears to be shifting toward a systems-oriented environment. These basic realities hold the key to understanding corporate strategies in the computer industry, and they will dictate, to a great extent, the industry's future structure. The origin of these underlying forces are emerging primarily from the intense rivalry between U.S. and Japanese industries for leadership in this critical sector.

American firms continue to dominate world markets in each segment of the computer industry, despite attempts by foreign competitors to displace them. Eight of the ten largest firms in the industry are American companies. Only in Japan do U.S. producers hold less than half of any data-processing market. Despite continued European efforts to expand their activities, Japanese firms are likely to be the only major source of competition for U.S. producers in the foreseeable future.

THE JAPANESE COMPUTER INDUSTRY

The Japanese computer industry is dominated by six companies: Fujitsu, Hitachi, Nippon Electric (NEC), Mitsubishi, Toshiba, and Oki. These firms, plus a larger number of secondary companies, have established themselves as major forces in the Japanese information-processing market. Much of these firms' success can be linked to government efforts to encourage technological development.[12] However, official efforts to control the structure of the computer industry have been less successful. The partnerships established by MITI in the early 1970s are no longer in existence. Hitachi and Fujitsu have ceased joint research and development and now offer different operating systems for their collaborative models. Toshiba has withdrawn from the NEC- Toshiba mainframe venture, and Oki is no longer collaborating with Mitsubishi. U.S. affiliates of IBM, Honeywell, and Sperry Univac, among others, remain powerful independent forces in the Japanese computer industry, where these firms still account for over 40 percent of the installed base in the Japanese mainframe market. In addition, a large number of new entrants have appeared. Ricoh, Canon, and Minolta from the camera and copier sectors are aggressively entering the industry, as are calculator and consumer electronics companies such as Sony, Casio, Sharp, and Matsushita. Over sixty new domestic producers entered the market in the last five years, further fragmenting domestic industry.

Although government activities have been critical, it would be dangerous to apply the "Japan Inc." concept to the Japanese computer industry. MITI has been unable to control and dictate completely the structure or direction of the industry in recent years. In the 1960s and early 1970s, large mainframes accounted for the bulk of Japanese computer sales. Today, although mainframes are still important, other segments of the industry are growing much more rapidly. Established firms are increasing their emphasis on chips, peripherals, personal and small business computers, and new entrants are emerging in each of these areas. The Japanese computer industry has grown beyond the control of government agencies.

Despite this fragmentation, it is possible to make certain generalizations about the Japanese computer industry. Corporate priorities, in terms of segments slated for emphasis, are highly consistent. There is also a degree of uniformity in the strategies developed by individual companies to pursue these segments. This consistency is clearly demonstrated in the field of semiconductors, where the six major vendors control almost 90 percent of the domestic market.

Peripherals

In 1969 MITI used its powers to establish a peripheral manufacturers cartel. The cartel allocated production and standardized designs for selected equipment. A coordinating committee composed of the six major firms administered production levels and product lines for individual companies. Despite the formation of the cartel, however, a large number of smaller Japanese companies have been successful in entering the industry. Attracted by the high rate of growth of the market, companies such as Seiko (Epson printers), Brother Industries (electronic typewriters), Toray, and C. Itoh (terminals) are now important players in the peripheral industry.

Exports of peripherals are growing at a rate in excess of 50 percent per year and exceeded $2 billion in 1983. The greatest growth has occurred in the low-priced, dot-matrix printer segment. Seiko's Epson dot-matrix printer is the largest selling printer in the world, and Oki's Okidata printer is second. Japanese firms held an estimated 42 percent of the world microcomputer printer market in 1982.[13] Sales of data-storage products and especially of microcomputer disk-drive units, have also grown sharply in recent years where Japanese firms hold an estimated 27 percent of the market.

Microcomputers

American companies first introduced personal computers to the Japanese market in 1977. That first year Tandy, Apple, and Commodore sold 5,000 units in Japan. By 1980 there were over seventy firms producing personal computers for the Japanese market. Unit sales exceeded 100,000 in 1980 and rose to 720,000 in 1982. In 1979 Tandy, Apple, and Commodore represented 80 percent of the Japanese market, but the market share of these American companies declined rapidly as Japanese companies entered the industry.

The major Japanese producers of microcomputers are NEC and Sharp. NEC's PC-8000 alone represents over 40 percent of the unit sales realized by Japanese companies, with Sharp's MZ-80 being the second most popular model. Together the top five Japanese producers accounted for over 80 percent of the personal computers sold in Japan in 1981. But exports of personal computers have grown very slowly. While NEC enjoys a small share of the U.S. market and Epson is expanding its efforts outside Japan, Japanese producers have yet to achieve any significant penetration of foreign markets for microcomputers.

Minicomputers

Minicomputers are often thought of as general-purpose computers of a certain size. In fact, the term principally refers to machines that are sold on an OEM basis to "systems houses" and end-users, generally for industrial applications. The systems house or the end-user develops the software and customizes the system for a special purpose, such as process control, communications, or scientific use. In Japan, minicomputers were first designed to meet internal process-control needs of the computer makers themselves. The range of applications has expanded from this original base. Minicomputers are now used widely for office work, measurement and analysis, research, and control purposes.

The minicomputer market in Japan is small by comparison to other segments of the computer industry. The market is growing rapidly, however. In 1982 sales of minicomputers exceeded 16,000 units with a value of almost $1.5 billion. By contrast, the 1982 U.S. market for minicomputers was estimated between $4 to 5 billion.

The leading Japanese producer of mini's, with about 25 percent of the Japanese market, is PanaFacom Ltd., a joint venture among Fujitsu, Fuji Electric Works, and Matsushita. The company supplies mini's to its parent companies and markets them externally.

Hitachi and NEC follow closely, each with about 15 percent of the market. Digital Equipment, Yokogawa-Hewlett- Packard, and Nippon Mini Computer, a subsidiary of Data General, each have lines of minicomputers from small micros to large 32-bit machines. Exports of minicomputers from Japan were insignificant in 1982.

Small Business Systems

Small business systems (SBS) range from desktop microcomputers to stand-alone mainframes that control distributed-processing systems. An SBS is defined here as any general-purpose business computer costing between $5,000 and $200,000 (1983) for the basic configuration. Users of these computers fall into one of two groups—small companies buying their first computer and large enterprises that already have a large general-purpose computer. Small companies use these systems for inventory control, billing, mailing lists, or figuring payrolls. Large companies purchase these systems principally as departmental data-processing subsystems.

Although over seventy companies produce small business computers for the Japanese market, the top five producers account for 50 percent of the units sold. With the exception of Fujitsu and Hitachi, the major computer makers are now placing primary emphasis on small computers. Mitsubishi, NEC, Toshiba, and Fujitsu are the leading competitors in the small-system market.

Optic-camera companies and consumer electronics/calculator companies are beginning to enter this growing market. Ricoh, Minolta, and Canon, for example, are aggressively expanding in this area, as are the calculator companies, Casio and Sharp. Consumer electronics companies such as Matsushita and Sony have also introduced small business systems. More entrants and further fragmentation of the market can be expected in Japan in coming years.

The primary distribution channel for these systems in Japan has traditionally been through independent dealers (*dairiten*). But, as companies such as Ricoh, Casio, and Sharp enter the market, the distribution pattern is beginning to change, with an increased emphasis on direct retail sales. Toshiba and NEC have developed networks of retail electronics outlets. Japanese companies are placing a great deal of emphasis on the sale of small business systems in foreign markets, through independent dealers and direct through sales efforts. Fujitsu and NEC have been particularly successful, but Mitsubishi and Toshiba are also expanding rapidly. Exports of small systems exceeded 10,000 units through 1983.

General-Purpose Mainframe Computers

Mainframes are the largest single segment of the computer industry. Worldwide sales exceeded $25 billion in 1982; in Japan, 1982 mainframe sales exceeded $3 billion. Hardware represents only a fraction of these total sales figures. Installation, education of operating personnel, maintenance agreements, service, and software development account for over half of the total cost of these systems. Because Japanese firms have traditionally been weak in these nonhardware components of the data-processing system, many of these services are provided by independent software and systems houses in Japan. With the support of these agents, Japanese vendors have been able to sell complete systems in Japan. But in foreign markets Japanese weaknesses have been pronounced since external services are not as readily available to the Japanese computer manufacturers. In response to this problem, Japanese vendors have tended toward OEM distribution agreements and plug-compatible (PCM) strategies in foreign markets. A plug-compatible strategy permits direct interface with equipment and software designed to fit a widely used standard, in this case IBM's.

In their effort to penetrate world markets, one of the principal challenges to Japanese firms in the mainframe industry will be software development. Many observers point out that although Japanese firms are competitive in mainframe hardware, they are significantly behind U.S. competitors in this aspect of the industry. Since software represents as much as 40 percent of mainframe systems cost (and the percentage is rising), this area poses an important problem for the Japanese computer industry.

The Japanese have responded to their software shortcomings in several ways. In addition to major government-sponsored software development projects, individual companies are spending heavily to make up for this deficiency. Fujitsu, for example, devoted over half of its R&D budget in 1983 to software development and has built a large software "factory" next to its principal mainframe assembly plant. This center employs 1,300 software engineers. Other firms are carrying out similar measures.

The number of software engineers employed by Japanese manufacturers appears small relative to leading U.S. companies who employ many thousands of software design specialists. This difference can be deceptive since major firms rely heavily on external software houses for development purposes in Japan. While nominally independent, these houses are in fact closely tied to individual vendors. Fujitsu, for example, works closely with thirty software houses. These houses do most of Fujitsu's customer application design and implementation work. Other firms have similar relationships.

There are about 1,900 software houses in Japan, but the top 50 firms account for about 50 percent of the industry's total sales. Most of these top software houses are, in turn, directly owned or tied to one of the six major computer firms. For example, the two largest software houses, each of which employs more than 4,000 people, are owned by Hitachi and NEC. Hitachi and NEC control other houses in addition to these flagship firms. Hitachi formed a total of eleven software subsidiaries between 1978 and 1982, each designed to serve a different market segment.

In addition to the traditional software houses, independent systems houses are becoming an important factor in computer marketing. Such parties have long accounted for the majority of minicomputer sales, but they are now becoming increasingly important in the mainframe market. These houses tend to be specialized along industry or application lines, and their growth has become a key trend in the computer market.

Although software will continue to be a weakness for Japanese firms, especially in foreign markets, further steps are being taken to reduce or avoid the problem. Joint software development and distribution agencies formed with government assistance are expanding rapidly. JECC, the public computer-leasing agency, serves as a clearinghouse for software programs. Packages filed with JECC increased from 327 in 1978, to over 2,000 in 1983. Rentals rose from 127 to over 12,000 during this same period. The Joint Systems Development Corporation, a government-backed consortium of 124 software houses employing 16,500 programmers, develops common packages for use by Japanese hardware users. These efforts are closing the gap in software capabilities; in some areas the gap has already closed. Although Japanese vendors are particularly weak in English applications packages, they excel in other areas, such as operating systems, manufacturing control, robotics, advanced utility programs, and data-base management packages.

Another means of addressing software deficiencies has been increased emphasis on sectors where software is less important. The personal computer and stand-alone small business system markets, for example, do not require sophisticated or customized software. Software vendors can also be used to meet customer needs in these sectors more readily than in the mainframe market.

Japanese Activities in the United States

Japanese vendors are traditionally viewed as pursuing a plug-compatible (PCM) strategy in the United States. Their mainframes can interface with IBM peripheral equipment and software and, of course, with other equipment and software designed to IBM standards. This approach allows the Japanese manufacturer to penetrate the mainframe market without incurring the extensive costs associated with systems design, software development, customer training, or service delivery. By producing a machine compatible with IBM's systems, PCM suppliers gain access to the bulk of the data-processing market. Industry observers estimate that at least 60 percent of the installed mainframe base in the United States and 40 percent worldwide use IBM standards. However, as market followers, PCM competitors must be able to adjust rapidly and at great cost whenever industry standards change.

The history of Itel, an American computer-leasing company, illustrates the problems of such a strategy. Itel's computer-leasing revenues grew from $204 million in 1975 to $650 million in 1979, based on an IBM plug-compatible product supplied by Hitachi. When the new price performance standards represented by the IBM 4300 were established, many of Itel's leased machines were returned. With no market for the used machines, the company filed for bankruptcy in 1981. Following Itel's failure, Hitachi's U.S. marketing activities were assumed by National Advanced Systems (NASCO), a subsidiary of National Semiconductor Company. Hitachi's 1982 sales in the United States were 60 to 80 large mainframe units.

Fujitsu's initial approach to the U.S. market was only slightly different from that of Hitachi. Fujitsu acquired a 27 percent interest in Amdahl Corporation in 1973. This company was formed by Eugene Amdahl, formerly one of IBM's top systems designers, to sell PCM mainframes in the United States. Fujitsu's relationship with Amdahl focused on mastery of Amdahl's systems design. In 1976 Fujitsu formalized a sourcing agreement with Amdahl that led to growing Japanese participation in Amdahl systems. Today, Fujitsu assembles the current Amdahl line in its facility at Numazu and exports the mainframes virtually intact to the United States. Both Fujitsu and Hitachi mainframes are sold under an American brand name by an American distributor. These arrangements have advantages, but they also involve problems, such as a lack of control over marketing activities, the short-term orientation of U.S. partners, and the loss of continuity when partnerships are terminated. Plug-compatible approaches also have drawbacks, primarily in terms of vulnerability to technological change. In order to reduce their vulnerability to changes in computer technology, Japanese vendors have aggressively pursued the development of their own semiconductor divisions. As a result, Japanese firms have achieved cost and technical parities with their U.S. competitors.

Japanese firms have also begun to emphasize direct distribution activities. Fujitsu, for example, formed a joint venture with TRW in 1980 to sell Fujitsu's medium and small computer systems under a common brand name. Fujitsu initially owned 51 percent of the new partnership; after some conflicts, Fujitsu acquired the remaining 49 percent in 1983. In addition, Systems Formulate Corporation, a Fujitsu spinoff, sells personal computers in the U.S. market. Several other firms have more direct arrangements. NEC Information Systems is a wholly owned subsidiary located in Waltham, Massachusetts. Its principal products include the NEC Spinwriter printer and the PC-8000 personal computer. NEC Electronics of America is another wholly owned subsidiary formed to produce and sell semiconductors. In addition, Hitachi, Mitsubishi, and Toshiba produce and sell semiconductor products in the United States through wholly owned affiliates.

While there is thus a growing tendency toward direct control of U.S. distribution activities, existing agreements block direct activity in some areas. NEC, for example, was barred from entering the U.S. mainframe market by the terms of a 1970 licensing agreement with Honeywell. That agreement expired in 1981 and NEC recently licensed Honeywell to sell its large computers in the United States. Amdahl also has exclusive rights to Fujitsu's M series mainframes. Despite these exceptions, direct distribution arrangements will continue to be a key element in future plans for penetration of the U.S. market.

Other Foreign Activities

Japanese firms are widely active in other foreign markets as well. For example, European markets accounted for over 20 percent of total Japanese exports of computers, components, and communications exports in 1983. Marketing intermediaries are also important in Europe. Fujitsu sells large mainframes through Siemens on an OEM basis. Fujitsu entered into an agreement in October 1981 whereby ICL agreed to market Fujitsu's computer mainframe line in exchange for access to semiconductor technology.

Japanese activities in Europe can be expected to increase sharply in coming years despite the constant threat of protectionism. The indigenous European computer industry is not highly developed, and the Japanese appear willing to enter into local partnerships. Increased emphasis on production and assembly within the EEC also reduces the problem of protectionism. The EEC contains the second largest computer market in the world after the United States, and there is a high degree of interest in penetrating this lucrative market.

Another principal area of interest to the Japanese has been the Australian market. Fujitsu's share of the Australian market, for example, has increased from 1 percent in 1978 to 11 percent in 1982. Mitsubishi has followed a similar approach for its line of small business systems. Hitachi has six sales offices in Australia, and NEC formed NEC Information Systems Australia to handle its Astra line of small business systems and minicomputers. Many observers view Australia as an incubator for defining future Japanese activities in other world markets.

In the Middle East, Japanese activities are largely focused on telecommunications markets. In Latin America, markets are limited but growing. Hitachi produces control systems in Brazil, and NEC manufactures telecommunications equipment in Brazil and Mexico. Fujitsu is currently planning a minicomputer facility in

Brazil. Brazil and Mexico are two of the fastest growing markets in the world, but the Japanese have so far had little success in these cases.

The Japanese Computer Industry in the Future

A variety of opinions exist about the future activities and impact of Japanese vendors in the world computer market. Many observers do not believe that Japanese competitors can do to the computer industry what they have already done to the consumer electronics and automobile industries. Important differences can be cited that distinguish computers from these sectors. But despite the industry, market, and environmental differences, few participants fail to treat the Japanese as a serious factor in the future of the computer industry. Their impact on the industry is already being felt indirectly as existing computer companies take steps to anticipate Japanese penetration of world markets.

It is not difficult to project the nature, scope, and emphasis of Japanese activities in the global information-processing industry. Clearly, Japanese vendors will not be limited to a PCM product strategy with OEM distribution and marketing arrangements. Japanese firms are now in a unique position to benefit from the convergence of computer and communications technologies with video, audio, and printed-transmission technology. While only three or four U.S. firms possess the technology and resources to combine these segments into an extended information-processing system for office or home application, each of the major Japanese vendors possess such capabilities. They are certain to play a major role in determining the future nature of these markets.

THE AMERICAN COMPUTER INDUSTRY

Recent developments within the U.S. computer industry have led to rising competition within traditional markets. Microcomputer companies have expanded upward into minicomputer markets, and the latter have upgraded themselves into segments of the mainframe market. The number of firms producing computer equipment has risen each year. New companies such as Prime,

Apple, Commodore, Datapoint, Tandem, and Cray have captured significant market shares in certain niches. Another generation of competitors such as Altos Computers, Apollo Computer Company, Synapse, and Convergent Technologies, benefiting from the recent venture-capital boom, emerged as serious contenders. While new entrants will continue to appear, partially due to the high mobility of personnel in this industry, key segments of the computer industry are likely to experience increasing concentration. Several forces support this prospect. Growth rates in the mainframe market may have peaked, for example, and capital requirements in almost all segments of the industry are rising rapidly. In addition, the spiral of accelerating technology cycles will limit the range of activities of many competitors. The most immediate result of these pressures may be seen in the withdrawal of some firms from secondary or marginal lines of activity. Many firms' ability to offer a full line of products will become strained in the face of rising capital and technology requirements and shortages of skilled people. Retrenchment will also reduce the number of competitors in many segments.

Mergers and acquisitions can also be expected in the computer industry as a result of these pressures. Motorola's acquisition of 4-Phase Systems, Schlumberger's acquisition of Applicon, and General Electric's purchase of Calma are just a few examples of this trend. Cooperative agreements between computer manufacturers can also be expected in response to industry pressures. This response, long followed in Europe and Japan, is now being practiced widely in the United States. The Microelectronics and Computer Technology Center, which consists of thirteen major U.S. corporate sponsors, is the best known example. Many two-party agreements have also been developed recently. IBM, for example, formed joint development agreements with Motorola and Texas Instruments. Other collaborations, both informal and formal, can be expected in the coming years.

At the same time that industry pressures are forcing consolidation and increasing collaboration, new competitors will continue to enter the market. The fertile venture-capital fields of San Francisco, Boston, Texas, and elsewhere will spawn new entrants in many segments of the computer industry, in addition to the expansion of foreign competitors, such as Olivetti, Philips, Plessey, Nixdorf, and Siemens, in the United States. The presence of these firms will put additional pressure on marginal domestic competitors and increase the internationalization of the industry. The net result of these countercurrents may be fairly constant industry concentration ratios, but with a changing cast of participants.

Two other broad trends deserve reemphasis. The first is the convergence of formerly distinct markets. In addition to a growing overlap between semiconductor, minicomputer, and mainframe producers, the personal computer market is closely related to the small business systems segment. The office equipment and telecommunications segments are converging as well. This trend will continue, but several important considerations must be kept in mind. The expansion of many firms into adjacent segments will be discouraged by competitive pressures, capital requirements, and counterattacks. Only the largest and most able firms in any segment will be able to venture successfully into adjacent markets. Despite these forces of resistance, however, further integration of market and industry structures appears inevitable. Vertical and horizontal integration will be powerful trends in the market. The ability to spread marketing, production, R&D, and personnel costs across a wider range of business and the need to make new investments will be primary concerns for firms attempting to expand their sphere of activities into adjacent segments. One of the best examples of this process is occurring in the field of personal computers.

Personal Computers

The personal computer market was initiated by Apple and Tandy, who together sold over 2 million units by the end of l983. These two leading firms are currently experiencing rising competition as companies from other sectors enter the personal computer market. Major new entrants include IBM, Hewlett-Packard, and DEC. In addition, a number of consumer electronics and semiconductor companies are stepping up their activities in this rapidly growing sector.

The personal computer market includes four distinct user categories: business, home, professional, and education. In addition, three broad product categories can be outlined. The low end of the market, costing $300 or less, is dominated by Commodore. Commodore's principal product, the 64, is manufactured in Japan, the United States, and Europe. Annual sales exceeded 500,000 units in 1983, with Europe and Japan accounting for 10 to 20 percent of total sales. Texas Instruments and Atari floundered and ultimately withdrew from this market in 1984.

The second segment of the personal computer market is dominated by the Apple II and Tandy's TRS-80. Products in this segment typically offer 48k-64k RAM capacity plus disk storage of 200–300k, disk drives, a monochrome display, and a printer selling for under $2,500 in 1984. This segment of the industry has been the principal target of IBM, DEC, and Hewlett-Packard product entries. A second threat to the existing producers of this segment originates from the lower tier of the personal computer market, such as the Commodore 64.

The third tier of the personal computer market includes systems generally retailing for $3,000 to $12,000. These systems offer additional memory, greater capacity, speed, a wider range of functions (including graphics and word processing) and more powerful printers and displays. Although Apple (Lisa) and Tandy are upgrading into this market, other competitors such as Hewlett-Packard, DEC, and IBM have been active in this area for several years. Burroughs and NCR entered the personal computer market in 1981 as OEM distributors, and AT&T introduced a workstation manufactured by Olivetti in 1984.

Minicomputers and Small Business Systems

Established American producers hold a dominant position in the world minicomputer market. The largest competitor in this segment is DEC, with an estimated 28.4 percent of the U.S. market. IBM, with about 15.0 percent of the U.S. market, is the second largest supplier of minicomputers. Other leading competitors are Hewlett-Packard (9.3 percent), Data General (9.0 percent), and Honeywell (7.5 percent). Each of these firms is active in this market on a global basis.

The traditional minicomputer market, which consists primarily of industrial and scientific applications is expected to continue as the dominant segment in the United States (see Table 11–8). Over 50 percent of all sales in this segment are to OEMs or systems

Table 11–8.   Minicomputer Market Segments.

Segment	Percent of Market 1980
Traditional Minicomputers	60.3
Small Business Systems	23.3
Data-Entry Systems	9.5
Intelligent Terminals	2.5
Office Systems	4.5

Source: *Datamation.*

houses. However, the office systems segment is expected to exhibit the highest rate of growth. Office systems include computer units sold as distributed-data-processing machines. These machines can be sold as stand-alone units, but they more often are hooked up to a central mainframe to permit exchange of data and processing flexibility. Here, compatibility with IBM equipment is particularly important.

The key growth segments of the minicomputer industry at present, in addition to office systems, are distributed-processing, 32-bit machines and nonstop systems. Distributed processing involves connecting a minicomputer to a large mainframe through telecommunications links. This practice permits transfer of data, flexibility in system capacity, preprocessing, and more efficient usage of machine time. IBM is the largest supplier of distributed minicomputer systems, but others with significant activity in this area include Datapoint, Honeywell, Texas Instruments, and Hewlett-Packard (in order of 1982 placements). Shipments of mini's for distributed-processing applications were growing at an annual rate of 65 percent in 1982.

The new generation of 32-bit minicomputers is dominated by DEC with a 56 percent market share in 1982. Other contenders include Prime (12.5 percent), Data General (7.4 percent), Perkin-Elmer (6.3 percent) and Wang (4.5 percent). This market is in the initial stage of expansion at the present time and has shown high growth rates in the early 1980s.

The nonstop computer market was initiated by Tandem Computer Company in 1979. Tandem machines offer dual processors so that downtime can be eliminated. These units have sold well to users whose operations are sensitive to computer failure. Tandem has a virtual monopoly in this market, but new competitors such as Synapse are emerging.

It is difficult to differentiate between the minicomputer and small business system markets in the United States. Products such as the IBM System 34, 38, 36, and 4300, for example, sell in both. IBM is the dominant supplier of small business systems, with DEC and Hewlett-Packard tied for a distant second position. In addition to IBM and the major producers of minicomputers, other mainframe computer companies such as Burroughs, Honeywell, NCR, and Control Data are also very active in this market, which reached a volume of 900,000 systems in 1984.

Mainframes

Competitive pressures are particularly severe in the mainframe market. Capital requirements for facilities modernization and expansion represent only part of the problem for existing producers. The need to develop or acquire micro- electronics and communications expertise is also imperative. NCR, for example, opted to develop its own semiconductor expertise at a cost of $155 million, and Burroughs acquired a producer of semiconductors in l982. Honeywell and Control Data are attempting to· develop similar in-house capabilities in the semi- conductor industry.

One important trend in the mainframe market, as already mentioned, is the rising importance of software costs, while hardware prices have declined sharply over time. Software "production" is largely a labor-intensive affair, with no economies of scale. In fact, small teams of independent software engineers have consistently outperformed larger and better-funded development groups. This suggests that external software vendors will begin to play a far more important role in this industry than they have in the past. If this does occur, it could work to the advantage of secondary competitors who do not have well-developed, internal software resources. Those companies whose hardware costs were highly competitive with more established competitors would be particularly helped. And if external software vendors expand their activities into field support, service, and sales, even greater benefits would accrue to such suppliers.

However, if all software development were done by independent external vendors, the greatest benefits might accrue to those established computer producers with large market shares. The variable costs associated with sales of software packages are very small. Volume purchasers would receive a substantial reduction in unit costs. Only in the area of customized software would there be no advantage to established competitors.

Office Equipment

The traditional office equipment market is dominated by office copiers, typewriters, dictation, and accounting equipment. The key growth areas at present are in office systems and local area networks (LANs). These products are replacing existing word-processing and office communications products. As recently as 1979, IBM and Xerox together controlled 64 percent of the rapidly growing word processing market. Their positions have declined sharply, though, to the benefit of smaller competitors.

The emergence of network office systems, however, could limit the activities of secondary suppliers. Networks provide not only word processing, but electronic mail, data communications, distributed data-processing, electronic filing, and other office functions. Those firms that sell network-oriented work stations, such as Wang, Datapoint, Harris, IBM, Xerox, and Mohawk Data Sciences all offer such extended services. In most office applications, word processing will be but one of many functions performed by office equipment systems. Entry into this segment of the market will require systems capabilities. The systems approach to the office equipment market represents one of the most powerful forces in the overall information technology sector. This area of activity is currently a focal point for the convergence of technologies, markets, and competitors, and rivals from virtually every segment in the broad information technology sector are expected to confront each other in this area of the market in the future.

The Role of the U.S. Government

While U.S. corporations remain vigorous competitors in all fields of information technology, the U.S. government has taken on an increasingly supportive role in this sector. In addition to Defense

Department programs such as the VHSIC, Supercomputer, and Gallium Arsenide projects, other agencies of government have taken steps to promote the industry. The Commerce Department, for example, negotiated a voluntary semiconductor import quota in 1982, while another agreement was reached opening Nippon Telephone's procurement activities to U.S. suppliers.[14] After dropping suits against IBM and AT&T, the Justice Department filed a predatory pricing suit against six Japanese semiconductor makers. The Federal Trade Commission also filed a monopolistic pricing suit against the same six companies.[15] The Federal Bureau of Investigation has been heavily involved in industrial espionage investigations involving Hitachi and Mitsubishi. Broad public support for the information technology sector is strongly in evidence. This sector presents the first indications of the potential power of a focused industrial policy in the United States.

THE EUROPEAN COMPUTER INDUSTRY

Although European computer markets are dominated by affiliates of American companies, there are a large number of effective indigenous companies that are privately owned and funded. Government support has been a factor in many but not all of these cases.

The leading European producer of personal computers is Sinclair Ltd. of Great Britain. Its ZX-81 model, introduced in 1981, sold more than 500,000 units in 1982. Another small British competitor in the mid-range personal computer segment is Acorn, Ltd., which sold over 100,000 units in the United Kingdom in 1982. Although Acorn is very much a private entrepreneurial venture, it received substantial indirect support from the British government. The British Department of Education, for example, offers a 50 percent rebate to all schools purchasing computers for educational use if they acquire an Acorn computer.

The continental market for personal computers is largely dominated by Commodore, with over 50 percent of total unit sales in 1982. Apple and Tandy have been relatively slow in penetrating the European market, although Tandy entered into a joint venture with Matra Corporation in November 1981 to assemble and market personal computers in Europe. The goal of this joint venture was to sell 25,000 units in 1983, with 80 percent outside of France. Other European entrants in the personal computer market include

Triumph-Adler, Olivetti, Philips, Olympia (AEG), Siemens, and Luxor, a Swedish television producer.

Minicomputer and Small Business Systems

European producers of minicomputers and small general-purpose systems have been highly successful in retaining control of a large share of these markets. One source estimates that indigenous European producers control 65 percent of this market. The leading sellers of minicomputers in Great Britain are ICL, Ferranti, GEC Computers, Systime Ltd., and Plessey. ICL, better known as a seller of mainframes, is also active in the minicomputer and small business system market. Ferranti's computer 1982 sales of $175 million were entirely in the areas of production control and military application, while GEC's minicomputer sales of $45 million were based in the commercial market. Systime Ltd. began in 1972 as a OEM suplier, but it now produces its own mini's and realized sales of $60 million in 1982. The National Enterprise Board owns 26 percent of Systime's equity. The remainder of this highly profitable and growing company is privately held. Plessey's minicomputer line is highly regarded in some circles, although sales have yet to reach a significant level. These five firms together control over half of the British minicomputer market.

The German small computer market is also dominated by European suppliers. Nixdorf holds 29.5 percent of this market, followed by Kienzle, Philips, Triumph-Adler, Olivetti, Ruf, and IBM. Privately held, profitable, and growing, Nixdorf has expanded its operations in the U.S. market to sales of over $150 million in 1982. Global 1982 sales reached $1.1 billion. The Deutsche Bank took a 25 percent stake in the company in 1979. Triumph-Adler, the second leading German producer of small computers, is owned by Volkswagen. This company is expanding from its typewriter base into a range of data-processing and office equipment markets. Total sales in 1982 exceeded $700 million. Triumph-Adler acquired Pertec Computer Products, a U.S. producer of small computers in 1979. Kienzle, with computer sales of over $400 million in 1982, ranks in the top 20 European vendors, ahead of rivals such as Data General. In addition to these German firms, Siemens also entered the small computer market in 1979.

The French small computer market also exhibits strong domestic firms. Thomson holds 21 percent of the French microcomputer market. The great majority of Thomson Informatique's 1982 sales of $497 million were in the minicomputer market. CII-Honeywell-Bull and CGE also are active in the French small and minicomputer markets.

Additional European producers of minicomputers include Nokia of Finland, which has sold more than 4,500 minicomputers, and Norsk Data, which offers one of the most efficient 32-bit minicomputers in the world. Norsk Data sales exceeded $100 million in 1982. Mycron, another small Norwegian producer, offers one of the first multiprocessor minicomputers, on the market. L. M. Ericsson recently acquired DataSAAB, whose 1980 sales of $276 million rank it among the larger European computer makers.

The success of European competitors in the small- and medium-sized computer segments is even more important in light of growth patterns in various segments of the market. The market for medium-sized computers is expected to grow at a 20 percent rate in 1983–84, while mainframes are growing at only an 8 percent rate. The fastest growing market, however, is for small-size systems priced under $50,000, which enjoyed a growth rate of 26 percent in 1983 (see Table 11–9).

Mainframes

The mainframe market has long been the focus of government support in Europe. ICL and CII-Honeywell Bull are both creatures of the state. Neither company has been financially successful, but

Table 11–9. Growth Trends in the European Data Processing Market.

Segment	Sales ($ million)				
	1979	1980	1981	1982	1983
Large Systems ($400,000+)	$2,850	$3,025	$3,750	$3,500	$4,000
Medium ($50,000–$400,000)	1,950	2,300	2,950	3,800	4,500
Small ($50,000)	1,100	1,450	1,950	2,400	3,100

Source: *Data Processing* (November 1983): 36.

both have established significant market positions, primarily but not completely in their home countries.

A constant theme in the mainframe industry has been attempts by major European producers to combat scale inefficiencies and capital requirements through collaborative ventures, such as Unidata, formed in 1976 by CII, Philips, and Siemens. CII's withdrawal to form a joint venture with Honeywell scuttled this agreement. More recently, collaboration agreements with Japanese producers have been common in Europe. For example, Fujitsu sells medium and large mainframes on an OEM basis to Siemens. Another agreement was signed with ICL in 1982, which commits ICL to marketing Fujitsu mainframes in exchange for access to semiconductor technology. Hitachi mainframes are sold by Olivetti and BASF.

Mainframes are the core market for Europe's largest computer companies. These companies are expanding their activities in other areas very rapidly, however. Siemens, which already owns an internal semiconductor business, has acquired four U.S. producers of semiconductors since 1979. The largest of these companies, Advanced Micro Devices, is a leading firm in the U.S. industry. Siemens is also expanding its activities in the medium and small computer segments in Europe and the United States, with its 6000 series of office computers.

Olivetti, while relying heavily on Hitachi for its mainframe product line, is a leader in the small computer segment. It recently acquired Docutel, a leading U.S. producer of automatic bank tellers, and has been a leader in this market in Europe. Olivetti is also a leader in the emerging European word processing market. The firm is somewhat unique in that 80 percent of its sales are generated outside of its home market. Olivetti's recent linkage to AT&T will greatly strengthen its access to U.S. markets, and broaden its product offerings in Europe.

ICL has also been successful in developing foreign markets for its products. Approximately half of its sales were realized outside the United Kingdom in 1981. The 1977 acquisition of Singer's installed base contributed to its presence in the U.S. computer market. In addition to its agreement with Fujitsu, ICL also owns 20 percent of Computer Peripherals Inc., a joint venture with Control Data and NCR.

CII-Honeywell-Bull's future is intimately tied to the strategy of the Mitterand government in France. The socialist government has nationalized literally every major French participant in the information technology sector and it is certain that further restructuring will take place, possibly with a larger role for CII. An integrated producer of components, computers, and communications equipment is expected to emerge in France, and CII may provide the nucleus for its formation.

THE CONVERGENCE WITH COMMUNICATIONS

A number of computer producers are presently active in the communications market. In Europe, Siemens, Philips, Olivetti, and France's CIT-Alcatel (a CGE affiliate) are leading telecommunications vendors. In addition, communications companies such as Plessey, Ericsson, and Ferranti are increasing their activities in the computer market. Japanese computer makers, especially NEC (36%), Fujitsu (21%), and Oki (31%) derive a large share of their total turnover from communications markets.

The role of the national telephone and telegraph authorities is particularly important in the communications industry. In Japan, NT&T accounts for 95 percent of all telephone set sales, 66 percent of all phone systems, and 18 percent of all PBX unit sales. The same pattern holds true in most European markets. In Great Britain, for example, all PBXs smaller than 100 lines have had to be purchased from the national British Telecom Board. The market for large PBXs is open to competition, but the primary customer for such systems is British Telecom itself. The small PBX market accounts for 50 percent of all switching-system sales in the United Kingdom. British Telecom serves this market on an OEM basis, purchasing systems from Mitel, Philips, and Plessey.

Japan's NT&T, unlike AT&T, does not manufacture its own equipment and depends for over 80 percent of its equipment purchases on the five leading Japanese computer companies. As a result, equipment purchases often involve significantly nationalistic biases. The recent AT&T fiber-optics contract involving Fujitsu was reversed under political pressure.[16]

The market for communications equipment is opening up, however. In the United States, communications deregulation is offering increased opportunity to independent vendors and U.S. imports of communications equipment soared in 1984. Japan's NT&T has opened its procurement doors to foreign suppliers, and British Telecom's monopoly was removed in 1982. These steps will increase the internationalization of the industry significantly. AT&T is already operating in markets outside of the United States for the first time since it was forced to divest foreign affiliates such as Nippon Electric Company and IT&T in the early 1920s.

The PBX Market

In the United States, the leading producers of PBXs are Rolm, GTE, Northern Telecom, ITT, Mitel, Stromberg-Carlson, and of course AT&T. As recently as 1975, AT&T held over 80 percent of the U.S. PBX market but its share had fallen to 54 percent by 1980. In addition to foreign entrants such as Ericsson, Fujitsu, and NEC, several major new U.S. competitors have recently entered this market. Companies such as Wang, Harris, Micom, and Datapoint have developed innovative PBXs with extended features, primarily voice and data communication. IBM, which has sold PBXs in Europe for some time, recently won approval from the FCC to offer a PBX system in the United States. Honeywell acquired a producer of PBX's in 1981 and entered into a joint venture with L.M. Ericsson in 1983.

Leading European makers include L.M. Ericsson, Philips, Siemens, AEG, and CIT-Alcatel. Several companies are making concerted efforts to enter the European PBX market. Olivetti, for example, adopted a licensing agreement with Northern Telecom in 1981 to manufacture small PBXs. In Great Britain, Plessey produces small PBXs under license from Rolm, GEC holds a license from Northern Telecom, and Ferranti is active in a joint venture with GTE. All were thus prepared for the elimination of British Telecom's monopoly on small PBXs in 1982.

Videotex

Videotex systems are highly developed in Western Europe. The most aggressive projects are operating in France, under the sponsorship of the Direction Générale des Telecommunications

(DGT). This communications authority has launched several innovative programs. The Teletel project, for instance, is an experimental videotex system conducted in the Parisian suburb of Velizy. While this experiment involves only 2,500 videotex terminals, a larger but more basic project consisting of 250,000 user terminals is being launched.[17] Plans call for equipping each of France's 30 million telephone subscribers with a free videotex terminal by 1992.

One immediate result of this effort has been the stimulation of videotex terminal production in France. CIT-Alcatel was given a contract to produce the first batch of 300,000 terminals in April 1982. The company plans to produce 1.5 million terminals in 1984. Alcatel recently signed an agreement with Source Telecomputing Corp., the largest supplier of home videotex services in the United States, to sell its products in the American market. Source, with a rapidly growing subscriber list approaching 100,000, hopes to sell 250,000 terminals by 1985. Other videotex projects of smaller scale are underway in virtually every European country.

In the United States, videotex services are dominated by private enterprises. While AT&T's videotex system is still in the experimental stages, two companies, Source and Compuserve, are selling primarily to users of personal computer rather than to videotex terminals.

Local Networks

The single most significant change taking place within the communications industry is the development of local networks. The term is somewhat misleading because local networks include not only interbuilding systems but intrabuilding, regional, and worldwide communications systems. Interbuilding systems, such as the Xerox Ethernet network, are hand-wired and entail installation of a separate set of cables. Linkages for more extended systems include microwave links and satellite earth station installations. These systems permit the development of worldwide private communications networks involving transmission of voice, video, and data signals.

Much of the conflict between system suppliers and niche-oriented competitors will take place in this increasingly important market, which deals in PBX equipment, satellite earth stations,

Many smaller niche-oriented competitors, for example, will be prime candidates for acquisition by systems oriented competitors in the years ahead. A large number of such acquisitions have already taken place. One advanced example of this strategy is Macom, which has pieced together an extended information technology enterprise through such acquisitions.

SUMMARY

Our analysis has focused on broad trends and key participants in the microelectronics, computer, and communications markets. The convergence and internationalization of these markets stand out sharply amidst the complexity and dynamism of this sector. The continued role of national governments in structuring and supporting indigenous industry also stands out.

These broad trends do not bode well for small, national, niche-oriented producers, with the notable exception of the service and software market, where such enterprises are likely to prosper. Many such firms will have to expand their operations in new markets if they are to survive in the information technology sector. Mergers, collaborations, acquisitions, public rescues, and bankruptcies can be expected in the future. Despite this prospect, however, new entrepreneurial enterprises will continue to make their mark in this sector and many are likely to originate outside the United States.

Competition among the global systems suppliers will increase significantly over the next decade. Competition will increase as AT&T expands abroad, as IBM diversifies its product line into new areas, as Japanese competitors broaden their operations, as France defines its national policies in the industry, and so on. Only the prospect of continued market growth alleviates the prospect of massive confrontation.

The ultimate competitive equilibrium in this market depends as much upon national will as any other factor. The United States is increasingly aggressive in protecting and promoting its information technology sector. Defense Department funding has risen rapidly; the Commerce Department reached an agreement with Japanese producers to limit chip exports to the United States in May 1982; and the courts have resolved antitrust suits against IBM and AT&T. A truly focused national effort by the United States in this sector would be a formidable force. There is every indication, in viewing both corporate and governmental activities, that U.S. competitors will strongly defend their leadership in the information technology sector.

Nonetheless, Japan's coordinated thrust in the sector promises to be very powerful. As has been shown, Japanese firms possess outstanding semiconductor, computer, and communications technology, and although the structure of the Japanese industry is becoming more fragmented and diffused, it is still the most focused and integrated of any national industry. Dominance of the information technology sector is a national goal for Japan. Japanese competitors will be committed to the industry with far more than the customary zeal, patience, and willingness to accept lower returns.

The European industry has strengths in many areas, but notable weakness in focus and integration. The European semiconductor industry is particularly weak. European efforts to compete in the information technology sector are likely to exhibit the highest level of direct government support and protection. So far, Europe's record of such activity has not been singularly positive. Nonetheless, government promotion and protection of domestic competitors will be an important force in shaping the future structure of the information technology sector.

NOTES

1. "World Market Survey and Forecast," *Electronics* (January 13, 1984).
2. Captive production of semiconductors totalled about $4.1 billion in 1982. The sales of leading producers appear below.

Company	Production Value ($ million)
IBM	$2,100
Western Electric	385
General Electric	225
Delco (GM)	185
Honeywell	180
Hewlett-Packard	160
NCR	70

Source: *Electronics* (May 19, 1982): 135.

3. "World Market Survey and Forecast."

4. For an excellent primer on semiconductor technology, see W.G. Oldham "The Fabrication of Microelectronic Circuits," *Scientific American* (September 1977): 110–28 and T.M. Fredericksen, *Intuitive IC Electronics* (New York: McGraw-Hill, 1982).

5. The history of the microprocessor is presented in R.N. Noyce, and M.E. Hoff, Jr., "A History of Microprocessor Development at Intel," *IEEE Micro* (February 1981): 8–21.

6. For a detailed review of early French efforts to create a national semiconductor industry, see M.P. Gadonneix, "The Influence of the State on Industrial Strategies: A Study of the Computer Industry in France" (Ph.D. dissertation, Harvard Business School, 1974). See also "Le Plan Français des Circuits Integrés," *Telecommunications* 41 (October 1981): 34–41. In late 1983, a plan was announced whereby Thomson would adopt most of CGE's components operations. "French Government Approves Asset Exchange Between Thomson, CGE," *Electronic News,* September 26, 1983, p. 45.

7. The five-year plan is designed to make France the "third largest force in world electronics": J.P. Chevenement, Minister for Research and Industry, quoted in *Financial Times,* January 21, 1983, p. 1. See also "Honeywell in France," (A and B), UVA-BP-234, Colgate Darden School, University of Virginia, 1984.

8. The VHSIC Project recently entered its second phase to produce a sub- micron device. See "2d-Steps Bids on VHSIC," *Electronic News* (May 30, 1983): 39. The Defense Department recently announced a new program to be patterned after the VHSIC project. See *Electronic News* (May 16, 1983): 92.

9. According to a recent Defense Department analysis of electronics purchases, requirements for computing equipment, semiconductors, and are scheduled to increase from $3.2 billion, $2 billion, and $3.3 billion in 1981, respectively, to $7.9 billion, $5.7 billion, and $6.4 billion in 1986. "Military Electronics," *Electronic News* (June 13, 1983): 4.

10. See *Electronic News* (July 18, 1983): 29.

11. "Texas Instruments' Problems Show Pitfalls of Home Computer Market," *Wall Street Journal,* June 17, 1983, p. 29.

12. See "The Development of the Japanese Computer Industry," in E.J. Kaplan, ed., *Japan: The Government-Business Relationship* (Washington, D.C., Department of Commerce, 1982). See also H.J. Welke, *Data Processing in Japan* (New York: North-Holland Publishers, 1982).

13. "Japanese (printer) firms to expand U.S. offerings," *Management Information Systems Week* (December 8, 1982): 14.

14. For a more detailed discussion of these developments, see W.H.

Davidson, *The Amazing Race* (New York: Wiley, 1984), ch. 6; also, "Japan to Cut Export of Chips," *New York Times,* April 8, 1982, p. D1.

15. "U.S. Probes Japanese Chip Makers," *San Jose Mercury,* July 27, 1982, p.1.
16. "Japan's High-Tech Sales Hit a U.S. Snag," *Business Week* (January 25, 1982): 40.
17. "France goes flat out for clever telephones," *Economist* (March 15, 1983): 83–84; "Videotex," *The Economist* (October 31, 1981): 90; *Financial Times* (January 1, 1981): 10.

12 THE AEROSPACE INDUSTRY

Milton Hochmuth

Free-world competition in aerospace is markedly different from that in most other industrial sectors, and the characteristics of competition between manufacturers of large military and commercial aircraft, particularly the latter, are unique. In 1984 some thirty-six firms in sixteen market-economy nations manufactured commercial passenger aircraft, but only three firms—Boeing and McDonnell Douglas in the United States and the European conational consortium of Airbus Industrie—were developing and building the large commercial transports that carry the majority of the world's passenger traffic.

About 600 commercial airlines in the free world are customers for these passenger aircraft, however, less than 100 fly the large airliners (roughly 100-seat or more capacity). Of these, only 15 airlines had fleets of eighty or more such large aircraft.[1] In the military field, no more than a dozen firms in the free world independently develop and manufacture first-line fighters and bombers. Nine operate in the United States and one each in Britain, France, Sweden, and Israel. Potential customers for these aircraft numbered, in 1984, some fifty countries.

Profitability in the manufacture of the large civil airlines has been rare. In 1981 Lockheed—one of the four remaining manufacturers—announced it was abandoning production of its sole entry,

333

the 300–400 passenger L-1011 "Tri-Star." And McDonnell Douglas gave signs of faltering when in late 1983 it abandoned new development. Only Boeing appeared to be making a profit on commercial planes.[3]

For manufacturers of military aircraft, profitability has been much easier to achieve, largely because of national military procurement policies. But the capital investment required to develop even a light combat aircraft is such that only a handful of national treasuries outside the three major manufacturing nations (the United States, Britain, and France) can afford to support industries that manufacture their own or licensed designs. West Germany has rebuilt an aerospace industry of respectable size but, partly for political reasons and partly for economic ones, has chosen to produce large military aircraft only jointly with Britain, France, and Italy. Of the other non-East Bloc countries, only Sweden has independently developed and built a first-line fighter, the JA 37 Viggen. The engine for the Viggen was a licensed derivative of the U.S. Pratt & Whitney JT 8D commercial engine. (In 1983, Israel launched the development of a multipurpose fighter, the Lavi, with lavish support from the U.S. Treasury.)

Of the eight firms that develop and manufacture jet engines for either large military or civilian planes, only three—two U.S. and one British—had an across-the-board capability, and these three supplied all large commercial engines either directly, through license, or through joint ventures.

In space technology and applications, the Europeans had mounted a challenge to U.S. domination of commercial applications in telecommunications. While considerably smaller in scale that U.S. activity, this European effort was persistent and vigorous.

Competition in private/corporate planes, commuter/regional transports, and helicopters can only be briefly touched on in this chapter, but it has been growing rapidly in importance. Deregulation of the U.S. airline industry in 1978 gave a strong impetus to second- and third-tier airlines, which flew the small planes of ten, twenty, forty, and even ninety seats. In 1982, when the U.S. industry shipped $6.2 billion worth of large airliners, it also shipped $2.0 billion of small commercial and private aircraft and $597 million of civil helicopters. Relatively few of the U.S. small commercial aircraft were for airlines, however.

In 1981 U.S. imports of small commercial aircraft almost doubled from $496 million (in 1980) to $913 million, exceeding U.S. exports for the first time. Many of these imports were commuter aircraft for airlines and came from the Netherlands, Canada, Northern Ireland, Spain, and, surprisingly, Brazil. Indeed, so successful has been the Brazilian eighteen-seat Bandeirante aircraft manufactured by Embraer that the U.S. Fairchild Company, whose Swearingen subsidiary manufactures a competing plane, petitioned the U.S. government to impose on Embraer countervailing duties of 40 percent of the Bandeirante's price. During the first five months of 1982, Embraer captured a 35 percent share of this particular market niche, largely at Fairchild's expense.

If we look at the global statistics in Table 12–1 for 1983 (excluding East Bloc and People's Republic of China aircraft), U.S. dominance of the large-aircraft industry was overwhelming. Yet the United States was not always in such a lead; in fact, the U.S. lead is comparatively recent. Although the Wright brothers are the acknowledged founders of today's aerospace industry, it was in Europe that aeronautical technology advanced most rapidly through the end of World War II. The most recent examples are jet engines (the heart of modern aircraft) and large rockets (the basis of all space technology). Not until early after World War II did the United States become dominant in aerospace technology and production. By the end of the 1960s, the U.S. industry seemed to both Europeans and Americans so dominant that little hope (or fear) existed that any European nation or Europe as a whole could ever compete with U.S. industry on an equal footing.[4]

An examination of the trends in industry sales, however, puts a somewhat different light on the picture. Whereas in 1967 U.S. production, as reflected by sales, totaled $25 billion, compared to only $3 billion for the Common Market countries (including Britain), the Europeans put the years following 1967 to good use (see Table 12–2).[5] Clearly, the world competitive picture in this industry has changed dramatically, with the United States losing its economic lead.

But how should competitive strength, success, or potential in the aerospace sector be measured and compared? Are the usual statistics a reliable index? In most industries the customary indicators are current figures and trends for sales, profits, market shares, financial resources, or a combination of these parameters. However, the world aerospace industry differs from most other indus-

Table 12–1. Approximate Number of Large Aircraft in Service or On Order (end of 1983) by Country of Origin.

	United States	United Kingdom	France	Joint Programs		
				United Kingdom/ Germany/ Italy/	United Kingdom/ France	France/ Germany/ United Kingdom
Military Combat Aircraft (excluding trainers, transports & helicopters)	16,000+	800	2,000	880	500	—
Large Civil Transports (100+ seats)	6,000	162	10	—	14	375

Sources: *Flight International* (December 17, 1983): 1,609 ff.; and Ibid. (May 26, 1984): 1407 ff.

Table 12–2. Aerospace Sales, 1967 and 1981 (in millions of current dollars.)[a]

	1967	1981	Percent Increase
Belgium	27	475	1,760
France	1,250	8,085	647
Germany	261	3,702	1,418
Italy	160	1,703	1,064
Netherlands	60	492	820
United Kingdom	1,510	9,099	602
Total European Economic Community (EC)	3,368	23,557	
Final EC (excluding intracommunity transactions between EC aerospace companies)	1,810	18,471	1,020
Japan	n.a.	1,326	—
United States[b]	24,688	52,327	212

Notes:

a. Excludes intracompany sales within a country but includes reexports to other countries—engines, electronic equipment, etc.

b. Excludes non-aerospace sales of aerospace companies

Sources:

a. European Economic Community: Collection Etudes, Serie Industrie, no. 4, 1971, vol. 2 pp. 871ff; EEC Commission Document III/202/84-EN, (Brussels, 1984)

b. Aerospace Industries Association of America, *Aerospace Facts and Figures:* 1976/1977 and 1983/1984

tries in many important respects, and international comparisons require a careful look behind the usual parameters. To explain the competitive context, this chapter will examine the factors that shape competition and then look at the source of the current major challenge to U.S. dominance—European collaborative or conational programs.

KEY FACTORS SHAPING COMPETITION IN THE AEROSPACE INDUSTRY

Competitive factors in aerospace can be divided into three categories: the usual economic ones, technical factors that are industry peculiar, and political factors. Of these, the political factors are the most powerful.

Political Factors

Industrialized nations have attached ever-increasing importance to their aerospace industries since World War II, and this importance has been heightened by a subjective perception of glamour in the notion of high technology itself and a willingness among nations to pay for it. For example, in the United States, the $30 million spent in 1983 for a single-seat fighter aircraft raised hardly a murmur, but paying $1 million for a heavily armed tank to carry four soldiers could trigger a congressional investigation. Sweden was willing to pay $31 million for the JA 37 Viggen fighter, and relatively less wealthy nations such as Ecuador or Morocco have also readily paid $5 million and more for less sophisticated fighter aircraft.

Because of their importance to defense, national aerospace industries have always had a symbiotic relationship with their governments. In Europe this relationship was strengthened in the 1920s and 1930s because civil air transportation was seen as a means of stitching far-flung colonial empires together, "showing the flag," and also of buttressing commercial and political links with distant trading partners. Still, it is remarkable that, from the earliest days, the industries' military sales, and more recently military-plus-space sales, to home and foreign governments have steadily hovered between 60 and 80 percent of their total sales, despite the coming of age of civil air transportation. As a result, governments have had more than a casual interest in the continuing health of these industries and have supervised them closely, whether the firms were state-owned or not. Given this strong interest, it is not surprising that political relationships and pressures, domestic and international, exert a profound influence on both military and civilian industry sales.

The advent of the large jet transports with their comparatively lower fares caused an explosive growth of international air travel and made commercial air transportation very big business indeed. With such large revenues involved, European governments were induced to use all their political powers to support and promote their national industries. European aerospace (and air transportation) firms thus became both politicoeconomic tools and, in a good many cases, economic liabilities.[6]

Not the least politically relevant feature of this industry is the importance of its labor force in the national economics of the United States, Britain, and France, which have the largest industries. Table 12–3 describes employment trends in the industry; the figures quoted do not include supplier-industry employment, which is sizable.

Comparison with the auto industry in the United States demonstrates the aerospace industry's importance: At the end of 1982, employment in the U.S. auto industry was 669 thousand compared to 1.15 million in the U.S. aerospace industry. Auto production workers numbered 490 thousand compared to 535 thousand aerospace production workers [U.S. Department of Labor data].

Because aerospace products, particularly military and civil transport aircraft, are so costly, they play an important role in tilting foreign trade balances. Aerospace is the single largest U.S. export industry and is a major positive contributor to French and British trade balances. Therefore political pressures of all sorts are frequently used to promote export sales. When Valery Giscard d'Estaing visited India in January 1980, for example, one of his announced tasks was to encourage exports of French aircraft. Sale of the proposed Mirage 2000 fighter was said to be part of a broad trade package including an aluminum plant, offshore oil exploration, financial support for irrigation projects, electric power development, and so on.[7] Egypt had already ordered twenty Mirage

Table 12–3. Aerospace Employment Trends (in thousands).

	1967	1972	1977	1981
West Germany	35	52	52	69
Belgium	5	5	5	7
France	101	109	103	114
Italy	17	29	32	41
Netherlands	6	7	7	10
United Kingdom	254	208	219	250
European Economic Community	418	409	418	490
United States	1,168	912	893	1,207
Canada	n.a.	29	29	45
Japan	n.a.	26	24	27

Source: EEC Commission, Document III/202/84-EN, (Brussels, Jan. 1984).

2000s at a price of $40 million (1982) per plane (including spares and other equipment).[8] Part of the agreements with both India and Egypt (which typified many such military and civilian export orders by European firms and, to a growing extent, U.S. firms) was that France would help these countries develop their ability to manufacture the plane under what are known as "offset" arrangements. Such arrangements specify transfer of technology, including production equipment, and the manufacture of part or even all of the plane domestically.

In negotiating the sale of civil airliners abroad, countless additional bargaining chips are used that may or may not have anything to do with the merits or price of the aircraft itself. Complex financial concessions (often state-provided), landing rights, flight schedules, purchase of unrelated products or services as part of the trade package are but a few of the typical tie-ins. A much discussed example was the extraordinary financial inducement offered to Eastern Airlines by the conational French and West German government-backed Airbus Industrie to crack the U.S. commercial airline market. In 1977 Airbus offered Eastern Airlines four of the new 240-seat A-300 B4 aircraft on a rent-free trial basis for six months. Then, after the aircraft proved to be highly reliable and more economical and technologically advanced than the older U.S. competitive aircraft, Eastern bought twenty-three in April 1978. What startled observers were the financial terms of the sale. Airbus Industrie lent Eastern $96 million (General Electric, whose engine powered the plane, lent Eastern $45 million), $250 million at 8.25 percent interest was provided by European bank loans guaranteed by European governments, and Airbus Industrie agreed to pay Eastern a subsidy for a (negotiable) period during which the A-300's seat capacity was greater than Eastern's stated need of only a 175-seat capacity.[9] Eastern's chairman, Frank Borman, was quoted as telling an employee gathering, "If you don't kiss the French flag every time you see it, at least salute it. The export financing on our Airbus deal subsidized this airline by more than $100 million."[10]

In space and the related military missile technology, nation states were, until the beginning of the 1980s, the sole sources of funds, and industry-state relations in this subsector were identical to those in the military aircraft subsector so far as financing was concerned. Funds, though, might come from a national space agency as well as the military. With the advent of commercial communication satellites this situation began to change, but the state was still the dominant force—providing launch vehicles, allocating satellite positions in space (under international agreement), communication frequencies, and providing significant R&D support. Because of the enormous commercial market potential in satellite communications, all governments (except perhaps the U.S.) became active, even aggressive as both suppliers and users. As a result, this segment of the aerospace industry also became highly politicized.

In sum, national and, above all, international politics permeate every aspect of the air industry. In the words of a French deputy:

> The aerospace industry is completely global in nature. The aeronautical world market is the opposite of pure and simple world trade between equals. More than anything, it is a power struggle between nations, each player using all his strengths—economic and political. And more than any other industry, aerospace is highly dependent on noneconomic factors. That is to say that, no matter how advanced your technology, how accurate your market estimates, how skillful your marketing effort, the adroit employment of political power is essential to break (to the degree deemed necessary) American dominance of the aeronautical market.[11]

Many American aerospace executives who felt the pinch of foreign competition wished that their government attached equal importance to the need for political leverage in the intense and increasingly competitive international arena.

Technological Factors

As in all industries, a number of technological factors influence the dynamics of competition in aerospace:

- Division of the industry into four product-specific, but interdependent, subsectors that differ according to technologies, barriers to entry, etc.
- Dependence of the industry on extensive, costly R&D for improved products and processes.

Table 12–4. "Final" Aerospace Sales by Country and Sector, 1967 (percentage of total sales).

Country	Total[a] (millions 1967 dollars)	Airframe	Space & Missiles	Engines	Equip-ment
France	1,267	47.9%	18.5%	23.0%	10.6%
Germany	419	64.0	13.0	23.0	18.1
Italy	160	58.1	0.0	23.8	18.1
Belgium	62	40.7	0.0	59.3	0.0
Netherlands	60	100.0	0.0	0.0	0.0
United Kingdom	1,566	47.5	4.8	37.8	9.9
EC and Great Britain	3,534	50.3	10.2	29.9	9.6
United States	24,688	39.7	20.4	17.7	22.2

a. The 1967 data are for final sales to user within each country, excluding intrafirm sales (e.g., equipment to airframe manufacturers), but do include international sales of components that are then included in importing-countries final sales.

Source: EEC Commission: Collection Etudes, Serie Industrie, no. 4, 1971. (SORIS), pp. 411 & 432

- A steady incorporation by the industry of these state-of-the-art products, resulting in costs that rise faster than inflation.
- The relatively lengthy time between development of a major new idea or program and its entry into service (anywhere from five to seventeen years).
- Considerable variation in the useful life of products among subsectors.

The average life of a military aircraft varies from less than twenty to as much as twenty-five or more years, while the average life of a commercial transport ranges from twenty to thirty or even more years. (In mid-1982 a small U.S. airline was flying a Douglas DC-3 transport which was 42 years old.) The median age of transports in the fleets of large carriers, however, is normally limited from 7 to 10 years.

Before the rocket, missile and space age, the aircraft industry consisted primarily of three subsectors: airframes, engines and a smaller equipment subsector (e.g., wheels, brakes, pumps, generators). With the advent of missiles and space vehicles, the product

range expanded considerably, especially in the area of rocket motors, electronics, and complex electro-mechanical and hydraulic-
mechanical equipment. At the same time, the sophistication of
these subsectors with respect to materials, product complexity,
and manufacturing processes increased at an almost unbelievable
pace. This accelerated pace was due largely to a subordination of
cost to performance by the industry's largest single customer, the
military.

By 1982 the industry was composed of four subsectors, each of
which required a different set of engineering, production, and
marketing skills. Tables 12–4 and 12–5 show the size of these
subsectors as they related to to the total market in 1967 and 1981.
The data for the United States and Europe are based on different
statistical methods, so they are not fully comparable, but the
figures do demonstrate relative changes for those countries with
the largest sales. (By the end of the 1980s helicopters will have
grown sizable enough to constitute a separate subsector: helicopters are included here in the Airframe and Engine categories.)

Literally hundreds of firms in the United States currently oper-

Table 12–5. "Overall" Aerospace Sales by Country and Sector,
1981 (percentage of Total Sales).

Country	Total[a] (millions 1981 dollars)	Airframe	Space	Engines	Equip- ment
France	9,844	63.5%	2.6%	16.6%	17.3%
Germany	4,591	61.5	4.9	10.8	22.8
Italy	1,962	69.5	2.5	13.7	14.3
Belgium	478	33.1	4.3	51.0	11.6
Netherlands	497	44.6	3.2	0.0	52.2
United Kingdom	10,962	38.3	2.3	27.7	31.7
EC	28,063	53.2	2.8	20.0	24.0
United States	65,000 (est.)b	47.7	17.7	14.6	20.0

Notes:

a. 1981 data are for "global" sales (e.g., they include the sales of all separate firms and
therefore are much larger than "final" sales).

b. "Global" data for the United States is not readily available.

c. The important Missile subsector is included in Airframes for the EEC and in space for the
United States

Source: EEC Commission, document III/202/84-EN (Brussels, 1984), p. 83

ate in the equipment subsector, and at least thirty or more could be considered major companies. Dozens of others are active in Europe and in Japan. This proliferation results from weak barriers to entry (capital investment required, cost of R&D, time for development) and a tendency for firms to specialize in particular products. But airframes, aircraft engines, large rockets and spacecraft are another matter. In the category of major military and large civil transport aircraft, only four firms exist in all of Western Europe— Messerschmitt Bölkow-Blohm (which has yet to develop and produce an entirely West German large aircraft, military or civilian), British Aerospace, and in France, Aérospatiale and Dassault. Japan also has yet to develop a world-class competitive industry. In the United States, nine firms are actively engaged in combat military aircraft development, but as was earlier mentioned, only Boeing and McDonnell Douglas are still in the large civil transport business (see Figure 12–1).

Only three firms in the world develop and build a complete range of large aircraft engines: Pratt & Whitney (United Technologies Corp.) in the United States, General Electric (U.S.), and Rolls-Royce (U.K.). This subsector illustrates one of the most important features of the aircraft industry—its historic dependence on improved engines as a basis for improved aircraft. While there have been tremendous strides in aerodynamics, airframe materials, and airframe production processes, the fundamental factors allowing development of improved aircraft performance have been increases in the efficiency and power of engines. Greater thrust and a corresponding reduction in the relative weight of the engine have permitted aircraft designers to develop larger, and at the same time more efficient, aircraft. Given higher engine temperatures and pressures, aircraft now burn less fuel per hour for a given thrust. Engine improvements of military aircraft over the past decades, while striking, cannot be strictly compared to civil-engine improvements because of the different performance characteristics the military seeks.

Despite what on the surface appear to be marginal performance improvements, a truly new engine such as the PW 2037 (Pratt & Whitney) represented more than five years of intensive development and a development and production tooling cost of over $1 billion (1982). Even more common incremental design improvements, known as derivatives, can cost $150 million and up.

Figure 12–1.   Major World Aircraft Manufacturers 1930–1985.

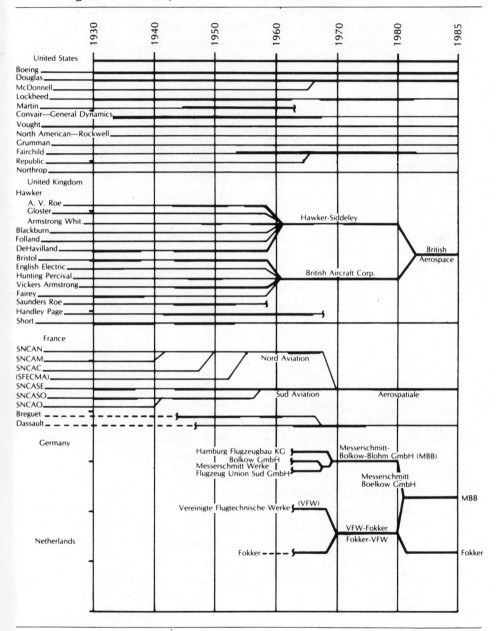

Note: Heavy lines denote development or manufacture of large commercial transports.

Jet engines for large airliners cost from $2 million to $5 million or more in 1982 (not including spare parts). The cost of an engine developed by General Electric and SNECMA, the French national engine concern, for the Airbus A-300, together with spare parts, was more than $6 million per engine (1982), which represented about one-fourth of the aircraft price.[12] Because of the high development costs, lengthy development times, and comparatively limited global market for jet engines, international cooperation was the only route for engine manufacturers other than the three mentioned previously. France's SNECMA was cooperating with General Electric in the development of two modern airliner engines—the CF6 series for wide-bodied airliners and the CFM 56 engines for smaller or short-range transports—while also independently developing and building engines for France's modern military aircraft. West Germany's Motoren-und-Turbinen Union (MTU) and Japan's three manufacturers had also been forced to enter into joint-development ventures with one of the big three for developing new large engines or into building existing engines under license. In 1983 it became evident that even the "big three" would be forced into conational ventures for future major developments.

Once widely adopted, an engine stays in production for as long as thirty years, undergoing incremental improvements with time. Because of price competition, payback periods for the engine proper can reach fifteen years before the cumulative cash flow becomes positive. But thereafter a widely adopted engine can become very profitable. The long payback period does not operate in the case of repair parts, which some customers maintain can be globally profitable in a few years.

With development costs so high, substantial technological progress occurs primarily in government or military-funded engine designs. These improvements, in turn, provide the technological basis for new civil engines. One major attempt at a technological breakthrough in civil engines was Rolls-Royce's use of carbon-fiber turbine blades in their RB-211 engine for the U.S. Lockheed Tri-Star. The failures and delays that resulted in Rolls-Royce's bankruptcy and subsequent nationalization brought Lockheed to near bankruptcy in 1971.

The aircraft engine subsector is therefore a bitterly competitive world oligopoly heavily supported by national governments, with new developments rare and costly enough to rival development costs for new planes. The United States, with by far the largest number of military and civilian aircraft in the western world, dominates this sector and appears likely to continue to do so unless international joint ventures become the rule.

Economic Factors

Economic factors are almost as powerful as political factors in shaping competition in the aerospace industry, and these economic factors can be ordered in terms of importance as follows:

- The high and constantly increasing unit costs of the end products, both military and civilian.
- The enormous size of the market.
- The ever-increasing costs of R&D and production tooling (including all nonrecurring costs).
- The relatively long development times (from program launch to first flight), causing a long period of negative cash flow for civil aircraft.
- The fact that the market for civil transports is primarily a function of the increase in passenger and cargo traffic, which, in turn, is largely influenced by general economic conditions. The market is secondarily a function of the age of existing fleets, technological advances that result in improved performance, and the ability of the airlines to finance new purchases. External factors, such as the multiplying cost of fuel, also have a very great effect.
- Total operating costs. So far as airliners are concerned, the most important single parameter influencing the choice between two or more competing transports is the total operating costs, including depreciation. These costs, in turn, are primarily a function of the price of the plane and the air-seat kilometers per liter of fuel.
- The importance of the home government as the largest customer and therefore the political interest the home government takes in the industry.

The preceding factors combine with the political and technological factors to produce certain corollary characteristics of the industry:

- By 1982 aerospace had become a world oligopoly as far as large combat aircraft were concerned, and a very small world oligopoly so far as large civil aircraft, large aircraft engines, and space materiel were concerned.
- Because of the huge costs involved, the aerospace industry has always been dependent on government R&D spending for advanced military aircraft to provide the basis for improved civil airliners.
- Careful timing of the introduction of a new airliner to avoid economic slumps has grown extremely important.
- Exports of both military and large civil aircraft have become crucial to the U.S., British, French, and to some extent the West German, industries to help amortize development costs. As a result, government backing of national industries' sales abroad have led to intense, even predatory, financing of exports by national agencies and financial institutions.

With the foregoing factors in mind, the structure of industry competition can be depicted and its evolution traced.

STRUCTURE OF AEROSPACE INDUSTRY COMPETITION

The cost of combat military aircraft has always been a function primarily of what technology could provide and, secondarily, of what governments could afford. If necessary, quantity has usually been sacrificed in favor of more advanced technology. Since combat aircraft are by definition products that "compete" with each other, the result has been a constant upward trend in unit costs significantly greater than inflation rates, as shown in Table 12–6.

Understandably, governments have found these financial burdens harder and harder to bear. For example, nonrecurring costs, including both development and production tooling, for the F-13 Grumman fighter were about $2 billion (1973).[13] In 1981 the Anglo-German-Italian Tornado advanced fighter, development of

Table 12–6. Approximate "Fly-away"[a] Cost or Cost Estimate of First-Line Fighter Aircraft (in millions of constant 1980 dollars).[b]

	1950	1955	1960	1965	1969	1976	1979	1982
Average Cost of all fighters purchased during year	1.1	2.2	5.9	5.3	—	—	—	—
U.S. F–4 Fighter	—	—	—	—	6.0	6.3	12.3	—
U.S. F–15 Fighter	—	—	—	—	—	9.1	12.5	17.1
U.S. F–14 Fighter	—	—	—	—	—	13.6	20.8	29.1 (1983)
Anglo-German-Italian Tornado	—	—	—	—	8.0[c]	—	18.0	22.0

Notes:
a. Cost of plane and equipment, excluding development, spares, etc.
b. price deflator for U.S. Federal Government purchases used.
c. Estimated
Source: *Aviation Facts & Figures,* various issues; *Fortune* (Feb. 1977): 82; *Financial Times* (April 11, 1982): 8.

which began in 1969, started coming off the production line; it was said to have cost $3.2 billion to develop and prepare for production (including the engine).[14] As a consequence of these financial loads on the national treasuries, the number of successful, large firms in Europe steadily diminished until, in 1984, only one major firm operated in each European country. This diminution in military manufacturers was much less marked in the United States, where in 1984 all nine principal aircraft firms were still active in the military aircraft market due to the military's and government's desire to finance a large production base (see Figure 12–1).

There was an additional cost restraint on some European manufacturers because of sales to Third World countries, which simply could not afford the most advanced technologies. The French, especially, had been delighted at the beginning of the 1980s to see over 60 percent of their military aircraft production exported. These exports have long been considered a "must" for the French economy, but because their customers were mostly Third World countries less expensive if slightly less performing aircraft were developed for both the home and export markets.

France, much to the credit of Marcel Dassault's genius, was able to keep the costs of combat aircraft development at a fraction of

U.S. and British costs—particularly in the 1950s and 1960s. Always using his previous plane as a stepping stone and keeping his staff very lean, Dassault designed new models and readied them for production much more quickly (and hence at lower cost) than U.S. firms. For example, in 1955–1956 the Mirage III was developed in thirteen months with a staff of only 25 engineers, while at the same time, Lockheed was converting an existing civil transport for antisubmarine duty with a staff of 439 engineers.[15] By the 1970s French development costs had increased but were still considerably less than those in the United States. Development times at the beginning of the 1980s for U.S. military aircraft seemed to range from five to seven years.

For civil transports, the underlying market factors have been quite different. Because air travel is so much faster than surface transportation, the air market grew quickly. Perhaps the best single parameter to measure the growth of the market is revenue passenger-kilometers traveled, since this is the basis for airline revenues.[16] From 1950 to 1970, passenger travel increased at a relatively steady rate of about 14 percent per year compounded. (This figure does not include Eastern Bloc or Peoples Republic of China data, and it masks important differences among domestic, international, and intercontinental travel.) Seat-kilometers offered increased even more rapidly than actual passenger travel, which reflected an overcapacity that resulted from increasing competition on all routes.

To capture market share, airlines kept adding large and faster aircraft to their fleets and increased the numbers of flights. Load factors (percentage of seats filled) fell from between 55–60 percent in the 1950s to barely 50 percent in 1970 and 1971. After dropping to around 10 percent through 1973, the annual passenger-kilometers growth rate dropped precipitously—to 6 percent in 1974–1975 because of the oil crisis—but then rose slightly in 1976–1977. In 1978 the rate jumped to 14 percent, and that year both Boeing and Airbus Industrie formally launched their multi-billion-dollar new transport developments—the Boeing 757 and 767 and the Airbus Industrie's A-310, which was in direct competition with the 767. The arrival of these aircraft was greeted with a rash of orders from the world's airlines for delivery beginning four years later at the end of 1982.

Unfortunately, the traffic growth rate in 1979 began falling; in

1980 it was only 6 percent and it actually dropped to -0.3 percent for domestic travel worldwide. In the intense competition for passengers, the airlines could not cover their rising costs and most had massive deficits in 1980 and 1981.[18] The year 1982 witnessed a rash of cancellations of airplane orders and the threat of more cancellations for the new airliners continued on into 1983. Lockheed had already terminated the L-1011 Tri-Star, McDonnell Douglas sold but a few more DC-10s, and only Airbus and Boeing appeared ready to weather the storm. This episode demonstrates how timing, largely a matter of luck, is a crucial factor in the success or failure of new civil transport.

By any measure, the world aerospace market is huge. Boeing's estimate for civil transport sales for the period 1983–1995, for example, was $167 billion (1983 dollars), with $58 billion going for replacement (most replaced planes enter the used-plane market) and $109 billion estimated to be required for new traffic growth. About 60 percent of these sales would be outside North America where European and other competitors were making the heaviest inroads into U.S. market shares.

Estimates of the military market varied more widely, from $100 billion to $300 billion (1983) for the decade of the 1980s (not including helicopters, missiles, etc.). The total world aerospace market is thus comparable to the world steel market for the 1980s but considerably smaller than the world car market for this period, which is estimated by the author at $2.3 trillion.

Civil airliners may lack the weapons, electronic fire control, and radar complexities of military aircraft, but they have their own complexities arising out of requirements for economy, comfort, safety, durability, and sheer size. While much of the process and product technology can be borrowed from military programs (especially in engine design), development costs have still been huge and increasing—as have prices (see Table 12–7 and Table 12–8).

In 1984 development of a completely new large civil transport was estimated at $2 billion. A major improvement or "derivative," which might include a stretched fuselage, improved wings, and more efficient and less noisy engines, was estimated to cost from $100 million to $800 million or more. Such derivatives can be delivered in two to three years after the decision to go ahead has been made, as opposed to the five to seven years or more required for a truly new design.

Table 12–7. Approximate Aircraft Development Costs between 1933 and 1982 (in millions of current U.S. dollars).

Plane	Time Period	Development Costs (nonrecurring costs prior to production)
DC–1, DC–2, DC–3	1933–1936	$ 1.5
Canberra (U.K. military)	1945–1951	50
Caravelle	1953–1959	140
Douglas DC–8	1955–1959	300
Concorde (Anglo-French) (including engine)	1962–1979	3,000+
Boeing 747	1965–1969	1,000+
Airbus A–300 (Franco-German)	1969–1974	600–1,000
A–310 (variation of A–300)	1978–1982	1,000
–320 (projected 150–seat Airbus)	1983–1988	2,000 (est.)
Boeing 757	1976–1982	600–1,000[a]
Boeing 767	1976–1982	1,500–2,000

a. Low development cost due to use of 727 fuselage.

Sources: Peter W. Brooks, *The Modern Airliner* (London: Putnam, 1961), pp. 82, 86; Great Britain, Committee of Inquiry into the Aircraft Industry, Cmnd. 1853 (1965), p. 6: Frederic Simi and Jacques Bankir, *Avant et après Concorde* (Paris: Seuil, 1965), pp. 49, 106; R.G. Hubler, *Big Eight* (New York: Duell, Sloan and Pearce, 1960), passim; Commission of the European Communities (Brussels), A Policy for the Community for the Promotion of Industry and Technology in the Aeronautical Industry, p. 49 (Annex III); *Wall Street Journal,* August 31, 1978; John Newhouse, *The Sporty Game* (New York: Alfred Knopf, 1982); and *Flight International* (February 27, 1982): 477.

With up-front development costs of this magnitude, either governments must finance airliner development or firms must sign up sufficient customers before heavy expenditures begin in order to provide cash flow through advance payments or demonstrate enough product acceptance to enable firms to obtain additional private financing. This requirement is notwithstanding the growing practice, begun by Boeing with the creation of the 747, of demanding that suppliers and subcontractors share up-front risks.

Unlike military aircraft sales to a home government, transport prices are not a simple function of cost topped by a "reasonable" profit. Civil aircraft prices are based on an aggressively—some say viciously—competitive market. Since actual delivery of a transport may take several years, sales contracts usually call for price adjust-

Table 12–8. NEW COMMERCIAL AIRCRAFT PRICES (AVERAGE) millions current dollars (may include initial stock of spare parts).

AIRCRAFT	YEAR							
	1965	1970	1972	1974	1976	1978	1980	1983/4
small								
McDONNELL DOUGLAS DC-9/MD-80 series	3.5			6.	7.	8.	9–15	18–22
BOEING 737 series	3.4			5.3	7.	8.5	12	18–22
medium								
BOEING 727 series	4.5		8.	8.2	10	11	17	21
BOEING 757							26	39
large								
McDONNELL DOUGLAS DC-10 series		17	19.5	21	25	33	35–47	?
LOCKHEED L-1011		17	20.5	20	22	30	36	X
AIRBUS A300/310				18	21	27	32–38	45–55
BOEING 767							32	38–45
very large								
BOEING 747 series		24	28	31	32	42	59	85–100

Source: Flight International and the Wall Street Journal (various issues).

354   REVITALIZING AMERICAN INDUSTRY

ments based on some price index (such as the producer price index and/or labor cost index). Moreover, price is but a part of the acquisition cost because financing terms, often government-supported, can make a big difference.

True competition between U.S. manufacturers has existed because the long-run profit potential of a successful airliner has generally been greater than for a combat aircraft program procured under government regulations. The air transport market has also grown much faster than the military market. Obviously, since every major aircraft manufacturer has had the technical capability to develop and build large civil airliners, they have all been tempted to explore this growing and potentialy very lucrative market. The stumbling block, however, has always been the heavy financial risk. But the temptation has been hard to resist, and especially for those firms that once succeeded when the stakes were lower. Consequently, airlines have always had a choice of two or three aircraft that were more or less suited to their current needs.

Because route structures may vary considerably among airlines, the airlines' needs also vary. And just as with military aircraft, constant technological improvements have periodically permitted manufacturers to propose more "desirable" planes, which could involve technical improvements, larger capacity, longer range, greater speed, and more recently, quieter and more fuel-efficient engines. From 1973 on the airlines' chief concern has been to cut operating costs (including depreciation) for a given route and schedule pattern. Aside from low purchase prices, this need meant seeking more seat-kilometers per liter of fuel. But matching these requirements with the airlines' additional need to remain competitive by offering more seats and more frequent flights than their rivals leads to shifting needs for specific aircraft sizes and performance. Large commercial transports available in the early 1980s are shown in Figure 12–2.

In 1981 Delta Airlines asked the world industry to develop a small, 150-passenger, short-range transport that would meet the needs of the bulk of its flights (less than 1,000 miles in length.) Delta felt that such a plane, using the latest technology, could achieve 78.6 air-seat miles (ASM) per gallon. This figure would be an 86 percent improvement over the 150-passenger 727–200, 43 percent over the 140-passenger DC9–80, and 25 percent over the 130-passenger 737–300. (The latter two were the newest and most

Figure 12–2.   Commercial Air Service

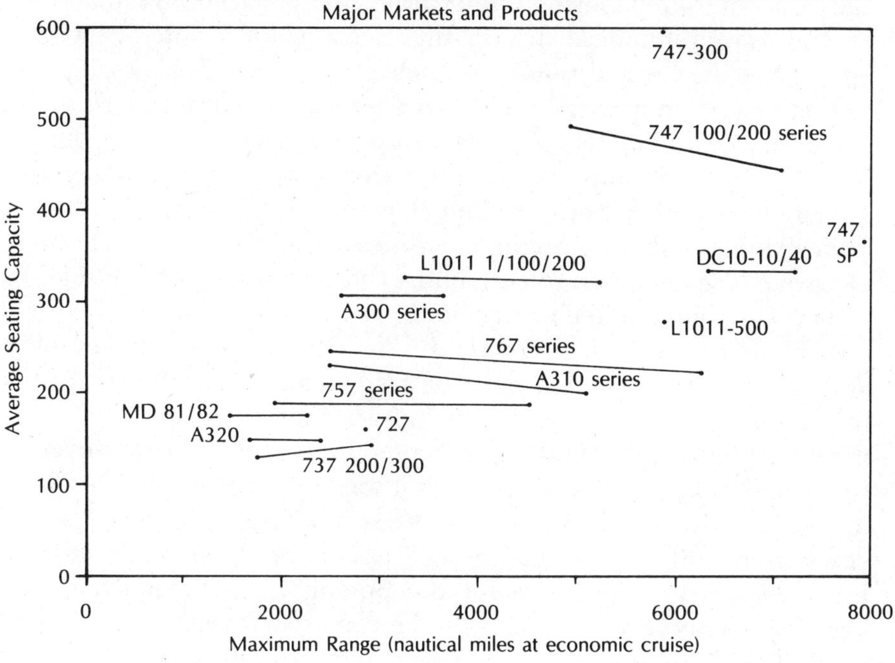

Major Markets and Products

Source: *Flight International* (October 15, 1983).

efficient smaller transports then on the market.) The improvements sought were technologically feasible, but a completely new plane would have to be developed at a cost estimated at $2 billion for the airframe and $1 billion for the engine. Given the economic climate (with Lockheed abandoning the market, McDonnell Douglas with its DC-10 problems, and Boeing having invested heavily in the 757 and 767), American manufacturers were understandably reluctant. Only the European Airbus Industrie seemed really interested. Meanwhile both Boeing and Douglas prepared derivatives that, while not having the performance of a completely new plane, nonetheless were significant improvements over existing small airliners. Taking advantage of available engine improvements, these derivatives were far less expensive to develop and would be available much sooner. But so weak was the market that in 1982 Douglas abandoned its major derivative.

Whether they appear on the market singly as did the 747 and Concorde, or in pairs, as the DC-10 and L-1011, the timing of new airplanes has not always suited the majority of the airlines, who always seem to be laboring under heavy unamortized investments or who were in financial straits. But once a major airline orders a new plane, the competition is compelled to follow. Tax laws allow fast amortization and tend to allow fleet rejuvenation before the useful life of a plane is over. Taxes aside, however, airlines purchase new aircraft only if they offer the competitive advantages already mentioned. Because their fleets could, if necessary, continue flying without replacement, airlines can afford to wait in hope of paying a lower price for the improved performance they seek.

This situation had led to ferocious price competition among the few manufacturers of civil aircraft. As a result, the number of aircraft of a new type that must be sold to amortize costs before the cumulative cash flow becomes positive has risen steadily over the years. In the late 1960s, an accepted figure for this break-even point was 250 to 350 unit sales, but it was not until the 400th sale in 1978, twelve years after the program was launched and seven years after its first flight, that the 747 was believed to have reached break-even.[18] One estimate for the Boeing 727's break-even of over 700 seems very high.[19] It would mean break-even was reached in 1970, ten to twelve years after program launch (see Figure 12–3). The 727, launched in 1959, has been the largest-selling transport in history, with 1,831 sold through 1983. It is now out of production.

An estimate by Airbus Industrie management of the combined break-even point for the Airbus A-300 and its A-310 derivative (a direct competitor to the Boeing 767) was 870 aircraft.[20] If plans are successful, this figure could be reached by 1990–1991. Initially the "official" break-even point for the A-300 B alone had been set at 360.

Manufacturers have been understandably wary in launching the development of a new aircraft. For even after intensive scientific planning of future traffic requirements and assessment of technological risk, an element of chance has always remained that could cause failure. A plane can come on the market too early (as the A-300) or too late (as the Concorde SST). Economic conditions change, and the market may dry up due to enormous airline deficits, as the world market did in 1981–1982. Chance, combined with extremely keen competition, makes a successful outcome far from certain. Hence, for the private-enterprise U.S. manufacturers, it

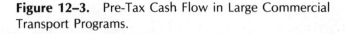

Figure 12–3. Pre-Tax Cash Flow in Large Commercial Transport Programs.

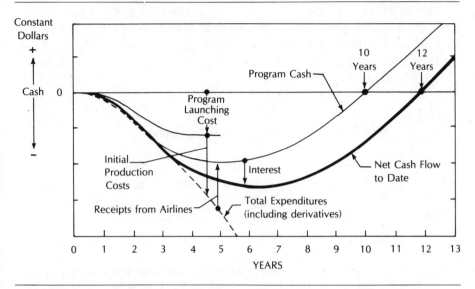

Source: Aerospace Industries Association of America. 1982.

has long been what John Newhouse calls a "sporty game." However, for the government-subsidized Airbus Industrie, failure to crack the key U.S. market or to register adequate sales during the first few years was less traumatic. They could afford to wait until "time and tide" finally came.

As previously stated, the net price to the buyer is not the stated sales price but the totality of the financial terms of the offer. Extremely attractive financing terms, often "concessionary" or even "predatory," usually involve a national export financing agency such as the U.S. Export-Import Bank, France's COFACE, or Britain's Export Credit Guarantee Department. Given the intensity of competition, the almost infinite number of ways governments can alter the true cost of a politically important export product, and the historic inability of nations to legislate good intentions, "predatory" financing appears to be here to stay.

The only large European transports purportedly to achieve break-even were Aerospatiale's Caravelle jet with 280 sold (first flight in 1955, last production 1972), the Vickers Viscount turboprop with 440 sold (last production in the early 1960s), and the smaller but remarkably successful Dutch Fokker F-27 turbo-prop, a regional transport, some 530 of which have been sold since it first flew in 1955 and which is still in production in 1985. The Fokker F-28, a 65–85 passenger twin jet that first flew in 1967 has since sold over 190 and should eventually break even. At the end of 1983, Fokker announced the launching of two major derivatives of the F-27 and F-28.

The Rise of International Cooperation

To share the financial burden entailed in launching new programs, to share the risks involved (even national treasuries have their limits), to widen "home markets," and to increase political leverage for export sales, the Europeans have had to enter into international joint ventures in both commercial transports and military aircraft.

Airliners. The first European airliner collaboration was the Franco-British Concorde supersonic transport. Launched officially in 1962 after years of discussion, the program cost the two countries over $3 billion (current) to develop and ultimately only sixteen aircraft were built. Fourteen years passed before the aircraft flew commercially. A brilliant technological feat over tremendous marketing and organizational problems, the program was a commercial failure.[21]

Back in the 1960s, when the Concorde still looked promising, it had been considered insufficient by itself to break the United States monopoly in civil aircraft; to reach such a goal was believed to require a successful, new European subsonic transport as well as a supersonic plane. British efforts had been unsuccessful: Hawker-Siddeley's medium-range Trident jet transport was launched in 1957, almost two years before Boeing launched the similarly sized 727, but the 727 entered service in 1962, a full year ahead of the Trident. And the latter, tailored to fit British requirements, simply could not compete. In 1961 the British Aircraft Corporation had launched the BAC-111, a smaller 80-passenger transport, which also turned out to be a an ineffective rival of the like-sized Douglas DC-9 and, later, the Boeing 737.[22]

Pursuing a determined Gaullist national policy, France refused to concede the overwhelming U.S. dominance in this critical industrial sector (90 percent of the world transport fleet in value at the end of the 1960s). Smarting over their continuing series of more or less unsuccessful aircraft ventures, the British were also seeking a way to regain their former position as the leading European aerospace power. West Germany's aircraft industry was another eager candidate for a large civil aircraft project. Anglo-French discussions about a large subsonic plane began in 1965 and led to a 1967 Anglo-French-German agreement to develop the Airbus.

Military Aircraft. In the military arena, the late 1960s and early 1970s saw France assume the European lead from the British by dint of Dassault's amazing export success with the Mirage III/5 fighter series—amazing because at the end of World War II France's industry was virtually nonexistent, while Britain's industry was technologically equal to that of the United States and second only to the United States in industry size. Desultory planning during the 1970s resulted in Britain falling behind France in successful airframe development and construction.[23]

Despite her growing success, France, for political and economic reasons, felt it prudent to seek joint programs for military aircraft. (This feeling was not shared by the intensely independent and self-confident Dassault.) In 1965 a joint light-fighter project, the Jaguar, was launched with Britain. This reasonably successful program was the only major British military effort during the 1970s, aside from a specialized vertical take-off fighter, the Harrier (which was later to earn its spurs in the Falklands against Argentina). Some 500 Jaguars were ordered but only a few were exported— to India, Ecuador, and Oman—for as the French saw how attractive their all-French Mirage had become, they only half-heartedly participated in the Jaguar joint-export effort.

Britain was thus left with no truly modern first-line fighter under development, and worse, it had been obliged to purchase U.S. F-4 Phantoms to maintain an adequate military capability. In the military as in the airliner domain, and in the face of steeply rising development and unit costs, Britain was therefore forced to consider another joint venture and joined with West Germany and Italy in the already mentioned Tornado program.

Unfortunately, conational cooperative programs appeared to require more money and more time than purely national ones. Most estimates placed the cost penalty at around 20 or 30 percent. Effective management, a thorny problem in equal partnerships, might have substantially reduced these penalties.

The 1970s thus saw large civilian programs limited to a decreasing number of firms in the United States and to international cooperative ventures in Europe, while in the military field, only France was able to maintain a significant, purely national effort of international significance. In this context, the political factors tended to dominate; and only the U.S. government in 1984 continued to believe that market forces should be allowed to determine the structure of the industry.

Space. The development of large booster rockets and their application in long-range ballistic-missiles, space probes and satellites followed a pattern similar to that for aircraft. Spurred by successful U.S. and Soviet programs, the Europeans (and Japanese) were determined not to be outdone in this area of technological sophistication. Here, more than in the aircraft sector, combined economic and technological factors made international cooperation in Europe imperative. The 1960s gave birth to two such endeavors —the European Space Research Organization (ESRO), now the European Space Agency (ESA), and the European Launcher Development Organization (ELDO). The former has been a steadily successful venture with many solid accomplishments to its credit. The latter was a total failure by 1971, after the fifth straight EUROPA satellite launcher blew up on takeoff. In each case, the success or failure of these European space ventures can be traced to management organization.[24]

Undaunted by the failure of ELDO, France saw space as too important to leave solely to the Soviets and Americans, although too expensive to be pursued on a purely national basis. France therefore roused a new international program that appeared, in 1984, to be destined for success. This program, the ARIANE satellite launcher, was placed under the ESRO umbrella in 1974 soon after ELDO's demise, and was first successfully launched in December 1979. On the eve of Ariane's launch, the director of the French National Space Agency asked the rhetorical question:

Why, after the technical difficulties and political unpleasantness of the EUROPA program, did we doggedly persevere in our conviction and do everything in our power to convince our European partners to join with us? . . . Should we regret this commitment? No! Because this political commitment is also an economic necessity.[25]

Here it is worth noting that a major impetus to the European program was NASA's refusal to launch European communication satellites, which the United States considered to be competing with the U.S. sponsored, if conational, INTELSAT.

No sooner was the first Ariane launched than French officials announced the creation of a "private" French corporation, ARIANESPACE, to commercialize the rocket for satellite launchings. With production to be taken over from ESA after the tenth launching in 1983, the firm announced it hoped to start making a profit after thirty launchings at a 1980 price of $28 million per launching. Since this figure was lower than NASA's price, orders were not long in coming in from INTELSAT, ESA, the Colombian government, RCA, Western Union and others. This aggressive marketing on the basis of price represents a European governmental commitment to wrest market shares from the United States.[26]

This situation demonstrates again the difference between U.S. and European governmental approaches to the aerospace industry. In Europe, governments that believe in state intervention use market forces as a tool to gain political and economic ends. The United States, which believes in giving full play to market forces, acted, until mid-1983, as if competition were nonexistent. At that time, prodded by Ariane's aggressive marketing, NASA began its own marketing efforts.

Engines. By the 1980s it had become clear that even the largest U.S. aerospace firms could no longer launch a major program without financial partners from abroad. Even Boeing needed Italian and Japanese partners for the 757 and 767, though Boeing remained the dominant partner.

Most large U.S. commercial jet engines entail some degree of foreign participation. The increasingly successful ten-ton thrust CFM-56 engine, previously mentioned, is a 50–50 partnership between U.S. General Electric and France's SNECMA. It powers Boeing's 737–300 and is used to re-engine older jet planes.

In 1983 a major new ten-ton engine for the "150 seater" launched by a conational consortium of U.S. Pratt & Whitney, Rolls-Royce, and Japanese, German, and Italian firms. At the same time numerous other international engine agreements were signed.

The Rocky Road to Successful International Industrial Collaboration

International joint ventures in which ownership is shared on a more or less equal basis between two or more national firms or agencies have been termed conational programs or enterprises.[27] Because the world aerospace industry (including the U.S. industry) has been inexorably driven to the formation of more and more conational programs, a closer look at the growth of one such endeavor, the European Airbus, is instructive.

In the early 1960s, American and European firms began thinking of producing larger transports, made possible by the larger jet engines then being developed. In October 1966, after laborious negotiations, the Europeans reached agreement on developing their entry in the race. Three governments (acting as bankers) and six firms had decided on a design and how the work would be shared. The Airbus A-300 would have the same passenger capacity as the competing U.S. DC-10 and L-1011, but a somewhat shorter, "European" range of 2,200 miles maximum, and—an important difference—it would have only two large engines instead of three. It took until September 1967 for the governments to sign a formal go-ahead. In 1968 the size of the A-300 B was reduced to avoid competing head-on with the U.S. wide-bodies, to make a lower price possible, and to permit a wider choice of engines.

Successfully wooed by Lockheed to become the primary supplier of motors for the L-1011, Rolls-Royce chose certain sales in the U.S. market rather than continuing in an A-300 program that could then only be viewed as high risk. Rolls-Royce was instrumental in having the not unwilling British government then withdraw from the A-300 program, leaving Hawker-Siddeley as a private supplier, with West German financial guarantees, to continue wing development. Britain's excuse was that the program costs had gone too high. So France and West Germany were left to go it alone.

In May 1969 the two governments signed a new agreement for the Airbus. A multitiered organization was created with key operational responsibility centered in a newly founded French firm, Airbus Industrie, which was equally owned by Deutsche Airbus GMbH and Aerospatiale. As expected, assignment of responsibilities within Airbus Industrie did not, initially, go smoothly. The West Germans felt that not only were they obliged to follow French leadership in program management, but they were even being frozen out of such key areas as marketing, in which they were anxious to gain experience. In time a *modus operandi* was reached. Airbus Industrie seemed to function remarkably, but it was under a single leadership, a French one. Airbus Industrie may be conational but it was not coequal in 1984.

However, the larger Boeing 747 entered service with Pan Am in January 1970. Then, in August of that year, the DC-10 flew its first test flight, followed soon after by the L-1011. Two of the three competitors were thus going well, though Lockheed's Rolls-Royce engine caused production delays resulting in order losses from which Lockheed would never recover. Again we see the importance of timing.

Airbus made Herculean efforts to sell, but to little avail. In November, 1971 the Spanish government, in an effort to modernize its industry, agreed to take a 4.2 percent share in the Airbus program. A condition for entry was an order by Iberia for four A-300s with options for eight more. A year later, in December 1972, Lufthansa placed an order for only three aircraft and took options on four—while placing substantial orders in the United States for five more DC-10s and three more 727s. Boeing remained active. The 727, whose capacity would ultimately reach 180 passengers, was stretched so as to be able to offer a plane with only 30 percent less capacity than the A-300 and at half the price. Moreover, the 727 was proven, available, and a best-seller.

In March 1974, 58 months after program launch, the Airbus was certified for commercial use, but by the end of the year, only 18 had been ordered as opposed to 1,200 727s, 142 L1011s and 233 DC-10s. There ensued in France the usual parliamentary investigations and all sorts of recriminations, and in West Germany murmurs were heard at all levels. In a U.S. private firm, the program would never have been launched without sufficient start-up orders from airlines and would have been canceled after such disastrous initial sales. Yet the European governments held fast.

By 1973 the oil crisis had intervened and fuel economy had suddenly become much more important. The A-300's modern, fuel-efficient General Electric CF-6 engines began to make a difference, giving the A-300 25 percent more air-seat-miles per gallon than the Boeing 727. Moreover, the engines were quieter and there were only two of them, making maintenance simpler. The cumulative orders for the A-300 began to rise slowly, while sales of DC-10s and L-1011s began to slip.

Nevertheless, in 1977 Western Airlines, which had been tempted to buy the Airbus, decided instead on the DC-10. Europeans snorted that the United States was being chauvinistic and politicoeconomically motivated (to boost employment in the U.S. industry).

Then occurred the celebrated "give-away" to Eastern Airlines described earlier. The sale to Eastern marked a watershed. During 1979, 131 A-300/A-310s were ordered worldwide, versus only 24 DC-10s and 30 L-1011s (see Table 12–9). Then in 1982 Lockheed announced it was abandoning the transport market; the L-1011 never would break even. Thus, without truly "cracking" the largest market, Airbus Industrie had become the second largest supplier of transports in the world.

Much of the Airbus success was along the so-called silk route—Japan, Korea, Singapore, India, and the Arab states. International politics, with France shrewdly exploiting American Middle Eastern policy, was no small part of this success. Boeing, if its total line is considered, might still have been ahead in both numbers and in dollar value of sales, but these aspects did not bother the Europeans, who were more than pleased to be leading in their market niche and who were preparing to capture the next major open-market niche—the new generation 150-seat medium-range transport that the airline industry claimed it needed. Airbus's success caused increasing concern in the U.S. industry.[28]

From Table 12–8 it is clear that Boeing was hardly threatened in the medium-range aircraft market. However, a heavy rash of order cancellations in 1982 and 1983 darkened Boeing's picture considerably. Reporting a sharp decline in earnings for 1981, Boeing announced in February 1982 a cut of 5,000 employees, on top of a previous drop from 81,500 to 76,000 in 1981.

Additional evidence of Boeing's concern and the seriousness with which the European and other foreign challengers were viewed was a Boeing "White Paper" published in March 1982.[29] This report pointed out that, during 1970s, Europe had increased its share of the total world commercial market to almost 25 percent, while the U.S. share had dropped correspondingly from an

Table 12–9. Annual Orders for Large Airliners.[a]

	1975	1977	1978	1979	1980	1981	1982	1983	1984
Boeing									
707	2	2	—	—	—	—	1	—	—
727	30	118	156	153	23	25	10	—[b]	—
737	34	39	115	125	108	79	42	154	169
747	23	43	76	89	38	19	14	24	22
757	—	—	—	40	9	33	—	26	2
767	—	—	30	64	42	11	11	16	10
Lockheed									
L–1011	0	2	30	30	15	2	—	4	1
McDonnell Douglas									
DC–9/MD-80	28	60	66	46	22	10	83	44	100 (est)
DC–10	14	16	26	24	12	3	1	1	7
Airbus Industrie									
A–300/310	13	20	69	131	49	45	17	6	21

Notes:
a. There were numerous cancellations of previous orders in 1982.
b. Out of production.
Source: U.S. Aerospace Industries Association. Economic Data Service series 23-02, periodic, and press reports.

almost 90 percent peak. U.S. government intervention was essential, the report stated, to "eliminate" all foreign export subsidies, limit government intervention in financing aircraft to guarantees and political-risk insurance, limit credit terms to the "useful life" of the product, make financing a "neutral" element in aircraft selection, and apply diplomatic leverage to ensure compliance with agreements reached concerning these subsidies. But until agreement is reached in these matters, the paper urged the United States to "maintain" a strong and "competitive" U.S. Eximbank (of which Boeing had consistently been the largest customer). It is hard to believe that U.S. manufacturers were so naive as to think that European and other competitors, all government-backed and all strong positive contributors to their national balance of payments, would submit to such pressures.

Marché du Siècle. The major European combat aircraft developments in the 1950s and 1960s took place in Britain and France. As earlier noted, British efforts, except for vertical takeoff fighters such as the Harrier, were relatively unsuccessful or aborted.[30] The French efforts, on the other hand, were increasingly successful.

The West German military aircraft industry had been reborn with the coproduction of the U.S. Lockheed F-104G Starfighter. Some 1,800 of these planes were built in West Germany, Italy, Belgium, and Holland by 1965, with a total value of almost $3 billion (1967).[31] Given the technological advances of Soviet aircraft, NATO deemed it necessary by the late 1970s to replace the F-104s with modern planes. This represented a very large potential market that attracted major U.S. manufacturers and, in particular, the French, who felt that the new fighter should be of European origin, even though they had partially withdrawn from NATO. The French set out to win.

What was needed was a replacement that was far less expensive than the all-purpose, super-sophisticated U.S. F-14 and F-15 planes that, by 1972, had reached systems procurement costs of $20 million per plane (including development) or fly-away costs of well over $10 million. In early 1972 the U.S. Air Force requested industry proposals for a development program to be chosen through a "fly-off" between contending prototypes.

For an overall market estimated at $20 to $30 billion over the 1975–1990 period (4,000 planes at $5 to $7 million each), the competition—and infighting—became serious. Europe required

350 planes, and the United States about 500. At the same time, Marcel Dassault continued steady incremental improvements on the Mirage, and announed in March 1973, a "new" Mirage F-1 with a superior engine, the French SNECMA M-53. This plane was now touted as an ideal replacement for the F-104G. The "new" F-1 was an excellent performer, but for budgetary reasons had not been bought by the French Air Force.

Sweden viewed the plane as an opportunity to save her excellent but miniscule aircraft industry, France saw it as an opportunity to break the "American Monopoly," and U.S. firms envisioned a golden opportunity. Most fittingly, the French dubbed the Mirage F-1 "the sale of the century."

In 1972 Belgium, Holland, Norway, and Denmark, the four remaining customers, sent observers to the United States to examine the two U.S. prototypes. The French entered the fray by promising production offsets for the new F-1 whereby 60 to 80 percent of the buy would be produced in the purchasing countries through a "single international production line." And, of course, they offered to purchase the F-1 for their own use to ensure greater economies of scale. The battle was rapidly becoming a melange of financial bargaining, horse-trading, and political arm-twisting. "The problem is not competition between the U.S. and France," said a French official, "but of maintaining our own (European) aircraft industry. If you don't act properly now, the next time you may not have a choice."[32]

By early 1975 the estimated price for the General Dynamics YF-16, finally chosen by the U.S. Air Force (with inputs from the NATO customers who had been busy bargaining price and production "offsets"), had risen to more than $5 million. The newly planned U.S. buy of 650 planes (a domestic purchase the French could not duplicate) would supposedly reduce costs. Belgium seemed to favor the Mirage because of previous Mirage purchases and long coproduction experience with the French. Holland had shown a preference for the Northrup YF-17. Quite naturally, offer followed offer, charge followed charge, and promise followed promise.

Then on April 4, 1975, the Defense Ministers of the four NATO customer countries tilted in favor of the U.S. YF-16 in Europe. Belgium held the pivotal decision, and as the contest's end neared, pressures and tempers rose. With Holland, Norway, and Denmark solidly in the F-16 camp, the French wondered whether Belgium would join the others as the "dynamiters of Europe".[33] Meanwhile, a bland announcement from Washington stated that the United States had decided on a Belgian machine gun as standard for the F-16 and would buy 160,000 of them. And Mr. Claude Valliere, president of Avions Marcel Dassault, wrote a personal note to the Dutch Minister of Defense accusing him of presenting arguments that were " . . . half truths, partial, deceiving and incomplete." "I hope," said another senior French executive sarcastically, "that those officials who chose the American F-16 won't have to be present when they will have to be used. Weapons are made to fight wars, not to play politics."[34] Strange words from the French, but they reflect the bitter competitiveness characteristic of the aerospace sector.

It was estimated to have cost 30 percent more to coproduce the plane than to buy it off-the-shelf from General Dynamics in the United States. But coproduction does create jobs; in January 1982 the Belgian government announced its decision to procure an additional eighteen aircraft to keep the Belgian production line (with 2,500 jobs) going after 1984. This move was made despite very attractive overtures from France to purchase late-model Mirages. And the battle is a never-ending one. In November 1983, the Dutch government ordered an additional fifty-seven F-16s, extending production of the aircraft at Fokker until 1992.

CONCLUSIONS

The first and foremost conclusions to be reached concerning the aerospace industry is the crucial role played by the state. The home government provides the core military (and space) market, which serves as the base and framework of the industry. It also frequently provides various types of financial assistance. Furthermore, every first-rank industrial nation in the world—and any that aspires to be so ranked—must actively support an aerospace industry, for defense purposes if no other. Successful civil programs, in addition to this government base, serve to reduce the financial burden while providing political and economic benefits to the nation. Aerospace is therefore intensely political in nature.

A second conclusion can also be drawn that concerns the nature and importance of profit at the company level and the relationship of profit to government support. With regard to military or government products, the situation, though complex, is reasonably clear. A profit is almost always assured. As concerns large civil transports, however, the situation is more complex. As revealed in the case of the A-300, European governments do not view short- or even medium-term profits as necessary to success. The governments of the major industrialized countries (other than the United States) are prepared to pursue implantation in the market, and even to sell at a loss in order to wrest a market share that might or might not ultimately result in profits. Despite years of poor or no sales, the Europeans perservered with the Airbus, for example, and this pertinacity appears to have finally paid off.

In the United States the role of profit is paramount and the role of government supposedly negligible. This view would appear substantiated by Lockheed's 1981 decision to terminate production of the L-1011 Tri-star when orders dried up during the 1979–81 airline crises. But after having been saved by government guarantees from the Tri-Star-triggered bankruptcy, Lockheed abandoned the airliner market in favor of the more comfortable and less risky role of government contractor. McDonnell-Douglas, with DC-10 sales similarly languishing, also threatened to discontinue its production unless more orders were forthcoming. These materialized in the form of a U.S. Air Force decision to purchase a total of sixty DC-10s, thus assuring production through the 1980s.

At first glance, one might cite Boeing as an example of a firm that has shown significant and profitable growth in the large civil transport sector without government support. But an examination of the roots of Boeing's success shows that the initial springboard was the 707 military tanker/transport, which started Boeing on its road to industry leadership. Such investment in military forerunners of civil products is ignored in break-even calculations. Even the 747 was made possible to a great extent by Boeing's earlier response to the Air Force's request for a large military airlift plane (where, paradoxically, Boeing lost to Lockheed's C-5).

Obviously governmental involvement is intrinsic to the aerospace industry, and only in the United States has the government's role been blurred by a simplistic belief that the government has no business financing private ventures.

A third conclusion is that the technological know-how to develop and build modern aircraft is widespread among the world's nations. Brazil, with its 18-seat Bandeirante transport is a case in point, although the economy has constrained Brazil's industry to attempt only lighter military and civil aircraft. Japan, too, is apparently planning to play an increasingly important role in this sector. It certainly now has the financial resources and technical competence, but the aerospace market is structured quite differently from the consumer electronics, steel, or motor vehicles market.

The fourth conclusion begins with an observation: development and unit costs of large commercial aircraft have reached a point that makes it extremely difficult for a single firm or one nation independently to launch a major new civil airliner or civil engine program. On can conclude that either the risk must be shared or underwritten by a munificent home government, or that the risk must be shared by several manufacturers (many with government support) from more than one nation. The latter approach has the additional benefit of broadening the captive, "home" markets. Because the driving force is politicoeconomic, the decision as to which nations and firms become partners and under what circumstances, can become very complex. In countries where the airlines or the aircraft industry or both are either nationalized or under tight government control (which means most of the world except the United States), the decision is usually based on which manufacturer offers the most attractive production "offset" to that nation's industry in addition to attractive financial terms. Here again the role of the government is fundamental. Because of their size, experience, and market strength, U.S. manufacturers will insist on being the leaders in such international joint endeavors. But sooner or later some foreign partners (and their governments) will demand more equitable sharing of power and project leadership, leading to true conational endeavors with all the attendant problems.

Given the high costs involved, the relatively small number of potential customers for large new aircraft, and the fact that ferocious competition within the small aerospace oligopoly will continue for the foreseeable future, it is likely that fewer and fewer truly new large aircraft and engines will be launched in the next few decades. Instead, those manufacturers still in the market will concentrate on offering less costly derivatives with minor improvements. Such a scenario will further increase the barriers to entry for a newcomer and make it very difficult for an existing manufacturer, such as Airbus Industrie, to sell an all-new but much costlier plane.

Lastly, no industry is likely to grow faster than the world's GDP in perpetuity. The growth in world air travel and cargo has so far, on the average, outpaced the world economy in general. But airlines have been instrumental in reducing the net demand on the industry by selling amortized-planes on the used-plane market after seven to ten years that still have fifteen to twenty years of useful life left. As the market becomes saturated, the demand for new aircraft is bound to drop, further aggravating the competition between the remaining national firms.

NOTES

1. *Flight International* (October 17, 1981): 1,152 f.; Ibid. (April 3, 1982): 794 ff.
2. *Flight International* (June 12, 1982): 1,522 ff.
3. See John Newhouse, *The Sporty Game* (New York: Alfred Knopf, 1982)
4. For a concise discussion of the evolution of the U.S. and European aviation industry until the early 1970s, see M. S. Hochmuth, "Aerospace," in Ray Vernon, ed., *Big Business and the State* (Cambridge, Mass.: Harvard University Press, 1974), pp. 146–69.
5. Ibid., p. 147; and "The European Aerospace Industry, Trading Position and Figures," EEC Commission Document III/202/84 EN (Brussels: 1984).
6. State ownership of the air industry in France and Britain magnified the industry's political significance. France had nationalized its air industry prior to 1940 and consolidated it into one large state-owned firm and one successful postwar private firm, Dassault, which specialized in military aircraft. (Dassault was also nationalized in 1982.) Britain nationalized its air industry in 1977 and then denationalized it in 1981 (but continued to provide substantial government financing).
7. *Financial Times* (July 23, 1980): 4.
8. *Flight International* (January 9, 1982): 46.
9. *Flight International* (April 15, 1978): 1,030; *Fortune* (April 21, 1980): 138; and *Air Transport World* (July 1978): 25.

10. *Business Week* (January 11, 1982).
11. Jacques Limouzy, Deputé/rapporteur, *Rapport, Commission d'Enquete Parlementaire,* Document no. 2815, Assemblée Nationale, Paris, 1977.
12. Accurate cost data for commercial aircraft and engines are difficult to obtain because of the complexity of the financial arrangements, the fact that engines are usually purchased together with spares, and the intense competition that leads manufacturers to guard such information closely. The estimates for aircraft in this chapter are obtained largely from *Flight International* which periodically publishes a list of such figures (e.g., see September 27, 1981 : 1,272 ff., and occasional prices that appear in other issues of *Flight International* (e.g., July 31, 1982: 248), and *Aviation Week and Space Technology* (e.g., December 8, 1980.
13. *International Herald Tribune,* March 12, 1973, p. 2.
14. *Aviation Week and Space Technology* (April 27, 1981): 107; and *Flight International* (June 6 1981): 1,703.
15. Jack Gee, *Le Mirage* (Paris: Editions Albin Michel, 1971), p. 33.
16. Comprehensive statistics are available for the world's airlines in the annual reports of the International Civil Aviation Organization, an intergovernmental agency located in Montreal, Canada.
17. *Flight International* (October 31, 1981): 1,207.
18. *Flight International* (May 27, 1978): 1,632.
19. *Flight International* (February 27, 1982 and December 19, 1981): 1,837; also see *The Economist* (August 30, 1980): 11.
20. The Economist (August 30, 1980): 12.
21. For a complete discussion of the Concorde program, see M. S. Hochmuth, *Organizing the Transnational* (Leiden: Sijthoff, 1974).
22. For a broader look at this time-frame see M. S. Hochmuth, "Aerospace," in Raymond Vernon, ed., *Big Business and the State* (Cambridge, Mass.: Harvard University Press, 1974).
23. Ibid., p. 158 ff.
24. Hochmuth, *Organizing the Transnational,* p. 59 ff.
25. *Le Monde,* December 12, 1979, p. 13.
26. For a detailed discussion of Ariane marketing policy and launch prices, see *Flight International* (August 28, 1982): 582.
27. See M. S. Hochmuth, *Multinationals, Transnationals and Now Conationals, European Research in International Business,* in M. Ghertman and J. Leontiades, eds., (Amsterdam & New York: North Holland, 1978), pp. 169–87.
28. See *The Challenge of Foreign Competition* (Aerospace Industries Association of America, December 1981).

29. *International Competition in the Production and Marketing of Commercial Aircraft* (Seattle: Boeing Aircraft Company, March 1982).
30. See Hochmuth, "Aerospace."
31. *Les Industries Aéronautiques et Spatiales de la Communauté, comparées à celles de la Grande Bretagne et des Etats-Unis,* Prepared for the EEC Commission by Soris, July 1969, vol. 4 (Brussels: Collection Etudes, Serie Industrie, no.4, 1971), pp. 871 ff.
32. *Business Week* (August 10, 1974), p. 156.
33. *Les Echos,* June 5, 1975, p. 12.
34. Ibid.

13 ANALYSIS AND SUMMARY

Milton Hochmuth

At the outset, this inquiry posed two interrelated questions: How have the economic strengths of the world's principal industrial powers changed with respect to each other over the past two decades, and how has their relative competitiveness in the world market place evolved over this period? As the title of the book suggests, the implicit questions were more tantalizing; namely, to what extent has U.S. industry lost its post-World War II pre-eminence; what are the factors involved; what should be done; and by whom?

At this point readers will have begun to form their own answers to these questions. Struck by this or that argument in one of the preceding essays or by one of the many statistics cited, they will have been comforted in their own prior convictions or, perhaps, seen their preconceptions altered. Two major observations are clear and inescapable, however: Not only has the "American Challenge" vanished, but the U.S. industrial base is showing dangerous signs of following in the unenviable footsteps of Britain, a condition starkly described in Professor Hood's essay.

As for the world economy as a whole, long-range prospects in 1985, despite many positive economic signs in the United States, were not bright. In addition to the plight of the world's "have-not" nations, whose continuously suffering economies are outside the

375

purview of this book, all of the industrialized countries were still feeling painful recessionary and "stagflation" pressures. Record trade and current account deficits in the United States, unemployment in the United States and Europe, the inability of Brazil, Mexico, other third world countries, and the East Bloc satellites to meet international debt payments, and a budgetary crisis in Japan all were disquieting signs for the long term. Whether these signs represented but a downward lurch in basically upward-bound economic charts or foretold a deep crisis was too early to tell. But this begs the question so cogently raised by Professor Vernon in his essay: Do these signs really pose a problem? Is the weak competitive posture of U.S. industry a long-term trend, destined to continue and end in changes such as befell eighteenth century Spain? Or will the 1983–84 recovery show it to be but a temporary phase?

Although the standard of living in the rest of the industrialized and newly industrialized world increased at a much faster rate than in the United States (Britain excepted), the fact remains that the well-being of the average individual in the United States nevertheless increased over the period under consideration. (Note, however, that were it not for the flood of low-cost consumer goods imported into the United States from Japan and newly industrialized countries (NICs), which helped those countries increase their standard of living rapidly, the U.S. standard would have grown at an even lower rate than it did, which tends to confirm the advantages of free trade.)

On the other hand, what if the United States follows Britain and experiences an actual decline in the standard of living? Argentina's plight demonstrates that Britain is not a unique case in recent history. Can the United States afford to continue vying with Britain for last place among the industrialized economies in growth of real per capita income during the rest of this century?

The indicators gleaned from the industry essays are not heartening for the United States. In both mature industries such as steel, autos, and apparel and in advanced technologies such as aerospace and information technology, the U.S. lead has either disappeared or is in the process of shrinking. However, the industry essays also show that it is hazardous to generalize, for there are significant differences among the different mature industries, and between the traditional industrial and the "high technology" sectors. Even within a given industry, the competitiveness of specific products or firms varies considerably. Equally onerous, as borne out by the country essays, is the task of separating the effects of national macroeconomic policies from the more direct governmental actions that influence a nation's industrial competitiveness. Yet it seems to me that there are enough threads common to all the essays to suggest some broad conclusions.

THE PERVASIVENESS OF THE STATE

No other single factor has had more influence in determining a nation's competitiveness, hence relative industrial strength, than the action or inaction of the national governments. Simplistic calls by some U.S. politicians and businessmen to "get the government off the backs of business" fly in the face of the evidence presented in these essays. The United States, unlike our competitors, does not have an integrated set of long-range policies to ensure coordination in planning between government and industry, nor for that matter a broad framework for such coordination. As far as the central issue of international competitiveness in manufactured goods is concerned, the United States is unique in that it has no industrial policy whatsoever.

We in the United States call for "unfettered free trade", yet our own macroeconomic policies, as those of our competitors, shape and constrain trade in countless ways. All governments—the United States included—intervene directly through tax, fiscal, and monetary policies, government procurement, tariffs, import quotas, innumerable nontariff barriers, and subsidies (direct and indirect) and by exerting political pressure to obtain contracts for their firms. Despite rapidly growing international economic interdependence, our world of separate, sovereign nations has not known free trade for centuries and certainly does not enjoy it now. True free trade can realistically occur only within a framework of political unity, as between the states in the United States. It does not yet even exist in the European Common Market.

Aside from the notion that the United States ought to have a realistic, broad, national set of long-range policies these observations do not offer guidance on *how* the nation should act. Long-range policies are no cure-all, nor do they always achieve their stated goals, as evidenced in the country essays. Nevertheless, they do appear to perform a number of crucial tasks that cannot otherwise be accomplished.

OTHER KEY FACTORS AFFECTING INDUSTRIAL COMPETITIVENESS

As important as it is, the state is but one of the partners in the national complex that, over time, determines a nation's industrial competitiveness. Management and labor, of course, directly control several key factors. How these have affected U.S. competitiveness is best understood by examining some questions triggered by the industry studies. Why did the steel and auto industries become less competitive while the textile industry was able to remain relatively competitive? Why has the U.S. textile industry (excluding apparel) been a lower cost producer (at least until 1982–83) than Japan and Europe?

Labor

Initial penetration of the U.S. market by European and especially Japanese steel and auto producers was accomplished on the basis of price and price alone. These lower prices were almost wholly the result of lower wage costs. Quality factors, subjective or real, and fuel economy in the case of autos did not play an important role in their penetration of the U.S. market until the 1970s. In the earlier years, these lower wage costs more than compensated for lower productivity—physical or unit output per man-hour—in Japan and even in Europe. (It is important to remember Professor Vernon's admonition about this "slippery concept . . . tricky numerator and tricky denominator.") Then, by the end of the 1970s, when productivity in Japan exceeded that in the United States for both steel and autos, while Japanese wage costs were still much lower, her grip on world market share tightened (see Table 13–1).

The data above clearly reveal why the European and Japanese steel and auto industries were able in the 1960s to penetrate U.S. and other foreign markets. The data further show that the labor cost differences between the U.S., West German, and Japanese textile industries was smaller than those in steel or autos. Equally

Table 13–1. Hourly Total Compensation of Production Workers (current U.S. dollars).

Industry	1965			1983		
	U.S.	West Germany	Japan	U.S.	West Germany	Japan
Average all Manufacturing	3.14	1.40	0.48	12.26	10.41	6.20
Automotive	4.24	1.70	0.55	19.07	13.29	7.79
Steel	4.36	1.69	0.80	21.19	11.31	10.69
Textiles[a]	2.14	1.23	0.34	7.35	8.08	4.15

a. Textile data is for 1965 and 1982.
Source: U.S. Bureau of Labor Statistics unpublished data, April, 1984.

striking are the large differences within the United States between textile and both steel and auto wage costs.

If U.S. textile costs in 1983 were, surprisingly, lower than in West Germany, they were still higher than in Japan and dwarfed Korean textile wage costs of $1.00 an hour, which explains the Japanese investments in Korean and other Asian textile industries pointed out by Professor Arpan. However, the low wage costs in the United States only partially explains the U.S. textile industry's ability to compete successfully.

Despite much lower wages than in steel and autos, the U.S. textile industry has had far more harmonious labor relations as evidenced by rare and less severe strikes. The U.S. textile industry appears to have escaped what Professor Hood called the "British Sickness," one aspect of which is the extremely hostile relationship between management and labor. Unbelievably long and costly strikes have occurred in Britain over the length of tea breaks or two or three minutes of paid wash-up time at the end of shifts. In the U.S. steel and auto industries, similar labor disaffection, and resultant poor-quality work and lack of assiduity, has not been uncommon. When U.S. union officials were discussing attempts to unionize the new Japanese/U.S. auto assembly plants (where Honda and Nissan were trying to install Japanese-style harmonious labor-management relations), they were quoted as believing that employees would soon sour on the Japanese-run companies as readily as they would on an American company. One union official stated, " . . . American workers are just more contentious by nature."[1] Strongly reminiscent of the "British Sickness," this attitude is in sharp contrast to the situation in West Germany and Japan.

Raw Materials

During the early 1960s, raw material and energy costs for steel were somewhat higher in Europe and Japan than in the United States. At the beginning of the 1970s, these costs were significantly lower for Japan and somewhat lower for Europe than for the U.S. industry. Because the auto industry's structure is more complex than steel's, comparable data are difficult to obtain, but its material costs in the 1960s were probably lower in Europe and Japan than in the United States. By 1980 they were significantly lower.[2] By and large, however, raw material costs have not played as significant a role in competitiveness as have wage costs—except in the textile industry.

Although natural fiber costs have generally been about the same for all countries, a distinct advantage developed for the U.S. textile industry at the end of the 1970s in the case of synthetic fibers. At that time, the U.S. industry captured a significant share of the European market, and there was an outcry abroad about unfair competition. Europeans felt that the U.S. industry was being subsidized by the lower raw material (petroleum feedstock) costs resulting from U.S. government control of petroleum prices.

Modernization and Economies of Scale

Until the 1970s, the cost of capital was somewhat lower in the United States than in Europe or Japan, except—and it is an important exception—in cases where the state subsidized or arranged for low-cost loans, or permitted such indirect subsidies as rapid tax write-offs. Since the 1970s, the cost of capital has been lower in Europe and Japan, although the huge Eurocurrency market has tended to even these costs out. But again, as Professor Davidson pointed out in the case of Japanese computer and electronic components industries, low-cost financial backing for "critical" industries has been commonplace in Japan and Europe. Of course the U.S. government has also occasionally intervened financially, as when the existence of Lockheed and Chrysler was threatened, but these cases were rare, *in extremis,* and not part of a long-range industrial policy.

Another financial factor that plays an important and direct role in international competitiveness is the exchange rate. A basic tenet of international economics and a cornerstone of the argument for free trade has long been that trade imbalances eventually result in exchange-rate adjustments that tend to rectify the imbalance. Historically, the international value of the British pound tended to corroborate this theory (until North Sea oil began to flow). But since the abandonment of the gold standard and the more recent departure from fixed parities, exchange rates have been influenced by a complex host of factors. Currency manipulation by national authorities, in the short and medium term, and national macroeconomic policies in the longer term, "distort" exchange rates. Additional distortion results from other nontrade-related capital flows, including foreign investments and the flight of capital in the search for politically safer havens. In the latter instance, the United States has been a particularly privileged beneficiary.

A specific example of the effect of exchange rates is Volkswagen's decision to establish first one, then a second automobile plant in the United States. By the end of the 1960s, the firm had been faced with wage rates that were rising more rapidly in West Germany than in the United States, while the dollar was steadily weakening against the Deutschmark. That combination had threatened the price advantage of West German cars in the U.S. market. In fact, when the dollar reached a low in the 1978–80 period, the cost of labor and materials in the West German auto industry briefly surpassed the seemingly exorbitant U.S. auto wage and parts costs in dollar terms. Later, in 1981, when the exchange rate swung sharply in favor of the dollar, West German auto manufacturing costs in dollar terms fell and, by 1982, were only two-thirds of comparable U.S. costs. This circumstance partially explains Volkswagen's decision to cancel plans to open a second U.S. plant and to rely increasingly on importing certain models and components for its remaining U.S. production. Unfortunately for Volkswagen, its U.S.-made cars were still higher priced than comparable Japanese cars.

Industry Structure

If the preceding discussion of factor inputs explains some of the success of the West German and Japanese auto and steel industries, it does not explain *why* their U.S. counterparts failed to modernize soon enough or on a sufficient scale to be competitive. Nor does it explain why the U.S. textile industry did. But it appears that differences in the structure between the industries played an important part. In the United States, the basic steel and motor vehicle industries have long been tight oligopolies with a handful of well-ensconced firms dominating their respective markets. In 1983 three motor vehicle manufacturers accounted for the bulk of the industry's 727,000 employees, the seven largest steelmakers accounted for the bulk of steel's 336,000 employees, while the twelve largest of some 5,000 U.S. textile firms accounted for only about one-fourth of that industry's 744,000 employees. Competition clearly is and has been keener in textiles and must be a major factor in maintaining its international competitiveness.

Still, neither Professor Arpan's essay nor the above discussion fully explains how the U.S. textile industry successfully fended off equally modern and potentially lower cost Asian competition. In completing our search for an explanation, we must conclude that the factor most instrumental in keeping the U.S. textile industry competitive was probably the umbrella of import protection it has long enjoyed. Recent protection accorded the U.S. steel and auto industries pales in comparison. As early as the late 1950s, a series of bilateral agreements were negotiated with foreign governments limiting textile imports under the provisions of the "Agricultural Act of 1956." Protection was further extended through the "Long Term Arrangement Regarding International Trade in Cotton Textiles" of 1961, and then through a series of Multi-Fiber Agreements (MFA) in 1974, 1978, and 1982. Frequently changed, the quotas, together with back-up tariffs, have provided for an orderly growth of textile imports without serious injury to the U.S. textile (or apparel) industries or damage to the U.S. consumer. This situation contrasts sharply with the situation in the U.S. steel, auto, and electronics industries, in which protective measures are a relatively recent phenomenon, always *ad hoc* in nature, and generally resorted to after the damage has been done.

Management

One must not conclude from the previous discussion that labor is the chief culprit of U.S. industries suffering from foreign competition. Management must shoulder its share of the blame. Decisions as to which products to manufacture, where to manufacture, and how to market, and in general how to compete, are all management prerogatives and duties. Above all, the decisions to invest (or not), when, where, and how much follow from the product decisions and are also management prerogatives. And, within the framework and limitations of the national socio-cultural context, or what Bernard Cazes described in his essay as the national *société civile*, labor relations are also a management duty.

Both in autos and steel, wage costs were allowed to rise much higher than the national manufacturing average in the 1965–83 period, 1982–83 "givebacks" included. The growth figures were 486 percent for steel, 450 percent for autos, and only 340 percent for textiles (versus a 390 percent growth for the average wage costs in all manufacturing industries). During that period the consumer price index rose less than 316 percent. The oligopolistic and geographically concentrated nature of steel and autos, pointed out earlier, made those heavily unionized sectors much more acquiescent in meeting wage demands to avoid crippling strikes than the relatively nonunion, fragmented textile industry, geographically dispersed throughout low-wage-cost parts of the United States.

It is easy, with hindsight, to criticize U.S. auto and steel managers for too long allowing their industries to stagnate through atrophied management practices, burdening themselves with uneconomic labor agreements, and complacently watching foreign competition bypass them commercially and technologically. It is also somewhat unfair. As Professor Doz stated, much of the Japanese success in motor vehicles was attributable to fortuitous circumstances. The timing and impact of the 1973 oil crisis was virtually impossible to predict. And in steel, president after president since World War II pressured the U.S. industry to keep prices down as wage costs skyrocketed. For managers to have risked crushing strikes by militant unions in order to keep these heavy industries internationally competitive would probably have been unrealistic. The textile industry could make the (relatively smaller) investments; many other sectors could not. Still, managers have some latitude within these constraints. Recent steel industry investment decisions provide a vivid example of how managements reacted quite differently to the need for investment in new plants. At the beginning of the 1980s, Bethlehem Steel, though closing some plants, reaffirmed its commitment to staying in the steel business and initiated substantial new investments. But U.S. Steel, the largest firm, followed a strategy that drastically changed the nature of the company. In 1979 U.S. Steel ordered fifteen antiquated plants closed, trimmed product lines, and scrapped plans for a $4. billion investment in a new plant—the first in 26 years. Instead of the new steel plant, it acquired the Marathon Oil Company in 1982 for $6 billion in one of the largest mergers in U.S. corporate history. One could understand management's rationale; the steel side of the business was losing $1.2 billion a year. Later, in 1983, in order to become competitive but to avoid massive investments for modern basic steel facilities, U.S. Steel was negotiating with the British Steel Company to buy 3 million tons of semifinished steel a year for its Philadelphia plant.[3] The negotiations foundered, in part due to union objections.

The question of whether and how to go international is another key management decision. While the U.S. steel industry did export modestly before World War II, its only export success since then was during the steel-starved postwar reconstruction era. Moreover, this sector never invested significantly in foreign production facilities. The reasons were many: the heavy capital investments required, the existence of a strong, rebuilt European industry, a long tradition of a world cartel to which the U.S. industry had at least tacitly adhered, and most important, the unwillingness of developed and developing foreign nations to see an industry considered crucial to their national defense and sovereignty held under foreign control.

Unlike steel, the U.S. auto industry has a long history of international involvement. With relatively smaller capital investment requirements, both Ford and General Motors began exporting and assembling cars abroad in the 1920s, while Chrysler began somewhat later. Their competitive advantage, pointed out by Professor Doz, was the product and process technology inherent to the low-cost, mass-produced car developed for the large U.S. market. For several decades these foreign subsidiaries evolved separately from their U.S. parents, developing and building quite different products and with relatively little international flow of product technology until the 1970s. Since the 1973 oil crisis and the Japanese challenge, these foreign investments and innovations may well turn out to be the U.S. auto industry's salvation.

Although slow to import small fuel-efficient cars from their European subsidiaries, the U.S. auto industry has reversed the flow of product technology, bringing to the United States European designs and, of far greater significance, importing foreign components and assemblies. Ford's Escort is one example, but a more striking example is the import of car engines from Mexico and Brazil for assembly into "U.S.-made" cars. A U.S. government agency estimated that in 1982–84 about 2.5 million engines and 1.7 million front-wheel drive transaxles, among many other car parts, would be imported annually. Most of these parts would come from modern U.S., European, and Japanese subsidiaries in Mexico and Brazil.[4] Mexico alone was to ship 1.7 million engines per year by 1984. This figure should be viewed against a background of a 1983 market of less than 10 million cars a year, of which 37.5 percent had already been captured by imports in 1983.[5] The portent of this development is all the more disquieting when one compares the following 1983 auto industry hourly wage costs.[6]

United States	$19.07
West Germany	13.29
Japan	7.79
Brazil	2.37
Mexico (1982)	2.55
Korea	1.66

INTERNATIONALIZATION OF PRODUCTION AND THE TRANSFER OF TECHNOLOGY

In the 1950s and early 1960s a vast number off U.S. manufacturing firms acquired or established subsidiaries abroad, particularly in Western Europe and to a lesser extent in Latin America. Among the many reasons for this development was a strong demand for newly developed U.S. products of high quality, a favorable exchange rate making imports costly and investment attractive, lower manufacturing costs, especially labor, and increasing tariff and nontariff barriers to imports from the United States. Where it was unfeasible or difficult to establish subsidiaries U.S. firms granted licenses to local firms. Toward the mid-1960s, U.S. firms accelerated the establishment of subsidiaries or the granting of licenses in the low labor-cost but industrious Pacific Basin countries of Taiwan, Hong Kong, and Korea, subsequently spreading to Singapore, Malaysia, Thailand and Sri Lanka. As the competition from these countries increased, Japanese and European firms also increased their investments in these new "export platforms."

Sooner or later such transfers of technology result in the "know-how" being spun off and used by independent foreign competitors. Japan's current success began with the purchase of licenses and some copying. The resulting influx of low-cost imports into the United States, aided considerably by the duty-free or very low duty status accorded "developing" nations under the U.S. Generalized System of Preferences, forced many U.S. firms to increasingly resort to manufacturing all or part of their products in these low-labor-cost countries to remain competitive. In 1983, for example, there were over 200 U.S. firms assembling high technology electronic products in Ireland, Mexico, and Malaysia, among other developing countries. The U.S. General Electric Company had some 14,000 employees in Singapore alone. In many cases, this "off-shore" effort consisted of shipping semi-finished goods from the United States for completion of the labor-intensive part of the production process. This type of activity is very common in the U.S. apparel and electronic industries because under item 807 of the U.S. Tariff Schedule, duty on the returning products is assessed only on the value added abroad.

When technology is transferred through subsidiaries, the host country usually requires a certain amount of "local content" in the finished product. While local content may initially consist of low-technology hardware, paint, and simple parts, continued host country pressures usually result in the transfer of increasingly sophisticated portions of the product previously reserved for production in the home country. Where the transfer is through licensing, the acquiring country usually seeks to protect the fledgling industry by quotas, tariffs, nontariff barriers and frequently outright bans on importation of the product. Brazil has long prohibited automobile imports. In 1978 foreign firms sold 80 percent of the computers assembled in Brazil, but by imposing harsh import regulations on small computers and their components, Brazilian-owned companies controlled 60 percent of the domestic market in 1982, and Brazil now has Latin America's largest computer industry. Most Brazilian-made small computers have 94 percent Brazilian components. Though the technology is not the latest, an industrial base has been established that can ultimately result in a world competitive industry as in the case of Brazil's success in commuter aircraft, auto engines, and armaments.

For "export platforms" such as Hong Kong and Taiwan, the situation is different. Their initial acquisition of technology in electronics and computers was the result of spin-offs from local subsidiaries of multinational firms from industrialized countries. Later, licensing and outright copying resulted in highly competitive products. Digital watches are an example. And facsimiles of Apple computers (which in 1983 sold for around $1,500 in the United States) could be bought in Taiwan for $250.[7]

Advanced Technology

Computers and related products are often cited as the archetypical high-technology products which the United States can turn to in order to compensate for the loss of world market share in mature industries. It is true that the computing equipment sector enjoyed an employment increase of 193 percent from 1965 to 1983. But this could not compensate for losses and low increases in other manufacturing sectors. Employment in the overall U.S. manufacturing industry rose by only 3 percent in the same period. And in the other advanced-technology sector discussed in this book—aerospace—employment actually decreased by 2 percent between 1965 and 1983 (see Table 1–4, p.). Aircraft and computers are the two leading U.S. manufactured exports. Therefore, from these statistics it is clear that advanced technology has far from compensated for the loss of manufacturing jobs in the United States when compared to the growth of the population (20 percent) and the economy as whole (59 percent in constant dollars) over the same period.

More ominous still are the trends in international competition in advanced technology. One such trend is the drop in U.S. research and development expenditures as a percentage of gross domestic product as compared to corresponding increases for

Japan and Germany. Another is the threat posed by the growth of Japanese and European computer and electronics industries traced by Professor Davidson. With strong governmental support, this foreign competition will become increasingly aggressive as Japan, Europe, and the newly industrialized countries such as Brazil not only become more self-sufficient, but capture larger shares of the total world market. This is already being felt in the exploding, very low-cost home computer market; the Atari Company recently closed down its U.S. factory with a loss of 1,700 jobs and announced it would build the product in Hong Kong or Taiwan.

The sector of solid state semiconductors, especially large and very large integrated circuits, is another particularly noteworthy example of competitive change. Developed and first manufactured in the United States, these circuits are the heart of large and small computers as well as of countless other electronic and mechanical products. U.S. semiconductor shipments were about $14 billion in 1983, of which $4.2 billion were exported. But $5.0 billion worth were imported, either from U.S. subsidiaries abroad or from competing foreign (mostly Japanese) firms. In the 1972–83 decade, exports grew at a compounded annual rate of 22 percent, but imports grew at a rate of 28 percent, a trend that is not at all comforting.[8]

In aerospace the situation is somewhat less alarming, although clouds are gathering. Chapter 12 documented how the European AIRBUS has broken the near monopoly the United States long held in the large commercial airliner market. The essay also cited the threat to U.S. manufacturers of small business and commuter aircraft. For example, Brazil, which in 1974 was the largest export market for U.S. light planes, imposed severe restrictions on imports of light planes and forced their manufacture in local joint ventures. Total light plane imports to Brazil from the United States in 1976 were 411; by 1982 only 48 light aircraft were imported from the United States, mostly expensive corporate jets of a type not yet being assembled in Brazil. Meanwhile Brazil was successfully competing in the U.S. and world markets with the twenty-passenger Bandeirante commuter described in the aerospace essay and, in a joint-venture with Italy, was developing and preparing to manufacture a jet fighter aircraft.

A more mundane information-technology product further demonstrates the problem for the United States. When General Electric entered the consumer phone market in 1983 it boasted that its phones were "GE designed." The company was more reticent about the fact that their phones were to be manufactured in Taiwan and Hong Kong—except for the cordless model, which was to be assembled at a GE plant in Singapore.

Newly Industrialized Countries (NICs)

The previous examples of the growing role of NICs in the world market place are but the tip of the iceberg. Professor Coutinho's discussion and the statistics given in Table 1–2 attest to the amazing and rapidly growing industrial prowess of the NICs. With technology being transferred so rapidly, the list of competitive NICs is sure to expand—with consequences difficult to foresee. The television industry provides another graphic example.

In 1953, 7 million TV sets were produced in the United States, a little more than 1 million in Britain; 41,000 in West Germany; and 41,000 in Japan (under U.S. and European licenses). By 1970 Japanese manufacturers had captured 51 percent of the U.S. black and white and 18 percent of the U.S. color television market. To survive, U.S. television manufacturers moved the majority of their labor-intensive operations to low-labor-cost countries. In 1976 Japan shipped over 4 million sets to the United States, which gave rise to cries for import restrictions. The result was an "orderly marketing agreement" whereby the Japanese agreed to limit their shipments to 41 percent of the 1976 levels. Not surprisingly, the NICs rushed in to fill the void. Korea, which did not even produce television sets as late as 1965, exported over 500,000 color televisions to the U.S. market alone in 1978. Korean manufacturers then increased their production capacity to 1.2 million color sets a year —all for export, because South Korea still did not permit domestic color television broadcasting![9] Ergo, another set of "orderly marketing agreements" with South Korea and Taiwan. The industrial challenge from NICs is a permanent feature of the changing economic world order.

WHAT CAN BE DONE?

We have asked the question of what the United States can do about these challenges, but perhaps a more basic question is whether anything should be done at all. That the peoples of the NICs have benefitted from America's free-trade policies cannot be denied, despite the continuing income and debt problems in Brazil and Mexico and the developing world. The Western industrialized democracies, especially Japan, have also benefitted. And, of course, the average American has been rewarded by being able to enjoy less expensive clothing, shoes, television receivers, and automobiles, just as classic free-trade economics maintains. But the case of Britain should be a warning that loss of industrial competitiveness can be seriously damaging to a nation's economic health. I must conclude that continuing a laissez-faire, *ad hoc* policy toward U.S. international industrial competitiveness will lead to a similar economic disaster for the United States.

Many observers and analysts have refused to become alarmed at the decline in U.S. industrial competitiveness. They are reassured, as mentioned in the introduction, by the possibility that the rise in service industries and agriculture will offset manufacturing declines. However, doctors, lawyers, accountants, bank tellers, custodial personnel, sales clerks, and government employees all want and must buy clothing, home appliances, automobiles, and so forth. Even the most optimistic estimates of service exports would not balance the potential negative trade balance (not including petroleum imports, which further darken the picture) that comes from a decline in industrial competitiveness. Ultimately a nation's standard of living is determined by its success in the industrial, not service, arena. Neither is compensating for the manufactured goods imbalance with agricultural exports a promising alternative. Aside from powerful national defense arguments, a United States that willingly accepts relative industrial inferiority generates decidedly uncomfortable feelings.

Industrial capability is sprouting up in all corners of the previously underdeveloped world, and technology is traveling at unheard-of speeds, as difficult to control as a drop of mercury with a finger. The result is that there are very few products that cannot be manufactured more cheaply abroad. Still, a means must be found to keep the United States industrially competitive without endangering the worldwide benefits that have accompanied increasing international interdependence. From this book it is apparent that reliance on the law of comparative advantage, itself rooted in the monolithic eighteenth and nineteenth century economic concepts of free trade and laissez faire, is *not* a solution. Moreover, in this world of independent sovereign states, neither fully developed nor developing nations appear willing to abide by the law of comparative advantage whereby they would produce only those products they most efficient in producing.

The evidence presented in these essays shows that broad, coordinated action by the state is both necessary and inevitable. Put differently, it is not a question of *if* the state should play a major role in ensuring a healthy industrial base, but *how* the state should intercede. Those of our competitors who have been successful, most notably Japan, have laid out long-range industrial policies that build on their nation's competitive advantages. The state's formal role in West Germany, while less obvious than in Japan, has been to ensure that the innate strengths of West Germany industry are developed and sustained. The fact that the state cannot solve every problem, as is evident from the West German guest-worker situation which went from boon to bane with the worldwide recession at the beginning of the 1980s, is no excuse for inaction.

The experience of France, with its long tradition of formal state intervention in these matters, has been reasonably successful. From a highly protectionist, inward-looking economy, France became a keen competitor in the world market place. Archaic sectors were modernized; new, high-technology sectors were nurtured and intelligently protected. During the trying early postwar years and on through the difficult adjustments incident to joining the Common Market, France benefitted greatly from its formal long-range planning system. As the economy adjusted, the need for and impact of this planning system naturally diminished. What the 1983 turmoil in France has shown is that state intervention may not always be wise intervention.

Britain's lagging economy further corroborates the need for a consistent, long-range industrial policy. I need only repeat Professor Hood's comments concerning the " . . . instability and *ad hoc* nature of industrial policy in Britain . . . [where] The observer looking for the comprehensive planning framework within which such [governmental] policy measures have been devised and implemented would be sorely disappointed."

In the United States, where there has been a complete absence of a national industrial policy (in fact a hostility toward this sort of state intervention), *ad hocism* has reigned supreme. In those areas in which the government has intervened, the action has usually been taken after the fact, in response to damage already inflicted. In his essay, Professor Davidson sees a " . . . very good approximation of a focused, vigorous industrial policy" in the information technology sector. Even here, I would maintain, *ad hocism* outweighs focus.

After-the-fact *ad hocism* is not a satisfactory response. By the time remedies are tried, the competitor is entrenched. This issue raises an important point frequently neglected in the static analysis of economists—the industrial dynamics of market share. The successful capture of more and more market share by a new competitor feeds and strengthens the gainer, whereas the converse is true for the loser. The success of SONY television receivers and Toyota cars in the United States are but two examples. They gained market share on the basis of price; after a strong market position was established these products could command a premium, thereby generating even larger profits to be plowed back into research, production, and more marketing—a golden circle as it were. Their U.S. competition was faced with dwindling cash flow—a vicious circle—until "orderly marketing agreements" were reached.

One can point to the awesome international debt predicaments and resulting tribulations of Brazil and Mexico to belittle certain aspects of the industrial policies and long-range planning of those countries. Nevertheless, it is hard to refute the enormous success of their industrialization: the recapture of domestic market share in sectors as diverse as the mature automotive, advanced technology small aircraft, and computer industries.

Any solution suggested by the preceding essays and discussion must be considered in the light of what Bernard Cazes termed the *société civile* in his essay. In essence the essay states the obvious—that the totality of a nation's socio-cultural forces and institutions are more powerful than the actions of the government in determining a nation's destiny. This does not mean that guidance, pressure, or restraint from the state have a negligible effect. What it means is that the state can only act as a catalyst to marshal the strengths and guard against the weaknesses of the *société civile*. The role of the state must be analogous to that of a leader, i.e., the style of leadership must be in harmony with the *société civile*. Translated to the workshop floor, for example, this means that starting the morning shift in a company uniform and singing the company song may not work as well in Tennessee as in Japan. Translated to the national level it means that an industrial policy dictated by the administration in power, *à la* France, may not be suitable for the United States.

Aside from the need for a national industrial policy in harmony with the *société civile,* these essays suggest other courses the United States can follow. Two are concerned with labor.

The adversarial relationship between management and labor, a byproduct of the intensive industrialization of the late nineteenth and early twentieth centuries, must be replaced with a relationship based on the simple fact that management's welfare and labor's welfare are inextricably entwined. The relationship is not a zero-sum game in which labor's gains must always be at the expense of management. In the long run, it is a cooperative game where, if properly played, both sides can win. If improperly played, both sides—and the nation—are sure to lose. Britain's experience has been dismal; in many cases, so has the United States'. This is not to say the situation is hopeless. Management-labor accords abounded in 1983, and there even have been encouraging signs within the automobile industry.

In 1981 the Chrysler Corporation determined that it could save well over $1 million a year by buying seat covers from an outside vendor rather than making them in their Detroit trim plant. Faced with Chrysler's decision to close yet another old Detroit plant, the local union and management reacted in a positive manner. Work rules were changed, old practices abandoned, unnecessary workers laid off, work output norms raised as much as 28 percent, and the plant became competitive—without "givebacks" or reductions in pay for the remaining employees.

The other labor area that is a proper concern of an industrial policy is wage levels. Here I do not suggest that setting wage levels by *diktat* is appropriate to a U.S. industrial policy; rather, we must have a mechanism to determine which classes of U.S.-manufactured products are not competitive in the domestic market because their wage costs are abnormally high (e.g. autos and steel) or because their "real" productivity (e.g., units produced per man-hour) is lower than foreign competition. Such sectors or subsectors should be exposed to greater import competition from abroad to encourage them to become more competitive. The adjustments such as those described above for Chrysler could not have happened without the pressure of outside competition.

Some other possible facets of an industrial policy might be the following:

- Given the ability of NICs, and especially the export platforms, to capture overwhelming market share in the United States if allowed free access, some means must be found to tread the delicate line between unfettered free trade and pure protectionism. Here, for example, an industrial policy might require a bilateral balance in merchandise trade with the NIC over a rolling five-year period in exchange for relatively free access to the U.S. market.
- The British, French, Brazilian, and Mexican situations show that cases may well exist that require strong government support if an industry is to survive. The cases of Chrysler and Lockheed demonstrate that the United States is not exempt from this need.
- U.S. manufacturing firms should enjoy greater economies of scale than their competitors abroad because of the larger U.S. domestic market and should be therefore able to compete effectively at home and abroad, even with higher wages. This may require "enlightened protectionism," as in the textile industry.

In summary, we can answer Professor Vernon's query affirmatively: the threat is real and long term. To respond, the United States needs a long-term industrial policy that takes into consideration its *société civile*, encourages cooperation between labor and management, and recognizes when free trade is beneficial and when enlightened protection is necessary.

NOTES

1. *The Wall Street Journal,* March 23, 1983, p. 33.
2. William J. Abernathy, James Harbour, and Jay Henn, "Productivity and Comparative Cost Advantages: Some Estimates for Major Automobile Producers," Harvard Business School Working Paper 13, February 1981, p. 82.

3. *The Wall Street Journal,* December 12, 1983, p. 2.
4. *The New York Times,* December 6, 1981, p. 2F, quoting the U.S. Transportation Systems Center.
5. *Summary of Trade and Tariff Information,* Automobiles, Trucks, Buses . . . , United States International Trade Commission Publication 841, June 1984, p. 47.
6. U.S. Bureau of Labor Statistics, *Hourly Compensation for Production Workers in Motor Vehicles and Equipment Manufacturing, 14 Countries, 1975–1982,* "unpublished data," April, 1984 (issued annually).
7. *1984 Industrial Outlook* (Washington, U.S. Department of Commerce, January, 1984), p. 30–5.
8. Ibid:
9. *Financial Times,* September 24, 1979, p. 3.

INDEX

ABOUT THE CONTRIBUTORS

Jeffrey Arpan is Professor of International Business at the University of South Carolina and director of USC's Center of Industry Policy and Strategy. He has recently completed a major research project on the fiber, fabric and apparel complex in the Asia Pacific area.

Bernard Cazes is Director of long-range planning at France's *Commissariat au Plan.* He is widely esteemed in France as a "philosopher-economist." He is the author of several books and numerous articles.

Luciano Coutinho teaches economics at UNICAMP in Sao Paulo, where he was in charge of graduate programs in economics for several years. He is just finishing a major research project on the topic of "Changes, Crises, and Trends of the World Economic Order."

Yves Doz is Associate Professor of Business Policy at INSEAD in Fontainbleau. From 1976 to 1981 he was on the faculty of the

409

Harvard Business School, where he received his doctorate. He has published extensively in the area of corporate strategy in the international domain and on the world auto industry in great depth, particularly in Europe and Japan.

Neil Hood is Professor of Business Policy and Associate Dean at Strathclyde University. For the past several years he has been actively involved in comparative international business studies. In 1978–79 he was Visiting Professor of International Business at the University of Texas at Arlington.

Klaus Macharzina is Dean of the business faculty at Hohenheim University in Stuttgart. In 1980 he was chosen by the American Accounting Association as distinguished lecturer for that year. The author of five books, he is one of Germany's most prolific writers in the area of business and management. He is also Editor of the journal *International Management.*

Hans Mueller is Professor of Economics at the Middle Tennessee State University. He has been Visiting Professor at the Fundacao Getulio Vargas in Brazil and at several other Brazilian universities. He has done extensive research on the world steel industry and, in particular, on the comparative analysis of national industries.

Brian Toyne is on the faculty of the University of South Carolina and has long specialized in the apparel and textile industries.

Yoshi Tsurumi is currently Professor of Marketing and International Business at Baruch College of the City University of New York. He has taught at Columbia University and at the Harvard Business School, where he obtained his doctorate. Until recently he directed the Pacific Basin Studies Center of the University of California at Los Angeles. He is the author of *The Japanese are Coming* and numerous other publications concerning Japanese industry and economy.

Raymond Vernon is Clarence Dillion Professor of International Affairs at Harvard and recently retired as Herbert F. Johnson Professor of International Business at the Harvard Business School.

Stephen Young is on the faculty of Strathclyde University and has been heavily involved in research in international business.

ABOUT THE EDITORS

Milton Hochmuth was Visiting Professor of Business Administration at Dartmouth's Amos Tuck School of Business when the colloquium which launched this book was held. He was Director of the Institute of International Business at Georgia State University and Professor of Business Policy and International Business at the Centre d'Enseignement Superieur des Affaires. He is currently teaching and writing in France.

William Davidson is on the faculty of the University of Virginia's Colgate Darden School of Business. He has published books and articles on the management of the multinational firm and foreign direct investment.